American Mennonites and Protestant Movements

A Community Paradigm

American Mennonites and Protestant Movements

A Community Paradigm

Beulah Stauffer Hostetler

HERALD PRESS

Harrisonburg, Virginia

Herald Press
PO Box 866, Harrisonburg, VA 22803
www.HeraldPress.com

American Mennonites and Protestant Movements
A Community Paradigm
By Hostetler, Beulah Stauffer
© 2018 Herald Press
ISBN: 978-1-5138-0560-3
Originally published, ©1987 Herald Press
ISBN: 1-57910-906-3

*To Hannah Rittenhouse Clemens
whose reminiscences
led me beyond the stereotypes*

Contents

Editor's Preface 15
Author's Preface 17

1. COLONIAL MENNONITES AND PIETISM 23
    Mennonites and Pietists in Pennsylvania • 32
    The Search for Unity • 42
    The Resurgence of Sectarianism • 53
    Pietism and Fragmentation • 65

2. THE CHARTER 75
    The Initial Charter • 77
    The Seven Articles • 81
        Article I. Concerning Baptism
        Article II. Concerning the Ban
        Article III. Concerning the Breaking of Bread
        Article IV. Separation from the World
        Article V. Shepherds in the Church of God
        Article VI. Concerning the Sword
        Article VII. The Oath
    The Charter in America • 93
        Documentation
        The Setting in America
        The Seven Articles
    Conclusion • 123

3. BROTHERLY UNION AND SCHISM 125
    The Oberholtzer Division • 126
        Events of the Division
        The Issues and the American Environment
        The Issues and Charter Values

The New Mennonites and Subsequent Schisms • 140
　　　　　The Hunsicker Division
　　　　　The Evangelical Mennonites
　　　　　The Johnson Mennonites
　　　Schism and Americanization • 146

4. THE ENCOUNTER WITH REVIVALISM 150
　　　The Second Great Awakening • 150
　　　　　Camp Meetings
　　　　　Perfection and Holiness
　　　Mennonites and Revivalism • 157
　　　Revivalism and the New Mennonites • 164
　　　Mennonites and the Third Great Awakening • 167

5. THE ENCOUNTER WITH INSTITUTIONALIZATION 176
　　　Institutionalization in the American Churches • 177
　　　New Mennonites and Institutionalization • 180
　　　The Structure of Franconia Conference • 183
　　　Resistance and Fragmentation • 188
　　　Institutionalization in the Mennonite Church • 193

6. THE ENCOUNTER WITH FUNDAMENTALISM 201
　　　Development of Fundamentalism • 201
　　　Concerning Biblical Interpretation • 210
　　　　　History versus Dogma
　　　　　Obedience and Inerrancy
　　　　　Precedence of the New Testament
　　　　　Literal Interpretation
　　　Mennonites and Millenarianism • 226
　　　Leadership Patterns • 234

7. DEFENSIVE STRUCTURING
　　　AND CODIFICATION OF PRACTICE 245
　　　Authoritarian Control over Members • 250
　　　Cultivation of Cultural Identity Symbols • 255
　　　Formal Limits on Structural Associations • 258

8. CHANGE AND THE NONRESISTANT FAITH 272
   Growing Peace Emphasis • 273
   New Wine in New Wineskins • 279
   Separation and Structural Associations • 287
   Schism and the Sword • 293
   Authoritarian Control Challenged • 295
   Change Affirmed • 303
   Accommodation and Dissension • 307
   Witness and Peace • 317

Bibliography .... .331
Index .... .351
The Author .... .368

Editor's Preface

Not every interpreter of history knows what questions to ask. Of those who do, not every such interpreter is willing to ask those exact questions, knotty and uncomplimentary as they always can be. Beulah Hostetler is aware of the need, and has been able to ask such deeper questions. She has stayed with the task of following the answers through the decades—and indeed centuries—of the eras of one group, the Franconia Mennonite settlement.

"What has been written creates," Olga Freidenberg wrote to Boris Pasternak in 1949. "What is unwritten brings chaos and separation."[1] Applying this to the Mennonite tradition, it would seem that too often, that which was not adequately chronicled and interpreted has come back to haunt us. In this volume the author is attempting, in effect, to wrest an ongoing community and its expressions of faith and life from chaos, and from being separated from its past.

This volume traces the religious history of the oldest Mennonite conference in North America—the Franconia Conference—which had its beginnings in Germantown, Pennsylvania, in 1683. Yet it is not strictly a narrative history of the conference. J. C. Wenger had courageously attempted this step already in 1937 under the title *History of the Mennonites of the Franconia Conference*. Nor is this volume a cultural-literary story of the Mennonites in eastern Pennsylvania, the great contribution of John L. Ruth in his *Maintaining the Right Fellowship* (1984). Yet again, it is not a source volume, or a general sociohistorical interpretation of the same people in the vein of Richard MacMaster, who with others so ably brought together two such tomes: *Conscience in Crisis* ... (1979) and *Land, Piety, Peoplehood* ... (1985).

The volume at hand probes history from a unique set of perspectives. At the heart of this probing, in its larger sense, lies the question of faith: individual and corporate. Beulah Hostetler charts the attempts, conscious and subconscious, at continuity—and discontinuity—of those realities that together spell the continuing degree of health of one particular community of

---

[1] *The Correspondence of Boris Pasternak and Olga Freidenberg, 1910-1954* (Harcourt Brace Jovanovich, 1982), p. 297.

gathered believers. Such particularity, however, lends itself to a certain universality: much within the Franconia tradition runs parallel to the experiences of other Mennonite communities in Lancaster (County), Maryland, Ontario, and Virginia, but equally to those experiences of Mennonites west of the Alleghenies, in later times.

The author dares to ask basic questions. She also dares to suggest some surprising conclusions that help cap a thesis which by definition is difficult to substantiate, except in the form of a cause-and-effect interpretation of the larger centuries-old tradition. Indeed, simply to have asked questions in the light of the several generations of the twentieth-century Mennonites would have missed the whole point: there is, to be sure, a larger, vital tradition which has existed over the centuries (and which continues to this day) undergirding a strong note of community still in existence, and a spirit passed on from one generation to the next. It is rooted in the Schleitheim tradition of the Gospel of Peace. It finds corporate expression in continuing adherence to the Seven Articles of the Brotherly Union, and goes all the way back to 1527—460 years ago.

The editors of Studies in Anabaptist and Mennonite History (SAMH) are grateful to be able to include this volume in its series. Similar studies could—and should—be undertaken for other conferences within the Mennonite Church, and within other groups making up the larger Anabaptist-Mennonite heritage in North America. These include the Hutterites and the Old Order groups as well. As already noted above, these would also include the traditions underlying Lancaster, Maryland, Ontario, and Virginia—the oldest groups and conferences. The Amish-Mennonite traditions, then, further west, would probably combine in slightly different ways, for study and comparison.

In any case, Beulah Hostetler has paved the way with her pioneering efforts in this unusual and essential opening-up of what too often only lies hidden in the heart, what one particular group feels in its corporate bones as being right. The author's approach and its outcome fulfill magnificently the vision that Walker Percy holds out to all writers:

> The primary business of literature and art is cognitive, a kind of finding out and knowing and telling, both in good times and bad; a celebration of the way things are when they are right, and a diagnostic enterprise when they are wrong.[2]

—Leonard Gross, SAMH Editor
Goshen, Indiana

---

[2] "The Diagnostic Novel: On the Uses of Modern Fiction," by Walker Percy, *Harper's*, June 1986, p. 41.

Author's Preface

This book is about continuity and change in the religious life of a Pennsylvania Mennonite community. It is not a chronology or history in the usual sense, but focuses on basic beliefs that underlie Mennonite customs and religious forms. Because it is concerned with religious thought, published works that were written to shape perceptions and practice are frequently examined. The settlement, Franconia Mennonite Conference, was initially selected because of proximity to our residence, since I am a wife and a mother as well as a researcher. My own community of origin, across the continent and in another country, was at Tofield, Alberta, Canada.

Observations concerning Franconia Conference in this volume are frequently compared to events in the wider Mennonite Church and contrasted with dominant emphases of American Protestant movements. The comparisons show that belief patterns in Franconia frequently (but not always) represent widely accepted emphases in the Mennonite Church. The contrasts with Protestant movements place beliefs in context, and help to make key values that were otherwise implicit stand out in clear relief. By making these comparisons there is no intention of promoting narrow sectarianism. Rather, it is hoped that delineating differences will foster dialogue among persons and groups with diverse understandings.

The Franconia Mennonite Conference is composed of 52 congregations located in the area surrounding Souderton, Pennsylvania, about 30 miles north of Philadelphia. It is the oldest permanent Mennonite settlement in America. Church membership in 1985 was 6,345; in 1940 there were 4,471 members, and in 1800 approximately 2,000 members.

It was long held that little could be known about Pennsylvania Mennonites before the twentieth century because of the lack of source materials. My first task, therefore, was to find out what early sources were available, and what could be learned from them. In the initial stages of the research, Wilmer Reinford, who has collected Franconia documents for decades, provided invaluable aid by freely sharing with me his accumulated materials. My second task was to discern the key beliefs of the group and to determine whether they served as a continuing norm, undergirding both resistance to outside influences and the adaptations that were made by the group.

The search was at first discouraging. A strong community, discipline, and separation from the world were marked characteristics of the group, but these could be simply ethnic demarcations. A few extant documents expressed a spiritual warmth and wisdom that belied the standard assessment of the group as backward and petrified.

Gradually I became aware that beliefs were imbedded in patterns of life and were largely nonverbal in character. It was the repeated references to Matthew 18, verses 15 to 17, as a guide for dealing with dissension, that first sparked the idea that religious expression might be guided by the Seven Articles of the "Brotherly Union" first agreed upon at Schleitheim in 1527. Testing this hunch began to yield positive results, and this book is the outgrowth of that search.

I have chosen to call the sum of beliefs and values expressed in the Seven Articles the "charter" of the community. While I consider the concept of a charter very useful for delineating key Mennonite beliefs, I do not reify the charter, nor do I consider this model an exclusive one. Other frameworks can be, and have been, used for understanding Mennonite beliefs.

In my comparisons of Mennonites with American Protestant movements, I pay particular attention to Pietism, Revivalism, Institutionalization, and Fundamentalism with its often accompanying millenarianism. Following the turn of the twentieth century, Mennonites attempted to protect their identity by codification of practice. Then, following 1950, there was very rapid acculturation in Mennonite communities. These trends will be assessed, together with an examination of the growing emphasis on the traditional peace stance.

This book does not treat the mission movement. The mission movement in both the Franconia Conference and the Mennonite Church has been ably treated elsewhere. The conference program has been recounted by John L. Ruth in "The Story Behind Franconia Conference's Outreach," published in the *Franconia Conference News* from October 1976 to November 1978. Theron F. Schlabach's *Gospel Versus Gospel* tells the story of mission in the Mennonite Church from 1863 to 1944.

Following a major division in the Franconia Conference in 1847, for a few decades trends are compared with the activities and directions of the new Oberholtzer group. Oberholtzer's New Mennonites affiliated with several Iowa immigrant congregations from Germany in the 1860s and then with additional congregations in Ohio. The majority of congregations from the large Mennonite immigration from Russia in the 1870s united with this small nucleus, becoming the General Conference Mennonites of North America. The book does not treat this conference, composed largely of Mennonites whose pilgrimages took them from the Netherlands to Prussia and Russia before their major migrations to Canada and the United States in the 1870s, 1920s, and the 1940s.

Two excellent histories of Franconia Conference are available. J. C. Wenger's *History of the Mennonites of the Franconia Conference* (1937) thoroughly documents persons, places, and events and frequently served as a sourcebook for the present work. John L. Ruth's *Maintaining the Right Fellowship* (1984) is a narrative account to 1947 that is rich in human warmth and episodic commentary. The reader's understanding will be greatly enriched by combining the use of these volumes with the present work.

This study is dependent on the previous work of a number of individuals and groups. Wenger's *History of the Mennonites* ... already mentioned, was an invaluable aid, as was his reading of the manuscript and the suggestions which he offered. Those whose work and contributions made possible the "Oberholtzer Division Issue" of the *Mennonite Quarterly Review* deserve thanks. Joseph Miller, archivist at the Eastern Pennsylvania Mennonite Historical Library and Archives during the writing of the book, also provided significant aid. Carolyn Charles Wenger and the staff of Lancaster Mennonite Historical Library made available helpful materials, and the membership committee of the Lancaster Mennonite Historical Society granted me a Research Stipend Award. I also gratefully acknowledge a 1981 National Endowment for the Humanities Summer Stipend, and a 1984 National Endowment for the Humanities Fellowship for Independent Study and Research.

I am indebted to Professor Don Yoder of the University of Pennsylvania, supervisor of my dissertation, which is the kernel from which the present book grew. He provided continuous encouragement and gave basic guidance with his rich knowledge of the sources, careful attention to detail, and knowledge of the period and the area. The probing questions of Professor Van A. Harvey, then chairman of the Department of Religious Thought, aided significantly in the shaping of the work. Professor Donald F. Durnbaugh of Bethany Theological Seminary served as a reader for the dissertation, and more recently his critical reading of the first chapter was greatly appreciated.

John E. Lapp, longtime minister, bishop, and overseer in the Franconia Conference, patiently answered many questions and read the entire manuscript in various versions. Elmer G. Kolb, secretary of the conference from 1950 to 1972, assisted considerably by making available his carefully organized records. The late Hannah Rittenhouse Clemens granted numerous interviews. Karen Leidig assisted with the bibliography and with other important tasks. Gerald C. Studer and James C. Juhnke read the entire manuscript and made helpful suggestions. Leonard Gross, executive secretary of the Mennonite Historical Committee and director of the Archives of the Mennonite Church, Goshen, Indiana, has given valuable encouragement and guidance both as SAMH editor for the book and in providing materials from the Archives.

Finally, I want to thank John A. Hostetler for his support in numerous ways throughout the entire project.

—Beulah Stauffer Hostetler
Elizabethtown, Pennsylvania

American Mennonites
and Protestant Movements

1
Colonial Mennonites and Pietism

William Penn's Sylvania began as a "Holy Experiment." The youthful Penn in 1681 persuaded King Charles II to repay a debt owed to his father, Admiral Sir William Penn, with a land grant in the New World. Penn received his land charter on March 14, 1681. Soon after this formal agreement was issued, a short announcement concerning the new province appeared in London, and a newsletter in German circulated on the continent. Especially noteworthy was the manner in which freedom of conscience was to be handled in the laws of the land. They were reported to forbid godlessness, vanity, frivolity, and scandalous living, but no one was to be forced to attend religious services. Tournaments, card playing, comedies, masquerades, swearing of oaths, lying, scandalous gossip, adultery, harlotry, dueling, and stealing were not to be allowed. The laws of the land promised to be strongly oriented to the Decalogue.[1]

Penn's objective was to establish a colony where unwanted religious groups could find refuge. Penn himself belonged to one of these factions, the English Society of Friends, or Quakers. In the decades following 1650, the Quakers had been quite active in spreading their message in England, the Netherlands, and parts of Germany. Mennonites in Germany and the Netherlands felt a kinship with these Quaker missionaries similar to that which they felt with a growing number of Pietists.

A year after Penn received his land grant, March 9 and 10, 1682, a Krefeld Mennonite merchant named Jacob Telner and two of his acquaintances, Dirck Sipman and Jan Streypers, each purchased 5,000 acres in Pennsylvania with the expectation that the land would be made available to settlers. Telner had visited America at least once prior to this purchase. Within a year 13 Quaker and Mennonite families from the Krefeld area in North Germany near the Dutch border were planning to emigrate to Pennsylvania.[2] Shortly

---

[1] Friedrich Nieper, *Die ersten deutschen Auswanderer von Krefeld nach Pennsylvanien* (Buchhandlung des Erziehungsvereins Neukirchen Moers, 1940), p. 78.

[2] Numerous works have treated the Mennonite immigration to Pennsylvania: C. Henry Smith, *The Mennonite Immigration to Pennsylvania in the Eighteenth Century* (Norristown, Pa.: The Pennsylvania German Society, 1929); John L. Ruth, *Maintaining the Right Fellowship* (Scottdale, Pa.: Herald Press, 1984); Nieper, *Die ersten deutschen Auswanderer*; Harold S. Bender, "The Founding of the Mennonite Church at Germantown, 1683-1708," *Mennonite*

before their departure, on April 11, 1683, the Krefeld emigrants were visited by Daniel Francis Pastorius (1651-1720), deputy for a small group of Pietists from Frankfurt on the Main that was also planning to migrate to Pennsylvania.

The young Pastorius, an only son, had recently completed his studies in jurisprudence, followed by the customary grand tour of Europe. His spiritual search brought him into contact with a number of Pietists of the Spener circle and eventually resulted in his decision to go to America. In a farewell letter he expresses his motives for the venture. Satiated with the luxury and wantonness he had observed on his tour, he "yielded to the special guidance of the Supreme Being to journey to Pennsylvania." He continues:

> Accordingly I have entered upon this journey and passage across the great ocean under God's guidance the more cheerfully, in order to escape temporal and eternal ruin, and together with the nine persons attached to me, in company with a number of respected families, from Deal, the 7th of June, 1683, in the hope that the Lord, who till this hour has so richly blessed me and commanded his angels to keep watch over me, will so rule my outgoing and incoming that thereby His most Holy Name may be praised in unknown places beyond the sea.[3]

Pastorius and his party landed in Philadelphia on August 20, 1683. The Krefelders, arriving six weeks later, had a "wonderfully prosperous voyage" from England to America. Their journey took only six weeks. No lives were lost during the voyage and two babies were born, a son and a daughter.[4] Pastorius wrote a brief but detailed account of their arrival and settlement:

> On the 6th of the eighth month [October] arrived likewise in Philadelphia Dirck and Herman and Abraham Isaacs op den Graeff, Lenert Arets, Tunes Kunders, Reinert Tisen, Wilhelm Strepers, Jan Lensen, Peter Keurlis, Jan Semens, Johanes Bleickers, Abraham Tunes, and Jan Lucken, with their respective children and servants, together thirteen families.[5]

Considerable debate has focused on the religious affiliation and identity of these immigrants.[6] The initial group of settlers appears to have been composed largely of former Mennonites who before the time of their emigration had espoused Quaker beliefs. Jan Lensen was a Mennonite when the group arrived and remained a Mennonite. Two of the op den Graeff brothers in time rejoined the Mennonite Church. Both Jacob Telner and Isaac Jacob van

Bebber who had helped to arrange the immigration and joined the group in Germantown in 1684 were Mennonites.[7] The settlers named their village Germantown, suggesting that although some persons were of Dutch extraction the group identified itself as German.

Pastorius became an important leader of the group as they established their settlement. He and the settlers "without delay requested of William Penn that he should have laid out and surveyed in one tract on a navigable stream all the land bought by the above mentioned High and Low Germans."[8] The land offered by Penn was some miles above the falls of the Schuylkill, not far from the city of Philadelphia in what is now Manayunk. The settlers examined the land but deemed it unsuitable because of its high hills. They then requested of William Penn that he

> grant . . . the township on more level ground in the wooded region, to which he agreed and afterwards on the 24th of October had fourteen lots or heredity shares, surveyed by Thomas Fairman, for which the above mentioned thirteen families drew lots on the 25th of the same month, and began forthwith to construct cellars and houses, in which they spent the winter, not without great hardships.[9]

Although the village was named Germantown, their initial poverty soon invited the nickname Armentown or Poortown, for many of the settlers had no means with which to purchase the supplies necessary for their survival

---

Quarterly Review (hereinafter *MQR*) 7 (October 1933): 227-250; Helmut E. Huelsbergen, "The First Thirteen Families," *Yearbook of German-American Studies* 18 (1983): 29-40; C. J. Dyck, "European Mennonite Motivation for Emigration," *Pennsylvania Mennonite Heritage* 6 (October 1983): 2-9; John L. Ruth, "A Christian Settlement 'In Antiquam Silvam,'" *MQR* 57 (October 1983): 307-331; and Robert Ulle, "Materials on Mennonites in Colonial Germantown," *MQR* 57 (October 1983): 354-387; and "Sources on Germantown History," *MQR* 57 (October 1983): 332-338.

[3] Learned, *Pastorius*, pp. 116-117. The ship was apparently delayed and left the 10th, not the 7th.

[4] Letter written by one of the three immigrant op den Graeff brothers. See William I. Hull, *William Penn and the Dutch Quaker Migration to Pennsylvania* (Swarthmore, Pa.: 1935), pp. 215-216.

[5] *Grund und Lager Buch* (Archives, The Historical Society of Pennsylvania, 1300 Locust Street, Philadelphia, Pa.) The *Grund und Lager Buch* is treated in detail with translations in Marion Dexter Learned, *The Life of Francis Daniel Pastorius* (1908). The quotation was taken from Franz Daniel Pastorius, "The Beginnings of Germantown," *Mennonite Historical Bulletin* (hereinafter *MHB*) 33 (April 1972): 2. Learned presents Pastorius' account in both the original German and in English translation, pp. 268-274.

[6] See especially Hull, *The Dutch Quaker Migration*, and Bender, "Founding the Mennonite Church."

[7] See Bender, ibid., and Smith, *Mennonite Immigration*, pp. 84-94.

[8] Pastorius, "The Beginnings of Germantown."

[9] Ibid.

through the winter. According to Pastorius, who continued to live in Philadelphia, the needy settlers in Germantown that first winter received frequent encouragement and actual assistance from William Penn.[10]

A letter from one of the Germantown settlers to the homeland, dated the following February 12, reports on the situation of the immigrants including the type of land, vegetation, the city of Philadelphia and " 'our city of Germantown' with its rivers and valleys." "The Indians," the writer reports, "show themselves very kind and friendly, and we live together very quiet and peaceable. We travel night and day through the forest without the least fear of them. Most of us already have our own habitations and every day more houses are being built, all of which pleases us greatly.... We have begun to spin flax."[11] Then, a dissonant note: Moors or blacks, the writer says, work as slaves in Philadelphia.

Hard physical labor was necessary for the development of the province. Pastorius discovered quickly upon his arrival that his nine aides and servants lacked the physical strength and skills needed to clear the forest, build houses, and do agricultural work. The Krefelders, too, were poorly suited for taming Penn's Woods. They were weavers, and although within a few years they brought prosperity to Germantown, there was initially no market for the product of their looms. Pastorius' letter to the homeland in March 1684, states that their greatest need was for builders and agricultural workers. He wished for a dozen strong Tyrolese to cut down the thick trees, for Penn's Sylvania was all forest.[12]

One accessible solution to the constant labor demanded for survival in the wilderness was to acquire slaves. Some Philadelphians, including Quakers, adopted this solution. To at least some of the Krefelders, the practice was objectionable. In 1688 several of them wrote a protest against slavery addressed to the Quaker monthly meeting at Richard Worell's. The document was signed by Garret Hendricks, Derick op den Graeff, Abraham op den Graeff, and Francis Daniell Pastorius and was written in Pastorius' hand.[13] All four signatories were Quakers at the time the document was written, but that it reflects Mennonite influence has been acknowledged by both Mennonites and Quakers.[14] The document confronts Quakers who are slaveholders, explicating the reasons why the signatories oppose the practice.

> These are the reasons why we are against the traffik of menbody, as followeth. Is there any that would be done or handled in this manner? viz., to be sold or made a slave for all the time of his life? ... we hear that ye most part of such negers are brought hitherto against their will and consent, and that many of them are stolen. Now tho they are black we cannot conceive there is more liberty to have them as slaves, as it is

to have other white ones. There is a saying that we should do to all men like as we will be done ourselves; making no difference of what generation, descent or colour they are. And those who steal or rob men, and those who buy or purchase them, are they not all alike?[15]

That slaveholding often leads to adultery and the forcible breakup of families is pointed out. The document goes on to say "This makes an ill report in all those countries of Europe, where they hear off, that ye Quakers doe here handle men as they handle there ye cattle. And for that reason some have no mind or inclination to come hither."[16] The writers further inquire whether owners would retain their nonresistant principles in the face of a slave uprising:

> will these masters and mastresses take the sword at hand and warr against these poor slaves, licke, we are able to believe, some will not refuse to doe; or have these negers not as much right to fight for their freedom, as you have to keep them as slaves?[17]

The discussion is concluded with an invitation to the recipients to demonstrate that Christians have a right to hold slaves.

The document was carried to the Quaker Monthly Meeting at Dublin, Pa., the second day of February 1688, but the Dublin Meeting "considered it a matter of too great importance to 'meddle with it here.'"[18] The Philadelphia Quarterly Meeting also considered it too important to act on, and passed it on to the Annual Meeting. Nothing more concerning the document is to be found in the official records.

A trickle of Mennonite settlers arrived almost annually after 1683.[19] By the end of the decade they were meeting separately from the Quakers for worship, and in 1698 they organized formally, electing William Rittenhouse

---

[10] Ibid.

[11] Letter, Hull, *Dutch Quaker Migration*, p. 215.

[12] Francis Daniel Pastorius, *Sichere Nachricht auss America, wegen der Landschaffe Pennsylvania, von einem dorthin gereissten Teutschen/ de dato Philadelphia, den 7 Martii 1684*. Reproduced in Learned, *Pastorius*, pp. 128ff. See also pp. 156-157.

[13] For the full text of the document see Smith, *Mennonite Immigration*, pp. 106-110. The names are spelled here as they appear on the document.

[14] *MHB* 33 (April 1972): 8. See also C. Henry Smith, *The Story of the Mennonites*, 3rd ed., revised by C. Krahn (Newton, Kans.: Mennonite Publication Office, 1950), p. 534; and J. Herbert Fretz, "Germantown Anti-Slavery Protest," *Mennonite Life* 13 (October 1958):183-186.

[15] Smith, *Mennonite Immigration*, p. 107.

[16] Ibid., p. 108.

[17] Ibid.

[18] Ibid., p. 109.

[19] Smith, *Mennonite Immigration*, pp. 94-96.

as minister and Jan Neues as deacon.[20] In all likelihood, this was simply an election, not an ordination with the laying on of hands, for there was no elder in America to perform this rite. A second election was held on October 8, 1702, and two additional preachers were chosen, Jacob Godschalk from Goch and Hans Neues from Crefeld.[21] The Mennonite belief in the priesthood of all believers was expressed in a practical way. Shepherds of the flock were chosen from the congregation and served for life, without pay. Seminary training was not a prerequisite for ordination. Choosing two or more ministers to serve a given congregation was a means of making the office less burdensome to any one minister.

At the turn of the century, almost two decades after the founding of the community, the basic rites of baptism and the Lord's Supper had not yet been observed, for there was no properly ordained elder to officiate at these services. A number of persons had requested baptism, and a letter was written to the congregation in Altona, near Hamburg, Germany, apparently requesting that an elder come to Germantown in order to ordain a leader who could then appropriately administer baptism and the Lord's Supper. The letter is no longer extant, neither is the reply, except for a passage that was copied, signed, and preserved in the Archives of the Mennonite Church in Hamburg-Altona.[22]

The Altona elders recognized the exigencies of the situation in Germantown, advising that it be publicly discussed with the entire congregation. Following this discussion they recommended a period of prayer, asking that God would look graciously on the weakness and shortcomings inherent under existing conditions yet bless the administering of baptism and communion under these circumstances. The elders cite a number of New Testament instances in which, upon the expression of faith and belief, baptism or communion was given apart from the usual structural framework. Hesitation appears to have continued at Germantown, however, and it was not until early in 1708 that Rittenhouse and the congregation made plans to proceed with baptism and the Lord's Supper. Before the anticipated service, on February 2, 1708, Rittenhouse died.

A group of Palatine Mennonites had arrived in Germantown in 1707. For an entire year they kept to themselves, holding their own services.[23] Following the death of Rittenhouse the two Mennonite groups united. They chose three additional men as overseers on March 22, 1708, and a month later, on April 20, 1708, two more preachers were chosen. The congregation then decided that the long-proposed baptism should take place. "It fell to Jacob Godschalk to do this, and so the first members to be taken into our church in this country by baptism were received, eleven in number."[24] This service took place on May 9, 1708. The Mennonite Church at Germantown then had 45 members. Infants and children were not baptized, and only baptized persons were counted as members, so the total community consisted of a considerably larger number of persons.

In the meantime Mennonites began settling not only in Germantown but also along the Skippack Creek in what is now Montgomery County. A tract of 6,166 acres of land was purchased by the Mennonite Mathias van Bebber on February 22, 1702, and resold to persons wishing to relocate in the area. Between 1702 and 1709 at least the following Mennonites took advantage of this opportunity: Hendrick Pannabecker and his brother-in-law Johannes Umstat, Johannes Kuster, Klas Jansen, Jan Krey, John Jacobs, Hermanus Kuster, Christopher Zimmerman, and Jacob, Johannes, and Martin Kolb.[25] Initially this settlement was considered an extension of the Germantown community and church.

The first American Mennonite meetinghouse was built in 1708, standing on the same site on Germantown Avenue as the present stone structure which replaced it in 1770. Mennonite immigrants continued to arrive, so that by April 6, 1712, the "church at Germantown and as far as Skippack had grown to the extent that it consisted of 99 members in number,"[26] a community of possibly 250 persons. The migration of Germans to Pennsylvania was slow in the first decades of the settlement. As immigration increased, the expansion of the settlement moved in a northerly direction into the more rural areas along the Skippack and Perkiomen creeks, and the local Germantown Mennonite community and church remained small.

Mennonite settlers began arriving in much larger numbers following 1710. They formed two settlements, one at Pequea, which developed into the Lancaster County settlement; the other, an expansion of the beginning settlement along the Skippack. The new arrivals were Swiss Brethren, who for a period of time, varying from a few years to a half century, had found refuge in the Palatinate. Persecution of the Anabaptists in Switzerland had been particularly intense during the second half of the seventeenth century. Concurrently, rulers of the Palatinate were seeking skilled, industrious

---

[20] Our source is an account of the settlement written by Jacob Godschalk and preserved in a 1773 letter written to Holland. "A Letter from Pennsylvania Mennonites to Holland in 1773," *MQR* 3 (October 1929):225-234.

[21] Ibid.

[22] "An Interesting Document in the Early History of Germantown," Research Notes, *MQR* 6 (October 1931):284-285. One of the four signatories was Gerrit Roosen, author of a widely used catechism among Mennonites.

[23] "Letter from Pennsylvania Mennonites to Holland," p. 228.

[24] Ibid.

[25] Smith, *Mennonite Immigration*, p. 106.

[26] "Letter from Pennsylvania Mennonites to Holland," p. 228.

farmers as both their land and population had been devastated by the Thirty Years' War (1618-1648).

Many Swiss Anabaptists responded to the invitation from Palatine rulers and with thrift and industry rehabilitated the land. All went reasonably well for the Swiss Mennonite immigrants to the Palatinate from about 1650 to 1700. During this time rulers in the Palatinate were Lutheran or Reformed. Recognizing the economic value of the Mennonites, they tolerated their religious deviancy.

At the turn of the century Catholics came into power and the zealous Jesuits again made circumstances very difficult for the Mennonites. They were no longer permitted to purchase land, and for a time, that which they owned could be repurchased by the former owner at the price for which he had sold it, disregarding improvements that had been made. Officially, Mennonites were not permitted to marry, which meant that their children were not legitimate and could not receive inheritance; nor were they permitted to bury their dead in the common burial grounds.[27] As a consequence many Mennonites migrated to Pennsylvania in the early 1700s.

Mennonite families were typically the organizers of the migrations from Palatinate villages. Young persons from the Lutheran and Reformed churches frequently requested permission to accompany the migration.[28] These persons sometimes served as hired hands for the Mennonite families upon their arrival in Pennsylvania, later marrying into the family and joining the Mennonite Church. The progenitor of the Alderfers in the Franconia area is said to have been a Lutheran immigrant, as was Nicholas Stoltzfus to whom the numerous Stoltzfuses of Lancaster County trace their ancestry.

As the century advanced, Catholic rule in the Palatinate, harsh taxation, and bad economic conditions also motivated increasing numbers of German Lutherans and German Reformed to migrate to Pennsylvania. Since both groups were organized on a state-church pattern and these migrations had no official sponsorship, no one was responsible for the spiritual welfare of the immigrants upon their arrival. Both groups encountered problems of organization during their first years in America. There were four ministers for 15,000 German Reformed settlers in the Middle Colonies in 1741 and three Lutheran clergymen for a similar number of communicants.[29] In a letter pleading for additional pastors, an early leader in the Reformed Church in Pennsylvania complains that because of the lack of pastors, "the number of those who ... have gone over to the Tumplers [Brethren], Sabbatarians, and Mennonites and others is so large that it cannot be stated without tears in one's eyes."[30]

The charter's provisions made it possible for Penn's Sylvania to quickly become a home for religious separatists of varying national origins and denominational loyalties. Some of the immigrants were craftsmen who soon became merchants, others were farmers who had been landowners when not restricted by religiously based economic sanctions. Following 1710, a large portion of the immigrants were German-speaking. The sectarians among them were devout, sometimes extreme in their beliefs, plain in dress and manner of life. The church people as well, whether Lutheran or Reformed, as already noted came without official sponsorship and therefore without church structures. Establishment travelers were dismayed at the variegated religious scene and confounded by the religious confusion in Pennsylvania. A harbinger of American religious patterns to come, the situation was appalling to eighteenth-century observers.

Both under conditions of persecution in Europe and frontier life in America there developed a hospitableness between groups that amounted to fluidity. Mennonites migrated with, hosted, settled alongside, and sometimes worshiped with German Quakers, German Lutherans, German Reformed, and German Schwenkfelders. Church buildings were shared by Mennonites, Lutherans, and Reformed at a number of sites; in one instance the Mennonites worshiped with Lutherans and Reformed in the same house for over 100 years.[31] The Schwenkfelders were spiritual descendants of Caspar Schwenkfeld (1498-1561), a small remnant of whose followers came to Pennsylvania in 1734, aided by Dutch Mennonites and Moravians.[32] Amish settlers, a distinct, conservative group of Swiss Anabaptists dating from a schism in 1693, began to arrive in 1727, settling in areas now part of Berks and Lancaster counties. Radical Pietist separatists soon also found refuge in Pennsylvania. More exclusivist in their beliefs and ready to proselytize, they sometimes posed a serious threat to the Mennonites.

---

[27] Smith, *Mennonite Immigration*, pp. 29-48.

[28] Personal conversation, Karl Scherer, director, *Heimatstelle Pfaltz*, Kaiserslautern, Germany.

[29] John B. Franz, "The Awakening of Religion Among German Settlers in the Middle Colonies, *William and Mary Quarterly*, 3rd Series 33 (1976):270. The congregational organization of the Mennonite churches, the practice of ordaining ministers from the congregation, and the absence of seminary requirements for ordination meant that Mennonites did not suffer the acute lack of ordained ministers experienced by the German Lutherans and the German Reformed in the early colonial period. For a discussion of this situation and its attendant complications, see also Martin E. Lodge, "The Crisis of the Church in the Middle Colonies," *The Pennsylvania Magazine of History and Biography* 95 (April 1971):195-220.

[30] Letter from John Philip Boehm to the Dutch Deputy Vellinguis, October 23, 1734, quoted in Donald F. Durnbaugh, ed., *The Brethren in Colonial America* (Elgin, Ill.: The Brethren Press, 1967), pp. 132-133.

[31] John D. Souder, "The Life and Times of Dielman Kolb, 1691-1756," *MQR* 3 (January 1929):39.

[32] For a series of letters in which the persecuted Schwenkfelders seek aid from the Dutch Mennonites, see Peter C. Erb, "Dialogue Under Duress: Schwenkfelder-Mennonite Contact in the Eighteenth Century," *MQR* 50 (July 1976):181-199.

Mennonites and Pietists in Pennsylvania

Mennonites in both Europe and America were open to fellowship with Pietists at the beginning of the eighteenth century, interacting with a freedom that was not to be seen again until well into the twentieth century. Pietism found expression in a variety of forms and virtually the complete spectrum was to be found among the Pennsylvania Germans by 1750. Except for the Mennonites and Amish, the German sectarians who came to Pennsylvania before 1745 were Pietists, as were a considerable number of church people as well. Pietism tended to blur denominational boundaries, for all of the Awakened shared a common "experience," and that experience was considered paramount. Some Mennonites found the zeal of the Pietists compellingly attractive and were drawn into their fellowships. The mingling of the varied groups climaxed in 1742 with a series of conferences on spiritual union led by Count Zinzendorf.

In its early phases Pietism bore a close kinship to Anabaptism: both called for a voluntary religious response, a personal religious experience, and included an ethical dimension. Both emphasized the study of the Scriptures in small groups, and both experienced censorship by the established church. The first Mennonites to come to Pennsylvania had been in close contact with Pietism before their emigration. Johann Arndt's *True Christianity*, published in 1615 and one of the first writings of proto-Pietism, was a favorite devotional book of the Mennonites, particularly in Switzerland. Pietists as well as Mennonites had found refuge in the Krefeld area of North Germany from which the first immigrants came. The German Quakers, from whom the first Mennonites in Pennsylvania are distinguished with difficulty, had a close affinity to Pietism.

Pietism began as a renewal movement in the Lutheran and Reformed churches on the continent. In the state church context where it began, Pietism awakened church members to the possibility of the individual personally experiencing the presence of Christ in his or her own life. It stressed the necessity of a conversion experience for each person and frequently called for basic reforms in church practice and personal living. Pietism as a movement dates from the appearance of *Pia Desideria* (Pious Desires) written by Philip Jacob Spener (1635-1705) and first published in 1675 as the "Introduction" to a new edition of Johann Arndt's *True Christianity*.[33] Spener was a Lutheran pastor and identified his concerns with Luther's teachings. He proposed six reforms: (1) increased Bible reading and study; (2) the priesthood of all believers; (3) that faith consists of practice, including love for one's enemies; (4) that purity of doctrine is maintained by holiness of life, not only by disputations and the writing of books; (5) that ministers themselves must be Christian—proper ordination and knowledge of pure doctrine alone do not suffice; and (6) that sermons should be a means of bringing salvation to the hearer, not merely exercises in erudition. Spener's statement was received with so much enthusiasm that it was republished as a book within a year.

During his years of growth to maturity, and at the time *Pia Desideria* was written, Spener was living in an area of Alsace where asylum was being given to a substantial number of Anabaptists. Spener's godmother, Countess Agatha of Salm, was married to one of the benefactors of the Anabaptists, Eberhard of Ribeaupierre. A decade and a half after the appearance of *Pia Desideria* Jacob Ammann, an Anabaptist leader of the area, deplored that the Anabaptists in Alsace were attending the state churches and holding that half-Anabaptists could be saved. This strongly suggests significant interchange between Anabaptists and Pietists in the region.[34]

Spener's points closely parallel Anabaptist teaching. Yet there were differences. Spener intended that his followers should remain within the state church, baptize infants, and support the state in warfare—all of which were contrary to Anabaptist positions. Pietism was a heart religion, valuing feeling and emotional warmth. Anabaptism emphasized free will, freedom of choice, and the necessity of obedience to the commandments of Christ. In contrast to Pietism, it sometimes appeared to be cold, legalistic, and "dead," and was frequently said to be so.

Although Pietism developed primarily as a renewal movement within the churches, Radical Pietist groups separated from the state church in the eighteenth century. They soon experienced persecution and numbers of them migrated to Pennsylvania, including the Contented of the God Loving Soul, the Dunkers or German Baptist Brethren, Inspirationists, and the Moravians. The Ephrata community which developed on American soil was also pietistical. All of these groups were active in Pennsylvania by 1742. Pietism was represented in the Lutheran and Reformed churches as well. The first outstanding leader of the German Lutherans in Pennsylvania, Henry Melchior Muhlenberg (1711-1787), who arrived in 1742, was a Pietist, as was Michael Schlatter (1716-1790), who arrived in 1746 and was highly in-

---

[33] Johann Arndt (1555-1621). See Philip Jacob Spener, *Pia Desideria*, tr., ed., and with an introduction by Theodore G. Tappert (Philadelphia: Fortress Press, 1964). While Pietism as a movement is dated from Spener's *Pia Desideria*, the phenomenon had appeared considerably earlier. See F. Ernest Stoeffler, *The Rise of Evangelical Pietism* (Leiden: E. J. Brill, 1965), pp. 1-108.

[34] Jean Séguy, *Les Assemblées Anabaptistes-Mennonites de France* (Paris, La Haye, Moulton, 1977), esp. pp. 126-128; Milton Gascho, "The Amish Division of 1693-97 in Switzerland and Alsace," *MQR* 11 (October 1937):235-266; and John B. Mast, ed., *The Letters of the Amish Division* (Oregon City, Oreg.: C. J. Schlabach, 1950).

fluential in the German Reformed Church.

The Radical Pietist Separatists who sought refuge in Pennsylvania had been influenced by the teachings of Jacob Boehme (1575-1624), a Protestant mystic. Boehme's activities and writings were strongly censored during his lifetime but they quietly spread their influence for a century. Boehme claimed insight through special revelation into the divine nature and harmony of the cosmos. He believed that the Living Word, the Christ within, takes precedence over the written Word. Apart from the Christ within, the Scriptures are a dead letter. Some of his ideas reappeared in the sermons of the Lancaster Mennonite revival preacher Martin Boehm in the 1760s and 1770s, as we shall see later. Jacob Boehme held that Adam was created androgynous, and that the desire to become male and female like the animals constituted the Fall. Boehme's followers valued celibacy, considering it a higher spiritual state than marriage, and they often gave apocalypticism considerable emphasis.

In 1694 a group of about 40 eminent German scholars who had been strongly influenced by Boehmist theosophy arrived in Philadelphia. They were mathematicians and scholars, but above all Pietists and theosophists. They located first in Germantown, then settled nearby along the Wissahickon in what is now Fairmont Park. They named themselves the Contented of the God Loving Soul but were also called the Society of the Woman in the Wilderness or simply the Hermits of the Wissahickon. Their youthful leader, Johannes Kelpius (1673-c.1708), chose to live in a cave that can still be visited in Fairmont Park. A common house was built for the remaining members. The group had journeyed to Pennsylvania with the anticipation of meeting Christ there in the wilderness at his second coming, which they believed was imminent. From a tower atop their residence, members of the group maintained a continuous watch for signs of his appearing.

The German Baptist Brethren or Dunkers were the next group of Pietist separatists to arrive in Germantown. The Brethren had been in close contact with Mennonites in the Rhineland both before and after their organization as a group in 1708 under the leadership of Alexander Mack (1679-1735). Some of the persecuted Dunkers found refuge in the Krefeld area, where they attracted numerous Mennonites to their fold. In America, the Brethren similarly established settlements close to the Mennonites and many Mennonites joined the Brethren church.[35]

The Brethren combined Pietist and Anabaptist principles in their belief.[36] Like the Anabaptists, the Brethren emphasized the importance of the disciplined community, and the principle and practice of not resisting violence with force. Unlike the Mennonites, they insisted on triune immersion (three times forward, in a running stream) as the only form of baptism. It was this practice that invited the name Dunker or Tunker.

When the Dunkers came to America, beginning in 1719, they came first of all to Germantown, where some of their members settled. Others found homes in the hinterland. During the ocean voyage tensions had arisen in the group and these stresses, compounded by the problem of geographic distance between settlements, resulted in a delay of several years in the resumption of Dunker congregational life.

A spiritual awakening among the Dunkers, beginning in 1722 and climaxing several years later, is recorded in the *Ephrata Chronicle:*

> The next spring, of 1724, however, when they resumed their meetings there was given to them such a blessing that the whole region roundabout was moved thereby. Particularly among their youth was this movement felt, who now, to the great edification of their elders, began to walk in the fear of the Lord and to love the Brethren. And as the fame of this awakening spread abroad, there was such an increase of attendance at their meetings, that there was no room to contain the majority. The following summer again many of them were moved, and love feasts were held, through which many of them were impelled to join them, and so their communion experienced a steady increase.[37]

In the fall of 1724 male members of the Germantown Brethren congregation set out in pairs to take their renewal message to the hinterland. The Seventh-Day Baptists of the Ephrata community, one of the most colorful and best-known Pietist groups in colonial Pennsylvania, developed indirectly as a result of this mission endeavor. In 1720 a young man named Conrad Beissel (1690-1768) had journeyed to America with the expectation of joining the Kelpius group along the Wissahickon. Upon his arrival he learned of the gradual demise of the group following the death of Kelpius in 1708. Beissel apprenticed himself for a year to a weaver, Peter Becker (1687-1758), a Dunker preacher. For several years following his apprenticeship Beissel lived in the forests of Lancaster County, sometimes with a few companions. As a result of the mission activity of Dunker itinerants in this area in the fall of 1724, several acquaintances of Beissel were baptized by Becker. Beissel was at

---

[35] Donald F. Durnbaugh, ed., *European Origins of the Brethren* (Elgin, Ill.: The Brethren Press, 1958) pp. 121, 203-214; Durnbaugh, "Work and Hope: The Spirituality of the Radical Pietist Communitarians," *Church History* 39 (1970):72-90; C. Henry Smith, *The Mennonites of America* (Goshen, Ind.: The Author, 1909), p. 178.

[36] Donald F. Durnbaugh, "The Brethren in Early American Church Life," in F. Ernest Stoeffler, ed., *Continental Pietism and Early American Christianity* (Grand Rapids, Mich.: Eerdmans, 1976), pp. 222-265.

[37] *Chronicon Ephratense: A History of Seventh Day Baptists at Ephrata, Lancaster County, Penn'a,* tr. J. Max Hark (1889), p. 23.

Rittenhouse homestead in Fairmont Park, Philadelphia

first reluctant to receive baptism from someone he considered spiritually inferior, but, remembering that Jesus was baptized by John the Baptist, he, too, requested baptism from Becker.[38] The newly baptized were given considerable autonomy because of the distance from the mother church, and Beissel became their leader.

The following spring, May 1725, Beissel baptized seven additional persons at Conestoga, including a former Mennonite minister, Rudolf Nägele and his wife, and Michael Wohlfahrt, Beissel's former companion in the wilderness.[39] After their baptisms Nägele and Wolfahrt set out on an evangelizing tour, mainly through the Oley and Schuylkill areas.

The small group at Conestoga was initially considered a Dunker congregation, but differences quickly became apparent. Beissel's mystic speculations of occult theosophy confounded his followers. Some deemed him inspired, others thought him demented. "Thus matters went on until it became imperative for him to sacrifice his beloved solitude and take up an abode among his people."[40] Beissel moved into a cabin erected for him on the land of the former Mennonite, Rudolf Nägele, and his example was quickly followed by others. "In a few months the land in the vicinity of Nägele's house was dotted with small log cabins of persons who wished to live in closer communion with the new leader."[41]

Additional baptisms took place at Conestoga on Christmas Day, 1726, and on Whitsunday, May 21, 1727. At the latter meeting "extraordinary powers were manifested." Antiphonal singing, for which the Ephrata community later became renowned, was introduced. The singing was "pentecostal and heavenly; yea, some declared that they heard angels' voices mingled with it."[42] Ecstasy at these meetings was inadvertently the harbinger of controversy. The day after the initial baptisms at Conestoga, quarreling was pronounced.[43] On Easter Sunday, 1726, controversy arose concerning the judgments of God. Difficulties multiplied, for Beissel believed in direct inspiration apart from written Scriptures, was a Sabbatarian, and advocated celibacy. By 1728 the Conestoga followers of Beissel and the Dunkers had severed relationships with one another.

Significant numbers of Beissel's early followers had Mennonite ties. Speaking of early followers, the *Ephrata Chronicle* records:

> It is yet to be remarked that these same good people, who were mostly descended from the Mennonites, had, after the manner of that people, a certain simplicity and lowliness of life; and the Superintendent [Beissel], in spite of the fact that he had had experience in the world of vanity and show, could so thoroughly adapt himself to their ways that his clothing, dwelling, and household were fashioned on the poorest scale. It was not long, however, before persons of social position landed in the Community, among whom the Eckerlins were the first.[44]

The Eckerlins, too, had experienced contact with the Mennonites. In his account of migration and conversion, Eckerlin says that "for a time we adhered to the Mennonites, because their simplicity of dress pleased us; but to their mode of worship we never could adapt ourselves." While some Mennonites were absorbed into the Ephrata community, others were critical. Eckerlin continues: "Then we inquired about the new congregation and its Superintendent, but heard of nothing but whoredom and lewdness, which were said to prevail there."[45] In spite of these reports, Eckerlin joined the community, and soon became its prior.

---

[38] Ibid., p. 24.
[39] Ibid., p. 33.
[40] Julius Friedrich Sachse, *The German Sectarians of Pennsylvania, 1708-1742* (Philadelphia: Printed by the author, 1899), p. 121.
[41] Ibid., p. 120.
[42] Ibid., pp. 127-128.
[43] *Chronicon*, p. 26.
[44] Ibid., p. 55.
[45] Ibid., p. 41.

Evangelists and missionaries spread out in all directions from Ephrata, convincing and converting former Mennonites, Brethren, Lutheran, and Reformed. The Reformed Church became alarmed when their eminent scholar and pastor John Peter Miller (1709-1796) joined the Ephrata community, taking a significant number of members with him. Several years later it was Miller who translated the *Martyrs Mirror* from Dutch into German for the Mennonites. Peter Lehman, a former Amishman, became leader of the Snow Hill branch of the Ephrata community and served in that capacity for 40 years.[46]

It was during this time of ferment that the Mennonites of Pennsylvania held their first-known conference, in 1725. It was a conjoint meeting of the two settlements, and its intent was to select a confession of faith that could be printed in English and circulated among the English-speaking colonists. They chose the accessible Dordrecht Confession of 1632, *The Christian Confession of Faith of the harmless Christians, in the Netherlands, known by the name of Mennonists.*[47] A note of explanation was included on the reverse side of the title page:

To the Christian Reader

We lovingly desire thee, not to look so much on the meanness of the wording of this little book; because we are of Dutch Extraction, and therefore willingly will own, that we are not exquisite in the English Language, but to look on the Grounds and Truths therein: And also kindly desire thee to Read the Same without Partiality; and consider the Exhortation of the Apostle Paul I Thes. 5:21. Prove all things, hold fast that which is "good."[48]

The document is signed by leaders from the Mennonite congregations at "Shipack," "Germantown," "Canastoge," "Great-Swamp," and "Manatany." The stimulus for publishing a confession of faith at this time was evidently the need for clarification of beliefs in the face of a very real external threat. All of the sectarians were experiencing an identity crisis and the appeal of the Radical Pietists was great.

The Ephrata community grew rapidly. A monastic-type organization was developed, and a special garb adopted. An order for men and an order for women was supplemented by an adjunct order for householders. Under the administrative leadership of Israel Eckerlin, large buildings were erected, orchards and mills developed, and the community made into an economic and cultural center for eastern Pennsylvania. *Fraktur* writing and choral singing became highly developed arts. In 1745 the community purchased a printing press and began job printing for the German colonists. The Mennonites were among their most active customers.

Separatists, who were not affiliated with any religious body, represented another strand of Pietism in America. Christopher Sauer (1693-1758), the influential Germantown printer, was a Separatist. Sauer, commenting on the religious scene in Pennsylvania in a letter to Schwartzenau dated August 1, 1725, says:

> There are still, to be sure, many souls who have a pleasing understanding. Most, however, have barricaded themselves into sects and groups. The Brethren have erected a fence around themselves; they admit and expel, and are jealous and quarrelsome with others. The Mennonites conduct things somewhat more honorably.[49]

Sauer's wife became a leading participant in the Ephrata community.[50] His son and namesake became a leader in the Church of the Brethren.

The Inspirationists, too, were Radical Pietists who as a result of their contact with the traveling French Prophets, or Camisards, came to believe in direct Inspiration, usually while the "Instrument" was in a trance.

One such Inspirationist, John Adam Gruber (1693-1736), had in Germany been associated with the Community of True Inspiration which a century later founded the well-known Amana community in Iowa.[51] It was through the youthful Gruber as Instrument that the "Twenty Four Rules of True Godliness" for the Inspirationists were pronounced on July 4, 1716.[52] Gruber lost the gift after a serious disagreement with his father. Within a few years he married, and came to America in 1726. He settled in Germantown with his family and a decade later contributed significantly to discussions concerning spiritual union.

Yet another Pietistic group made itself felt in Pennsylvania when the Moravian missionary August Gottlieb Spangenberg (1704-1792) arrived in 1736 with a commission to minister to the German-speaking Christians in Pennsylvania. The Moravians were a gathered remnant of the *Unitas Fratrum*, a Protestant group dating from the fifteenth-century reforms of

---

[46] Sachse, *The German Sectarians*, p. 365.

[47] Printed, and Reprinted and Sold by *Andrew Bradford* in Philadelphia, in the Year, 1727. Original in the Historical Society of Pennsylvania. For a commentary on the confession see Irvin B. Horst, "The Dordrecht Confession of Faith: 350 Years," *Pennsylvania Mennonite Heritage* 5 (July 1982):2-8.

[48] Sachse, *The German Sectarians*, p. 132.

[49] Durnbaugh, *The Brethren in Colonial America*, p. 36.

[50] *Chronicon*, pp. 55-56.

[51] For a detailed account of Gruber, see Donald F. Durnbaugh, "Johann Adam Gruber, Pennsylvania-German Prophet and Poet," *The Pennsylvania Magazine of History and Biography* 83 (October 1959):382-408.

[52] Ibid., p. 387.

John Huss. In 1722 a few scattered members of this group found a refuge on the Berthelsdorf estate of Count Ludwig Nicholas von Zinzendorf (1700-1760), a devout Pietist. The sanctuary drew others, and soon several hundred had gathered.

Zinzendorf took a paternal interest in their welfare, and though a Lutheran, was soon recognized as their religious leader. Under Zinzendorf's leadership the Moravians became active missionaries, establishing missions in foreign countries and with equal zeal sending out missioners to "awaken" members of existing denominations.

The Moravians placed great emphasis on unity, and when Spangenberg came to Pennsylvania with a group of missionaries, he was appalled at the religious fragmentation, calling Pennsylvania a "veritable Babel."[53] During his stay in Pennsylvania he wrote detailed reports of his observations and experiences to European associates including the prominent Dutch Mennonite Pietist John Deknatel (1698-1759) with whom he had become acquainted when he visited Amsterdam in December, 1734.[54]

Spangenberg carried on his work among the German colonists from the farmstead of Christopher Wiegner. They were responsive, for "Spangenberg ... was greatly respected by the German Separatists and sectarians because of his piety, humble manners, earnestness, and winsome personality. They were much impressed at the willingness of the former professor at Halle to labor in the fields with his hands."[55] Tactfully, Spangenberg tried to organize the separatists into a group. John Adam Gruber was among the convinced and circulated an anonymous appeal for union. Out of these efforts a group for devotion, prayer, and mutual edification was formed, known as the Associated Brethren of the Skippack.

The Associated Brethren of the Skippack were active as hosts when the young evangelist George Whitefield (1714-1770) visited eastern Pennsylvania in 1739 and 1740. Whitefield was merely 24 years of age when he began preaching to large outdoor assemblies in the colonies. Six thousand persons gathered to hear him preach in Germantown in 1739. On the morning of April 24, 1740, he was in Montgomery in eastern Pennsylvania. Later that day he spoke to a crowd of 2,000 at Wiegner's in Skippack, and in the afternoon at Henry Antes' with 3,000 in attendance. A second sermon was preached in German at both places by George Boehler, a minister who had come to Pennsylvania on Whitefield's ship with fellow Moravians.[56]

Whitefield's *Journal* gives an account of the day:

> Thursday, April 24. Was hospitably entertained with my friends last night at Montgomery, about eight miles from Neshaminy, whither I came to make this day's journey the easier. Preached at Skippack,

sixteen miles from Montgomery, where the Dutch [German] people live. It was seemingly, a very wilderness part of the country but there were not less, I believe, than two thousand hearers. When I had done, Peter Bohler, a deacon of the Moravian Church, a dear lover of our Lord Jesus Christ, preached to his countrymen in Dutch [German]. Traveling and preaching in the sun again, weakened me much and made me very sick; but by the Divine assistance, I took horse, rode twelve miles, and preached in the evening to about three thousand people at a Dutchman's plantation, who seemed to have drunk deeply of God's holy Spirit. The German Brethren were exceedingly loving to me, and I spent the evening with many of them in a most agreeable manner. The order, seriousness, and devotion of these people in common life, is most worthy of imitation. They prayed and sang in their language, and then God enlarged my heart to pray in *ours*.[57]

The "Dutchman's plantation" was Henry Antes' farm. Antes was an elder of the Falkner Swamp Reformed Church and a member of the Associated Brethren of the Skippack. In light of the many negative comments being made at the time it is interesting to note that Whitefield speaks positively of the religious life of the Pennsylvania Germans and of the fellowship he experienced with them. Whitefield sang and prayed with his own friends and the German Brethren before daybreak the next morning, then he and his party traveled 35 miles to another meeting, at Atwell in the East Jerseys. When they arrived Gilbert Tennent and a Mr. Rowland had already preached three sermons. Whitefield preached a fourth.[58]

Whitefield experienced warm spiritual fellowship with the Germans, but he also became aware of their desperate need for pastors and wrote a letter to Zinzendorf sharing this concern.[59] Zinzendorf responded by calling Spangenberg back to Europe, and in the fall of 1741, he set out for Pennsylvania with a contingent of aides.

[53] Frantz, "The Awakening of Religion," p. 268. Quoted from "August Gottlieb Spangenberg to the Congregation at Herrnhut," May 14, 1736, Ms., Moravian Archives/Herrnhut.

[54] *Brethren in Colonial America*, p. 270f. Deknatel was also influential in the Palatinate. A letter which he wrote to the Friedelsheim congregation March 4, 1756, was later printed under the title *Der Weg zur Seligkeit* and widely circulated. See Robert Friedmann, *Mennonite Piety Through the Centuries* (Goshen, Indiana: Mennonite Historical Society, 1949), p. 61.

[55] Durnbaugh, "Johann Adam Gruber," p. 393.

[56] John R. Weinlick, "Moravianism in the American Colonies," *Continental Pietism*, p. 136.

[57] George Whitefield, *George Whitefield's Journals* (London: The Banner of Truth Trust, 1960), p. 412.

[58] Ibid., pp. 412-413.

[59] Nicolaus Ludwig Zinzendorf, *Pennsylvanische Nachrichten von dem reiche Christi, Anno 1742* (Büdingen: Johann Christoph Stöhr, 1742?), p. 9.

The Search for Unity

Zinzendorf perceived the spiritual stirring among the Pennsylvania Germans and their need for pastors as preparing the way for his ecumenical dream. The concept was somewhat nebulous, but Zinzendorf's stated intent was to facilitate union without disrupting denominational ties. Zinzendorf's hope was to unite the German-speaking churches of Pennsylvania into one church of God in the Spirit.

Zinzendorf had already promoted his ideas concerning spiritual union among the Mennonites in the Netherlands. When Zinzendorf was in Amsterdam in February and March of 1736, he had been in touch with Deknatel, and upon returning to Amsterdam in 1737 he celebrated communion in Deknatel's home. For a time it appears that Deknatel was highly sympathetic to Zinzendorf's ideas of spiritual union, conducting occasional services for the Moravians in Amsterdam and uniting with the Moravian congregation when it organized—at the same time retaining his Mennonite membership. Deknatel's sons for a time attended Moravian schools.[60] Zinzendorf's impressions of the Mennonites in Pennsylvania were no doubt influenced by his acquaintance with the Dutch Mennonites and his close friendship with Deknatel.

Zinzendorf landed in New York late in 1741. En route to Philadelphia he held discussions with awakening leader Gilbert Tennent (1703-1764).[61] From Philadelphia, Zinzendorf set out before Christmas to visit the Moravian settlement of Nazareth, and a second colony which during his visit he named "Bethlehem." On the journey from Philadelphia to Nazareth he visited a number of church leaders, most of them members of the Associated Brethren of the Skippack. The first night was spent in Germantown at the home of the Reformed minister John Bechtel. The next night he stopped at Christopher Wiegner's, and the following night at Henry Antes'. From Bethlehem Zinzendorf went to Oley, and then to the Ephrata community, where he failed to gain an audience with the leader of the community, Conrad Beissel.[62]

Soon after his visit from Zinzendorf, Henry Antes sent out letters to the various religious groups in Pennsylvania, inviting them to attend a conference to discuss religious concerns. One of the declared purposes of the conference was to combat widespread slander and criticism and, it was hoped, to create an atmosphere in Pennsylvania in which the bearers of such tales would experience remorse. It was a recurring problem for Pennsylvanians, and the criticisms should be understood in relation to the religious assumptions of the time. The established ideal was a territorial church, with all persons in a given region belonging to that church. The church, in turn, was supported financially by the political government. This pattern existed in most of the American colonies as well as in Europe. The sectarians in Pennsylvania had rejected this system, insisting on the voluntary nature of the true church. Their religious interpretation had been rejected by those in authority and by opinion makers before any of them had set foot in Pennsylvania. Moreover, the church people who came to Pennsylvania were without customary sponsorship and hence lacked structures for establishing religious life. The letter of invitation deals quite specifically with these concerns:

> Frederick Township in Philadelphia County
> December 15, 1741
>
> In the name of Jesus. Amen.
> Beloved [Friend and] Brother:
> Frightful damage is wrought in the church of Christ among the souls that have been called by the Lamb to follow Christ, mainly through mistrust and suspicion toward one another—and that, often without reason—whereby every purpose of good is continually thwarted although we have been commanded to love. It has therefore been under consideration for two years or more whether it would not be possible to call a general assembly, not to argue about opinions but to treat with one another in love on the most important articles of faith in order to ascertain how closely we can approach one another on fundamental issues, and for the rest bearing one another in love on opinions which do not subvert the ground of salvation; in order that all judging and criticizing might be diminished and done away with among the aforesaid souls, by which they expose themselves before the world and give occasion for it to be said that those who preach peace and conversion are themselves at variance.
> Therefore this very important matter has now been under advisement again by many brethren and God-seeking souls, and has been weighed before the Lord. It has been decided to meet on the coming New Year's Day in Germantown. Hence you are cordially invited to attend, together with several more of your brethren who have a foundation for their faith and can articulate it, if the Lord permits. It has been announced to nearly all of the others through letters similar to this one.
> There will probably be a large gathering, but do not let this deter you

---

[60] Christian Neff, "Deknatel, Jeme," *ME*, s.v. According to Neff, after 1751 Deknatel withdrew more and more from the Moravians.

[61] These discourses proved to be divisive rather than ameliorative. See Milton J. Coalter, Jr. "The Radical Pietism of Count Nicholas Zinzendorf as a Conservative Influence on the Awakener, Gilbert Tennent," *Church History* 49 (March 1980):35-46.

[62] Weinlick, "Moravianism in the American Colonies," pp. 139-140.

44   Colonial Mennonites and Pietism

In 1734 congregants chose between Beissel and the Dunkers at this barn along the Cocalico Creek near Akron.

for all will be arranged without great commotion. May the Lord Jesus grant us His blessing thereto.

Form your poor and unworthy, but sincere friend and brother, Henry Antes.[63]

Response to the letter was good, and the first conference convened in Germantown at the home of Theobald Ents on January 1 and 2, 1742, with approximately 100 persons present. Zinzendorf later published a report of this and subsequent conferences, which is our primary source of information about them.[64] We have no direct comments from the Mennonites concerning Zinzendorf, the conferences, or their participation in them. There are, however, a number of items relating to the Mennonites in the printed report.

The conference opened on the evening of January 1. Care had been taken in the arrangements to provide for proper parliamentary procedures and "representation from every known religion in Pennsylvania." This included Lutherans, Reformed, Moravians, Quakers, Mennonites, Baptists, Dunkers, Sabbatarians, Schwenkfelders, Separatists, Hermits, and Inspirationists. Zinzendorf called the group a worthy, unassuming delegation of persons that could, contrary to popular opinion, state their positions with clarity and understanding.[65]

Among the first items discussed at the conference was the widespread, unfounded slander of religious groups in Pennsylvania. The decadent state of the church in Europe was brought into the discussion as were the criteria for establishing the essentials of the faith. After considerable discussion the conference came to an agreement that there was more material than could be handled effectively, also that the discussions were becoming unnecessarily tedious and might be more hindrance than help. It was then noted that representatives from the Mennonite congregations had not stated their position "about some errors that had, with their knowledge, gained ground among others of their name [Mennonite], of which those in this country cannot be accused."[65] Someone in the gathered group, who was identified as having nothing to do with the Schwenkfelders, subsequently gave a warm testimony concerning some among the Mennonites, whose response appears to have been one of silence. After an agenda was prepared for the following morning and the hope expressed that it would be possible to discuss differences without giving offense, the meeting closed.

It appears to have been of some concern to leaders of the conference that an adequate statement of faith had not been obtained from the Mennonite delegation, for on January 13, before the second conference convened, the Syndic, or presiding officer of the first conference, paid a personal visit to some of the elders of the Mennonites to discuss the matter. The Syndic "cordially presented to the Mennonite elders how the Savior here and there in Europe was working a great redemption among their fellow believers," referring, no doubt, to the spread of Pietism among the Mennonites. He said that they "had among them scholarly tongues to preach everywhere of the deity of Jesus and his everlasting merits, and a large number of teachable ears and hearts to accept the true word of grace, without sectarian examination of from whence it comes." For this reason, "the conference is not indifferent to whether or not the Mennonites send their delegation."[67]

The Mennonite elders explained that unofficial representatives were present at the first conference because there had not been time to inform their congregations of the matter. It was because the representatives at Germantown were not fully authorized that they had not articulated their position. Furthermore, the elders stated, the leaders who would appear at the

---

[63] Donald F. Durnbaugh, *The Brethren in Colonial America*, p. 282. For a copy of the original letter see "Beylagen," *Pennsylvanische Nachrichten*, pp. 92-93.

[64] *Pennsylvanische Nachrichten*, pp. 48, 49, *passim*. Reports of the seven conferences were published by Benjamin Franklin and are available under "Church of God in the Spirit" in the chronological catalogue of the "William J. Campbell Collection of Benjamin Franklin Manuscripts" (Philadelphia: Curtis Publishing Company, 1918). Elizabeth Horsch Bender and Lydie Hege assisted with the translations.

[65] Ibid.

[66] Ibid., p. 51.

[67] Ibid., p. 67.

forthcoming conference would also be informal delegates. The Syndic accepted this condition, then suggested that the third gathering might be held in a Mennonite elder's home on the Skippack. The Mennonites willingly accepted this proposal.[68]

The Mennonite leaders were then presented with a strange rumor by the Syndic. The passage is ambiguous, but apparently accusations that needed clarification had been brought against the Mennonites at the first conference:

> Everyone who has the least bit of knowledge, knows that with respect to doctrine, those who do not have the courage to deny directly the merits and Deity of Jesus in Hungary and elsewhere also pass under the name of Anabaptists, and spread their doctrine throughout the Anabaptist communities as industriously as conditions at any place permit; but in fact an evil is in process of intruding to a great extent into the whole group, viz., of accepting for baptism the respectable and rich, and people of good reputation, just as they are accepted to the Lord's Supper in other faiths—whether they are converted or not; which is a terrible abomination.[69]

The Mennonite elders said they knew nothing of such a practice and that it did not exist among them in this land. The charges, which apparently had been aired at the first conference, may potentially have contained enough truth to make matters awkward for the Mennonite representatives and may explain their reticence to speak out. The rumor may have been brought by the Schwenkfelders, who within the decade had left Silesia, found temporary refuge on Zinzendorf's estate, migrated to America, and were casually acquainted with the Anabaptists of Hungary.[70] European Mennonites had been subjected to two contrasting influences: Pietism and Socinianism. The Socinians, or Polish Brethren, had many beliefs that were similar to the Mennonites: nonresistance, nonswearing of oaths, emphasis on the teachings of Jesus, and strict discipline in the congregation based on Matthew 18:15-17. They accepted that people were justified by faith, but held that faith really means obedience to the commandments of Christ.[71] They denied the Trinity and the deity of Christ. Socinians had contact with the Mennonites in the Netherlands and Germany, and with the Hutterites in Hungary.

The Syndic expressed the hope that his inquiry would not be taken as an impertinence; his desire was to elicit a due declaration of the truth which had not been brought to Germantown the first time. Instead, there the Mennonite representatives "in spite of frequent requests and inquiries had held

The Search for Unity 47

back with an unseeming timidity which cast suspicion on them."⁷² In response to the Syndic's queries and the rumor, the Mennonite elders stated the fundamentals of their faith:

> 1) That they regarded the reconciliation of the world through the blood of Jesus Christ fully valid and for all because they held the one who had atoned for their sins to be the eternal Son of God, equal to his Father in power and majesty;
>
> 2) That they knew nothing of the above practice, nor was it found among them.⁷³

The meeting ended on a friendly note. One of the Mennonite leaders accompanied the Syndic to Falkner Swamp so that it could be confirmed whether it was agreeable to transfer the site of the third conference to Skippack, and so that he could be given a printed report of the first conference.

The Second Synod met in the house of George Hübner in Falkner Swamp, January 25 and 26. Mennonites were present at both this and the Third Synod which met at Oley in the home of John de Türk, February 21-23, 1742. Several Indians were baptized at the third conference and the Ephrata mystics presented a paper on matrimony. The paper aroused intense dissension, leaving the remainder of the group with a feeling of unanimity after the departure of the Ephrata group. Zinzendorf made a number of contacts following the conference, returning to Philadelphia via Skippack, where the Mennonites asked him to preach.⁷⁴

The Fourth Synod met at Germantown March 21-23 in the home of Mr. Ashmead. Neither Mennonite nor Schwenkfelder representatives appeared at the conference. This was attributed to an oversight, but the statement issued by the conference also indicates concern that the purposes of the conferences were perhaps being misunderstood:

> Because of the absence of the Mennonites and the Schwenkfeldians, it was unanimously noted that they had received no information about it; and although the conference deputies and its Syndic failed only through misunderstanding, only they, not the Mennonite Church

---

⁶⁸ Ibid., pp. 67-68.
⁶⁹ Ibid., p. 68.
⁷⁰ Peter C. Erb, "Dialogue Under Duress: Schwenkfelder-Mennonite Contact in the Eighteenth Century," *MQR* 50 (July 1976):181-199.
⁷¹ N. van der Zijpp, "Socinianism," *ME*, s.v.
⁷² *Pennsylvanische Nachrichten*, p. 69.
⁷³ Ibid.
⁷⁴ Ibid., p. 119.

Ephrata Cloisters: *Sisters' House (left) and meetinghouse (right) of the Ephrata community.*

or the Schwenkfeldian friends were responsible; for that reason they very sincerely beg pardon for the truly unintentional error, and in order that there be no misunderstanding (in such an important matter, which has meanwhile already been brought before the Savior), they *herewith* again issue a sincere and direct invitation for the coming April 6, 7, 8 or 9 to a special or public conference in Germantown; when it takes place the Syndic for his own person [i.e., speaking for himself] offers to go wherever he is asked, to give them a thorough and adequate explanation of everything because he respects them sincerely for the sake of their fathers and seeks the best for his brethren and friends who are among them.[75]

When the subject matter for the conference was selected, the first question was submitted to the lot: "whether the coming conference should journey to the Mennonites or assemble in Germantown."[76] The lot indicated that the meeting should be held in Germantown. The Mennonites were not represented at this, or any of the subsequent conferences.

The Fifth Synod was held in the German Reformed Church, Germantown, April 20-27, and the Sixth Synod at Germantown, May 16-18. The Seventh and last of the Union Synods convened in Philadelphia on June 13 and 14, 1742. Unanimous conclusions were formulated at this conference. The fifth conclusion treated the Mennonites:

Concerning the Mennonite Church we are not to pass judgment. It is known throughout Holland that the blessing of the Lord has been with them there and many of their ministers are united with and faithful assistants of the invisible church,[77] whereas those in this land have from the beginning been more against us than for us. Now a part of the Mennonite Church in this land, to be sure, is not of the kind out of which the most oft-named servants of the Lord come forth; for they are from the Sun[78] where we have only slight acquaintance. But also it is a small, exclusive religion with boundaries and gates, and is therefore treated according to the regulations of the first conference, and is left entirely to the Lord. Only we must carefully consider, that we have not been commissioned or permitted, nor is it demanded of us to correct or guard what is theirs.[79]

The seventh conclusion of the conference suggested that it would seem natural for the Dunkers to unite with the Mennonites, if only they could agree on the question of baptism. That way there would be one less sect in the country.[80]

From the beginning Zinzendorf's reception in Pennsylvania was not what he had anticipated. In an open letter written in February 1742, he describes his experience: "At my arrival I was rather jarred: I had anticipated love and confidence, and found much hostility and distrust against me." Zinzendorf seemed to have thought that he could take up where Whitefield had left off, and called him "a son of our Church." "I had hoped for lasting fruit from my brother George Whitefield's work," he says, "however, I heard more praise for him than I was pleased with, and of what he found praiseworthy I did not see enough."[81] From the beginning, Zinzendorf said that his reception caused him heartfelt distress, as did the lukewarmness he perceived in his countrymen in Philadelphia. News of his problems in Europe had preceded him to America, and the Pennsylvanians were wary.[82] Though he soon had traveled throughout Pennsylvania, he related that he was invited to speak only at Oley. "I can tell you in a few words what I have done these two

---

[75] Franklin Manuscripts, p. 61.
[76] Ibid., p. 69.
[77] True spiritual believers of all denominations, in this case no doubt fellow Pietists.
[78] Conservative wing in a late seventeenth-century division in the Dutch Mennonite Church.
[79] Franklin Manuscripts, p. 114.
[80] Ibid., p. 115.
[81] *Pennsylvanische Nachrichten*, pp. 9, 11-12.
[82] John R. Weinlick, *Count Zinzendorf* (New York and Nashville: Abington Press, 1956), p. 167.

months," he wrote. "I have traveled, watched, prayed, wept, sought peace, and seek it still."[83]

Following the conferences, Zinzendorf spent some time among the Indians. On January 1, 1743, one year after the beginning of the First Synod, Zinzendorf left Philadelphia to return to Europe. In his party were two Dunker ministers who had become supporters of him. Both men had Mennonite as well as Dunker connections, and both visited Mennonite and Dunker communities in Europe, presumably as emissaries of the Moravians. The record of their travels illustrates the Moravian method of mission work and suggests considerable fluidity between denominational lines, as evidenced by sequential visits to Mennonite, Dunker, and Moravian communities. The accounts also point to frequent changes of church membership by some individuals. According to an excerpt from the American Reports of Herrnhut Matters:

> . . . Count Lewis [Zinzendorf] himself left Philadelphia on January 1, 1743, at nine o'clock in the evening. Among those who were taken along and went with him from this area was Andrew Frey. He had formerly been a Separatist, was later a Mennonite, was then a Sabbatarian but took offense at them and became a leader among the Brethren. He then became involved with this Moravian movement, and was made a leader.[84]

A second Brethren leader who accompanied Zinzendorf on his return to Europe was Joseph Müller (1707-1761). According to Müller's autobiographical account which is preserved in the Moravian Archives at Bethlehem he was born in Alsace near Werthe on October 23, 1707. "My father and mother," he wrote, "were natives of Switzerland and as Mennonites were expelled from there."[85] Müller accompanied Zinzendorf on his return journey to Europe in 1743. His account continues:

> After being in London for about two weeks I was sent to Holland; from there I visited Friesland and Groningen and the Mennonites and Brethren there. After four weeks I returned to Heerendyck. After several days I traveled from there to visit Gernfeld; I visited Brethren and Mennonites.[86]

It was while Müller was in Europe that the Moravians began to employ descriptive religious terminology that many other Christians found offensive. This was the so-called "Sifting Time." Müller uses some of these expressions in his autobiography. Of an early awakening he wrote, "For a time the Savior was so close to me by night and by day ... that no man can be closer to his wife. At night I thought I was lying in his arms; when I awoke I thought I still had him with me." The intensity of his spiritual experience passed, and he went through a period of dryness and distress. He joined the Moravians, eventually to be ordained a deacon. Describing the occasion he wrote, "My heart was so humbled and ashamed, and the streams from Jesus' wounds so penetrated me that I cannot describe it." He closed his autobiography with: "Now here I am, poor little worm, and wish in the end to be nothing but a blessed little mercy-gate enamored with the four little nails, and to hide in the split-open little side of Jesus and to be at home there forever. May the dear little mother help me thereto."[87] Müller traveled extensively during his stay in Europe. On March 11, 1748, he visited the Mennonites in the Palatinate. The following year he returned to Pennsylvania. He wished to go among the Brethren, as he had in Europe, but was strongly rebuffed by them.[88] The Brethren were no longer open to fellowship with Moravians.

Following Zinzendorf's attempts at spiritual union there was rapid withdrawal into denominational structures among the Germans in Pennsylvania. Zinzendorf's inability to win the confidence of the Pennsylvania Germans was perhaps partly because of his imperious manner, which they found offensive.[89] Although he had laid aside his titles when he came to Pennsylvania his manner and expectations soon gave him away. One is tempted to speculate how Pennsylvania religious history might have been different had Spangenberg, with his reputation for humility, remained in Pennsylvania and Zinzendorf in Europe. Although Zinzendorf was a great religious leader, he related more effectively to followers than to colleagues.

By the end of February, 1742, Mennonites, Dunkers, Schwenkfelders, and the Seventh Day Baptists of Ephrata had withdrawn from participation in the Pennsylvania Synods. The Dunkers began holding annual meetings, the Mennonites would soon begin ministers' conferences, and both the Mennonites and Dunkers began active programs of publication. Lutheran and Reformed representatives continued their participation in the synods, but promising young leaders were sent from Europe to America to organize both

---

[83] *Pennsylvanische Nachrichten*, p. 13.

[84] Donald F. Durnbaugh, *The Brethren in Colonial America*, p. 292. Frey became disillusioned with the Moravians while he was in Europe and renounced all connections with them.

[85] Ibid., p. 305.

[86] Ibid., p. 307.

[87] Ibid., pp. 306, 308-309.

[88] Ibid., p. 308. For a copy of the letter Müller wrote to the Brethren, and their reply, see pp. 309-315. The leaders of the Brethren left no doubt concerning their rejection of the Moravians, and of Müller as long as he was associated with them.

[89] Ibid., p. 285.

Avthentifche
NACHRICHT
Von der
Verhandlung und dem Verlaſs
Der am 14^{den} und 15^{den} Januarii Anno 174½

Im ſogenannten FALCKNER-SCHWAMM

An GEORG HÜBNERS Hauſe gehaltenen

ZWEYTEN
VERSAMMLUNG
Sowol
Einiger Teutſchen ARBEITER
Der EVANGELISCHEN RELIGIONEN

Als

Verſchiedener einzelen treuen GEZEUGEN und Gottsfürchtiger NACHBARN.

Nebſt einigen BEYLAGEN.

PHILADELPHIA,
Gedruckt und zu haben bey B. FRANKLIN.

Authentische Nachricht: *Benjamin Franklin printed Zinzendorf's accounts of the seven ecumenical conferences.*

groups. The Lutherans sent Henry Melchior Muhlenberg to Pennsylvania in 1742. That same year Michael Schlatter from Saint Gall, Switzerland, volunteered to come to America to help organize the German Reformed Church. One is reminded of Thomas Merton's assessment of many ecumenical endeavors, from which the participants "return to their several structures and bed down again in their own systems, having attained just enough understanding to recognize themselves as utterly alien to one another."[90]

Religious stirring among the German settlers both preceded and followed the Pennsylvania Synods. Michael Schlatter preached to a gathering of more than 600 persons on his first visit to Tulpehocken in 1746. In 1745 the crowd that gathered on a winter Sunday near New Hanover to hear Muhlenberg preach was so large that it could not be contained in the intended barn, and the service was moved outdoors. Large crowds were similarly reported at Lancaster, in Philadelphia, and New York City.[91] The awakening was alive; spiritual union had been rejected.

The Resurgence of Sectarianism

Why did the Mennonites participate in Zinzendorf's conferences? Why did they draw back? There had been close association between Mennonites and Pietists in both Europe and Pennsylvania. Both Mennonites and Pietists sought a personally meaningful religious experience and neither placed primary weight on theology or dogma. Both claimed to live according to the Bible. Both justified their policy on the basis of the leadership of the Holy Spirit who taught them correct understandings of the Scriptures. Both sought to include all of life in their religious systems, but differed on what this meant: Pietists placed emphasis on the devotional aspects, Mennonites emphasized the practical.

Yet there were significant differences. Most Pietists remained within the state church and continued to baptize infants. Representatives of the Lutheran and Reformed churches, who remained with Zinzendorf through all seven conferences, like him did not challenge basic ecclesiastical structures, but rather called for an adaptation of emphases. They, along with Zinzendorf, could accept the concept of an "invisible church" defined by individual experience rather than organizational boundaries. The Mennonites believed that the church must be a voluntary association separate from the state: a visible, gathered, disciplined group. Baptism of adults symbolized this voluntary choice and commitment. Most of the Radical Pietists also believed in a

---

[90] *Ben and the Birds of Appetite* (Abbey of Gethsemeny: New Directions, 1968), p. 3.
[91] Frantz, "Awakening of Religion," p. 284. See also Marti Pritzker-Erlich, *Michael Schlatter von St. Gallen (1716-1790)* (Zurich: Adag, 1981).

voluntary church and baptized adults, but they took an absolutist position as to mode, considering only baptism by immersion as valid. This was tantamount to holding that the rite of baptism conferred salvation, a position unacceptable to Mennonites. Pietists who remained within the state church did not reject participation in warfare, but some of the radical Pietists were pacifists. For Mennonites the rejection of all uses of violence was central to their understanding of the gospel of Jesus Christ.

The Mennonites began a concerted program of publication following their withdrawal from the Pennsylvania Synods. Several themes are dominant in the publications which they issued following 1742: suffering and martyrdom, the meaning of the cross, and baptism. Devotional literature, too, received fresh emphasis. Recent scholarship has pointed out that the colonial Mennonites were in an advantageous position with regard to church organization and publication when compared with the German Lutheran and the German Reformed churches. The congregational organization of the Mennonite churches, the practice of ordaining ministers from the congregation, and the absence of seminary requirements meant that the Pennsylvania Mennonites were free to move ahead with church life.[92]

In 1742 the Mennonites had their traditional hymnal, the *Ausbund*, reprinted at Germantown.[93] The republication of the *Ausbund* at this time was of considerable significance. Soon after his arrival in Pennsylvania, Zinzendorf also published a hymnal, *Hirten Lieder von Bethlehem*.[94] This small, 95-page hymnal was intended for wide usage. A note opposite the title page states that in Philadelphia the hymnbook is available from Benjamin Franklin, in Germantown from Christopher Sauer or John Bechtel, at Falkner Swamp from Henry Antes, and in Canada from John Hildebrand. The book supposedly "was prepared for publication within six days after [Zinzendorf's] arrival in the Province, and contained a small selection of old and new hymns suitable for the use of all denominations."[95] In 1744 the Dunkers also printed a hymnal, *Das kleine Davidische Psalterspiel der Kinder Zions* . . . (The Small Davidic Psalter). Their hope, too, "was to create an 'impartial' or nonsectarian hymnbook by choosing hymns from several sources."[96] Interestingly, the *Ausbund* also carried an ecumenical statement on its title page, as it had since 1564: "Most useful to all Christians of whatever denomination, impartial."

For both Moravians and Mennonites, and no doubt other Pietists as well, the function of hymns in the service was very significant. One scholar says that the religious life of the Moravians centered in their hymns, and calls the "hymn sermon" the distinctive invention of the Moravians.[97] The *Ausbund* could be said to contain hymns that function in a similar manner. However, the language employed by Pietists to express their devotion to

Christ was significantly different from that used by Mennonites, and nowhere is this more evident than in their respective hymns.

The songs of the *Ausbund* have both a historical and a doctrinal dimension. These songs are the spiritual story of a people, and the singing of them reinforces that identity. Each hymn is introduced with a brief statement. Sometimes it simply gives the theme of the hymn; frequently it also puts the hymn into historical context, giving the name of the author and the circumstances under which it was written. There is little subjectivism in the *Ausbund* hymns, according to Elizabeth Bender: "Hardly ever does a writer dwell on his own feelings, either of joy or of sorrow."[98]

The *Ausbund* was initially published by the Swiss and South German Anabaptists in 1564 and continues to serve as the hymnbook for contemporary Amish congregations. The archaic style of Amish singing and the continuous reprinting of the book in its ancient format suggests to the modern-day observer that the words and the themes of the hymns are likewise antiquated. While some of the hymns are martyr stories, a significant number are songs of praise or expound doctrinal themes: the meaning of the cross, love to one's fellowman, baptism, and nonresistance.[99]

The hymnody of the *Ausbund*, when compared with pietistic hymnody, reveals contrasting understandings concerning the cross of Christ. Both Mennonites and Pietists believed in "justification by grace through faith." Both accepted the centrality of the cross. However, their conceptions of how the cross was to be appropriated in the life of the believer differed markedly. Several hymns pointedly illustrate the contrast. The first is taken from the *Ausbund*. It was written by Michael Sattler (c. 1490-1527), an early Anabaptist leader to whom is attributed authorship of the "Brotherly Union of a Number of Children of God Concerning Seven Articles," written in 1527. The introductory statement to the hymn in the *Ausbund* reads: "Another song of Michael Sattler who, at Rottenberg on the Neckar, was torn

---

[92] See Lodge, "The Crisis of the Churches in the Middle Colonies," pp. 195-220.

[93] *Ausbund, Das ist: Etliche Schöne Christliche Lieder*. Germantown: Gedruckt bey Christopher Saur, 1742). The *Ausbund* was subsequently reprinted in Germantown in 1751, 1767, 1785, and 1815.

[94] The complete title reads *Hirten Lieder von Bethlehem, Zum Gebrauch Vor alles was arm ist, Was klein und gering ist* (Germantown, gedruckt bey C. Saur, 1742).

[95] Sachse, *The German Sectarians*, pp. 452-453.

[96] Durnbaugh, *The Brethren in Colonial America*, p. 353.

[97] John Jacob Sessler, *Communal Pietism Among Early American Moravians* (New York: Henry Holt and Company, 1933), pp. 108-109.

[98] Elizabeth Bender, "Teachings Stressed in the *Ausbund*," Paul M. Yoder, et al., *Four Hundred Years with the Ausbund* (Scottdale, Pa.: Herald Press, 1964), p. 24.

[99] For discussions of the *Ausbund* and its contents see Smith, *Mennonite Immigration*; Rosella Reimer Duerksen, "Doctrinal Implications of Sixteenth Century Anabaptist Hymnody," *MQR* 35 (January 1969):38-49; and Yoder, et al., *Four Hundred Years with the Ausbund*.

56 *Colonial Mennonites and Pietism*

apart with glowing tongs, his tongue cut out, and then burnt. In the year [15]27, the 21st of May."[100] Because the hymn is lengthy, representative stanzas which carry the theme have been selected:

When Christ with His Teaching True

1 When Christ with His teaching true
 Had gathered a little flock
 He said that each with patience
 Must daily follow Him bearing his cross.
2 And said: You, my beloved disciples,
 Must be ever courageous
 Must love nothing on earth more than Me
 And must follow My teaching.
5 Behold Me: I am the Son of God
 And have always done the right.
 I am certainly the best of all
 Still they finally killed me.
8 He it is who tests you as gold
 And yet is loving to you as his children
 As long as you abide in my teaching
 I will nevermore forsake you.
9 For I am yours and you are Mine
 Thus where I am there shall you be,
 And he who abuses you touches My eye,
 Woe to the same on that day.
12 O Christ, help Thou Thy people
 Which follows Thee in all faithfulness,
 That though through Thy bitter death
 It may be redeemed from all distress.
13 Praise to Thee, God, on Thy Throne
 And also to Thy beloved Son
 And to the Holy Ghost as well.
 May He yet draw many to His kingdom.[101]

In striking contrast is a Moravian hymn:

How happy, that my heart can view
The Lamb in all that bloody hue,
Upon the cross outstretched!
If from my eyes this should depart,

> My heart would feel a piercing smart,
> Yea I should be most wretched.
> If those dear wounds I did not know,
> Which now with blood's juice overflow,
> What else could satisfy me?
> But Blood, that's good
> Still to wash me, and refresh me;
> In that Ocean,
> I do ever find my portion.[102]

That this mode of expression was common not only among Moravians but other Pietists as well is strikingly illustrated by hymns sung among the Old Order River Brethren, a pietistic group originating c. 1778 in Pennsylvania.

> Hark! the voice of love and mercy
>   Sounds aloud from Calvary;
> See it rends the rocks asunder,
>   Shakes the earth and vails the sky!
>   It is finish'd;
>   Hear the dying Saviour cry.
>
> It is finish'd! O what pleasure
>   Do these charming words afford
> Heav'nly blessings without measure
>   Flow to us from Christ the Lord
>   It is finish'd
>   Saints, the dying words record.
>
> Finish'd all the types and shadows
>   Of the ceremonial law;
> Finish'd all that God had promis'd
>   Death and hell no more shall awe.
>   It is finish'd!
>   Saints, from hence your comfort draw.

---

[100] *Ausbund*, p. 46. Translation by the author.
[101] Verbatim rendering by John H. Yoder, *The Legacy of Michael Sattler* (Scottdale, Pa.: Herald Press, 1973), pp. 139-145. The German text appears opposite the English rendering.
[102] From *Collection of Hymns* (1754), Part II, No. 99. Printed in Sessler, *Communal Pietism*, p. 140.

> Happy souls, approach the table,
>   Taste the soul-reviving food;
> Nothing half so sweet and pleasant
>   As the Saviour's flesh and blood.
>   It is finish'd!
>   Christ has borne the heavy load.
>
> Tune your hearts anew, ye seraphs,
>   Join to sing the pleasing theme;
> All on earth and all in heaven,
>   Join to praise Immanuel's name—
>   It is finish'd!
>   Glory to the bleeding Lamb.[103]

These hymns graphically illustrate that Mennonites stressed that Jesus' followers must deny themselves and, like him, take up their cross.[104] Pietists, by contrast, focused on the bliss experienced by the believer as a result of Christ's suffering and death.

The 1742 and subsequent American editions of the *Ausbund*, unlike the European counterpart, contain two appendixes which were pertinent additions at this time. Baptism is the central theme of the first, focusing on Scriptures which the author understands to be in opposition to infant baptism. Written by the young Thomas von Imbroich for his captors while he was imprisoned in 1558, the statement of his faith failed to convince them, and he was martyred. The confession, however, was circulated widely, and reprinted in numerous collections, including three of the publications reissued by the colonial Mennonites in the 1740s.[105]

The second appendix is a firsthand account of the persecutions suffered by the Swiss Anabaptists between 1635 and 1645, written originally for the Dutch Mennonites who interceded on their behalf with the Swiss government. The account is highly personalized, giving names, dates, and graphic details of the persecutions. It relates, for example, how Felix Landis was indicted by the government and sent to Oetenbach, where he was incarcerated in a "horrible confinement under cruel and unnatural circumstances." For some time he was given nothing to eat. Near him were imprisoned some men who were moved to pity, and they passed warm broth to him through a coil in the wall. The caretaker discovered the procedure, and Landis was moved to another location. Finally, when he was near death from starvation, he was again allowed food.

For nearly four years his wife, too, was imprisoned. She was stuck in many fetid nooks and treated with utter shame and cruelty. For a time her captors undressed her each night and took away all her clothing. The children of the couple were placed with strangers and their house and farm sold; the financial loss was 5,000 guilders. This is but one of 40 biographical accounts included in the report, which is entitled *Ein Warhafftiger Bericht*.[106] Numerous Swiss Anabaptists found refuge in the Palatinate following this time of persecution, and many of their descendants later came to America. Others came directly from Switzerland, but for all of the Mennonites in the colonies these stories possessed an immediacy.

In 1744 Henry Funk (d. 1760), a Mennonite bishop, published a book on baptism, *Ein Spiegel der Taufe mit Geist mit Wasser und mit Blut* (A Mirror of Baptism with the Spirit, with Water, and with Blood).[107] Funk was called the "pious miller on Indian Creek"; the deed for his land, from the sons of William Penn, bore the date of October 20, 1718.[108] The book was written to reaffirm the Mennonite conception of baptism. The traditional Mennonite mode of baptism was by affusion (pouring), symbolizing the outpouring of the Holy Spirit. Funk reaffirmed this mode and its meaning. He held that men have been freed by Christ and again have the power of choice, enabling them to choose to follow Jesus.

> And if he is followed, then his will is done, and we shall not miss the way, but much more go the true way; for Jesus himself is the way and the truth.[109]

To choose to follow Jesus is not only a matter of heart devotion, but involves all of life. Mennonites saw the new birth as the call to an obligation and a task, to *Nachfolge* in the kingdom. The Pietists saw it as a peaceful possession.

Baptism, according to Funk, is threefold: with the Spirit, with water, and with blood. The latter symbolizes the baptism of suffering:

---

[103] Taken from *A Collection of Spiritual Hymns . . . Especially Designed for Use in the Old Order River Brethren*, 1971 (no address; no publisher), p. 273. See also Beulah S. Hostetler, "An Old Order River Brethren Love Feast," *Pennsylvania Folklife* (Winter 1974-1975):8-20.

[104] Mark 8:34.

[105] The *Ausbund*, *Martyrs Mirror*, and *Güldene*, *Aepfel in Silbern Schalen*. See Christian Neff, "Imbroich, Thomas V.," *ME*, s.v. See also Felix Reichmann, "An Early Edition of Thomas von Imbroich," *MQR* 16 (April 1942):99-107.

[106] The subtitle reads *Von den Brü dern im Schweitzerland, in dem Zuercher Gebiet, Wegen der Truebsalen welche ueber sie ergangen seyn, um des Evangeliums willen; Von dem 1635sten bis in das 1645ste Jahr*. The Landis account is found on pp. 26 and 27.

[107] (Germantown:) *Gedruckt (Bey Christoph Saur) im Jahr 1744*.

[108] Jacob C. Clemens, "Heinrich Funck," *GH* (January 10, 1929), p. 859.

[109] Henry Funk, *A Mirror of Baptism* (Skippack, Pa.: Printed by John M. Schuenemann, 1853), p. 71.

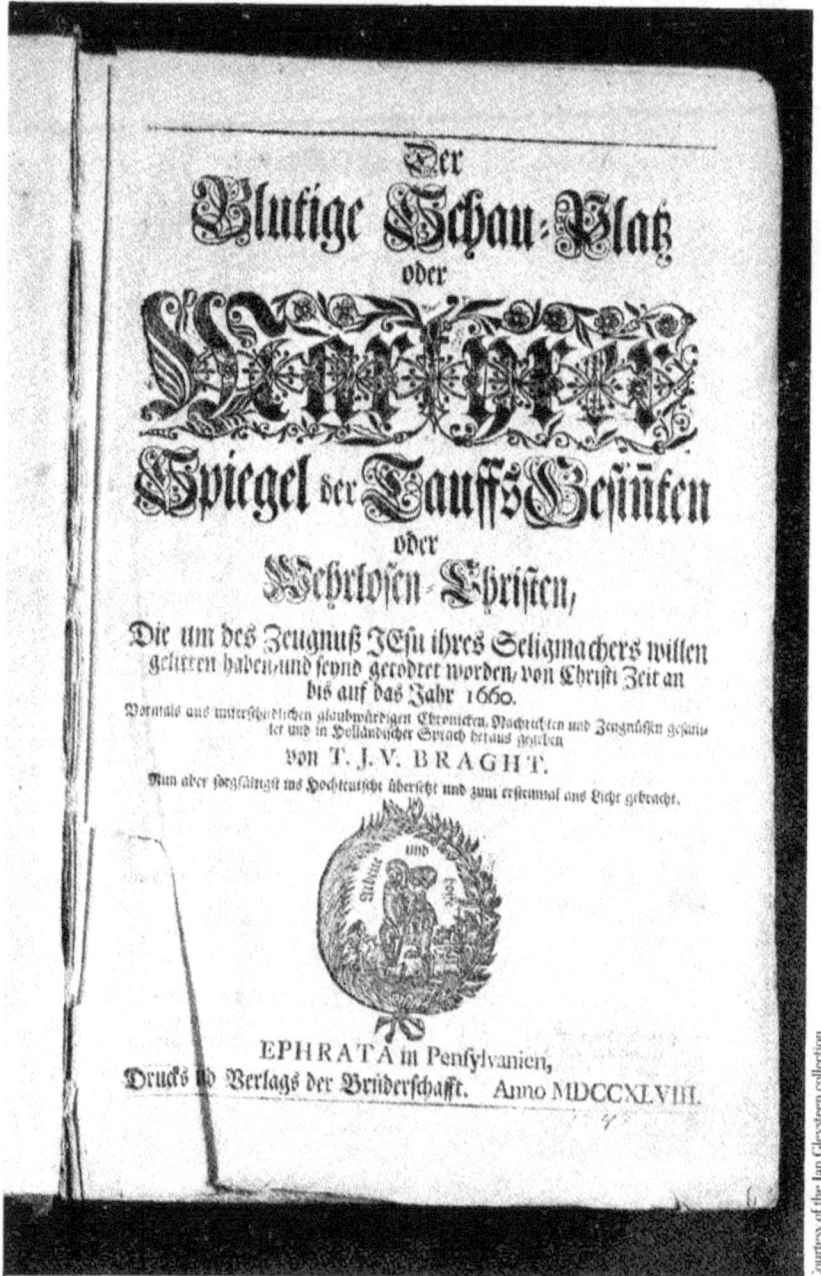

1748 Ephrata edition of Martyrs Mirror, *the largest book printed in the colonies.*

In the Gospel of the new Covenant there is named by Jesus a baptism of sufferings, in which baptism the Lord Jesus was the first subject of the New Covenant. Under this baptism hath Jesus conquered the Devil, the enemy and sin, and opened to us and paved the way into his eternal Kingdom, as he also bids all them that are his, to follow him.[110]

Both the Mennonites and the radical Pietists had theologies of suffering, but they differed in content. The radical Pietists understood suffering as *Anfechtung*, the spiritual struggle of the soul. At Ephrata asceticism, suffering through the deliberate denial of bodily comforts, was seen as desirable to spiritual growth. Mennonites understood suffering to be a natural consequence of following Jesus, of taking up the cross, and as something imposed on the believer externally.

Funk says that through baptism the individual becomes a member of a fellowship, one of the people of God, citing the scriptural passage, "I will dwell in them and walk with them; and I will be their God, and they shall be my people."[111] This self-conception stands in marked contrast to the Moravian Joseph Mueller's, "Now here I am, a poor little worm, and wish in the end to be nothing but a blessed little mercy-gate enamoured with the four little nails."[112]

Funk's book was highly important for strengthening Mennonite identity because of its emphasis on traditional, as opposed to pietistic, emphases. German editions were printed in 1744, 1834, 1850, 1853, and 1861; English editions in 1851, 1853, and 1890.[113] One scholar of Pietism has called *Ein Spiegel* "an unusually austere and effective book." The word "blessedness" (*Gottseligkeit*), commonly used by Pietists, does not occur at all in the book. "On the other hand," he continues, "the concept of the way of the cross, that is suffering for the sake of conscience, forms its very heart."[114]

The largest publication project by the Mennonites at this time was the translation from Dutch into German of Thieleman J. van Braght's *Martyrs Mirror* and its republication at Ephrata. Mennonite leaders shared their concern and intent with their Dutch brethren in October of 1745:

> It was ... unanimously favored by the brotherhood in this land, to see if we could manage to have Dielman Jans van Braght's *Bloedig*

---

[110] Ibid., p. 78.
[111] Henry Funk, *A Mirror of Baptism* (Mountain Valley, Va.: Joseph Funk and Sons, 1851), p. 67.
[112] See above, p. 51.
[113] Harold S. Bender, *Two Centuries of American Mennonite Literature* (Goshen, Ind.: The Mennonite Historical Society, 1929), p. 2.
[114] Friedmann, *Mennonite Piety*, pp. 232-233.

Tooneel (*Martyrs Mirror*) translated into German, especially since here in this country in our brotherhood many young people have grown up and greatly increase in number, so that our posterity may have before their eyes the traces of those loyal witnesses of the truth, who walked in the way of truth and have given their lives for it.[115]

Several problems hindered this project although they had "greatly desired to have this work published for a number of years." The quality of local paper was poor, and they were concerned that the translation be competent and accurate:

> We have for certain reasons not been able to entrust it to those who have volunteered and promised to do it, for however much we are concerned to have it translated, we are equally concerned that the truth remain unblemished by the translation.[116]

Eventually the Pennsylvania Mennonites contracted with the Ephrata community for its translation and publication. A portion of the work, *Das Andenken Einiger Heiligen Martyrer,* was completed in 1745.[117] The first copies of the entire work were released in 1748. John Peter Miller, famed linguist of the Ephrata community, did the translating. The translation was checked in its entirety by Henry Funk and Dielman Kolb (1691-1756), who supervised the undertaking. Kolb, a weaver from Wolfsheim in the Palatinate, had immigrated in 1717[118]; he and Funk had lived as neighbors in Germany. Funk and Kolb claim to have read every word of the translation, and make a signed statement to that effect at the end of the volume. They also write:

> We further believe that the best thing about this book will be that the Lord through his Holy Spirit will so kindle the hearts of men with an eager desire for it that they will not regard a little money but buy it, and taking plenty of time, read it earnestly with thought, so that they may see and learn in what way they should be grounded in belief in Christ, and how they should arrange their lives and walk in order to follow the defenceless Lamb and to be heirs of the everlasting Kingdom with Christ and his Apostles.[119]

The republication of the *Martyrs Mirror* has been consistently interpreted as a measure to strengthen Mennonite identity. The edition was, however, also appropriated by the Dunkers. Similarly, when *Golden Apples in Silver Bowls,* a Mennonite compilation of martyr epistles and prayers, was printed on the cloister press at Ephrata in 1745, the edition was used by both

Mennonites and the Ephrata community.[120] According to the imprint, the book was published by various members of the Mennonite fellowship. It had first been published in Switzerland in 1702 and again in 1742. Containing both martyr accounts and devotional material, the book's combination of Anabaptist and Pietist emphases may have seemed very timely in Pennsylvania in 1745 and account for the apparently wide distribution of this one edition in America. That both Mennonites and Radical Pietists took as their own both the *Martyrs Mirror* and *Golden Apples in Silver Bowls* suggests considerable intermingling of ideas between the groups. It is also possible that each group, in bringing its own assumptions to the material, read it with a somewhat different understanding.

In 1745 the Pennsylvania Mennonites reprinted a prayer book that was first issued by Mennonites in the Palatinate in 1702. This volume, *Ernsthafte Christenpflicht*, was also printed by the press at Ephrata. The book is intended for private prayer and edification, but this first edition printed in Pennsylvania added an appendix of martyr stories that appeared neither in the European editions nor in later American reprints.[121]

The program of publication which the Mennonites of eastern Pennsylvania sponsored in the 1740s turned once again to accounts of the suffering of believers—from New Testament times to the recent past. Many of these accounts relate suffering to voluntary adult baptism. They saw in these stories a continuation of that "vast cloud of witnesses" recorded in the Bible, and they understood the Bible historically, as the account of God's interaction with his people.[122] The choice of publications appears to have served them well, for when the next phase of pietistic, revivalistic religion developed among the German-speaking settlers following 1760, Franconia was minimally affected, although the movement made substantial inroads into the Mennonite churches of western Lancaster County, Virginia, and Maryland.

---

[115] "A Pennsylvania Letter of 1745 to the Mennonites in Holland," tr. by Elizabeth Bender, *MHB* vol. 23, no. 4 (October 1971), pp. 3-4.

[116] Ibid.

[117] Bender, *Two Centuries*, p. 2.

[118] John D. Souder, "Dielman Kolb, 1691-1756," *GH* (February 7, 1929), pp. 938-940.

[119] Statement by Kolb and Funk at the end of the Ephrata edition of the *Martyrs Mirror.* For a translation of the entire statement, see "A Contemporary Colonial Mennonite Statement," *MHB*, vol. 23, no. 4. (October 1971), p. 6.

[120] *Gueldene Aepffel in Silbern Schalen* (Efrata, Im Jahr des Heils 1745, verlegt durch etliche Mitglieder der Mennonisten-Gemeine). See Bender, *Two Centuries*, p. 2.

[121] Robert Friedmann, "*Ernsthafte Christenpflicht*," ME, s.v. See also Friedmann, *Mennonite Piety*, passim, and Bender, *Two Centuries*, p. 3. Bender gives the publication date as 1739. A copy bearing the date 1702 has since been discovered.

[122] For the development of this thesis, see pp. 210-226. Rodney James Sawatsky has seen the use of history by American Mennonites as a tool for maintaining identity. See his "History and Ideology: American Mennonite Identity and Definition Through History" (Ph.D. dissertation, Princeton University, 1977).

Güldene Aepfel: *A few Mennonites sponsored the printing of this devotional book in Pennsylvania in 1745.*

Pietism and Fragmentation

A widespread pietistic renewal movement spread among the German colonists in the latter third of the eighteenth century, climaxing in the formation of a series of new denominations: first the River Brethren under the leadership of Jacob Engle (about 1778 to 1784), the Evangelical Association under the leadership of Jacob Albright (about 1800), and the United Brethren in Christ under the leadership of Philip William Otterbein and Martin Boehm between 1800 and 1815. In each instance the organization was by gradual steps and thus the dates given are approximate. The United Brethren was by far the largest of these groups, and consisted principally of an amalgamation of former Mennonite and Reformed leaders and members.

The Pennsylvania German Revival, as this awakening to experiential religion was soon called, spread through Mennonite settlements in Virginia and Maryland, and to Lebanon, Northampton, and western Lancaster counties in Pennsylvania.[123] Methodist itinerants had considerable influence in arousing religious enthusiasm among the Pennsylvania Germans, especially in the fringe settlements, but they customarily declined to minister to the German settlers in their own language. German-speaking leaders who supported the revival attempted to spread the message among their own people in the German language. Some of these preachers invited opposition by their "enthusiasm" and the emphases of their preaching.

The content of Pietism began to blend with the techniques of Revivalism. Among the techniques used by the more stable leaders was the class system, borrowed from Methodist itinerants. Another was the big meeting or the great meeting. It became common practice for large crowds to gather wherever accommodations could be found and a commanding speaker—or speakers—was available. It was at such a meeting, at the Mennonite Isaac Long's barn on Pentecost Sunday, May 10, 1767, that the Reformed Church leader, Philip William Otterbein (1726-1813), recognized his spiritual kinship with a Mennonite bishop, Martin Boehm (1725-1812), as he heard him speak.

Otterbein had come to the colonies in 1752 in response to Schlatter's plea for pastors. Otterbein had been trained at the pietistic University of Herborn in Germany. Soon he began to introduce pietistic practices into his Lancaster congregation, such as encouraging members personally to see the

---

[123] This movement has been dealt with extensively by John B. Frantz, "Revivalism and the German Reformed Church in the United States to 1850, with Emphasis on the Eastern Synod" (Ph.D. dissertation, University of Pennsylvania, 1961). See also Sem C. Sutter, "Mennonites and the Pennsylvania German Revival, *MQR* 50 (January 1976):37-55. Paul Himmel Eller, "Revivalism and the German Churches in Pennsylvania, 1783-1816" (Ph.D. dissertation, University of Chicago, 1933), includes a widely cited chapter on the German revival. His chapter on "Mennonites and the Revival" is based mainly on sources that are biased.

pastor before communion. He also instituted prayer meetings, at which there was Scripture reading, prayer, meditation, and the singing of hymns. Otterbein was a competent, scholarly leader whose preaching was very effective, but not revivalistic.

Boehm had been ordained a preacher at Pequea Mennonite Church in 1758. Initially he felt his ministry was ineffective, but after an intensive spiritual struggle and a dramatic conversion experience in 1758, he apparently began to preach with great power. The following year he was ordained as a bishop in the Mennonite Church. In 1761 he visited the Mennonites in Virginia. The preaching of George Whitefield and the New Light preachers had created confusion among them, and the settlers had requested counsel from the mother settlement in Lancaster. Boehm responded to the call, and on his visit encouraged them to embrace the new emotional sensations they were experiencing. After the 1767 meeting in Long's barn, Boehm is reported to have spent much of his time preaching. He preached regularly at at least three places in the Lancaster settlement: Pequea, Donegal, and in an old house on his own property. In each of these locations the congregation was made up principally of Mennonites.

Boehm, Otterbein, and others of like persuasion worked informally within the German-speaking churches for an extended period of time, eventually organizing fellowship meetings for the leaders who were engaged in this work. They held their first conference in Otterbein's home in Baltimore in 1789, calling themselves the United Brethren. At this meeting 14 ministers were present: nine came from German Reformed backgrounds, and five from Mennonite backgrounds. A second conference was held in 1791, and a third in 1800.

The new fellowships accommodated a piety and emotionalism that seemingly were experienced with some frequency, but which the established churches could not or would not absorb. Christian Newcomer (1750-1830), Mennonite in his youth and sometimes called the apostle Paul of the United Brethren Church, represented this type of experience both in his own life and in his journal accounts. While traveling and preaching for 50 years he recorded his experiences, later published as *The Life and Journal of the Reverend Christian Newcomer, Late Bishop of the Church of the United Brethren in Christ/ Written by Himself/ Containing the Travels and Labors of the Gospel from 1795-1830.*[124]

Newcomer recounted: "My Parents were both members of the sect of Christians called Mennonites, and I believe as far as their information extended, they endeavored to lead a pious life. I do recollect perfectly well, that I have seen them both on their knees many a time before the bed, offering up their prayers or evening sacrifice to God, although in silence." While silent prayer was a preferred form among Mennonites, for Pietists and revivalists it was barely adequate. "At a certain time I was present," Newcomer continued, "when my parents held a conversation respecting my grandmother. They said she was very melancholy and sad, in great doubts about the salvation of her soul, and in distress of being lost;—adding, that she ought *not to do so*, but cast herself on the mercy of the Lord her God."[125] Mennonites had difficulty dealing with just this type of religious personality specifically with those who frequently found release in pietistic experiences. Martin Boehm, Christian Newcomer, and Jacob Albright all had experiences of melancholy, and all three had intense conversion experiences.

Newcomer tells of searching and distress in his own youth, climaxing one day during a tremendous thunderstorm which he thought was the day of judgment:

> I ran or rather reeled out of the house into the yard a few paces, to the garden fence, and sunk on my knees, determined to give myself wholly and without reserve to Jesus the Saviour and Redeemer of mankind; submitting to his will alone.
>
> Having in this manner humbled myself before my Lord and Master, unable to utter a word, a vivid flash of lightening darted across my eyes; at the same instant a clap of thunder. O! what a clap!—as it ceased, the whole anguish of soul was removed; I did not know what had happened to me, my heart felt glad, my soul was happy, my mouth filled with praises and thanksgiving to God, for what he had done for me, a poor unworthy creature. . . .
>
> For some time I continued in this happy state of mind . . . gradually I lost this pleasing sensation, fear returned and again took possession of my heart more and more, the confidence in God was lost. . . .[126]

Newcomer sought the counsel of a Mennonite preacher and was baptized and taken into the Mennonite Church. He married, and the following winter again experienced a cycle of melancholy and release.

Newcomer became acquainted with Otterbein and his associates and identified with their cause:

> Whereas these men preached the doctrine I had experienced, and which according to my view and discernment so perfectly agreed with

---
[124] Transcribed and Corrected and Translated by John Hildt (Hagers-Town: Printed by F. G. W. Kapp, 1834).
[125] Ibid., p. 1.
[126] Ibid., p. 5.

the doctrine of Jesus Christ and his Apostles; therefore I associated with them and joined their society: and blessed be God, although I withdrew myself from the Mennonite society, I never felt in any wise accused within for doing so.[127]

Newcomer became an outstanding leader; his experiences typify those of many Mennonites who identified with the new religious groups.

Some expressions of Pietism continued within the Mennonite churches. In 1767 Jacob Gross, a young man recently immigrated from the Palatinate, wrote a letter to the Pietist Mennonite preacher Peter Weber in the Pfaltz.[128] The letter effusively expresses devotion to Jesus and trust in him; yet from the standpoint of assessing Pietist influences, it is as significant for what it does not say as for what it does. It emphasizes devotion to Christ, love and submission, but there is no mention of blessedness, or the cross, or wounds, or the blood of the Lamb. These common pietistic expressions *were* used in Peter Weber's account of his visit to Amsterdam and Johannes Deknatel in 1757.[129] A later letter from Gross to Weber (1774) was written as Gross and his wife, Ingrid, were preparing to pay a visit to her parents in Maryland.[130] Gross speaks of unrest in the church. The letter is not specific, but it was written at the height of the stress in Lancaster, Maryland, and Virginia over the pietistic, revivalistic preaching of Newcomer, Boehm, and others.

The River Brethren, later known as the Brethren in Christ, were the first to organize as a distinct group as a result of the German Revival. The events of origin are obscure.[131] Jacob Engle (1753-1823), whose parents were Mennonites, and who himself probably had been baptized as a Mennonite, was active in leadership as the group was formed by mutual baptisms about 1784. Baptism by immersion, a crisis conversion experience, and disciplined congregations were considered essential by them. An account given by Winebrenner in 1848 states:

> Between sixty and seventy years ago, awakened persons of Mennonites, Lutherans, German Reformed, Brethren or Taeufer, "whose hearts were closely joined together—had a common interest, not only in regard to the general cause of religion, but in each other's edification," and they met in the capacity of a social devout band, from house to house, to make prayer and supplication for the continued influence of God's spirit—out of these social circles, was organized the Religious Association, now commonly known as the River Brethren.[132]

The second group to take definite organizational form was the Evangelical Association. Its founder, Jacob Albright (1758-1808), was of Lutheran background. Following his conversion in 1792, Albright joined a Methodist class which was English-speaking, but when he began to preach it was mostly to fellow Germans, largely in the German language. Albright was in contact with several persons who were associated with Boehm and Otterbein, yet he organized his followers independently into classes after the Methodist pattern. The first classes were organized at the home of Peter Walter at Rockhill, Bucks County, and in Northampton County. The group was very small at the beginning; the total enrollment of the classes in 1800 was 20 members.[133]

The United Brethren in Christ, the largest denomination to grow out of the German Revival, did not assume its final, independent form until after the death of Otterbein in 1813, although the organization is often dated from 1800. Otterbein, like Wesley, strongly resisted separation from the mother church. When the United Brethren in Christ did form a distinctive church body, both the initial leadership and the membership consisted largely of former members of the German Reformed and Mennonite churches. Their polity, too, accommodated both traditions, freely making room for adult and infant baptism, nonresistance or participation in warfare, and the option of observing foot washing in conjunction with the communion service. Interestingly, Mennonite reluctance delayed record keeping for a period of time.

Martin Boehm was active both in the German Revival and as a Mennonite bishop for a considerable period of time. He had worked independently in the revival for almost 10 years, then, after preaching at Long's barn in 1767, cooperated closely with Otterbein. Approximately 20 years after his conversion experience, c. 1778, Boehm was excommunicated by the Lancaster Mennonites. About the same time as Boehm was excommuni-

---

[127] Ibid., pp. 13-14.

[128] Historical Archives of the Mennonite Church (hereinafter *HAMC*), Historical Mss. 1-536, Box 1, Weber Collection.

[129] "... und der Grund davon ist die Liebe unseres Heilandes, sein Blut und Wunder für alle Sünder ..." and "die ihre Seligkeit in dem Blute des Lammes erkennen ..." Christian Neff, "Peter Weber," *Christliches Gemeinde-Kalender* (1930):64. Weber was twice silenced in the Palatinate soon after his ordination because of his strong expressions of Pietism.

[130] Weber Collection.

[131] For several of the best early accounts, see George R. Prowell, *History of York County*, vol. 1, p. 143; and A Familiar Friend, "History of the River Brethren," *History of All the Religious Denominations in the United States* (Harrisburg, Pa.: John Winebrenner, 1848), p. 553. The latter account is important because it is one of the earliest, and apparently written by someone with firsthand acquaintance with the group, probably Philip Boyle, a Dunker elder in Maryland according to Durnbaugh. See also Carlton O. Wittlinger, "The Origin of the Brethren in Christ Church," *MQR* 48 (January 1974):55-73.

A synthesis of these various views of origins is contained in Beulah S. Hostetler, "An Old Order River Brethren Love Feast," *Pennsylvania Folklife*, vol. 24, no. 2 (Winter 1974-1975), pp. 8-20.

[132] A Familiar Friend, p. 553.

[133] Raymond W. Albright, *A History of the Evangelical Church* (Harrisburg, Pa., 1942).

Germantown Mennonite meetinghouse, built in 1770.

cated, the River Brethren crystallized into a distinct group. Membership in the group cut across denominational lines, but Mennonites were predominant. Precisely in what way these events related to Boehm's excommunication we do not know, but the widespread unrest, coupled with the formation of a new religious group, probably contributed to precipitation of the crisis at this particular time.

The Lancaster brethren wrote a statement explaining their action in the expulsion. Apparently it was a controversial move, and they delineated their position with considerable care.[134] The points of difference between the Lancaster Conference and Martin Boehm were not peripheral, nor did they center primarily on concepts of conversion or techniques of revivalism. In their statement the Lancaster brethren reported that as Boehm's preaching and teaching expressed elements that differed from their own understanding, they had tried to counsel him, both as individuals and before the congregation. Boehm, they said, had denied certain accusations and said of others that if he had said such things he was sorry. But according to the brethren he had not mended his ways, but continued to do and say the same things.

Of primary concern to the Lancaster brethren was that Boehm had fellowship with those who believe in war, and the swearing of oaths, both of which, they said, are directly opposed to the teaching of Christ. In addition, Boehm received into fellowship persons under discipline by the conference, without first requiring them to settle their differences. Another complaint brought against Boehm was that he had said that the ministers and bishops lay so much stress on the ordinances of baptism and foot washing that people are led only to the devil and not to God. This accusation sounds very strange until it is compared with a letter written by a devout Pietist to ministers among the Dunkers. This letter declares:

> It displeases God when we adhere too much or cling to something if it is not Jesus and his death and wounds and bloody atonement. Everything else can become idolatrous for us, that is, baptism, Lord's Supper, feetwashing, going to meeting, vigils, praying, fasting, giving alms, and other deeds that can be performed.[135]

Another offense of Boehm which greatly troubled the Lancaster brethren was the way in which he explained evil. Later treatments of the incident typically pass over this charge or dismiss it as a misunderstanding on the part of the Mennonites. The concern, however, receives major attention in the document and is discussed very carefully. The position which the Lancaster brethren understood Boehm to be taking concerning evil was highly offensive to them. Boehm, they said, has held that Satan is a benefit to mankind, that the Scriptures are a dead letter and could be burned, that faith comes from unbelief, light from darkness, and life out of death.

The document deals with each of these assertions. The Lancaster brethren say:

> His first declaration, "That Satan was good and beneficial to man" was contradicted by many, because Satan is the great enemy of the human race, and through him sin and entire corruption was brought into the world, and it required the life and blood of Christ again to release us from the power of darkness.[136]

The Lancaster brethren carefully point out that God is light and that there is no darkness in him; that although Paul says God commanded light to shine out of darkness this is not to say that light comes from darkness. While they agree that the paper and ink of the Scriptures could well be destroyed by fire,

---

[134] John F. Funk, *The Mennonite Church and Her Accusers* (Elkhart, Ind.: Mennonite Publishing Company, 1878), pp. 41-56. The original document has not been located. The copy to which Funk had access was neither dated nor signed, but there seems to be no reason to consider it spurious.

[135] Durnbaugh, *Brethren in Colonial America*, p. 309.

[136] Funk, *The Mennonite Church*, p. 45.

Germantown Dunker meetinghouse, built in 1770.

they point out that "Christ teaches 'The words that I speak unto you, they are Spirit, and they are life.' "[137]

It appears that Martin Boehm had been influenced by the mystical ideas of Jacob Boehme. Boehme held that the Christ within was the only essential, that the written Word of God itself was indeed a dead letter; that the universe was one and that no reality could be manifested without its opposite. Thus without evil, man could not know good, and therefore both Satan and evil could be said to serve a useful purpose in the total scheme of things.

Each of the charges made by the conference against Boehm violated a key religious value of the group: unity within the brotherhood, the acceptance of mutual counsel, the importance of communion and baptism as commandments of Jesus, the belief in two separate kingdoms—the kingdom of Christ and the kingdom of this world, nonresistance, and nonswearing of oaths. For an extended period of time the Mennonites had interacted with the pietistic German Revival. Their withdrawal, when it came, appears to have been based on fundamental differences between the religious understandings of the movement and the beliefs of the Mennonites.

By the fourth quarter of the eighteenth century Mennonite communities were firmly established in Bucks, Montgomery, Lancaster, and adjoining counties in Pennsylvania, and small settlements were found in five counties in Virginia.[138] A new settlement was beginning in Allegheny County

Pietism and Fragmentation 73

in western Pennsylvania. In 1773 a group of Mennonite ministers wrote a letter to Holland, answering questions that had apparently been posed to them. They say that their communities are so numerous that they are not in a position to describe them accurately: "We cannot designate how many ministers or how many communities but according to our calculations there are at least eighteen confirmed ministers and fifty communities, some of which have more than one hundred and fifty members."[139] They say further:

> Our congregations increase rather than diminish. Through God's mercy we enjoy unlimited freedom in both civil and religious affairs. We have never been compelled to bear weapons. With yea and nay we can testify before our worthy magistrates. We accept no office under government because force is used therein. Besides, it is not found good among us that any member of the community should openly, much less secretly, keep an alehouse or an inn, because it leads to a great number of irregularities. Concerning marriage, it is not approved or permitted that one should marry outside the community, and in case it occurs, the person, whether Brother or Sister, is notified to withdraw from the fellowship, the brotherly council, the kiss of peace, and the Lord's Supper until they have made expiation to the community.[140]

The writers of the letter point out that primary emphasis is given to the Holy Scriptures in their church life, especially to the Evangelists, by which they mean the four Gospels of the New Testament. An offense against the community results in exclusion (the ban) from religious rites until expiation is made. Participation in the surrounding culture is limited, even in economic affairs. Being defenseless Christians, i.e., not bearing arms, is of paramount importance. No office under government is accepted because this would necessitate the use of force. Their refusal to take an oath has been respected: they are permitted to use simply "yea" and "nay" when testifying before magistrates.

During the American Revolution this idyllic picture faded as Mennonites and other defenseless Christians found themselves in very awkward circumstances. Their consciences did not allow them to participate in warfare of any kind. Furthermore, when they came to Pennsylvania they had promised (affirmed) loyalty to the king of England. They saw endorsement of the Revolutionary cause as a breaking of that promise. As the war progressed,

---
[137] Ibid.
[138] Page, Shenandoah, Frederick, Rockingham, and Augusta counties.
[139] "A Letter from Pennsylvania Mennonites to Holland," p. 229.
[140] Ibid., p. 230.

a loyalty oath was required of all citizens. Here the defenseless Christians encountered a third severe problem. They believed that Jesus had said "swear not at all," and from the inception of their movement they had refused to swear an oath of any kind. Their stand appeared very suspicious to those who were sacrificing and suffering as fighters for the Revolutionary cause. On the surface it appeared that the defenseless Christians were Tories, supporting the British. The situation made them unpopular, and coercive legal action against them became common. The story of the Mennonites during the American Revolution has been told elsewhere, and an assessment of the options open to nonresistant Christians has also been written.[141] Following the American Revolution a number of Mennonites, seeking cheaper land and loyal to the British crown, migrated to Canada. The majority simply accepted the new government and continued their quiet way of life.

---

[141] John L. Ruth, *'Twas Seeding Time* (Scottdale, Pa.: Herald Press, 1976); Richard K. MacMaster with Samuel L. Horst and Robert F. Ulle, *Conscience in Crisis, 1739-1789* (Scottdale, Pa.: Herald Press, 1979); Donald F. Durnbaugh, "Religion and Revolution: Options in 1776," *Pennsylvania Mennonite Heritage* 1 (July 1978): 2-9; Ruth, *Maintaining the Right Fellowship*; and Richard K. MacMaster, *Land, Piety, Peoplehood* (Scottdale, Pa.: Herald Press, 1984).

2
The Charter

By the middle of the nineteenth century Mennonite religious patterns appeared increasingly archaic and unevangelical in contrast to dominant Second Awakening emphases. Living in quiet rural communities, the Mennonites stood apart from the institutional and educational development which the Great Awakenings fostered. Furthermore, among Mennonites no introspective diaries traced inner spiritual pilgrimages, as they commonly did among neighboring Quakers and Moravians. Introspection concerning one's religious feelings was not encouraged by Mennonites, and they also frowned upon verbal expressions of these feelings in the form of testimonies. In an era when much religious expression was verbal and emotional, this seemed to indicate clearly that Mennonites were lacking in religious zeal.

For more than a century commentators wrote negatively about American Mennonites. They were depicted in the nineteenth century as "petrified"[1] or "in a low state of ignorance"[2] and generally thought of as legalistic during the first half of the twentieth. Careful study suggests that although these assessments contained elements of truth, perhaps the chief offense of the Mennonites was deliberately to stand outside the mainstream of American religious and cultural expression. American religious experience was commonly interpreted from a vantage point that saw America as an elect nation and revivalistic evangelicalism as the norm.[3] In this context, the Mennonites fared badly. They staunchly resisted combining religion and patriotism, and they shunned evangelical revivalism with an almost equal determination.

It was long held that little could be known about American Mennonites before the twentieth century, for they kept few records. Contemporary explanatory accounts appear mainly from the pens of those who rejected the group. Original publications were minimal. The sparseness of formal, first-hand accounts of group events has commonly been attributed to backward-

---

[1] Philip Schaff, *America* (Cambridge: Belknap Press of Harvard University, 1961), p. 167. First published in 1855.

[2] John H. Oberholtzer, "A Letter of John H. Oberholtzer to Unnamed Friends in Germany, 1849," tr. by Elizabeth Bender, *MQR* 45 (October 1972): 401.

[3] See Martin Marty, *The Righteous Empire* (New York: Dial, 1970); and Robert T. Handy, *A Christian America* (New York: Oxford University Press, 1971).

ness. Records that are extant tend to be perfunctory, rarely commenting on religious issues or feelings.

Why did the Mennonites resist dominant religious and cultural pressures? What enabled them to do so? Were they dead traditionalists, as their critics claimed, or did they have basic core values that undergirded belief and practice? What was the essential character of the group, the underlying sentiment that informed beliefs, customs, and practice?

Several recent studies have spoken to aspects of this question. Sandra Cronk, studying the Old Order Mennonites and the Old Order Amish, saw the embodiment of their ethos in yieldedness and surrender. Joseph C. Liechty noted that as Mennonites were confronted by the impact of nineteenth-century American Protestant movements, they reinforced their own identity with an emphasis on humility. Theron F. Schlabach described the cultural orientation of American Mennonites from 1683 to 1850 as traditionalist but increasingly pressed toward modernization. In the religious milieu of American revivalism, he noted, the humble became "aggressive workers," while growing institutional structures called for increasing centralization of power. Harold S. Bender, in his classic synthesis, saw the uniqueness of the Mennonite heritage in its Anabaptist understanding of discipleship, nonresistance, and the nature of the church.[4]

This study proposes that key values were functioning in the Mennonite group, and that these values were contained in a "charter" that gave fundamental support to religious forms.[5] *Charter* was defined by the social anthropologist Bronislaw Malinowski as "the system of values for the pursuit of which human beings organize, or enter into organizations already existing."[6] He included traditionally established values, programs, and principles of organized behavior in the charter. John Hostetler applied the concept of the charter in his study of Amish society.[7] He defines it as the fundamental values and common ends of a group, recognized by its members and accepted by them. *Charter*, for him, refers not only to a set of moral values, or what might be termed recognized beliefs. *Charter* indicates a blueprint for social organization and social relationships containing not only values but also practical procedures for institutional structure and daily living. While statements of belief are very important, so also is the body of pragmatic knowledge which can be used to adjust and confirm social arrangements by group decision. The charter is the accumulated body of definitions, practices, and traditions. He points out that the charter need not be written to be effective, and it need not be consciously vocalized by the group. Nonetheless, it informs behavior and governs the conception of what is appropriate and inappropriate.

Malinowski suggests that the understanding of a group may be substantially advanced by investigating the historical antecedents of the group and by establishing the existence of a traditional charter.

The Initial Charter

The first common statement of values and beliefs for the Swiss-South German Anabaptists who came to America was the Schleitheim statement of "Brotherly Union" in 1527. Although it had been the hope of the early Anabaptists to become a renewal movement within the church, by 1525 it became apparent to them that if they were to live according to their convictions it would be necessary for them to form an independent fellowship. In 1527 a group of their leaders met at Schleitheim in Schaffhausen, a small town on the German and Swiss border, and drew up a statement which all of them could endorse: the "Brotherly Union of a Number of Children of God Concerning Seven Articles."[8] The seven articles of the "Brotherly Union" treat Anabaptist positions which contrast with those of the Protestant Reformers: the points delineate matters of ethics and church order. On beliefs considered doctrinally essential, such as the authority of the Bible, the sacrificial work of Christ, and justification by faith, the Anabaptists and the Reformers were in essential agreement.[9] Yet the points of difference were considered so momentous by both sides that they became matters of life and death.

A cover letter accompanying the "Brotherly Union" acknowledges belief in God as Father, atonement through the blood of Jesus Christ, and the

---

[4] "Gelassenheit: The Rites of the Redemptive Process in Old Order Amish and Old Order Mennonite Communities" (Ph.D. dissertation, University of Chicago, 1977); "Humility: The Foundation of Mennonite Religious Outlook in the 1860's," *MQR* 54 (January 1980): 5-31; "Mennonites, Revivalism, Modernity 1683-1850," *Church History* 48 (December 1979): 398-415; "The Humble Become 'Aggressive Workers': Mennonites Organize for Mission, 1880 to 1910," *MQR* (April 1978): 113-126; *Gospel Versus Gospel* (Scottdale, Pa.: Herald Press, 1980); and "The Anabaptist Vision," *Church History* 13 (March 1944): 3-24.

[5] For the original presentation of this thesis, see Beulah S. Hostetler, "Franconia Mennonite Conference and American Protestant Movements, 1840-1940" (Ph.D. dissertation, University of Pennsylvania, 1977).

[6] *A Scientific Theory of Culture* (N.C.: University of North Carolina Press, 1944), pp. 52-53.

[7] *Amish Society* (Baltimore: Johns Hopkins University Press, 1968 ed), p. 47f. Following Hostetler, Paul Peachey used the term chapter in relation to Mennonites, but did not designate the content of the charter. Paul Peachey, "Identity Crisis Among American Mennonites," *MQR* 42 (October 1968): 243-259.

[8] For the full text of the "Brotherly Union," and the context in which it was written, see *The Legacy of Michael Sattler*, tr. and ed. by John H. Yoder (Scottdale, Pa.: Herald Press, 1973), esp. pp. 27-43.

[9] John H. Yoder, "The Contemporary Evangelical Revival and the Peace Churches," *Mission and the Peace Witness*, Robert L. Ramseyer, ed. (Scottdale, Pa.: Herald Press, 1979), pp. 98-99.

78   *The Charter*

Town of Schleitheim where Anabaptists affirmed the "Brotherly Union" in 1527.

gifts of the Spirit. It tells how unity was achieved concerning the Seven Articles in a gathered group that met to discuss differences. It calls fellow believers to "stand fast in the Lord as obedient children of God."[10] The Seven Articles treat Baptism, The Ban, Breaking of Bread, Separation from the World, Shepherds of the Flock, The Sword, and The Oath. Michael Sattler (c. 1490-1527), a former Benedictine monk who became an Anabaptist, is generally accepted as the original framer and final author of the "Brotherly Union of a Number of Children of God Concerning Seven Articles."

The crucial consequence of the "Brotherly Union" in the formulation and consolidation of the Anabaptist movement is pointed out by John H. Yoder. Yoder calls the Schleitheim meeting, and the subsequent "Brotherly Union," the most important event in the whole history of Anabaptism:

> That it could happen, that in the course of a meeting men could change their opinions and come to unity, is not only a striking rarity in the history of the Reformation; it is also the most important event in the whole history of Anabaptism. Had it not happened, the Anabaptism of Grebel, Blaurock, Mantz, and Sattler would have died out together with its founders. But now it has taken on a viable form and was in a position

to resist the licentiousness of the fanatics, the coercion of Christian governments and the persuasiveness of the preachers.[11]

The "Brotherly Union" circulated widely. Within a few months Zwingli had received four copies of it from four different sources.[12] "There is almost no one among you," he wrote, "who does not have a copy of your so well founded commandments."[13] He promptly responded to it in a letter, refuting it point by point.[14] Later he wrote a careful rebuttal in Latin which included sections of the statement in translation.[15] The confession continued to circulate widely despite efforts to confiscate and destroy all copies. Seventeen years later, in 1544, Calvin found himself pressed to write a response to it in spite of his reluctance:

> If any man marvel ... that I will occupy myself to answer a book which is unworthy to be spoken of or made mention of, ... it shall be sufficient excuse for me to allege that I have done it at the request and insistence of many good and faithful men who hath sent the book to me from far countries with the testimony that it was very needful for the health of many souls that I should take it in hand.[16]

In March 1636, when persecution in Switzerland resumed with vigor, arrested Anabaptists were confronted with articles of belief by their interrogators. The Fifth Article, they say, was allowed to pass without debate. Article VI was singled out for special attention. Several months later, in another location, a disputation was held concerning three articles, namely Baptism, The Ban, and Breaking of Bread. The continuing centrality of the Seven Articles is clearly suggested.[17]

---

[10] Yoder, *Legacy*, p. 35.

[11] Yoder, *Legacy*, p. 47. Tr. by Yoder from his *Die Gespräche zwischen Täufer und Reformatoren in der Schweitz 1523-1538* (Karlsruhe: H. Schneider, 1962), pp. 98f. See also Leland Harder, ed., *The Sources of Swiss Anabaptism* (Scottdale, Pa.: Herald Press, 1985); and C. Arnold Snyder, *The Life and Thought of Michael Sattler* (Scottdale, Pa.: Herald Press, 1984).

[12] Yoder, *Legacy*, pp. 13, 32-33.

[13] Ibid., p. 33.

[14] Ibid., p. 45, fn. 5.

[15] *Contra Catabaptistarum Strophus Elenchus*, ibid., p. 46, fn. 13. See also p. 45, fn. 5; pp. 32-33.

[16] *Briève Instruction pour armer tous bons fidèles contre les erreurs de la secte commune des Anabaptistes*, quoted in Willem Balke, *Calvin and the Anabaptist Radicals* (Grand Rapids, Mich.: William B. Eerdmans Publishing Company, 1981), p. 181.

[17] See *Ein Warhafftiger Bericht von den Bruedern im Schweitzerland, in dem Zuercher Gebiet, wegen der Truebsalen welche ueber sie ergangen seyn, um des Evangeliums willen; von dem 1635sten bis in das 1645ste Jahr*. Printed as Appendix II in the *Ausbund* (Germantown: Gedruckt bey Christoph Saur, 1742), pp. 5-8.

Oldest known copy of the "Brotherly Union."

A *Sammelband* (anthology) purchased in Pennsylvania by antiquarian Amos Hoover contains a copy of the Seven Articles of the "Brotherly Union." The book appears to have been a minister's manual. Measuring approximately four by six inches in size, it contains the Dordrecht Confession; prayers for various religious ceremonies, for the sick, and after meals; selected hymns; Michael Sattler's "Letter to the Church at Horb"; and the "Brotherly Union of a Number of Children of God Concerning Seven Articles." A hymn dated 1691 is included in the volume, indicating that it was assembled some time after that date. This volume provides material evidence that the Pennsylvania Mennonites had access to the "Brotherly Union" in written form.

The Seven Articles

Article I. Concerning Baptism

The first of the Seven Articles of the "Brotherly Union" concerns baptism, the ceremony of initiation into the Christian church. Like each of the articles, it relates not simply to belief, but to practical life. The article states that baptism may be given to all who have been taught repentance, amendment of life, and who truly believe that their sins are taken away through Christ. They must desire to walk in the resurrection of Christ, and be buried with him in death. Baptism may be given to all who, with such an understanding, themselves desire and request it. Hereby, they say, is excluded all infant baptism.[18]

The rejection of infant baptism was seen by the authorities as both heresy and sedition. At issue was the nature of the church, its relationship to society, and differing understandings concerning the relationship of Old Testament to New Testament Scriptures. Adult baptism upon confession of faith implied a voluntary church, one that stood apart from society. Zwingli himself had early in the Reformation questioned the practice of baptizing infants but because of practical considerations laid the matter aside.

Zwingli and his supporters held that every citizen was embraced by the church, just as all Israel was covered by the covenant with Abraham. The baptism of infants signified their inclusion in the church, just as the circumcision of male infants betokened their participation in the covenant with Abraham. Anabaptists believed that the New Testament took precedence over the Old Testament. In the Old Testament obedience to God's law was mandated. In the New Testament his love, as manifested in Christ, called for voluntary response and willing obedience. This implied an adult choice and a voluntary church.

While Anabaptists deemed little children to be recipients of grace without any outward ceremony, they believed that adults were justified by grace *through faithfulness*.[19] The article states that repentance must precede baptism, and that it is to be followed by "amendment of life." Luther's emphasis on justification by faith alone was interpreted by some of his followers as license to do as one pleased. Libertines were also found among the earliest sympathizers with Anabaptism. One of the purposes of the Schleitheim meeting was to confront this posture, and it was decisively rejected. The ensuing emphasis on ethics was seen by the Reformers as moralism and legalism. The conflicting views were not new. The apostle Paul speaks to the

---

[18] Yoder, *Legacy*, p. 36.
[19] John H. Yoder, *The Politics of Jesus* (Grand Rapids, Mich.: William B. Eerdmans, 1972), pp. 215-232.

issue in his letter to the church at Rome in a passage that was read by American Mennonites at baptismal services: "What are we to say then? Shall we persist in sin so that there may be all the more grace? No, no! We died to sin: how can we live in it any longer?"[20] As the passage continues, it develops another key Mennonite emphasis: baptism as incorporation into the death and resurrection of Christ:

> Have you forgotten that when we were baptized into union with Christ Jesus we were baptized into his death? By baptism we were buried with him, and lay dead, in order that, as Christ was raised from the dead in the splendor of the Father, so also we might set our feet upon the new path of life.[21]

The "Brotherly Union" states that persons who wish to be baptized "must desire to walk in the resurrection of Christ and be buried with him in death." In this conception of baptism, God's grace not only makes forgiveness possible, but also *regeneration*, resulting in a "New Creation," the rebirth of the entire person. This transformation occurs in the present as well as in the future. Through the indwelling power of the Spirit, this newness of life, often called "walking in the resurrection," is experienced in the daily life and conduct of the believer.[22]

Accepting baptism meant accepting Christ as Lord, *and* being joined to the brotherhood. It meant a covenantal relation to the community, and this was a community not simply of belief, but of practical life. The community was to be a disciplined community, and the discipline was enacted through mutual admonition and the ban.

Article II. Concerning the Ban

Article II of the "Brotherly Union" begins as follows:

> We have been united as follows concerning the ban. The ban shall be employed with all those who have given themselves over to the Lord, to walk after Him in His commandments: those who have been baptized into one body of Christ, and let themselves be called brothers or sisters, and still somehow slip and fall into error and sin, being inadvertently overtaken. The same shall be warned twice privately and the third time be publicly admonished before the entire congregation according to the command of Christ (Mt. 18). But this shall be done according to the ordering of the Spirit of God before the breaking of Bread, so that we may all in one spirit and in one love break and eat from the bread and drink from one cup.[23]

The ban is probably the most misunderstood of all Anabaptist tenets. Simply stated, the ban is disciplinary action, by the group, directed against a person who has formally committed himself to group standards and has later violated those standards. The commitment was made to the group, and if it appears that the commitment has been violated, it is the group that takes disciplinary action. The procedure to be followed is specified in the "Brotherly Union." It is to be done according to the command given by Jesus in Matthew 18:15-17.

> If your brother commits a sin, go and take the matter up with him, strictly between yourselves, and if he listens to you, you have won your brother over. If he will not listen, take one or two others with you, so that all the facts may be duly established on the evidence of two or three witnesses. If he refuses to listen to them, report the matter to the congregation; and if he will not listen even to the congregation, you must then treat him as you would a pagan or a tax-gatherer. (The New English Bible)

This was to be done before the breaking of bread (communion), so that all might in one spirit and one love partake from one bread and drink from one cup. Writing in 1527, Anabaptist leader Balthasar Hubmaier said that where such brotherly discipline is absent, there is no church even though water baptism and the breaking of bread are observed.[24]

Leaders as well as members were potentially subject to the rule of the ban. Banning, when it occurred, was to take place in the presence of the congregation and with its participation. The spiritual exclusion which it denoted was considered the only appropriate punishment for an errant member: "Within the perfection of Christ only the ban is used for the admonition and exclusion of the one who has sinned, without the death of the flesh, simply the warning and the command to sin no more."[25] The discipline of the ban

---

[20] Romans 6:1-2, *New English Bible*. Benjamin Eby says that Romans 6 was read at baptismal services. See *Kurzgefasste Kirchen-Geschichte und Glaubenslehre der Taufgesinnten Christen oder Mennoniten* (Berlin, Canada: Gedruckt bey Heinrich Eby, 1841).

[21] Romans 6:3-4.

[22] See Harold S. Bender, "Walking in the Resurrection," *MQR* 35 (April 1961): 96-110. For an illuminating treatment of this conception of baptism, and how it contrasts with classical Christian theology, see Van A. Harvey, "Resurrection of the Dead," *A Handbook of Theological Terms* (New York: The Macmillan Co., 1964), pp. 206-207.

[23] Yoder, *Legacy*, p. 36.

[24] For Hubmaier's discussion of discipline and the ban, see Donald F. Durnbaugh, *Every Need Supplied* (Philadelphia: Temple University Press, 1974), pp. 27-37. For a contemporary discussion of mutual discipline, see Marlin Jeschke, *Discipling the Brother* (Scottdale, Pa.: Herald Press, 1974).

[25] Yoder, *Legacy*, p. 39.

seemed extraordinarily mild at the time it was introduced. Later, when persecution had ceased and discipline was generally lax, it appeared severe.

In the early Reformation period church discipline was widely discussed. Both Luther and Zwingli considered the use of the ban, but found it unworkable in a territorial church. In the debates between Protestant church authorities and Anabaptists following 1525, the issue arose repeatedly. By 1530, Protestant authorities no longer considered discipline according to the rule of the ban workable.[26] At issue was not only discipline within the congregation, but church government as well. Hierarchical forms of authority and the disciplinary arm of the state were both rejected by the rule of the ban, or, as the Anabaptists called it, "the Rule of Christ."

Matters requiring the use of the ban were to be dealt with before the breaking of bread (communion), so that all might in one spirit and one love partake from one bread and drink from one cup. When the ban was invoked, it meant that the individual was barred from the breaking of the bread, sometimes called the Lord's Supper, until he had expressed contrition and been received back into the spiritual fellowship with the group. The ban did not imply social avoidance as later called for by the article on shunning in the Dordrecht Confession and practiced by some of the more conservative Anabaptist groups such as the Amish.[27]

The importance of love in the exercise of the ban was recognized from the time of its inauguration. Michael Sattler, in a letter written to his congregation at Horb shortly after the Schleitheim meeting, cautioned:

> Further, dear fellow members in Christ, you should be admonished not to forget love, without which it is not possible that you be a Christian congregation.... But if you love the neighbor, you will not scold or ban zealously, will not seek your own, will not remember evil, will not be ambitious or puffed up, but kind, righteous, generous in all gifts, humble and sympathetic with the weak and imperfect.[28]

Article III. Concerning the Breaking of Bread

Concerning the breaking of bread, we have become one and agree thus: all those who desire to break the one bread in remembrance of the broken body of Christ and all those who wish to drink of one drink in remembrance of the shed blood of Christ, they must beforehand be united in the one body of Christ, that is the congregation of God, whose head is Christ, and that by baptism. For as Paul indicated, we cannot be partakers at the same time of the table of the Lord and the table of devils. Nor can we at the same time drink of the cup of the Lord and the cup of devils....

So it shall and must be, that whoever does not share the calling of one God to one faith, to one baptism, to one spirit, to one body together with all the children of God, may not be made one loaf together with them as must be true if one wishes truly to break bread according to the command of Christ.[29]

For the Anabaptists the Lord's Supper was a memorial service, one to be observed in remembrance of the broken body and the shed blood of Christ. It also signified union with each other and with the risen Lord. Christ was thought to be present not in the elements but in the community of believers who were partaking of the elements. Throughout the statement the importance of unity and oneness among the followers of Christ is emphasized. The adjective "one" is used 10 times in two paragraphs: "Concerning the bread, we have become one and agree"; "one bread," "one cup," "one body of Christ," "the calling of one God to one faith, to one baptism, to one spirit, to one body ... one loaf together with them." The demand for unity of belief and commitment among those participating in the breaking of bread meant that anyone not participating in this unity must be excluded from participation in the Lord's Supper, and the need for such exclusion is plainly stated in the article.

Both the Anabaptists and Zwingli understood the Lord's Supper to be symbolic, a service of remembrance and commemoration signifying union with the risen Lord and among the participants. It was the continuing observance of the Catholic mass after Zwingli and his inner circle decided it was not based on Scripture that caused the initial rift. The Anabaptists decisively rejected Zwingli's judgment that faithful observance, according to their mutual understanding, must await the approval of the city council.

When Calvin wrote *Confessio Schlattensis*, a rebuttal to the "Brotherly Union," he only briefly refuted the article on the breaking of bread.[30] Like the Anabaptists, Calvin saw the Supper as a means "to unite the members of our Lord Jesus with their head and with one another into one body and one spirit," and he recognized the need for discipline in relation to the Lord's Supper.[31] Here, however, the agreement came to an end. Calvin, like the other Protestant Reformers, saw the "one body," the true church, as *invisible*, for no one knew who participated in the communion with genuine trust and

---

[26] Ervin A. Schlabach, "The Rule of Christ Among the Early Swiss Anabaptists" (Ph.D. dissertation, Chicago Theological Seminary, 1977), passim.
[27] Article XVII.
[28] Yoder, *Legacy*, p. 59.
[29] Yoder, *Legacy*, p. 37.
[30] Balke, *Calvin and the Anabaptist Radicals*, p. 192.
[31] Ibid., p. 77.

faith. It was expected that there would be hypocrites in the church: the wheat and tares would exist side by side until the final harvest. In contrast to this, the Anabaptists identified the body of Christ with the visible congregation of believers. For them the church was composed of those who were regenerated, lived a disciplined life, and were committed to participation in a fellowship of believers:

> The body of Christ is the faithful community of Christ. Whoever eats of this bread in the Supper of the Lord, testifies that he desires to have fellowship with and to participate in all things with the body of Christ. That is, he commits himself to the community in all things, in love and suffering, wealth and poverty, honour and dishonour, sorrow and joy, death and life, indeed, that he is ready to give life and limb for the brothers, as Christ gave himself for him. Similarly with the cup in the blood of Christ: Whoever drinks of this cup has first surrendered himself and testifies with it that he is prepared to pour out his blood for the sake of Christ and his church insofar as faith and the test of love demands it.[32]

This call for self-surrender to the group was illustrated with the elaboration of a prayer found in a second-century treatise, *The Didache* or *The Teaching of the Twelve Apostles*.[33] This second-century prayer, which concerns the Eucharist, asks that just as in the bread grains of wheat which were formerly scattered over the hills have been gathered together to become one, so might the church be gathered together from the ends of the earth into Christ's kingdom. The Anabaptist version incorporates a dimension of self-surrender: as many grains of wheat are ground together, giving up their identity to make one loaf, and many grapes are brought together and crushed to make the wine, so too the individual members of the congregation must surrender their will and identity so that they might become one. This parable is related in a communion hymn in the *Ausbund*, and was recounted during the distribution of the bread and wine at communion services in eastern Pennsylvania until well into the twentieth century.[34]

Article IV. Separation from the World
Article IV reads in part:
> We have been united concerning the separation that shall take place from the evil and wickedness which the devil has planted in the world, simply in this; that we have no fellowship with them, and do not run with them in the confusion of their abominations....
>
> To us, then, the commandment of the Lord is also obvious,

whereby He orders us to be and become separated from the evil one, and thus He will be our God and we shall be His sons and daughters.³⁵

Further, He admonishes us, therefore, to go out from Babylon and from the earthly Egypt, that we may not be partakers in their torment and suffering, which the Lord will bring upon them.

From all this, we should learn that everything which has not been united with our God in Christ is nothing but an abomination which we should shun. . . .³⁶

Article IV of the "Brotherly Union" unequivocally calls followers of Christ to be separated from the evil which the devil has planted in the world. The world here refers to both the established order and the people in it. The article implies two worlds or two kingdoms, contrasting good and evil, believing and unbelieving, darkness and light, God's temple and idols, Christ and Belial. Separation from the religious establishment was a rigorous judgment that invited the animosity of both Catholic and Protestant authorities.

Both severe persecution and the charter can be seen as motivations for the withdrawal into remote communities which became so characteristic of the Swiss Anabaptists and for which they have received so much criticism. The church as a disciplined, gathered community has two sides as it finds expression in the human community. The positive manifestation is the practice of brotherhood in the community; the negative aspect is standing apart from the larger society, or "separation from the world." Separation from the world does not necessarily mean *withdrawal* from the world, but it does frequently find expression in that manner.

Separation from the world as a mandate for the devout Christian was not a new idea when the Anabaptists framed the "Brotherly Union." From the period of the early church two strains of Christianity are evident: one is expressed in a close fellowship of committed disciples emphasizing the Gospels, including the Sermon on the Mount; the other sees the Gospel as an all-embracing ideal, a free gift expressed through institutional forms designed to include the masses.³⁷ Those stressing the need for separation frequently

---

³² Hans Schlaffer, "A Pleasant Letter of Comfort, 1527," quoted in Klaassen, *Anabaptism in Outline* (Scottdale, Pa.: Herald Press, 1981), p. 196.

³³ *Teaching of the Twelve Apostles*, edited with a translation, introduction, and notes by Roswell D. Hitchcock and Francis Brown (New York: Charles Scribner's Sons, 1884), p. 19.

³⁴ *Das 55. Lied*, verse 23, page 308. John E. Lapp said that Bishop Jonas Mininger always told this parable as he distributed the bread and wine, and that Abraham G. Clemmer said it had long been the custom in the conference. Personal interview, May 24, 1982.

³⁵ 2 Corinthians 6:17.

³⁶ Yoder, *Legacy*, pp. 37-38.

³⁷ Ernst Troeltsch, *The Social Teaching of the Christian Churches* (New York: Harper Torchbooks, 1960), pp. 328-343.

experienced persecution, yet the Catholic Church structurally accommodated both forms, incorporating into its institutional framework by means of the monastic system and church orders those who desired commitment to discipleship. The Protestant Reformers rejected monasticism, and as a result had no means for channeling the sectarian impulse. The reemergence of religious separatism in a structurally unified society threatened religious and social stability and provoked immediate persecution.

The withdrawal from the world which is characteristic of the sect does not necessarily mean the rejection of either force or the use of power structures. But Article IV of the "Brotherly Union" takes a natural step from separation from the world to the abandonment of coercion. It forbids the use of weapons of violence, either for the protection of friends or against enemies, since Christ commanded his followers not to resist evil. It reads:

> Thereby shall also fall away from us the diabolical weapons of violence—such as sword, armor, and the like, and all of their use to protect friends or against enemies—by virtue of the word of Christ: "You shall not resist evil."[38]

The immediate problem confronting the writers of the Seven Articles was not participation in warfare but the use of violence to enforce or resist conformity of belief. Only later did warfare become the central issue.

Article V. Shepherds in the Church of God

> The shepherd in the church shall be a person according to the rule of Paul, fully and completely, who has a good report of those who are outside the faith. The office of such a person shall be to read and exhort and teach, warn, admonish, or ban in the congregation, and properly to preside among the sisters and brothers in prayer, and in the breaking of bread, and in all things to take care of the body of Christ, that it may be built up and developed, so that the name of God might be praised and honored through us, and the mouth of the mocker be stopped.[39]

When the Anabaptists made worthiness a fundamental qualification for shepherding in the church, they reversed current religious values. Early in the fourth century in the Donatist controversy, the Catholic Church ruled that proper ordination, not the worthiness of the individual priest, determined the efficacy of the sacrament. The rule of Paul, referred to in the article, is found in 1 Timothy 3:7: "He must moreover have a good reputation with the non-Christian public so that he may not get exposed to scandal and not get caught in the devil's snare."[40] Calvin criticized the Anabaptist criterion, upholding the importance of office and minimizing the significance of conduct for the office holder.[41] Luther, too, upheld the priestly office sanctified by proper ordination. Menno Simons, like the framers of the "Brotherly Union," laid emphasis on conduct rather than office, repeatedly citing the example of Jesus and the apostles.[42]

A second point at issue was theological training for office. Calvin charged that the Anabaptist shepherds were "ignorant," for they eschewed formal training in the theological schools.[43] The key to understanding the Bible, according to the Anabaptists, was not theological training, but willingness to obey. This included a willingness to submit to the cross (obedience), willingness to be instructed by both the Spirit and the brethren, and an openness to personal application of the truths as they apply in everyday life.[44]

A third point of difference between the Reformers and the Anabaptists concerned the preaching of the Word. Both Lutheran and Reformed confessions placed great emphasis on the preaching of the Word, and on the power of the Word so preached. In contrast, the article on shepherds does not even include the word "preaching." The shepherd's duties were to read, exhort, teach, admonish, or ban in the congregation, and to preside at the breaking of bread and in prayer. Further, the shepherd was "in all things to take care of the body of Christ,"[45] a mandate calling the leader to a pastoral function.

Article V states that the shepherd is to be supported by the congregation: "He shall be supported, wherein he has need, by the congregation which has chosen him, so that he who serves the gospel can also live therefrom, as the Lord has ordered." Support was to come, not from the state, or a structured hierarchy, but from the congregation served. Zwingli's translation says that "the shepherd should be one from the congregation."[46] Whether or not this is the most appropriate translation, it is indeed the practice that was followed for several centuries in America. The article says nothing about the method by which a minister is to be selected, but it makes provision for the immediate selection of a new shepherd in case of arrest or martyrdom.[47]

---

[38] Yoder, *Legacy*, p. 38.
[39] Ibid., p. 39.
[40] *New English Bible*.
[41] Balke, *Calvin and the Anabaptist Radicals*, p. 235f.
[42] Henry Poettcker, "Biblical Controversy on Several Fronts," *MQR* 40 (April 1966):132.
[43] Balke, *Calvin and the Anabaptist Radicals*, p. 238.
[44] Poettcker, "Biblical Controversy," p. 115.
[45] Yoder, *Legacy*, p. 39.
[46] Ibid., p. 52.
[47] Calvin accuses the Anabaptists of ordaining in haste. Balke, *Calvin and the Anabaptist Radicals*, p. 237.

Article VI. Concerning the Sword

The longest article in the "Brotherly Union" concerns the use of the sword. It deals not with warfare, but with whether a Christian may exercise the powers of the magistracy. The article accepts government (the sword) as part of the order created by God, but holds that it is outside of the perfection of Christ. The Anabaptists did not envision the "conversion" of the social order; they did not expect more than a comparatively small number to make up the church.

Four questions concerning their position on the sword were frequently put to the Anabaptists. The first concerns the punishment of evil and the protection of the good:

> Now many, who do not understand Christ's will for us, will ask: whether a Christian may or should use the sword against the wicked for the protection and defense of the good, or for the sake of love.[48]

Christ, they answer, has commanded his followers to learn from him, and they cite the incident of the woman taken in adultery: Even though the law of the Father required that she be stoned, and although Jesus had said, "What the Father commanded me, that I do," yet he treated her with mercy and forgiveness, warning her to sin no more. "Exactly thus," they say, "should we also proceed, according to the rule of the ban."[49]

The second question frequently asked was: "Whether a Christian shall pass sentence in disputes and strife about worldly matters, such as unbelievers have with one another." Again, they cite the example of Christ as their answer: "Christ did not wish to decide or pass judgment between brother and brother concerning inheritance, but refused to do so. So should we also do."[50]

The third question was whether a Christian should serve as a magistrate if he is chosen for that office. They responded by pointing out that the crowds wanted to make Christ king, but he refused. Not only did he refuse kingship, but he also said, "Whoever would come after me, let him deny himself and take up his cross and follow me." They add that he further forbids the use of the sword when he says, "The princes of this world lord it over them, etc., but among you it shall not be so."[51] Government, they believed, was established to punish the wicked and protect the good, and secular rulers were established to wield this power. Within the perfection of Christ the ban was the only appropriate discipline. It dealt with the spirit, it did not harm the flesh. The rule of government is according to the flesh; that of Christians, according to the spirit. Their weapons of battle are carnal, those of the Christian are spiritual. Their concluding argument is that as Christ, the head, is minded, so the body must be minded, for any kingdom divided against itself will be destroyed.

Calvin rejected the arguments of the Anabaptists point by point, strongly taking issue with their interpretation. According to him, the incidents cited by the Anabaptists spoke only to relationships within the church, not to the Christian's relation to government.[52] Attitudes toward participation in government were among the main distinguishing features between Anabaptists and other free churches growing out of the Reformed tradition such as Baptists, Quakers, and certain branches of Puritanism.[53]

Article VII. The Oath

In their attempt to follow Jesus' teachings as given in the Sermon on the Mount, the Anabaptists also refused to take the oath. In the secular society of the twentieth century, where the oath has lost much of its significance except as grounds for perjury, it is difficult to comprehend its importance in the sixteenth through eighteenth centuries. The oath called upon God as witness to the promise or statement being made, and sometimes invited judgment on the person making the oath if he should renege on his promise. The oath was widely used in both civil and religious affairs. Their refusal to take the oath made normal life difficult for the Anabaptists and was the basis of the most significant persecution experienced by Mennonites in America.

The Anabaptist refusal to take the oath was based directly on Jesus' commentary in the Sermon on the Mount:

> Again, you have learned that our forefathers were told, "Do not break your oath," and "Oaths sworn to the Lord must be kept." But what I tell you is this: You are not to swear at all—not by heaven, for it is God's throne, nor by earth, for it is his footstool, nor by Jerusalem, for it is the city of the great King, nor by your own head, because you cannot turn one hair of it white or black. Plain "Yes" or "No" is all you need to say; anything beyond that comes from the devil.[54]

---

[48] Yoder, *Legacy*, p. 39.
[49] Ibid., p. 40.
[50] Ibid.
[51] Ibid.
[52] Balke, *Calvin and the Anabaptist Radicals*, pp. 260-265.
[53] For an analysis of the variant Protestant attitudes toward church and state and how they affect expressions of belief, see Thomas G. Sanders, *Protestant Concepts of Church and State* (New York: Holt, Rinehart, and Winston, 1964). His understanding of the Mennonite position is highly perceptive.
[54] Matthew 5:33-37, *New English Bible*. The passage in Matthew is echoed in the epistle of James 5:12.

The Anabaptist hermeneutic is clearly demonstrated in their position on the oath: the New Testament takes precedence over the Old. Catholics, Lutherans, and Reformed continued to place considerable emphasis on the Old Testament. Calvin defended the use of the oath, arguing his reasons in some detail in opposition to those of the Anabaptists.[55] The article recognizes the approved usage of the oath in the Old Testament, yet it stands by the initial assertion: "Christ, who teaches the perfection of the law, forbids his followers all swearing."[56] Numerous sects that preceded the Anabaptists took a similar position concerning the oath. These groups included the Cathari, the Waldenses, the followers of Wycliffe and Huss, and the Bohemian Brethren. All Mennonite confessions of faith, according to two Mennonite scholars, "without exception have included a prohibition of the oath."[57]

The religious beliefs which caused the early Anabaptists to break with the Protestant Reformers are pinpointed in the confessional statement adopted at Schleitheim in February 1527: "Brotherly Union of a Number of Children of God Concerning Seven Articles." We have chosen to call the Seven Articles the "charter" of the early Anabaptists, identifying them as the stated values for which they organized, and which expressed their common ends and purposes.

The Seven Articles both signaled consolidation and implied exclusion. Wolfgang Capito (1478-1541), a leading Strassburg Reformer, feared that the articles heralded "the beginning of a new monasticism."[58] The French scholar Jean Séguy saw in the meeting at Schleitheim "the beginning of a transformation from simple nonconformity and a fraternal lay movement to a 'clear tendency to legislate' behavioral patterns and a growing clericalization" among Anabaptists.[59] Already in 1527, two years after the first baptisms, Michael Sattler, likely the former prior of a monastery,[60] framed a polity which in subsequent years resulted in Mennonite communities that more than once would be likened to monastic orders with a family base.

The "Brotherly Union of a Number of Children of God Concerning Seven Articles" was the charter of the early Anabaptists, embodying the system of values for the pursuit of which they organized.[61] Its continuing importance for Mennonites is asserted by Samuel Cramer, a Dutch scholar, who noted that "almost every phrase of the "Brotherly Union" is found again later in Mennonite teaching and practice." Robert Friedmann listed all of the known editions of the "Brotherly Union," commenting that it had an astonishingly wide circulation. He also noted that the Swiss Brethren, when emigrating, took with them their most precious goods and a few old books like the Seven Articles of Schleitheim.[62]

The Charter in America

The Seven Articles of the "Brotherly Union" continued to serve as the charter for mid-nineteenth-century Mennonites, particularly those in the Franconia Conference of eastern Pennsylvania. The question may well be asked: Why the "Brotherly Union" of 1527, when it was the Dordrecht Confession of Faith of 1632 that the Mennonites had taken as their own in 1725?[63] We have already noted that the Dordrecht Confession was adopted at a time of religious ferment, and printed in English for distribution to neighboring settlers, not for use within Mennonite congregations. Further, there is some question as to the degree to which the Dordrecht Confession was internalized. Although the 1727 edition of the confession states that five Pennsylvania Mennonite districts (at that time the only established American Mennonite communities) have taken the confession to be wholly theirs, this appears to be something of an overstatement. Examination of religious forms shows considerable discrepancy (particularly in the Franconia area) between the articles of the Dordrecht Confession and these forms, discrepancies which are absent when religious forms are compared with the Seven Articles of the "Brotherly Union."

One of the most obvious ways in which practice in Franconia was at variance with the Dordrecht Confession concerns Article XI, the Washing of the Saints' Feet. The article calls for a literal observance of the practice,

---

[55] Balke, *Calvin and the Anabaptist Radicals*, pp. 253-260.

[56] Yoder, *Legacy*, p. 41.

[57] Christian Neff and Harold S. Bender, "Oath," *ME*, s.v. Quote taken from p. 4.

[58] "The Capito Letters," translated in full by Yoder, *Legacy*, pp. 86-99. Quote from p. 87.

[59] Jean Séguy, *Les Assemblées Anabaptistes-Mennonites de France* (Paris, The Hague: Moulton, 1977). Quote from review by Marlin E. Miller, *MQR* 55 (October 1981):388.

[60] Yoder, *Legacy*, p. 10. See also C. Arnold Snyder, "Revolution and the Swiss Brethren: The Case of Michael Sattler," *Church History* 50 (September 1981):276-287.

[61] Malinowski, *Scientific Theory of Culture*, p. 52.

[62] Samuel Cramer, *Bibliotheca Reformatoria Neerlandica* 5 (1909):593; statement quoted in *Legacy*, p. 47; "The Schleitheim Confession (1527) and Other Doctrinal Writings of the Swiss Brethren in a Hitherto Unknown Edition," *MQR* 26 (April 1942):82-99; *Mennonite Piety Through the Centuries* (Goshen College, Goshen, Ind.: The Mennonite Historical Society, 1949), p. 155.

[63] The Dordrecht Confession of Faith was a product of the Dutch and North German Mennonites. In 1660 it was adopted by a group of ministers from Alsace, and subsequently by the German and Palatine Mennonites. The Swiss Mennonites never endorsed the Dordrecht Confession. See J. C. Wenger, *History of the Mennonites of Franconia Conference* (Telford, Pa.: Franconia Mennonite Historical Society, 1937), p. 435f. For the history, context, and substance of the Dordrecht Confession, see Irvin B. Horst, "The Dordrecht Confession of Faith: 350 Years," *Pennsylvania Mennonite Heritage*, vol. 5, no. 3 (July 1982):2-8; and Gerald C. Studer, "The Dordrecht Confession of Faith, 1632-1982," *MQR* 58 (October 1984):503-519; and "What Place Confessions," *Pennsylvania Mennonite Heritage*, vol. 6, no. 2 (April 1983):2-6.

following the example of Jesus, and cites John 13:4-7 and 1 Timothy 5:9 and 10. Yet Franconia Mennonites did not observe this practice until late in the nineteenth century.[64]

Written documents for the Franconia Conference repeatedly mention Matthew 18 when issues of church discipline arise. Article Two of the "Brotherly Union," concerning the ban, focuses on Matthew 18. The Dordrecht Confession cites many Scriptures, and includes articles on expulsion from the church and on shunning, but nowhere refers to the relevant passage in Matthew 18 or to the procedure it recommends. It was these repeated references to Matthew 18 that first stimulated the idea that perhaps the Seven Articles of the "Brotherly Union" served as the charter.

Article XVII of the Dordrecht Confession calls for the shunning (social avoidance) of those who have been expelled from the church. The account of Christian Funk is sometimes cited as the sole evidence that shunning may have been practiced by the Franconia Mennonites. But even when Funk, in his *Mirror for All Mankind,* says his former brethren walked out of an eating house, refusing to eat with him, he adds that such an action had never been the custom among them. It appears that Franconia Mennonites practiced the ban (exclusion from communion), following the "Brotherly Union," but that they did not customarily practice shunning (social avoidance) as called for by the Dordrecht Confession.

One of the most widely recognized characteristics of American Mennonites was their emphasis on separation from the world. The "Brotherly Union," contains a prominent article on separation from the world; the Dordrecht Confession does not contain an article on separation.

These examples afford convincing evidence that although the Dordrecht Confession of Faith had been formally adopted by the Franconia Mennonites, it did not serve as their charter.

In the following pages we will examine a number of documents concerning the religious life of mid-nineteenth-century American Mennonites that have been publicly though somewhat obscurely available. We will demonstrate that most American Mennonites ca. 1840 expressed in their religious forms at least a modicum of the original Anabaptist charter as expressed in the Seven Articles of the "Brotherly Union." The tendency to routinize behavioral patterns, noted by Séguy, will also be evident.

Documentation

The most important sources of information for understanding Mennonite practice at mid-century are a number of formal letters and several books. The letters are those of Jacob Krehbiel, "A Few Words About the Mennonites in America in 1841: A Contemporary Document by Jacob

Krehbiel"[65]; John H. Oberholtzer, "A Letter of John Oberholtzer to Unnamed Friends in Germany, 1849"[66]; and John Geil, "Farewell Address of Pre. John Geil to His Congregation at Line Lexington, Penna.,"[67] written in 1852.

In 1838 Abraham Godshalk authored both English and German editions of a book entitled *A Description of the New Creature*. Henry Funk's *Mirror of Baptism*, initially published in 1744, was reprinted in 1834, 1850, 1853, and 1861, and therefore belongs to this period. Another helpful book, *Kurzgefasste Kirchen-Geschichte und Glaubenslehre der Taufgesinnten Christen oder Mennoniten*, was written by Benjamin Eby in 1841. The author had moved from Lancaster County to Canada. Krehbiel, in his letter, recommends the book as a source of information about the American Mennonites, and encloses a copy. He says, "I noticed that the last named work contains a description, beginning on page 204, of ritual and customs of the churches in this country."[68] Krehbiel points out several ways in which the practice in Bucks and Montgomery counties is at variance with that in Lancaster and Canada.[69]

Jacob Krehbiel, an immigrant of 15 years, addressed his letter to friends in Germany. In response to their questions concerning American Mennonites, he says that he has had more opportunity than any other immigrant of the past 15 years to observe the inner condition of church life among the American Mennonites. "I have attended the conference in Canada three times and in Pennsylvania once," he adds. "At these times I have frequently had the opportunity to observe what principles actually furnished the foundations for the work of these gatherings, and what really are the objectives of these regularly established annual conferences. I have also had much opportunity privately at the above-named places to become better acquainted with the conditions and to note quietly my own opinions about them."[70]

Krehbiel says that in order to understand conditions in America one must remember that "most of these early immigrants consisted of members

---

[64] Jacob Krehbiel discusses at some length the fact that the Mennonites in Bucks and Montgomery counties did not practice foot washing and that they say they never have observed this practice, although most of the other Mennonites in Pennsylvania did observe it. "A Few Words About the Mennonites in America in 1841: A Contemporary Document by Jacob Krehbiel," tr. and edited by Harold S. Bender, *MQR* 5-6 (April 1932):110.

[65] Tr. and ed. by Harold S. Bender, *MQR* 5-6 (January 1932):43-57; (April 1932):110-122.

[66] *MQR* 46 (October 1972):398-405.

[67] John F. Funk, tr., *Biographical Sketch of Pre. John Geil*, p. 34. Original broadside in the Heritage Center, Souderton, Pa.

[68] Krehbiel, "A Few Words," p. 115.

[69] Franconia Mennonites do not observe the foot washing ceremony, they have not introduced variant modes of baptism, they observe the Lord's Supper only once a year, and the ministers go to the seats of the congregants when they dispense the elements.

[70] Krehbiel, "A Few Words," p. 49.

Farewell Letter of John Geil, 1852.

of the Swiss churches who had been exiled from Switzerland and who, as is well known, held very strictly to their church regulations." He says that practically all of the Mennonite congregations in North America still hold to the old regulations, although this varies considerably from place to place.

One can sense that Krehbiel is responding to somewhat critical inquiries from the German Mennonites about the American Mennonites. At length he tries to explain how he sees and understands the condition of their inner life and how he views their practical Christian living. He says that judgments concerning the inner life of the Pennsylvania Mennonites and their practical Christian living will vary, depending upon whether the judgment is well considered, or merely based upon biased attitudes. The judgment of the new immigrants is often in the latter category, he says, for it cannot be denied that among the Pennsylvania Mennonites more or less emphasis is placed on outward forms and that these vary somewhat from community to community.

The letter written by John H. Oberholtzer in 1849 to unnamed friends in Germany is highly critical of the Franconia Mennonites. In 1847 Oberholtzer had been a key leader in a major schism in the conference. He outlines with some optimism the reforms that he has initiated. Oberholtzer's letter is an attempt to establish wider fellowship with the Mennonites. He says he has been much affected by reading the letters which van der Smissen had written to the Mennonites in Canada and America.[71] Oberholtzer's letter will be used to supplement and challenge the discussion. Certain points in his letter will be reserved for the following chapter which discusses at length the Oberholtzer division in which he was a central figure.

John Geil's farewell letter to his congregation, originally printed as a broadside, is one of fatherly spiritual concern. It is especially helpful in showing how a minister of a Franconia congregation for 42 years expresses his spiritual understanding and his concerns for his congregation.

The Setting in America

The fourth decade of nineteenth-century America was a period of religious fervor and ferment. The Second Great Awakening had stimulated unprecedented activity in the churches. Benevolent societies, political and social reform movements, congregational programs, and institutional structures all proliferated. More will be said about these developments in later chapters.

---

[71] Carl Justus van der Smissen (1811-1890), a university trained Mennonite minister serving the Mennonite congregation at Friedrichstadt in Schleswig-Holstein. Van der Smissen was a Pietist, and the manner in which he expressed his spiritual concerns apparently influenced Oberholtzer deeply. Don Yoder has published van der Smissen's 1838 letter in both the original and in translation: "Mennonite Contacts Across the Atlantic: The van der Smissen Letter of 1838," ed. by Don Yoder, *Pennsylvania Folklife*, vol. 19, no. 1 (Autumn 1969):46-48. The letter was first published by the *Canadian Museum*, pioneer newspaper of Berlin, now Kitchener, Ont. It was also published by Friedrich Schmidt, ed., *Lutherische Kirchenzeitung und allgemeines Schulblatt* of Easton, Pa., and by Benjamin Eby of Canada.

In 1868 van der Smissen emigrated to America to teach theology at the new seminary founded by the General Conference of the Mennonite Church at Wadsworth, Ohio. See H. P. Krehbiel, *The History of the General Conference of the Mennonites of North America* for an account of the early years of the seminary and van der Smissen's role in it. See also "Carl Justus van der Smissen," *ME*, s.v.

The religious enthusiasm of the times resulted in the mushrooming of unusual religious manifestations by 1830.[72] Spiritualism was coming to the fore, with the Fox sisters as the principal mediums. Joseph Smith was having visions and translating the *Book of Mormon*. William Miller was leading a growing movement that predicted Christ's imminent second coming. Communal societies were springing up in many locations. Those founded upon utopian idealism tended to emphasize either celibacy or group marriage. More permanent communes were made up of new immigrants, some of them inspirationists who were spiritual descendants of the French Camisards. Others had their roots in Radical German Pietism and were strongly influenced by Jacob Boehme.[73]

When John Geil addressed his Lexington congregation in 1852, he was speaking realistically of the times:

> Beloved in the Lord, we have come upon critical times, in which many sects and denominations have already arisen among the professors of Christianity, and many more may yet arise. We hear everywhere the cry, "Lo, here is Christ, or there He is." Here prudence, watchfulness, and caution are indeed necessary; for we are in danger of being turned from ourselves, to look abroad and see the Kingdom of God without ourselves, while it is to be established within us....[74]

The Mennonite community in eastern Pennsylvania for the most part stood aloof from the fervor and ferment. It appears to have quietly pursued the religious patterns it had maintained for a century. It is not surprising that the conference appeared to supporters of the Awakening to be ingrown or petrified. The group that formed a separate conference in 1847 almost immediately initiated organizational adjustments to the American environment.

The Seven Articles

In the following pages we will compare each article of the Brotherly Union with nineteenth century primary source material in order to see in what ways religious forms in Franconia and other American Mennonite communities contradicted or supported the separate articles. Customs and traditions will be observed, noting the relation of these customs and traditions to the early Anabaptist charter.

Baptism

The most direct statement on baptism comes from the pen of one of Franconia's early ministers, Henry Funk, who in 1744 published *Ein Spiegel der Taufe mit Geist, mit Wasser, und mit Blut.* That it continued to be much used is testified to by reprints in 1834, 1850, 1853, and 1861. Funk's view of baptism closely coincides with the charter statement. He says that teaching and repentance come before baptism, thus excluding infant baptism. Baptism is a symbol of the believer's dying with Christ, and rising again to walk with him in newness of life.[75]

Abraham Godshalk[76] assumes adult baptism, and that baptism follows belief and repentance. Baptism is not regeneration; it follows regeneration. Godshalk placed great emphasis on the godly walk which follows baptism. His discussion of baptism is primarily an argument against the position taken by immersionists. His aim is to convince the reader that when Jesus said one must be born of "water and of the spirit," water had a symbolic and spiritual meaning.

The "Brotherly Union" does not specify the mode of baptism, and the mode was not stressed by American Mennonites, except insofar as they insisted that immersion was not necessary. The Dunkers, the Seventh-Day Baptists, and the River Brethren, all German-speaking sectarian neighbors of the Mennonites, also believed in adult baptism, but insisted that the only correct mode was by immersion. Krehbiel's discussion notes variant modes or forms of baptism that have been considered in Canada, but he says that in Pennsylvania they still hold to the customary form of baptism, which is by pouring.

Krehbiel's letter confirms the continuing practice of adult baptism in the American communities. He says that in the United States and Canada there is no definite age for reception into the church through baptism. The candidate is supposed to feel the necessity of baptism himself and to come when he is ready. "It is understood of course," he says, "that baptism never takes place too early in life, not before the candidates themselves understand the meaning of the ceremony."[77] He states that sometimes candidates are baptized before the age of 20, and the implication is that he considers this a young age for baptism.

The charter holds that teaching is to precede baptism. Funk's book on

---

[72] Sydney Ahlstrom speaks of this period as "Sectarian Heyday," Sydney E. Ahlstrom, *A Religious History of the American People*, pp. 472-490. Philip Schaff, *America*, reporting to his European colleagues in 1854, indicates his disapproval of the confusion and fragmentation of the American religious scene at mid-century.

[73] Donald Durnbaugh, "Work and Hope: The Spirituality of the Radical Pietist Communitarians," *Church History* 39 (March 1970):72-90.

[74] Geil, tr. by Funk, p. 34. For strikingly effective glimpses of John Geil see John L. Ruth, *Maintaining the Right Fellowship* (Scottdale, Pa.: Herald Press, 1984), passim.

[75] See also above, pp. 59, 61.

[76] *A Description of the New Creature*.

[77] Krehbiel, "A Few Words," p. 57.

Ein Spiegel der Taufe,

mit Geist, mit Wasser, und mit Blut.

In neun Theile verfasset, Aufs neue aufgesetzt und ausgezogen aus dem Heiligen Fundament=Buch, dem Neuen und Alten Testament, und den Canonischen Büchern.

~~~~~~~~~~~~~~~~

Drey sind die da zeugen auf Erden, der Geist, das Wasser, und das Blut; und diese drey sind beysammen.   1 Epist. Joh. 5, 8.

Gedruckt im Jahr 1834.

Ein Spiegel der Taufe: *Funk explained the Mennonite understanding of baptism in 1744.*

baptism takes the same position. However, our contemporary documents suggest some disagreement concerning the adequacy of the teaching that was being given at mid-century. John H. Oberholtzer criticizes what he sees as a lack of spiritual preparation for baptism among the Pennsylvania Mennonites:

> Now I am going to tell you how new members used to be received into the church. If anyone requested to become a member, it was announced at the congregational meeting with the invitation that if there were others they were to make it known. These then met once or twice; they were then admonished. Then they were baptized. But they were never examined to see whether they had a correct conception of the way of salvation.[78]

To remedy this situation Oberholtzer says that he has initiated instruction among youth. Additional sources confirm some aspects of Oberholtzer's statement and seem to contradict others. Krehbiel acknowledges that circumstances in America for the education of youth are considerably different from those in Germany in that in America there is no catechetical instruction in the public schools. In America, young people do receive some such instruction in the German schools, which are conducted by the church, but Krehbiel admits that it is often inadequate. As to special instruction for those who are received into the church through baptism, he says: "In Pennsylvania ... I was told everywhere on my visit, such instruction is a regular custom. During the instruction the thirty-five questions of Gerhard Roosen's book are used as a basis."[79]

Benjamin Eby describes a regular instructional period for baptismal candidates.[80] He says that if anyone strongly desires to enter into the covenant with God through holy baptism he makes it known to the bishop (*bestätigter Prediger*). The bishop asks the candidate whether he is willing to yield obedience to the example of Jesus. If the answer is affirmative, this wish is made known publicly to the members of the brotherhood, who are then asked whether they have anything against the candidate, and whether they can anticipate in him or her a good prototype. Further action is delayed for several weeks, in case others may also wish to ask for baptism.

Eby describes the instruction meetings for candidates. These sessions were held in a designated meetinghouse on Sunday afternoons. The instruc-

---

[78] "A Letter of John H. Oberholtzer," p. 403. Oberholtzer's term is *Heils-Ordnung*, translated here as "way of salvation."

[79] Krehbiel, "A Few Words," p. 117. See also "Appendix VI, Roosen's Catechism," John C. Wenger, *The Doctrines of the Mennonites*, pp. 111-157.

[80] Eby, pp. 202-208.

Kurzgefaßte
Kirchen Geschichte

und

Glaubenslehre

der

Taufgesinnten=Christen oder Mennoniten.

Verfaßt und herausgegeben von

Benjamin Eby,

Mennoniten Prediger.

Berlin, Canada:

Gedruckt bey Heinrich Eby.

....

1841.

Kurzegefasste Kirchengeschichte: Benjamin Eby's brief church history described nineteenth-century American Mennonite ceremonies.

tion centered around the Confession of Faith. The candidates were encouraged to study the articles at home, to read the Scriptures on which they were based, and to learn as many of God's commandments as possible.[81] Instruction continued in this manner, with the aim of bringing the candidates to a maturity of understanding where they could direct their own belief, "their souls obeying the true creator in good works, and seeking happiness and salvation alone in the name of Jesus." The emphasis was on obedience to the example of Jesus and on commitment to the group.

Several weeks before baptism the candidates were brought before the congregation, and opportunity was given for the congregation to question them. If no objection was made against the candidates, they were ordered to come together once more on a Saturday afternoon when the confession was read again in its entirety and explained to them. Then they were asked if they were in unity with the entire confession. If the response was affirmative, they were told to be at the service the following morning at its very beginning.

Eby describes the baptismal ceremony step by step. Because critics of the Mennonites in the nineteenth century repeatedly charged that Mennonite members were ignorant of the "way of salvation," it seems appropriate to include in considerable detail the description of this ceremony. The account shows that to receive baptism meant a confession of belief in God and in Christ. It also meant committing oneself to obedience to the example of Jesus along with commitment to the brotherhood.

The baptismal service, always held on a Sunday morning, began with a song. Then a preacher or a deacon would read aloud John 1:1-36, after which one of the preachers gave an appropriate sermonette and directed a prayer. The entire congregation would then kneel for the prayer, and after the prayer the bishop *(bestätigter Prediger)* read Matthew 28:18, 19, and 20, which served as his text. Following the sermon, he would step before the candidates and bid them arise. They would form a semicircle, and he would then ask them the following questions: First, I ask you whether you believe in an all powerful God, who has created heaven and earth; and in Jesus Christ, the only begotten son of God, that he is our Redeemer and Saviour, who died for us on the cross, and in the Holy Ghost, who proceeds from the Father and the Son and leads us into all truth. If so, answer with "yes." Second, I ask you whether you are truly sorry for the sins you have committed and do you renounce your own will and all satanic works? If this is so, answer with "yes." Third, I ask you: Whether you promise by God's grace and his help to be

---

[81] It appears from Eby's account that instruction in Canada was based on the 18 articles of the Dordrecht Confession of Faith. As noted above, in Franconia Gerhard Roosen's shorter catechism was used as a basis for instruction.

obedient and true to the teachings of Jesus until death? If you so will, answer with "yes."[82]

The minister then knelt again with the candidates and prayed aloud. When the prayer ended, the preacher arose. The candidates, however, remained on their knees. A deacon would come with water, and stand at the right side of the bishop who then would step first in front of the male candidates, laying both hands flat on the uncovered head of each candidate, saying: On this confession of faith, repentance, and sorrow for your sins, you are (the preacher would form a concave with his outstretched hands and the deacon would pour water in the same) baptized with water in the name of the Father, Son, and Holy Ghost.[83]

In this manner the baptism of all the candidates was carried out, then the preacher turned back to the first one, reaching him his hand and bidding him to stand up, saying: "In the name of the community *(Gemeine)* I give you my hand, and point you to a new beginning; the Lord will transplant you out of your sinful state into the righteousness of his kingdom; I now say welcome as a brother in the church." He then would give him the kiss of peace.

The same procedure was followed for the female candidates, except that the wife of a minister or deacon stood beside the preacher, and gave to each the kiss of peace as she arose, saying "Welcome as a sister in the church."[84]

Following the baptism, the preacher again returned to the preacher's bench *(Predigtstuhl)*, and read from the sixth chapter of Romans. He preached a short sermon of admonition, then closed with an audible prayer. Each prayer was said with bended knees and closed with "Our Father." Another song was sung, the benediction given, and the service closed.

Eby says that when anyone from another confession wished to come into their fellowship, and had already received baptism in his faith, he would not again be baptized, but only instructed in their confession. If he expressed unity with it, and the brotherhood had nothing against him, he would be asked the following questions in an open meeting by the preacher: Do you confess that you are one with our confession of faith, rules and regulations; and do you say you will remain true and obedient to the same until death? If this is so, answer "yes." Then the preacher would give him his hand, the kiss of peace, and say to him "welcome as a brother in the church," and wish him God's blessing to endure in the good to the end.

Preacher John Geil makes no mention of baptism *per se*, but his letter shows that the concepts of "amendment of life," and "walking in the resurrection," have been retained and woven into the conception of being a follower of Christ.

Baptismal practice in America supported rather closely the concerns outlined in the "Brotherly Union." In both instances, baptism was to be given to those who had been taught, who had experienced repentance and amendment of life, who truly believed their sins were forgiven and requested baptism, and who desired "to walk to the resurrection of Christ." In both instances, infant baptism was excluded by the nature of baptismal requirements.

The Ban

In America the discipline of the ban continued. A congregational meeting was always held a week or two before the Lord's Supper was observed. Eby calls this meeting the *Umfrage*, or inquiry meeting; in Franconia it was called the counsel meeting. This special service was the occasion when any and all grievances in the brotherhood were to be made public if it had been impossible to settle them privately. The meeting was often long, and sometimes vexatious. If there were disagreements in the fellowship that could not be settled, it was sometimes necessary to postpone the breaking of bread until peace could be restored.

The "Brotherly Union" lays emphasis only on mutual admonition, but among Mennonites in America the counsel meeting also became a time of introspection. American Protestant churches on the frontier observed a period of self-examination preceding communion, and discipline for moral infractions was common. Presbyterians called the exercise "fencing the tables." Methodists could not participate in the sacrament of the Lord's Supper unless they had received their class ticket.[85] Eby, too, accents the importance of self-examination: care must be taken that a believer does not observe the Lord's Supper as an unworthy person, or with an unworthy person, either knowingly or unknowingly. He points to the writings of Paul in Corinthians as the foundation for this practice. "Examine yourselves. Are you living the life of faith? Put yourselves to the test."[86] In the Mennonite counsel meeting, great emphasis was placed on unity and oneness in the brotherhood, whereas in the Protestant churches the procedure was largely introspective.

Eby stresses the responsibility of the preacher in seeing that proper

---

[82] John E. Lapp says that in Franconia the candidates were asked three questions on their knees: (1) Are you truly sorry for your past sins and have you repented? (2) Do you believe that your sins are forgiven through the grace of Jesus Christ? (3) Do you desire water baptism?

[83] For baptism in Franconia Conference, the deacon held a pan of water. The bishop would dip his cupped hands into the water, carrying the water to the candidate's head with his hands.

[84] John A. Lapp, Executive Secretary of the Mennonite Central Committee, noted: "I was struck with how similar Benjamin Eby's description of a baptismal service was to the style I lived through (in Franconia Conference) during the 1940's and early 50's." Personal letter.

[85] William Warren Sweet, "The Churches as Moral Courts on the Frontier," *Church History* 2 (March 1933):3-21.

[86] Eby cites 2 Cor. 13:5; 2 Cor. 11:29; and 1 Cor. 5:11, 13.

preparation is made for the inquiry meeting so that it serves its purpose and does not deteriorate. Its purpose is to prepare the hearts of members so that they can approach the Lord's Supper in a spirit of love and humility, not in unworthiness or hypocrisy so as to invite the judgment of God where they should be receiving a blessing.

The inquiry meeting was traditionally long. At the close of the period of self-searching and confession, Eby says that the minister, or perhaps two ministers together, would go into the counsel room. One after another the members of the brotherhood would follow them into the room, each one reaching out his hand to show that he was at peace, saying, "I am at peace with God and all men. I desire also that all men be patient with me, because my desire is to go with them to the Lord's Supper, if no one holds anything against me."

According to Eby, when someone did have a grievance against a brother or sister, he was to deal with it first of all according to Matthew 18. If he brought his complaint to the counsel room and had not first sought reconciliation with his brother alone or with witnesses, his complaint would be rejected; if, however, he had attempted reconciliation, the complaint would be received and dealt with according to the regulations. When the inquiry was completed, the ministers reported the results to the brotherhood, namely, whether all were at peace, or whether there was discord, and between whom. Finally, God's grace and blessing was wished to each one who had examined himself, the day of the Lord's Supper was made known, and the meeting dismissed.

The manner in which the ban was observed, once it had been invoked, varied with the different groups. Among the Pennsylvania Mennonites it usually meant simply that the individual was barred from breaking bread, or participation in the Lord's Supper, until he had expressed contrition and had been received back into the group.

In 1846, considerable dissension was brewing in the Franconia Conference, and a specific reference to Matthew 18, or the rule of the gospel as it was commonly called, is found in a minute from the May 1846 conference:

> *Firstly:* That no complaint can be received at Conference, except when it has been dealt with beforehand in accordance with the Gospel, that is, as Jesus tells us: If your brother sins against you, then tell him his fault between you and him alone; if he will hear you, then you have gained your brother, etc.[87]

This minute likely referred to dissension between two ministers in the Skippack congregation, Abraham Hunsicker and Elias Landes. It does not prove that spiritual government, as based on Matthew 18 and the "Brotherly Union," was operating in the conference, but it does indicate that some of the members considered the rule of the gospel to be the proper method of procedure. It should be noted here that the Skippack congregation was centrally involved in the schism which took place in 1847, and that the majority of the members of this congregation became members of the new conference. Thus it may be that the apparent failure of the congregation to handle the difficulty according to Matthew 18, which the petitioning members believe they should have done, is an indication that this congregation was departing from the old customs and traditions.

Following the schism, Abraham Hunsicker, a principal in the above case, wrote a letter to Bishop Christian Herr of the Lancaster Conference, in an attempt to solicit the support of the Lancaster brethren. Herr's response was skeptical:

> If there were still other reasons for disunity among you, why then did you act so rashly and erect such a bulwark for a split? Why did you not much rather take in hand the teaching of Jesus in Matthew 18, especially from the 21st verse to the end of the chapter, and keep house accordingly?[88]

The minutes of the Franconia Mennonite Conference, which begin unofficially in 1880,[89] indicate that mutual admonition, as recommended in Matthew 18 and the "Brotherly Union," was an active part of church discipline in Franconia Conference following 1880. This method of church discipline is repeatedly illustrated in incidents reported in the conference minutes.[90] These same minutes also emphasize the need to deal with members in patience and brotherly love.

A farewell letter written by John Geil to his Lexington congregation in 1852 closely parallels the spirit of Sattler's 1527 counsel to his congregation:

> Above all things it is my wish, and I entreat you, that you strive to maintain love, peace, and unity among yourselves. Love is the badge of the disciples of Jesus; as He himself says, "By this shall all men know that ye are my disciples if ye have love one to another." If you have not love one to another, you are not the disciples of Jesus, but you must

---

[87] "The Mensch-Oberholtzer Papers," p. 365.
[88] Ibid., p. 347.
[89] Jacob B. Mensch, *Memorandum Book of Reverend Jacob B. Mensch and Proceedings of the Franconia Conference*. Tr. by Raymond E. Hollenbach.
[90] *Ibid.* See, for example, minutes for the conference held May 5, 1881; May 1, 1884; May 1, 1890; May 5, 1898.

follow after peace and holiness, without which no man shall see the Lord. Earnestly endeavor to maintain love and unity, and you shall be strong and stand firm. Let love run through all of your dealings with each other. Be not credulous. If you hear evil reports of your brothers and sisters, or anything which may injure their honor or reputation, believe, hope, and wish the best concerning them.... Bear with each other in patience and forgive one another, even as God has forgiven you in Christ.[91]

The practice of the ban was meant to facilitate a pure church, the discipline of the offender intended to be redemptive. Testimonies of persons who experienced the ban negatively are not infrequent. They have not been countered by positive testimony, for when the ban was experienced positively and forgiveness received, the offense was never again to be recounted. At its best, spiritual government served the community in a positive way. Sandra Cronk interpreted it as a means of helping the participants to handle interpersonal problems ritually. By finding the solution to problems in a mutual yielding of selfish claims, the building of a caring brotherhood was promoted.[92]

By the twentieth century, two developments undermined the effective use of the ban. The first was the institutionalization of the procedure so that the deacon was expected to confront the offending party with his offense, instead of this confrontation being made by the person offended; the second was the development of written disciplines. Admonition in the counsel meeting then centered on the reading of the Discipline and the citing of infractions. Both developments institutionalized the exercise of Matthew 18 and violated the original intent and spirit of the article.

The Breaking of Bread

The Mennonite communion ceremony of the mid-nineteenth century is described in detail by Benjamin Eby. The service, customarily, he said, began with a song, followed by the reading aloud of either the 26th chapter of Matthew or the 22nd chapter of Luke, both of which recount the story of the Last Supper and surrounding events. One of the preachers gave a short sermon explaining the chapter and the meaning of the Lord's Supper, then led from this to the prayer. The account of Jesus' trial and crucifixion was then read in its entirety from either Matthew 27 or Luke 22. A designated minister preached a sermon on the same chapter, telling of the great love of Jesus who suffered and bled on the cross as mankind's Savior and Redeemer. He earned mankind's redemption and eternal salvation and commanded his followers to hold the communion meal in memory of his suffering.[93]

Practice in Bucks and Montgomery counties was distinctive from Lancaster and Canada on at least three points according to Krehbiel: communion was observed once a year rather than twice, the ministers distributed the bread and wine while moving among the congregants, and the footwashing ceremony was not observed.[94]

Oberholtzer's proposed constitution, written in 1847, has three articles on commonunion:

> Article 9. Required, that a communion service or Lord's Supper shall be observed in the Mennonite brotherhood at least once a year as a memorial of the suffering and death of Jesus Christ.
>
> Article 10. Required, that the Lord's Supper shall always be celebrated with bread and wine.
>
> Article 11. No one is entitled to partake of the sacred Supper unless he has a correct comprehension of the teachings of Christ and agrees with them, believes them with all of his heart, and is willing to adorn them with a virtuous, God-pleasing and penitent walk and life. If aged or sick persons who are members in good standing desire to partake of the Lord's Supper when it is observed in the congregation, the preacher or deacon in that congregation shall give him of the same bread and wine which was given to the congregation, that all may be partakers of one bread.[95]

These articles on communion make no mention of unity among the believers or of their commitment to the brotherhood. They do mention "one bread" but the context suggests that the emphasis is on the elements all being from one source, not on unity in the congregation. This is in distinct contrast to the emphasis of the "Brotherly Union," where oneness within the brotherhood is of prime importance.

Documents following 1880 suggest that the traditional group continued its emphasis on the Lord's Supper as a symbol of unity, brotherly love, and submission to the group as well as to Christ. In practice, this sometimes made the time surrounding communion unpleasant, for differences and deviation were exposed and not always resolved amicably. Church discipline continued to be closely associated with communion until well into the twentieth century. As standards became increasingly codified, the conference discipline

---

[91] "Farewell Letter," pp. 29-30.
[92] Cronk, "*Gelassenheit*," p. 106.
[93] Eby, *Kirchengeschichte*, pp. 213-214.
[94] Krehbiel, "A Few Words," p. 110.
[95] "Constitution of the Mennonite Brotherhood," Tr. by Elizabeth Bender, *MQR* 46 (October 1972):394.

was read prior to communion in many churches. Only those willing to support its standards were to participate.

As late as the mid-twentieth century, American Mennonites continued to practice "close" communion, which meant that only members in full fellowship were allowed to participate.

Mennonite leaders pointed out that even those churches who claimed to have open communion set up requirements for participation in the Lord's Supper. These same Mennonite leaders also stated that they were not passing judgment on those who had different practices and were not permitted to participate in the Mennonite communion services. For their own congregations, however, they believed communion should be preceded by personal heart searching and collective examination, so that nothing would disturb or hinder the peace of the church and the unity of the body. The demand for unity meant that anyone not participating in this unity must be excluded from participation in the Lord's Supper, and the need for such exclusion is plainly stated.[96]

The rationale for this stance is explained in a 1955 *Gospel Herald* article that closely echoes the spirit and content of Article III of the "Brotherly Union":

> The primary meaning of the Lord's Supper, namely, the remembrance of Christ as a crucified and living Saviour, means not only that we memorialize what he has done for us, but that we testify that His life is in us, and that accordingly we are committed to His teachings, His program, His kingdom. It would be an empty form and hypocritical act if we should profess by eating of the emblems that we have the life of Christ in us, and then do not manifest that life in our conduct, our service, our devotion, our character. If this be true, how can we admit to the Lord's table those who do not carry out his teachings? How could we possibly testify to a unity of spirit and faith with those who do not obey Christ?[97]

As in the "Brotherly Union," American Mennonites considered Christ to be present, not in the bread and the wine, but in the community of believers who were partaking of the elements. By baptism they had been united into one body of Christ, which is the congregation. Spiritual government was to be exercised before the breaking of bread so that all might in one spirit and love break and eat from one bread and drink from one cup.

Separation from the World

An emphasis on being separate from the world has been perhaps the most widely recognized characteristic of nineteenth-century American Mennonites. One of the first conference discussions recorded by Jacob B. Mensch supports the opinion that separation from the world was strongly emphasized (but not consistently practiced) by the Franconia Mennonites.

> 2nd—Complaint was made of how pride rules everywhere, not only in clothes, etc., but in many other aspects and how the truth is rapidly turning to corruption on the broad road to heathenism. It is desired that every preacher bring this before his members, and their duty to warn their children and to themselves refrain from imitating the rest of the world. Brothers and sisters shall not raise their children in the finery and fashion of the world. It was also pointed out that the parents should in love ask their children to stay away from drinking places and singing schools, etc. It was pointed out that members should stay away from drinking places and that these places were solely for travellers and business people and not for the people of the local community, and further, it is considered for the best that members do not sign any petitions for licenses for places that sell liquor; also it was not considered good that members take shares in any new bank; further, the sisters are to be warned against finery, hair-do's, gold ornaments, and stylish clothes. Brothers and sisters are asked to keep away from surprise parties where things are carried on in "high style," etc.[98]

The Mennonites of the nineteenth century have been repeatedly criticized for their emphasis on separation. It has been looked upon as something superficial and external. While the manner in which separation was expressed may well have been superficial and external, Article IV of the "Brotherly Union" indicates that separation was not extraneous to Anabaptist-Mennonite belief and practice, but part of its basic conceptual framework.

By the time Krehbiel wrote his letter, there seems to have been considerable contrast between the Mennonites in America and the Mennonites in Germany. The German Mennonites seem to have considered the American Mennonites as ultraconservative, placing too much emphasis on outward forms. Krehbiel admits there is considerable emphasis on outer forms, especially dress, and that sometimes it is overdone. He says, however, that superficial contacts between European and American Mennonites often

---

[96] Letter from John E. Lapp to E. Jane Nyce, Bluffton College, Bluffton, Ohio, April 26, 1955. Lapp letters, Eastern Pennsylvania Mennonite Historical Library (hereinafter EPMHL), Lansdale, Pa.

[97] Harold S. Bender, "Communion, Open or Close," *Gospel Herald* (January 11, 1955):25-26.

[98] Minute for conference held May 1882.

Late nineteenth-century Franconia Mennonites dressed like their non-Mennonite neighbors

Above: Isaiah L. Lapp, c. 1890.
Right: Kate Clemmer, c. 1890.

result in complete misunderstanding: "In truth, one must have had several years of contact and must possess the gift of impartial judgment in order to give any judgment at all."[99]

Krehbiel indicates that the Mennonites emphasize simplicity in dress, but that the amount and type of emphasis varies from place to place. He says, "A major point of accusation against American Mennonites concerns the clothes question, and not altogether without justification. However ... in many places in Pennsylvania there is no difference between the costume worn by the Mennonites and that worn by other people in America and Germany." Krehbiel had moved to America just ten years earlier. He points out that fashionable dress is far more prevalent in rural America than it was in rural Germany, implying that the need for restrictions on dress in rural

America is greater than the need in Germany.[100] His letter suggests that there was consensus among the American Mennonites on the need to wear plain, simple attire, but that dress was not uniform. This view has also been taken by our best secondary sources on costume.[101]

It should not be overlooked that Geil makes no mention whatsoever of specific external forms in his farewell letter, either for dress or other behavior. Oberholtzer, although he takes great issue with a special coat for ministers, says nothing of specific dress requirements for other church members. Abraham Godshalk strongly emphasizes the Christian's conduct, quoting many Scripture passages, but says nothing of external forms that are to be observed. Thus, while separation was emphasized, it appears that practice was not codified, and it was not uniform.

Hannah Rittenhouse Clemens (1880-1977) states that dress patterns were not uniform when she was a girl, except for coats worn by preachers. However, separation from the world was very much emphasized. She says they were to be separate from the world not only in dress and appearance but in their homes as well.[102] The "world," however, seems not to have been as rigidly defined as in the "Brotherly Union." She reports social intercourse with church neighbors, including frequent attendance at all-day funerals and helping when neighbors were involved. Pulpits were also sometimes exchanged between Mennonite and Reformed ministers.[103]

The Mennonites of Pennsylvania were far from alone in what has been called their emphasis on external forms. They were surrounded by German sectarians who also emphasized distinction in dress and way of life. In addition, evangelical Protestantism in America had revived the austere standards of Puritanism during the Second Great Awakening. Emphasis on modesty in dress, and prohibitions by the churches against dancing, theater-going, lotteries, swearing, obscenity, Sabbath-breaking, and the drinking of alcoholic beverages were so widespread that this type of morality became identified with the Victorian Era.

Nonresistance to evil, also a part of Article IV, is another widely

---

[99] Krehbiel, "A Few Words," p. 51.

[100] Ibid., p. 52. Theron Schlabach has raised an interesting question concerning religiously prescribed attire in America: "I wonder whether the fact that, in America, local custom and class status did not dictate form of dress is what brought the dress question to the fore in America. I.e., did American social mobility and equalitarianism create the problem for Mennonites?" Personal letter. For a discussion of the function of dress in the folk community, see Don Yoder, "Folk Costume," *Folklore and Folklife*, ed. Richard M. Dorson, p. 308.

[101] See Melvin Gingerich, *Mennonite Attire Through Four Centuries*, and Mary Jane Hershey, "A Study of the Dress of the Old Mennonites of Franconia Conference, 1700-1953," *Pennsylvania Folklife*, vol. 9, no. 3 (Summer 1958):24-47.

[102] Personal interview, May 7, 1974. She commented that they had always had toilet soap in their home. Many people, she said, did not have toilet soap. It was considered too worldly.

[103] John E. Lapp, manuscript for Hatfield Township History, 1976.

recognized tenet of American Mennonites, and one of the most self-consciously held. This article demands the avoidance of evil, and forbids the resistance of evil and the use of weapons of violence—either for the protection of friends or against enemies, since Christ commanded his followers not to resist evil.

Nonresistance for the Franconia Mennonites was not something that was added to their understanding of the gospel. Rather, they spoke of the nonresistant gospel. This understanding is illustrated in depth in the writing of Abraham Godshalk, who devotes much attention to this theme, relating it to many aspects of life, including the care of animals.

In the course of the nineteenth century, attitudes toward government in Franconia Conference seem to have become more positive than those reflected in the "Brotherly Union," and the emphasis on nonparticipation in warfare received a more prominent role. J. C. Wenger holds that the emphasis of the Pennsylvania Mennonites by the late nineteenth and early twentieth centuries closely paralleled that taken in an apology written by T. T. van Sittert of the Dutch Mennonites in 1664 and available to American Mennonites as an appendix in various books.[104]

Although Franconia Conference Mennonites consistently took a position of nonparticipation in warfare, this position received its most severe test in World War I. The stand taken by the conference was reported in a Philadelphia paper.

> Souderton, Pa., September 3, 1917
>
> Mennonite young men called in the draft will respond on the dates fixed for their appearance at local board headquarters to entrain for mobilization camps. Moreover they will meekly travel to these camps with their fellows in the call. But when they arrive at the mobilization points, they will decline to wear a soldier's uniform or perform, as combatants or as noncombatants, any service in any way related to warfare. For this they expect to be sent as prisoners into detention camps, where they are resolved to remain, humbly but firmly obedient to the highest tenets of their faith—"thou shalt not kill" and "return good for evil."
>
> This was the decision of the Franconia Conference of the Old Mennonites held in the Souderton Church here today. When it was reached by a vote of the bishops, ministers, and deacons the nearly 1,000 conferees wept in their resignation to what they believed the will of the Lord, and they exhorted their parting youth to "go with a childlike faith in one another and a childlike love for one another and for the world and resist naught but temptation."[105]

Both separation from the world and nonresistance were severely challenged when many Mennonites identified with Fundamentalism in the 1930s and 1940s. Mennonite leaders who embraced Fundamentalism attempted to preserve nonresistance and separation from the world, but because these tenets were not a part of Fundamentalist theology, they tended to be appended to the Mennonite doctrinal structure that was developed at that time. Separation became nonconformity, expressed in codified forms; nonresistance, something that was taught *after* one had accepted the gospel. As their young men served in Civilian Public Service as conscientious objectors in World War II, Mennonites refocused their understanding of both nonresistance and separation, strengthening the former and gradually revising the latter.

Shepherds of the Flock

Blameless character and obedience to the commands of Christ, rather than formal training, continued to be seen as the essential qualifications for ministers among the nineteenth-century Mennonites in America. Charges of ignorance were repeatedly made against them, yet they continued to spurn theological training until well into the twentieth century. Krehbiel responded against insinuations of incompetence when he wrote:

> I must add . . . that I am almost constantly in correspondence with ministers and members in Pennsylvania and Canada, and that in many letters, which are also frequently written in quite good style, I can observe nothing else according to my opinion than the sincere desire to follow faithfully after the teaching of Christ and his apostles according to the pure meaning of the gospel in teaching and life by means of his Grace. . . .[106]

Some of the earliest reports from Pennsylvania Mennonites indicate that ministers, as mandated in the "Brotherly Union," continued to read and exhort and teach: to warn, admonish, and ban in the congregation. The 1773 letter says, "Our community, by God's blessing, has been cared for by such ministers as the Apostle Paul describes, who have administered baptism and

---

[104] Particularly the *Ernsthafte Christenpflicht*. See John C. Wenger, "T. T. van Sittert's Apology for the Anabaptist-Mennonite Tradition, 1664," *MQR* 49 (January 1955):5-21.

[105] *Public Ledger*. Reprinted in John C. Wenger, "Franconia Mennonites and Military Service, 1683-1923," *MQR* 10 (October 1936):222-245. Wenger's article provides a substantial treatment of the experience of the Franconia Mennonites in relation to war, and the relief of war sufferers. For a broader treatment of Mennonites and peace issues, see Guy F. Hershberger, "Historical Background to the Formation of the Mennonite Central Committee," *MQR* 44 (July 1970):213-244.

[106] "A Few Words," p. 116.

the Lord's Supper...."[107] We are told that Jacob Godschalk served the congregation by reading. In his letter Geil writes, "And we beseech you, brethren, to know them which labor among you, and are over you in the Lord, and admonish you ..."[108] clearly implying that one of the expected functions of the minister was to admonish the congregation.

By 1840 it was common for each congregation to have several ministers and a deacon or two. Occasionally, differences among shepherds in a congregation became serious, with negative consequences for the brotherhood. Article 5 recognizes that a shepherd might err, and we learn from the documents that the provision for reprimanding a minister guilty of an offense was at times employed.[109]

John Geil stresses the importance of love between the congregation and its ministers, for without love the congregation cannot be built up by their teaching. He admonishes congregants to honor their ministers, but at the same time the ministers are not to seek honor. Because their task is difficult, he urges the church to pray for them, "that the Lord may give them grace, and clothe them with power from on high, and bestow on them the needed gifts."[110]

The ideal of ministerial support by the congregation was retained in America, but in actual practice the minister was largely responsible for his own support and that of his family. Geil implies that he had supported himself according to the tradition handed down from the apostle Paul: "Ye yourselves know that these hands have ministered unto my necessities.... I have labored in your service freely with the gift that has been bestowed upon me...."[111] He also acknowledges gifts to him from the congregation: "And to each and everyone that has bestowed upon me the least benefit, or given me proof of his love and friendship, I feel heartily thankful."[112] Jacob C. Clemens says of his early ministry: "I was called to the ministry November 13, 1906.... We had three children then, I now had a double task and for two years I stayed in the bank and studied at night which exacted too much of my strength.... When I attended funerals during the week or special meetings I used to catch up on book work in the bank in the evenings and I did not get my rest.... I had to study hard to get Bible material ready for funerals, marriages, and regular preaching services.... In those days we didn't look for material support and in fact we didn't need it. There were some of the ministers in debt and the churches liquidated the debt."[113]

While the "Brotherly Union" implies that it is the congregation that selects the pastor and installs him into his leadership role, it does not specify the way this is to be done. Jacob Godschalk wrote that the first preacher at Germantown was chosen by a unanimity of votes in the congregation. A tradition reported by Krehbiel holds that the first American minister was selected by lot, in absentia, in a European Mennonite congregation, but the letter by Godschalk which has been preserved would cast some doubt on this tradition. Concerning the selection of ministers, Krehbiel says simply: "Preachers are chosen in the well-known way, by the lot. All those voted for are taken into the lot, even when only one vote is cast for a person. For the choice of a bishop, the ministers in a district cast lots among themselves under the leadership of their bishop or several bishops from other congregations. On the slip which determines the minister to be chosen, the following words from Proverbs 16:33 are always written: 'the lot is cast into the lap but it falls where the Lord wills'; the other slips are blank."[114]

John H. Oberholtzer objected to the practice of placing all nominees in the lot. He said poorly qualified individuals were often included, and sometimes selected. There were 15 candidates in the lot at the time of his ordination in 1834. Hannah Rittenhouse Clemens also acknowledged that the lot sometimes resulted in what seemed to be the selection of very unsuitable candidates, saying that sometimes "they couldn't preach at all."[115] Normally several ministers served any one congregation, and this no doubt helped to mitigate the negative effect of those less able to preach. Oberholtzer, however, considered the situation deplorable.[116]

Krehbiel's description of a mid-nineteenth century church service gives us some information concerning the function of the minister in the congregation.

> In the conduct of divine service, with the exception of a few minor differences here and there the procedure is as follows: at the beginning they sing several verses from a hymn or the whole hymn is sung, and then a chapter is read out of an Epistle (at Easter the passion story of Christ is used), then several verses are sung again from a hymn whereupon the opening address is given. This is short. Then a season of silent prayer is held; after this the real sermon is given and the text is read. Toward the end before the last prayer the preacher stops and gives liberty (in these very words) so that any brother present who wishes to

---

[107] "Letter from Pennsylvania Mennonites," p. 229.
[108] Funk, "Biographical Sketch," p. 30.
[109] See "Mensch-Oberholtzer Papers," *MQR* 46 (October 1972), especially VII, VIII, and IX.
[110] Funk, "Biographical Sketch," p. 31.
[111] Ibid., p. 28.
[112] Ibid., p. 34.
[113] From "Autobiographical Notes," Jacob Cassel Clemens, 1874-1965. Written c. 1954. EPMHL.
[114] "A Few Words," pp. 110-111.
[115] Personal interview, May 4, 1974.
[116] "Letter from John H. Oberholtzer....," pp. 401-404.

say anything may do so for the benefit of all present. If there is another preacher present, he will speak a few brief words. In the absence of the same, a deacon may speak, who usually only states that the address of the brother so far as he could understand was according to the gospel and he wishes the blessing of God thereto. After this the officiating preacher rises again and speaks a few brief closing words whereupon he leads in an audible prayer, minister and audience kneeling during the prayer. After this a few verses of a hymn are sung and then the preacher dismisses the congregation with an audible benediction.[117]

The fifth article of the "Brotherly Union" found continuing expression in the group, with the shepherd teaching, admonishing, and presiding at the breaking of the bread, baptism, and the exercise of the ban. We have evidence that when circumstances required it, shepherds were also disciplined by the congregation. Ministers were probably receiving less material support than the initial charter made provision for.

The Sword

Government in Pennsylvania in 1683 was significantly different from what it had been in Switzerland in 1527. The Quaker founders of Pennsylvania were closely related to both the Reformed and the Anabaptist traditions. Like Calvin, they envisioned the conversion of the social order and assumed the Christians' active participation in this task. But they also espoused nonviolence and believed that the Christian should not take an oath. William Penn saw his Sylvania as a unique opportunity to demonstrate the workability of his philosophy of government. From 1682 to 1756, Pennsylvania was governed by the Quakers. By then the tensions between their religious philosophy and the demands of government became so unbearable that there were no longer a sufficient number of Quaker candidates to maintain a majority in office.[118]

For a few years the Quaker-Mennonites ran the local government of Germantown, which was early granted incorporation as a borough. Here, too, problems in governing were experienced. Jan Lensen, the one original settler who continuously remained a Mennonite, on July 9, 1700, refused jury duty on the basis of conscience. The last court records for the borough of Germantown are for the year 1706. The charter was lost soon thereafter because an insufficient number of candidates was available for the elective offices. C. Henry Smith, who recounted the experience, concludes that the Mennonites who espoused Quaker beliefs "never entirely outgrew their earlier Mennonite convictions on office holding."[119]

"In the matter of the use of the sword and political office," Krehbiel says of the Mennonites of the mid-nineteenth century, "testimony is everywhere given against these two things."[120] One of the persons whom Krehbiel reports as having expressed dissatisfaction with the American Mennonite church was a minister from North Germany by the name of Risser who had settled in Ohio. Risser was bitter because he had been unable to maintain full fellowship with either of two nearby Mennonite congregations. A major point of dissension concerned holding public office. The Dutch and North German Mennonites had developed a more positive attitude toward office holding than the Swiss Mennonites, and Risser's desire to be actively involved politically was unacceptable to the Ohio congregations.[121]

"Suing at the law is likewise not permitted," Krehbiel reports, "in this case, however, there is no excommunication from the church but rather a simple 'setting back,' which may again be withdrawn upon confession of the transgression."[122] As this implies, lawsuits did occur, but invariably invoked censorship. Some infractions have been recorded, such as in the May 1, 1884, memoranda of Jacob Mensch:

> The question was brought up of a brother who sued another who is not a member, and the answer was he should take another person with him and go to the person sued and ask forgiveness.[123]

The constitution which Oberholtzer proposed in 1847 permitted members to defend themselves and their property by law. This was one of the most offensive articles of the constitution in the opinion of the Lancaster brethren to whom Abraham Hunsicker appealed for support.[124]

In the course of the nineteenth century, attitudes toward government in Franconia Conference seem to have become more positive than those reflected in the "Brotherly Union." Abraham Fretz (1793-1875) was elected Commissioner of Bucks County in 1837 and County Treasurer in 1841. He was nominated for the lot in 1840, but was not permitted to be in it because of his political activities. He was, however, ordained in 1843.[125] Abraham

---

[117] Krehbiel, p. 111. Patterns of church leadership and congregational organization will be dealt with in greater detail in chapter 6.
[118] See Guy F. Hershberger, "The Pennsylvania Quaker Experience in Politics, 1682-1756," *MQR* 10 (October 1936):187-221.
[119] *The Mennonite Immigration to Pennsylvania* (Norristown, Pa.: The Author, 1929), pp. 110-118. Quote on p. 118.
[120] "A Few Words," pp. 54-55.
[121] Ibid., pp. 118-121.
[122] Ibid., pp. 54-55.
[123] *Memorandum Book*.
[124] "Lancaster Conference on the Proposed Constitution," *MQR* 46 (October 1972):361-365.
[125] J. C. Wenger, *Mennonites of Franconia*, p. 260.

Hunsicker was also active politically before his ordination in 1847. His son, Henry, speaks of the political situation c. 1837 and tells of his father's participation in local politics:

> My father was an ardent Whig, and he supported the measures that looked for the lightening of the burdens the country was under.
> He attended the township primaries, the county conventions that framed the ticket, and attended political meetings, believing that as a good citizen it was his duty to do so.[126]

That Hunsicker's political activities were not considered normative for the conference is also indicated:

> He was waited on by Minister Eli Landis and Elder John Gotwals, warning him of offending the rules of the Meeting, assuming that such was the duty only of people of the world.[127]

These incidents indicate some ambivalence concerning the question of political participation by members of the conference c. 1840. Both Abraham Fretz and Abraham Hunsicker experienced a certain amount of censorship for their political activities, yet both were chosen to serve as leaders in the conference. Fretz apparently abandoned his political activities following his ordination in 1843. Hunsicker was one of the ministers who separated from the conference in 1847.

The political climate during World War I enhanced the stance of nonparticipation, even for local political office. A conference minute from October 4, 1917, urges that no political office be accepted, adding:

> Since we are going through the present crises (WW) we have learned that the world expects us to be separate. We therefore consider it advisable to abstain from voting.[128]

Earlier conference minutes had admonished only against public offices that conflict with the nonresistant faith, and voting had been a common practice.

Mennonites came closest to involvement in government when charter values were threatened. Prior to United States' involvement in World War II, Mennonite leaders carefully worked out and presented to government officials plans for alternatives to military service for their young men who were conscientious objectors to war. Eventually a mutually acceptable plan was agreed upon. It called for church operation and financing of alternative service camps that were ultimately under the military arm of the government. A generation later some assessed the resultant experience as a situation in which Mennonites *de facto* administered a program of the state and of the military.[129]

The Oath

During the American Revolution the Mennonite position on nonswearing of oaths became an acute problem for them, as it did for the Dunkers and Quakers. It was rumored that preacher Christian Funk took the oath of allegiance early in the Revolutionary Period, and he was subsequently excommunicated. Dunker ministers who yielded to pressure and took the oath were likewise unfrocked. Most Mennonites steadfastly refused to take the oath, and numerous fines and jail sentences were imposed between 1778 and 1781. A number of Mennonite men from Northampton County were banished from the state for refusing to take the oath of allegiance, and most of their property—including food, clothing, stoves, beds, and Bibles—was confiscated and sold at a sheriff's sale for 40,000 pounds. Copies of a petition sent by the accused men, and of one later sent by their destitute wives to the Representatives of the Freemen of the Commonwealth, are extant.[130]

Jacob Krehbiel points out the firm stand of the nineteenth-century American Mennonites against the taking of an oath:

> In the matter of the use of the sword and political office, testimony is given everywhere against these two things. The first is contrary to the principle of nonresistance and the second touches closely the swearing of oaths, although according to the constitution, the government cannot force the oath upon any official when he assumes office, but rather permits a simple affirmation in the case of conscientious scruples. It is really the lowest office, that of justice of the peace, which would be easiest for Mennonites in the country to occupy, but it is so closely connected with the oath that this official must constantly administer oaths to other people. Similar conditions exist with regard to many offices. Now if one holds that the oath is contrary to the teaching of Christ for oneself, how could one administer this same oath to others? For this reason such an official would be expelled from the church without hesitation.[131]

---

[126] Henry A. Hunsicker, "Church Division in 1847," *Mennonite Year Book and Almanac*, 1907.
[127] Ibid.
[128] Minutes of the Franconia Conference, 1907-1949, recorded by Jacob C. Clemens. Unpublished. Minute for October 4, 1917. *EPMIII*.
[129] Albert N. Keim, "Service or Resistance? The Mennonite Response to Conscription in World War II," *MQR* 52 (April 1978):141-153.
[130] See MacMaster, et al., *Conscience in Crisis*, pp. 394-457, especially pp. 438-444.
[131] Krehbiel, "A Few Words," p. 54.

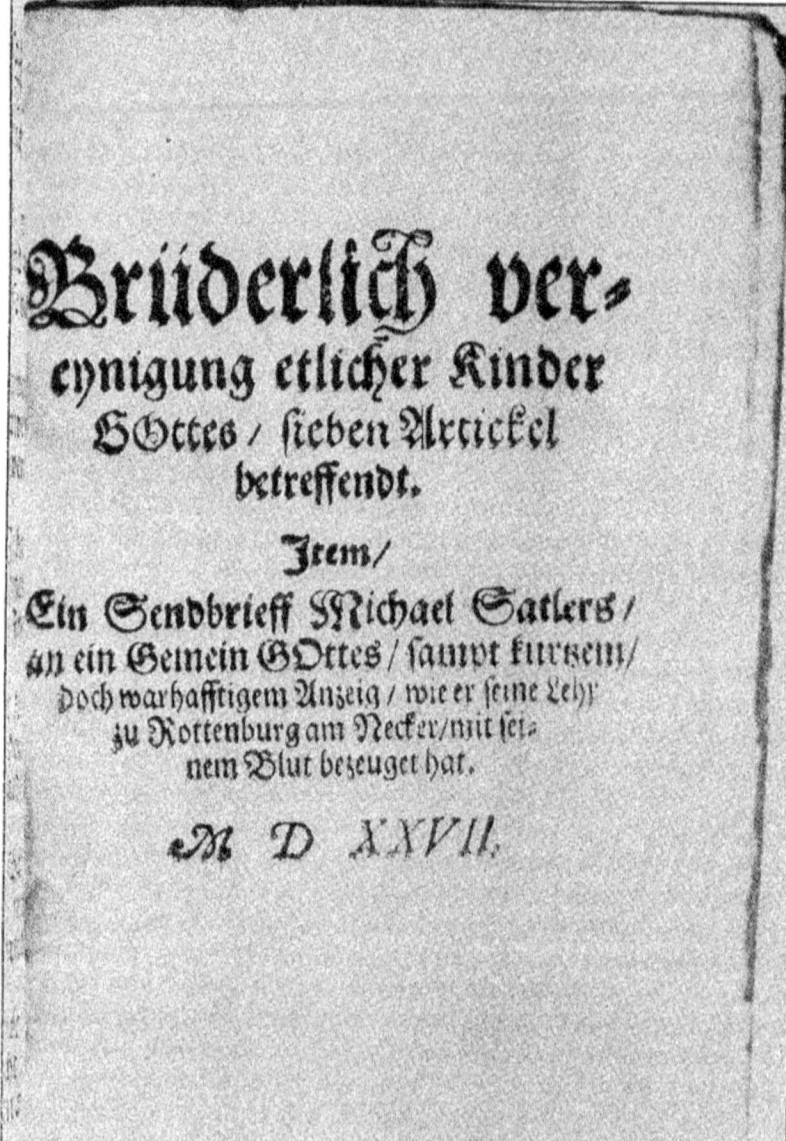

The "Brotherly Union" in a Pennsylvania handbook

The Mennonites in America held firmly to the original charter position which forbad all swearing of oaths. During much of their experience, they were allowed a simple affirmation in place of the oath, but under duress they refused to violate their consciences, suffering persecution rather than acquiescing.

Conclusion

We have compared American Mennonite documents with the Seven Articles and conclude that the main emphases of the Seven Articles were retained as key values from the eighteenth to the twentieth centuries and that they served to undergird, guide, and regulate behavior. The documents examined are more broadly based than the basic paradigm of Franconia Conference, and it appears that the charter served widely for Mennonites of Swiss-German descent in the nineteenth century.

This is not to maintain that these American Mennonites retained the original spirit and vitality of Anabaptism. It proposes only that the authoritative standard for practice found in the Seven Articles continued to undergird religious forms. The Seven Articles appear to have originally circulated with a brief document that gave directions to local congregations concerning frequency of meetings, content of services, etc. A scholar has recently called this document the "Congregational Order."[132] Practice among nineteenth-century American Mennonites bore limited relationship to its requirements. The Congregational Order called for brothers and sisters to assemble three or four times a week to "exercise themselves" in the teachings of Christ and the apostles, and to admonish and strengthen one another. Each time they met, they were to share the Lord's Supper, as well as a simple meal. Persecution and the necessity of living at great distances from one another early modified this pattern. In Franconia, the norm was for each congregation to assemble biweekly, and the Lord's Supper was observed annually. This one illustration indicates some of the distance that no doubt separated the early Anabaptists from American Mennonites.

The Seven Articles were recorded in verbal, written form, but they were largely relational in content, and were designed to inform behavior. They were not statements of dogma and did not result in systematic theological formulations. They spoke, rather, for those who ascribed to them, to relationships—to deity, to each other, to outsiders, to leadership, to law, and to the state. This is one of the things that made Mennonites so misunderstood. What was important to them did not sound like theology to their critics, and Mennonites had a great deal of trouble systematically verbalizing their

---

[132] Yoder, *Legacy*, pp. 44-45.

beliefs. But for them, Jesus' basic religious statements had been relational—to love God with all one's heart and one's neighbor as oneself. Also, Jesus had said that if any wished to give allegiance to him, they must take up their cross and follow him. This meant putting belief into action. The Anabaptists and Reformers differed not primarily in doctrinal or creedal matters, but in the expression of religion in congregational life and everyday relationships.

3
Brotherly Union and Schism

Schisms have been a recurring phenomenon among American Mennonites. In the preceding chapter we examined the Mennonite ethos in relation to brotherly union; in this chapter we confront the reality of disunity and division. Cleavages have occurred in a variety of ways. As noted in chapter 1, the interaction of Mennonites with Pietism and revivalism in the latter third of the eighteenth century resulted in the formation of new religious groups in western Lancaster County, western Maryland, and Virginia. The mid-nineteenth-century Oberholtzer division will be the concern of this chapter. This rift was a response to the growing trend in American churches to create organizational structures. Subgroups that quickly fragmented from Oberholtzer's supporters focused on other aspects of Americanization: higher education, ecumenicism, and revivalism. Within a few decades resistance to accommodation was expressed in the Wisler schism that began in Indiana and by the end of the century had spread to Canada, Ohio, Pennsylvania, and Virginia, resulting in the formation of the Old Order Mennonites. This schism will be examined in chapter 5.

While fragmentation has been a serious problem for Mennonites, the tendency of small, schismatic groups to divide and subdivide has made the problem appear even greater than it is in relation to the larger communities.[1] Furthermore, not all branches of Mennonites are the outgrowth of schism. In the American free-church setting many denominations find themselves divided into numerous groupings. At least five elements are operative in this process: (1) national origins, (2) time of migration, (3) type of church government, (4) emphasis on emotionalism, and (5) differences in doctrine. These factors have influenced transplanted churches, whether the denomination

---

[1] In 1776 Christian Funk of the Franconia Conference urged payment of the voluntary war tax requested by the revolutionary government following the Declaration of Independence. The conference held that willing payment of a *voluntary* war tax to a revolutionary government violated the nonresistant principles of the group. Funk and his followers withdrew from conference. Around 1950 two small groups again withdrew from the conference, one with Fundamentalist leanings, the other, an ultraconservative group. A small group broke away from the Lancaster Conference in 1812, becoming the Reformed Mennonite Church. In 1845 another group formed the Stauffer Mennonite Church. The Old Order Mennonites, sympathetic to Wisler in Indiana, withdrew in 1893 and have subdivided into numerous variants.

numbers 5,000,000 or 50,000. The two largest Mennonite bodies in America illustrate this process: (1) the Mennonite Church growing predominantly out of Swiss-South German migrations in the early eighteenth and mid-nineteenth centuries; and (2) the General Conference Mennonite Church rooted primarily in migrations from Russia beginning in 1870 and continuing to the 1950s but tracing initial origins to the Netherlands and North Germany.

The Mennonite form of church government was particularly vulnerable to schism. It was based on personal commitment and mutual counsel. It required complete unity before communion could be administered. Since no overarching authority existed as a final court of appeal, unresolvable differences could be accommodated only by excommunication or schism. The excommunication of a strong personality sometimes precipitated a schism as others withdrew in support of his position. The causes of Mennonite divisions have therefore frequently appeared to be petty concerns relating to personality conflicts. Although disagreements focused on practice, and were sometimes compounded by intransigence, the issues were not necessarily inconsequential. Careful examination indicates that frequently the issues represented charter concerns. Members sometimes found it difficult to articulate these concerns. Furthermore, since the charter related primarily to relationships and to practice, critics often did not see the issues of a schism as *theological*, and therefore considered them of little consequence. In the following discussion the apparently trivial issues of the Oberholtzer division will be examined in relation to charter values.[2]

The Oberholtzer Division

The Oberholtzer division in Franconia Conference in 1847 was one of the largest schisms to occur in the Mennonite Church. The recognized issues centered around the young minister, John H. Oberholtzer (January 10, 1809-February 15, 1895), by whose name the division has since come to be known. The new group was vocal about its actions and highly critical of the conference. The main body wrote nothing in its self-defense. Within the past decade and a half contemporary documents have become available which invite a new evaluation of this schism.[3] Several detailed studies have been made of the new conference[4]; our concern will be to understand the position of the traditional majority.

Oberholtzer was in contact with, and supported by, some of the most preeminent leadership in the conference. John Hunsicker (August 27, 1773-November 17, 1847), moderator of the conference and bishop at Skippack, stood behind Oberholtzer and gave him counsel. John's younger brother,

Abraham (July 31, 1793-January 12, 1872), ordained at Skippack in 1847, likewise supported Oberholtzer. Skippack was considered the most powerful congregation in the conference. Several of Oberholtzer's followers attempted to solicit the support of leaders in the large Lancaster Conference.

At their initial recounting, the issues of the division appear trivial. Examined in relation to contemporaneous American Protestantism, it becomes apparent that they were closely related to religious influences in the American environment. That the formation of the new conferences was largely a response to such influences has been recognized by historians C. Henry Smith, Samuel F. Pannabecker, and Robert Friedmann.[5] The thesis of this chapter is that the apparently minor issues of the division represented currents of thought that challenged the charter, and therefore posed a fundamental threat to the character of the traditional group.[6]

Events of the Division

In 1842 John H. Oberholtzer, a 34-year-old schoolteacher, was ordained as a minister at the Swamp congregation. It was customary for Mennonite ministers to wear frock coats without lapels. After ordination a minister commonly wore out his old coat, then replaced it with the regulation garb. Oberholtzer failed to make the expected transition, and at the conference held in May 1844, a resolution was passed saying that those who failed to conform to the usual garb would have no vote at conference. Oberholtzer did not attend the next several conferences. His refusal to wear the plain coat is usually referred to as one of the three main issues in the schism.

The second issue was a disagreement over whether or not the decisions made at conference should be recorded in the form of minutes. Precisely what happened concerning this issue is not clear. Our most complete source of information is a letter written by Abraham Hunsicker of Skippack to

---

[2] For a recent interpretation of the division that attempts to look at both sides, see John L. Ruth, *Maintaining the Right Fellowship* (Herald Press, 1984).

[3] The Mensch-Oberholtzer Papers. They are published in both the original German and in translation in a special issue of the *MQR*, The "Oberholtzer Division Issue," 46 (October 1972). The editors have included careful footnotes, identifying persons and issues, but have deliberately avoided interpretation of the materials.

[4] Samuel F. Pannabecker, "The Development of the General Conference of the Mennonite Church of North America in the American Environment" (Ph.D. dissertation, Yale, 1944); and Harder, "The Quest for Equilibrium in an Established Sect: A Study of Social Change in the General Conference Mennonite Church," Ph.D. Dissertation, Northwestern University, 1962).

[5] *Story of the Mennonites* (Newton, Kans.: Mennonite Publication Office, 1950); "The Development of the General Conference" and *Mennonite Piety Through the Centuries* (Goshen, Ind.: The Mennonite Historical Society, 1949).

[6] This is not to deny stresses, possibly caused by disequilibrium of norms, as proposed by Leland Harder in "Quest for Equilibrium."

128 *Brotherly Union and Schism*

John H. Oberholtzer (1809-1895).

Bishop Christian Herr of Lancaster Conference.[7] According to Hunsicker, at the May conference in 1845 John Geil (April 9, 1778-January 16, 1866), minister of the Lexington congregation, made the suggestion that in the future everything that was discussed at conference should be recorded.[8] Hunsicker says that at that time the suggestion was approved unanimously. At the same conference a resolution was passed which said that in the future it would be necessary to adhere only to "all the rules and usages of the forefathers that are based on gospel truths."

It appears that these two items were understood variously, for according to Hunsicker's letter, there was a reticence to stand by either decision at the next conference:

But when the next conference assembled they did not want to know much about the record-keeping. At the same time the decision was made that all proceedings should be written up, it was also decided that all proceedings should have Gospel foundation or that everything must be measured by the Gospel, so to speak. Everything then that is not according to Scripture—whether it be doctrine, faith, sacraments, worship services, or life—all must be measured by this unerring plumb-line and must in genuine godly fear without respect of persons be broken and brought to naught by this righteous, divine scepter.

Then when the next conference assembled somebody asked the question whether the Conference was still thus minded to go with the Gospel, and if they were so minded could they testify to it by standing. But the objections were raised that it would be dangerous to go with the Gospel, and one could not really determine this. Here you can well imagine, my dear brother, that the Conference broke up in confusion.[9]

Hunsicker says that by this time the conference had already divided into factions. He tried to arrange a meeting between representatives of the two factions, but Henry Hunsberger and John Geil, the two men to whom he had written proposing that they come together on the day before conference to discuss their differences, did not respond favorably to his suggestion.

In the meantime, in January of 1847, John Oberholtzer conceived the idea that it would be good to write a constitution for the conference. He had written a constitution for his Swamp congregation already in 1844. Bishop John Hunsicker of the Skippack congregation encouraged him in his plan, and during the last week of April and the first week of May 1847, he wrote a constitution.[10] He was also persuaded to buy, and wear, a coat of the cut customarily worn by ministers.

The night before the spring conference in 1847, Bishop John Hunsicker held a meeting at Skippack which was attended by seven ministers, besides Hunsicker, and five deacons. At this meeting they discussed and approved Oberholtzer's constitution, and the next day at conference, Oberholtzer, who was now wearing his regulation coat, offered to read the constitution. The discussion which followed was so long that Moderator John Hunsicker ruled that insufficient time remained to read the constitution. It was then proposed that it be printed and distributed so that it could be read. A vote was taken,

---

[7] "Letter of Abraham Hunsicker to Christian Herr, Lancaster, January 29, 1848," "Mensch-Oberholtzer Papers, I," *MQR* 46 (October 1972):333-341.

[8] He is the author of the "Farewell Letter" used extensively in the previous chapter.

[9] Letter from Abraham Hunsicker, p. 335.

[10] John H. Oberholtzer, "Testimony from the Boyertown Case," *MQR* 46 (October 1972):418.

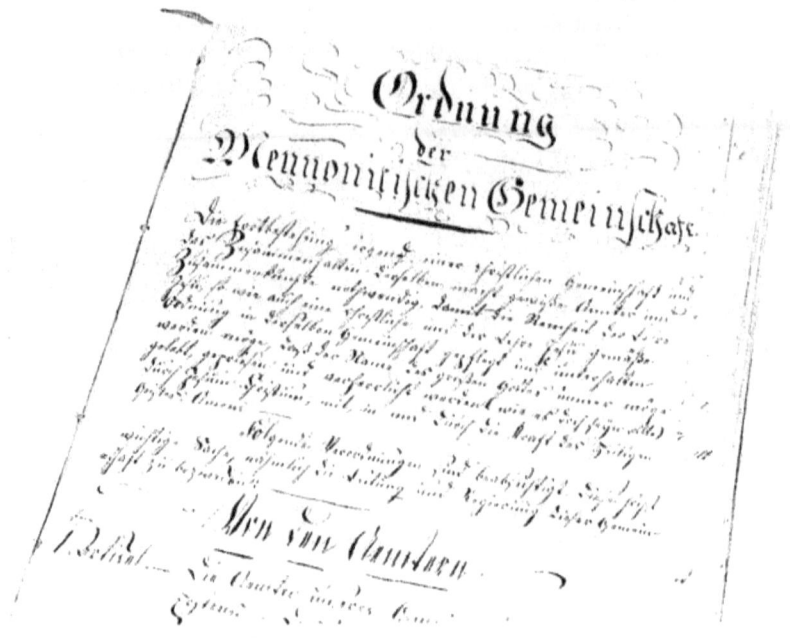

Constitution of the Mennonite Brotherhood, written in Oberholtzer's hand, begins New Mennonite record book in 1847.

rejecting this idea, but the supporters of the constitution had it printed and circulated despite the ruling.

When the fall conference convened, the supporters of the new constitution sat in a bloc on one side of the meetinghouse. That the division had already been largely precipitated is indicated by the fact that Bishop Henry Hunsberger was moderating the conference: John Hunsicker, according to custom the rightful moderator, was seated with the constitution bloc. Apparently the first action of business, under the direction of moderator Hunsberger, was to disfranchise those who had approved of the new constitution. They walked out of the meeting, and the division had taken place.[11]

The precise details of what occurred at the two final conferences, and the sequence of those events, is not clear from the records. It has been disputed whether or not a vote to have the constitution read was taken at the May 1847 meeting of conference. Apparently this was very soon a point of dissension, for in 1848, thirty members of the traditional group signed a statement to the effect that whether or not the constitution should be read had never come to a vote. According to them, the vote had pertained to whether or not the constitution should be printed.

The order of events on the day of the secession has also been in dispute. The seceding group argued that they were "read out of fellowship" before they walked out of the meeting. The traditional group claims that the group walked out of the meeting and were then read out of fellowship.

Sixteen ministers and deacons withdrew at the time of the division. Fifty-four remained with the conference. About one-fourth of the membership withdrew, which historian John C. Wenger estimated to have been about 500 persons.[12] Six meetinghouses were claimed by the new group, and seven were shared on alternate Sundays with the traditional group. The six meetinghouses claimed by the new group were Upper Milford, Schwenksville, Skippack, East Swamp, West Swamp, and Finland. Both groups shared the meetinghouses at Saucon, Springfield, Providence, Worcester, Hereford, Boyertown, and Rockhill. At Deep Run a new building was constructed for the New Mennonites.[13]

At Deep Run the segment of the congregation that followed Oberholtzer requested in writing that they be allowed to use the traditional meetinghouse on alternate Sundays, as had been arranged in a number of instances, and that they be allowed to bury their dead in the burial ground. Should the congregation refuse compliance, they threatened harsher measures. The request to use the burial ground was apparently granted, but the traditional congregation began to hold services every Sunday, making it impossible for the New Mennonites to use the building on alternate Sundays. The new group then requested recognition as a corporation, calling themselves Mennonites. This alarmed the traditionalists, for they feared that it was the intention of the new group to form a corporation and lay claim to the church property. The traditional group submitted a counterpetition, arguing that the new group could not claim to be Mennonite, for three of their signatories had been excluded from the Deep Run congregation, and a number of others had never been members. Further, the practices which they espoused were contrary to Mennonite teaching and practice. They pointed out that a large number of Mennonites are dispersed throughout the country and none has recognized the new group as brethren. To the contrary, the large Lancaster Conference, which was approached on the matter, unanimously refused such recognition. The petitioners acknowledged that they had not been incorporated, never having found it necessary to take such a step.[14]

The matter was finally settled with the New Mennonites constructing

---

[11] "Untitled Franconia Conference Minute of May 1848," "Mensch-Oberholtzer Papers, IX," *MQR* 46 (October 1972):367-369.

[12] "Franconia Mennonite Conference," *ME*, s.v.

[13] By usage Oberholtzer's followers soon became known as "New Mennonites." The New Mennonites in Lancaster and in Ontario were distinct and separate groups.

[14] The *Original Record Book of the Deep Run West Church*, EPMHL.

their own meetinghouse, Deep Run West, just a short distance from the meetinghouse of the traditional group. Plans for the construction of the new meetinghouse, as well as the selection of the pastor, aroused internal disagreements which resulted in the refunding of pledged contributions to dissenters. This was the only meetinghouse erected immediately by members of the new conference. The original cemetery was shared by both churches for a number of years.

The Issues and the American Environment

The cultural setting of any event is complex. In this section we will simply point out a few of those circumstances in the American environment that relate most directly to the specific issues at the center of the Oberholtzer division.

The first half of the nineteenth century was a time of great change and activity in the American churches. The Pennsylvania Mennonites were not alone in resisting this rapid accommodation in theology and church program. The German Lutheran and German Reformed churches in Pennsylvania also resisted the innovations.[15] In the decades before and after the American Revolution, individualism and rationalism widely affected both political and religious attitudes. Revivalism, too, contributed to change. The Second Awakening, with its great emphasis on the salvation of the individual, resulted in a type of reductionism. With the emphasis on conversion as *sine qua non* of the salvation experience, emphasis on theology waned. Finney revivalists stressed the reasonableness of Christianity. They encouraged individual Bible reading, and individual interpretation was the inevitable result.

Certain traditions, such as the wearing of clerical garb, were also on the wane. Finney writes in a somewhat derogatory manner of the earlier requirement that ministers wear clerical garb, pointing out that the practice is still required of Catholic clergy. Then he says:

> But now these things have been given up, one by one, by a succession of innovations and new measures, until now in many churches a minister can go into the pulpit and preach without it being noticed that he is dressed like other men.[16]

When Oberholtzer refused to wear a special coat he was following a trend in the environment and exercising both his individual prerogatives and his reason. When pressure was put on him to wear the regulation coat he said he would comply as soon as he could see that it was his duty to do so.[17] His argument was that no one had a right to impose on him a man-made regulation that was not specifically supported by Scripture.

When the matter first came up I had no idea it should bring about a division. I did not think conference would take such steps in matter in the shape of a coat [sic]. After it had come to the point that we were excluded on account of the coat, I thought it was against the scripture to exclude a member of the church on account of man's commandment.[18]

Oberholtzer's opinion in this matter can be seen as closely paralleling that of the early Anabaptists. John H. Yoder has pointed out that "the Anabaptists placed in a central position the text of Matthew 15, in which Jesus condemns the Pharisees for having created traditions which God did not command.... This particular text became the slogan which best expressed the Anabaptist's general attitude toward all religious tradition; it has no authority counter to the teaching of Scripture, nor can it even require with authority items to which Scripture does not speak."[19] However, also central to Anabaptist hermeneutics was the belief that Scripture should be interpreted by the gathered group. Thus one can argue both that Oberholtzer was supporting the true Anabaptist position by rejecting a tradition that was not supported by Scripture and conversely that he was defying the principle that Scripture is rightly interpreted by the gathered group.

The issue of keeping minutes, and the adoption of a constitution, were also related to the mood of the times. American independence had created an urgent need for indigenous organizational structures, both political and religious. Church denominations, freed of governmental structures, needed to create their own, and in doing so they tended to follow the national model of adopting a constitution. Similarly, the need to provide their own financial resources and operate their own institutions precipitated a need for record keeping, usually in the form of minutes. A careful examination of Oberholtzer's life and the events surrounding him suggests that he wanted preeminently to create an effective organization within which and from which the Mennonites could operate. A constitution, and the keeping of conference minutes were for him an essential part of organizational consistency.

---

[15] Don Yoder, "The Bench Versus the Catechism: Revivalism in Pennsylvania's Lutheran and Reformed Churches," *Pennsylvania Folklife*, vol. 10, no. 2 (Fall 1959):14-23; John B. Frantz, "Revivalism in the German Reformed Church in the United States to 1850, with Emphasis on the Eastern Synod" (Ph.D. dissertation, University of Pennsylvania, 1961); and John E. Groh, "Revivalism Among Lutherans in America in the 1840's," *Concordia Historical Institute Quarterly* 48 (February 1970):29-43. The Mercersburg Theology, which developed at midcentury, is the most obvious illustration of this resistance.

[16] Charles G. Finney, *Revivals of Religion*, (Chicago: Moody Press, 1962) p. 197. First published in 1935.

[17] "A Letter of John H. Oberholtzer to Unnamed Friends in Germany, 1849," *MQR* 46 (October 1972):402.

[18] "Testimony from the Boyertown Case," p. 421.

[19] "The Hermeneutics of the Anabaptists," *MQR* 41 (October 1967):302.

Extant documents indicate that members of the new conference were avid record keepers.

Constitutions served both as guidelines for the new structures and to protect the individuals operating within them. The individual's right to choose, his autonomy before the law or the church, and his right to legal protection were all a part of the Anglo/American legal concept of justice and constitutionalism. Oberholtzer intended his constitution to serve these purposes. In his trial testimony in the Boyertown Case, 30 years after the division, Oberholtzer suggests that he had intended to resolve the coat issue by means of the constitution:

> I thought it was against the scripture to exclude a member from the church on account of a man's commandment.... The constitution which I provided would settle the plain coat problem for the reason it contained nothing about the coat.[20]

The constitution also provided means whereby an individual might defend himself against the actions of a congregation or the leaders of the conference. Oberholtzer wrote:

> Article 8.—When anyone believes that injustice has been done him by a district ministerial meeting, he can appeal to the semi-annual conference but with the reservation that he has informed the regional meeting that he believes has wronged him in good time before the larger conference convenes, in order that it can prepare a self-defense. Unless he does this the complaint cannot be given a hearing and his charge cannot be accepted. If the complainant cannot prove that the decision is in contradiction to the Holy Scriptures or to this constitution the matter is left as it was decided. But if the complainant can clearly prove that an injustice has been done to him, then the conference shall without delay grant him his rights in such a manner as demanded by circumstances or as the conference may deem proper, but in every case the decision must not be in conflict with the Holy Scriptures or with this constitution; thus it shall be treated from the district meeting to the larger conference.[21]

The Issues and Charter Values

The three issues which precipitated the Oberholtzer division represent concerns that were closely related to key values as expressed in the charter. The first issue was Oberholtzer's refusal to wear the plain coat normally worn by ministers. From the vantage point of American cultural and religious values the pressure put on Oberholtzer to wear the plain coat appears authoritarian. Viewed from the standpoint of the value system of the traditional group in the mid-nineteenth century it is quite another matter. When pressure was put on Oberholtzer to wear the regulation coat he said he would comply as soon as he could see that it was his duty to do so.[22] His argument was that no one had a right to impose on him a man-made regulation that was not specifically supported by Scripture.[23] Oberholtzer placed the right of the individual to interpret Scripture and practice above the right of the group to determine standards for discipline. Oberholtzer's attitude involved disobedience, which was a serious offense in the eyes of the traditional group. Isaac Moyer, recounting the incident in court 30 years later, gives the following interpretation:

> In the conference some of the members objected to Mr. Oberholtzer wearing a coat outside of the regulation, as it was objectionable to the members of the church. Oberholtzer said they could not show him any scripture that prescribed what form of coat should be worn.... The reason given at the conference why they desired him to conform to the rules in the matter of dress was, that the people would have confidence in him, as it would appear he was disobedient to the rules.[24]

The matter of noncompliance with group standards is also brought out in a letter explaining the division, written to a friend by Jacob and Mary Mensch.

> Then it came about that a minister of the word in the Swamp congregation (Bucks County) by the name of John Oberholtzer did not want to yield himself under the old discipline and rules of the conference and congregations. It was requested of him to get a plain suit and show himself obedient to the counsel of the Conference. But he would not and began to rebel against the discipline and rules of the Conference.[25]

The central issue of the schism was not merely the coat, but *what is the source of authority recognized by the group?* Oberholtzer claimed only to

---

[20] "Testimony from the Boyertown Court Case," pp. 422-423.
[21] "Constitution of the Mennonite Brotherhood," tr. by Elizabeth Bender, *MQR* 46 (October 1972):384-397, Section IV, Article 8.
[22] See "A Letter of John H. Oberholtzer," p. 402.
[23] "Testimony from the Boyertown Case," p. 421.
[24] Ibid., p. 425.
[25] Letter from Jacob B. Mensch and Mary Mensch to John S. Kurtz (February 15, 1887), "Mensch-Oberholtzer Papers XII," p. 377.

recognize the authority of Scripture. His opposers felt that in addition to Scripture the discipline and rules of the conference were binding upon its members. Saying it in another way, the source of authority for the group was the Scriptures as interpreted by the brotherhood. In their opinion, Oberholtzer did not respect this brotherhood discipline. It is not the intention of this discussion to comment on the validity of Oberholtzer's position, but rather to observe how his actions were viewed by the traditional group in the conference. In light of the strong emphasis that was placed on commitment to the disciplined brotherhood in the charter, it is evident that his actions appeared as a threat to key values held by the group.

Whether or not a written record was to be kept of actions taken at the semiannual conferences was a second matter at issue. Apparently Oberholtzer had also been active in promoting this change. "The first I recollect of Mr. Oberholtzer in the conference," Moyer testified, "is that he wanted the proceedings of meeting put down in a book. No minutes of the proceedings of the conference had been kept before."[26] Oberholtzer believed that the keeping of minutes would promote objectivity in working with matters of discipline, making it possible to treat any offense exactly as it had been handled in a previous instance.

Flexibility in discipline was valued by the traditional group. Each disciplinary issue was ideally considered in relationship to the unique circumstances surrounding it. J. C. Wenger sensed the underlying cause for the objection to minutes among the more traditional members.

> There was more common sense in the opinion of these brethren than many people recognize. Behind the statement of the "old members" (the author believes) there was a deep and worthy conviction that the best way for conference to function is to decide every issue, in the light of that particular situation, on Scriptural principles.[27]

When one evaluates the conference position in light of the charter it becomes intelligible. It will be recalled that the charter places great emphasis on conducting church discipline on a face-to-face basis and in each instance in the context of the circumstances (Matt. 18:15-17). Reliance on written rulings and precedent would undercut this approach to discipline, and hence another important aspect of the charter.

The most concrete evidence that the new group was challenging established norms is to be found in the *Constitution of the Mennonite Brotherhood*, the constitution that was adopted by the seceding brethren on October 28, 1847, as a guide for establishing the new conference.[28] The contents of the constitution deviate from what we have termed the charter in specific, identifiable ways. However, it was not just to the contents of the constitution that the traditional brethren objected. The contents could have been modified. Basically, they objected to a constitution *per se*. While Oberholtzer argued that he wanted Scripture alone as the governing principle, to the traditionalists it appeared that a constitution would place man-made regulations above Scripture.

The supporters of the constitution tried to solicit the goodwill of the ministers of Lancaster Conference. Abraham Hunsicker apparently wrote to Bishop Christian Herr, then, failing to receive a reply, wrote again.[29] Henry Nice of Franconia Conference also sent a copy of the proposed constitution to the Lancaster brethren for their evaluation.[30] The responses to these letters are instructive, for we have preserved for us no detailed, contemporary response to the contents of the constitution by the ministers in Franconia Conference.

Christian Herr of Lancaster understood Abraham Hunsicker of Franconia to say that the constitution did not cause the division. Christian Herr says he cannot understand how Hunsicker can hold this position.

> You stated that it was not the printed constitution that divided the congregations. This seemed strange to me and to others. Even if it was not the start of the dissension, it is clearly evident that it was the main factor and conclusion of the Division, and it is also establishing a rupture between us and you if you are continuing with it.[31]

Hunsicker had presented the constitution to Herr as expressive of attitudes that were already widespread in Franconia. Herr finds it difficult to accept this evaluation. He says:

> You stated that as long as you can remember there were different customs kept up among you, which should simply have been dropped—that this was the opinion of many. But this seems strange to me, for it has now been well onto thirty years that I learned to know your father, and a great support he was to me. And many strengthening conversa-

---

[26] "'Testimony from the Boyertown Case," pp. 424-425.
[27] J. C. Wenger, *History of the Mennonites of Franconia Conference* (Telford, Pa.: Franconia Mennonite Historical Society, 1937), p. 354.
[28] Copies of seven editions of the constitution that were issued before 1880 are extant. For detailed comments on the various editions, see *MQR* 46 (October 1974):384-386.
[29] "Letter from Abraham Hunsicker."
[30] "Letter of Henry Nice to Abraham Grater, 1848," "Mensch-Oberholtzer Papers, V," p. 361.
[31] "Letter of Christian Herr, et al., to Abraham Hunsicker, April 17, 1848," "Mensch-Oberholtzer Papers, III," p. 345.

tions as well as sermons have I heard from him. And I still have in my possession more than fifty letters from your father and your brother John. And to the best of my knowledge I have never heard a word out of their mouths or read in their letters that they wanted to change the ground and discipline of their conference.[32]

According to Herr, he and his Lancaster brethren felt that attitudes represented in the constitution, and specific proposals made, would destroy their conference. In general the constitution probably recommended practices that had been customary. Certain emphases, nonetheless, were innovative.

The constitution provided for a more careful assessment of the qualifications of candidates for the ministry, and recommended that only the two most qualified be placed in the lot. Oberholtzer complained about the traditional Mennonite way the lot was used for the selection of ministers, bishops, and deacons. One vote from any member could place an individual in the lot. Oberholtzer felt that by this means too many persons were nominated, and often without their abilities having been sufficiently considered.[33] Furthermore, if a congregation by a majority vote was able to select a candidate, that method of selection was to be considered equally valid.[34] Deacons might be selected by vote without recourse to be the lot.[35] Financial support for ministers was strongly encouraged.[36]

Oberholtzer decisively objected to being excluded from participation in conference for disobeying what he considered a man-made regulation. In several places the constitution states that all church regulations must be based directly on the teaching of Scripture.[37] It will be recalled that at the October 1845 conference a resolution had been passed stating it would be necessary to observe only the rules and practices of the forefathers that were based on the gospel, and also that minutes should be recorded of actions that were taken at conference. Both actions were called into question the next time conference convened.[38] Section IV, Article 10 of the constitution seems to be designed specifically to prevent the recurrence of such a situation:

> Article 10. It is herewith ordained that no regulation can be rescinded that has been established by the semi-annual conference, if it coincides with the teaching of Christ and the Apostles: but any rule or resolution that cannot be proved by the clear Word shall and must be altered or rescinded as soon as it can be shown that it produced perverted or evil effects.

Six of the Lancaster ministers record their response to the constitution in a letter sent to Henry Nice.[39] First, they say, "the new regulation, whereby a chairman is to be elected, as well as a secretary who is to record all conclusions and rules of Conference in a book, would be imitating the worldly practice exactly. Therefore we cannot accept such a thing...." Second, they object that only the two brethren receiving the largest number of nominations would be placed in the lot, for this would make it appear that anyone who nominated someone else would have their nomination be null and void. Third, they object to preachers being paid. They acknowledge that it has always been the custom to help to support a minister, but to pay him they considered dangerous. Fourth, they believed the ruling in Section VII, Article 4, would soon lead to "foreclosures, lawsuits, and legal proceedings ... which would basically be totally contrary to the teachings, life, and walk of our Saviour and his apostles."[40] They strongly objected to easing restrictions on marriage with outsiders, and to what they interpreted as recognizing the baptism of infants.

Each of the items to which the Lancaster ministers objected was innovative. Later testimony suggests that the modification of the stand on nonresistance (i.e., permitting members to initiate lawsuits) and permitting marriage with outsiders, were among the most threatening of the changes proposed by the constitution, for the traditional Franconia group as well as for the Lancaster brethren.[41]

Oberholtzer and his followers insisted that they were not altering Mennonite beliefs.[42] In his testimony in court 30 years after the division, Oberholtzer's definition of being a Mennonite was: "A Mennonite is one who believes in the doctrine as announced by Menno Simons as far as the scripture goes."[43] For the Old Mennonites of the conference this definition would have been partially correct, but inadequate. In the same case Oberholtzer testified that "our conference was not opposed to go to law in a

---

[32] Ibid., p. 347.
[33] Fifteen persons had been in the lot at the time Oberholtzer was ordained. "A Letter of John H. Oberholtzer," p. 402.
[34] "Constitution," Section II, Articles 2 and 3.
[35] Ibid., Section II, Article 6.
[36] Ibid., Section III, Articles 10 and 11.
[37] Ibid., Section III, Article 1; Section IV, Article 8, Article 10.
[38] "Letter to Abraham Hunsicker," p. 335.
[39] "Attitude of the Lancaster Brethren on the New Constitution," "Mensch-Oberholtzer Papers, VI," pp. 361-365.
[40] Article 4 reads: Required, that in every respect we will be willing to grant the government all Christian dues; we also will call upon it for protection as God's minister, but only when it is necessary to protect and to save our honor and property. Any case where it can be shown that the government's aid was used with dishonest or malicious intentions is to be censured in the congregation. "Constitution," Section VII, Article 4.
[41] Isaac Moyer, "Boyertown Case Testimony," p. 427.
[42] John H. Oberholtzer, "Testimony from the Boyertown Case," pp. 414-424.
[43] Ibid., p. 422.

just cause. Every man determines whether his cause is just for himself."[44] Here again we note both a change in the traditional value system (suing at law is now allowed), and a new emphasis on individualism in determining whether or not the action is appropriate.

The articles on communion in Oberholtzer's constitution make no mention of unity among the believers or of their commitment to the brotherhood.[45] They do mention "one bread" but the context suggests that the emphasis is on the elements all being from one source, not on unity in the congregation. This is in distinct contrast to the emphasis of the "Brotherly Union" where oneness in the brotherhood is of prime importance.

Following the division the traditional group seems to have quietly continued its usual course. A letter written by John C. and Catarina Clemens in July of 1858, apparently in response to questions about the welfare of the conference, elicited the following response:

> The Old Mennonite Brotherhood continues in peace and unity, as also in growth as far as I know. On 11 July, seventeen persons were baptized in Franconia. On the same day thirteen in Skippack, and the next Sunday there was to have been a baptismal service in the Gehman meetinghouse—how many there were I do not know. On the 3rd of August they are planning to hold the Harvest Home Service in Franconia.[46]

The inquiry may have been spurred by news of more church trouble. Schisms occurred in the New Mennonite group in both 1851 and 1858, and trouble was already brewing for a third division.

The New Mennonites and Subsequent Schisms

The desire for adaptations among the New Mennonites went well beyond the obvious issues on which the Oberholtzer division focused. Although the division is known by Oberholtzer's name, and the overt issues are linked to actions which he took, events demonstrate that some of Oberholtzer's initial followers desired more adaptations than Oberholtzer himself was willing to accept. Unfortunately, this process of accommodation to the American environment was accompanied by considerable disruption in the new group. Three schisms occurred within the first 15 years: The Abraham Hunsicker division in 1851, the William Gehman division in 1858, and the Johnson division in 1861. Each of these schisms centered on an issue involving adaptation to American religious influences.

The Hunsicker Division

The minutes of the first conference of the New Mennonites list Abraham Hunsicker as *Vorsitzer* (chairman), and Johannes Oberholtzer as *Schreiber* (secretary).[47] Abraham Hunsicker was both capable and progressive. Even while a member of the traditional conference, before the Oberholtzer Division, Hunsicker had been an innovator. He gave his fourth son, Henry, a private school education.[48] In the year following the division, Hunsicker founded Freeland Seminary with his son Henry as principal. He had been politically active even before the division:

> He attended the township primaries, the county conventions that framed the ticket, and attended political meetings, believing that as a good citizen it was his duty to do so. He was waited upon by Minister Eli Landis and Elder John Gotwals, warning him of having offended the rules of the Meeting, assuming that such was the duty only of people of the world.[49]

Abraham's brother John, formerly moderator of the traditional conference, died on November 17, a few weeks after the schism. Abraham's son Henry, now principal of Freeland Seminary, joined the new group in 1848, believing "that under a revised and improved discipline, led by men of liberal views, the church would make a new start and bring into its fold an element that had stood aloof."[50] Henry was ordained to the ministry at Skippack on New Year's Day, 1850. It was not long until some in the new conference felt that the Hunsickers were moving too fast. The Hunsickers were interested in ecumenical interaction as well as education. Henry Hunsicker reported:

> In the full belief of a new and liberal church policy, I accepted frequent invitations from neighboring churches of other denominations to preach for them, and when the occasion offered shared communion with them. For doing this, strange as it may seem, I was called to ac-

---

[44] Ibid., p. 424.
[45] "Constitution," p. 394.
[46] Letter to Tobias Kolb and wife, July 28, 1858, from John C. Clemens and Catarina Clemens. Historical Archives of the Mennonite Church (hereinafter HAMC). Historical ms. 1-439.
[47] *Verhandlungen des Hohen Rathes der Mennoniten Gemeinschaft* (Abraham Hunsicker, Vorsitzer, Johannes H. Oberholtzer, Schreiber), Gedruckt bey Johann H. Oberholtzer. Broadside, 1848.
[48] See Susan J. Schnabel, "Freeland Seminary," *Bulletin of the Historical Society of Montgomery County, Pennsylvania*, vol. 14, no. 2 (Spring 1964):81-103.
[49] Henry A. Hunsicker, *Mennonite Year Book and Almanac*, 1907, p. 22.
[50] Ibid., pp. 23-24.

Original building of Freeland Seminary, founded in 1848 by Abraham Hunsicker.

count; for it was alleged that I thereby sanctioned infant baptism, and stood in with people who take up arms. I was warned of going too fast....[51]

A second issue concerned membership in secret societies, a controversy widespread in American churches of the time. Several ministers had been ordained by the new Mennonites shortly after the division. Opinions among them differed on numerous matters, including secret societies:

> Some of these ministers would make a test of fitness for preaching to be a tacit submission to the doctrine that no member may belong to any secret order. Most of us held such a Church edict was an invasion of conscience, besides superseding the one great and only true test of entire submission to the Word and the Christ Spirit in our hearts, yielding obedience to His commandments, and striving to do the Will of God.[52]

The New Mennonites and Subsequent Schism 143

The dissension appears to have come to a head when Abraham Grater, Abraham Hunsicker's newly ordained nephew, publicly preached in favor of open communion.[53] Grater and Henry Hunsicker were asked to acknowledge their error. When they refused to do so, they were excommunicated. Abraham H. Hunsicker and preacher Israel Beidler supported their position and were also excommunicated. This was in 1851. The majority of the members in Germantown and Phoenixville supported the Hunsickers, who continued to hold services in the Phoenixville and Germantown Mennonite Meetinghouses. Members from Skippack and Providence who supported the Hunsickers met in schoolhouses. In 1854 the group built a nonsectarian church at Freeland, where the seminary, founded by Abraham and Henry Hunsicker, was flourishing.[54]

Little attention has been paid to the Abraham Hunsicker division in accounts treating either the traditional group or the New Mennonites. This is likely because the group soon lost all direct affiliation with Mennonites. By 1890 all of the Hunsicker congregations had been absorbed into Protestant denominations with the exception of Germantown, which rejoined the Oberholtzer group. The church at Freeland became Reformed, the Lutherans acquired the Phoenixville property, and Henry A. and Francis R. Hunsicker became Presbyterians.[55]

Most of the initial members of the Hunsicker group a few years earlier had belonged to the traditional group. Hunsicker was 54 years old when the Oberholtzer division occurred, 58 when he formed his own group. He was fundamentally a product of the traditional group, even though it had had trouble containing his more progressive attitudes and actions. One of Oberholtzer's charges against the American Mennonites was that they were in a low state of ignorance.[56] The writings of Abraham Godshalk, John Geil, and Abraham Hunsicker suggest that there were capable, competent individuals among the Mennonites, although admittedly some of them could not be contained by the conference.

---

[51] Ibid.

[52] Ibid. Whitney R. Cross points out that although there was much Second Awakening opposition to secret societies many clergymen belonged to such societies. *The Burned Over District* (New York: Harper Torchbooks, 1950, 1965).

[53] Abraham Hunsicker points to this incident in his account of events in *A Statement of Facts and Summary of Views on Morals and Religion as Related with Suspension from the Mennonite Meeting, 1851* (Philadelphia: S. G. Harris, Printer, 1851). Grater defended himself with a vilifying tract, "An Explanation of Incidents That Took Place Among the So-Called Mennonites."

[54] When John F. Funk attended the seminary in 1855 there were 184 students. Helen Kolb Gates, *Bless the Lord, O My Soul* (Scottdale, Pa.: Herald Press, 1964), p. 36.

[55] Wenger, *Franconia Mennonite Conference*, p. 361.

[56] "Letter from John H. Oberholtzer ..." p. 401.

New Mennonites retained the Lower Skippack meetinghouse, built in 1844. It was claimed by the Johnson Mennonites in 1861.

The Evangelical Mennonites

The New Mennonites experienced a second schism in 1858, led by William Gehman, who was ordained to the ministry in 1849 at the Upper Milford congregation. Gehman had been raised in a German Lutheran family and after a conversion experience joined the Mennonites. He was only 22 years of age at the time of his ordination. Soon he began to advocate prayer meetings, receiving the personal approval of John H. Oberholtzer and Bishop Moses Gottschall for such meetings. The New Mennonites passed a resolution allowing prayer meetings, but opposition to these meetings soon developed and in 1856 the bishops reversed their decision. Gehman considered the decision of the bishops unevangelical, and continued to hold the meetings.

> Many that attended the meetings became awakened and deeply convicted of their sinful condition, found peace in the wounds of Jesus, and were transplanted into the freedom of the children of God.[57]

Whether the decision of the bishops to discontinue the prayer meetings had been unevangelical was discussed in the spring conference of 1857 and brought to a vote. Before the vote it was announced that all who voted against the bishops would be expelled from the church. Twenty-four negative votes were cast. These persons were excommunicated and subsequently formed the Evangelical Mennonite Church.

In order to carry on this work properly they appointed sabbath afternoon and evening to be spent with one another in prayer and religious exercises, and also prayer meetings to be held once during the week, and family worship to be held in every family, and also public protracted meetings where the word was for a time preached every evening—in purity and power.[58]

The program which they instituted—prayer meetings, protracted meetings, and family worship—closely followed accepted Second Awakening patterns. This congregation eventually merged with other like-minded groups in Canada, Ohio, and Indiana to form the Mennonite Brethren in Christ Church.[59]

The Johnson Mennonites

Shortly after the Oberholtzer division, on December 2, 1847, Henry G. Johnson was ordained as a minister for the New Mennonites at the Skippack congregation. Five years later, December 1, 1852, he was ordained bishop. The Skippack congregation had been split by the Oberholtzer division of 1847 with the Oberholtzer group retaining the meetinghouse. This group was rent by schism a second time when Abraham Hunsicker, Abraham Grater, and Henry Hunsicker were excommunicated.

There was to be yet a third schism. Henry G. Johnson, now bishop at Skippack, strongly favored the practice of foot washing. The new conference considered the practice acceptable, but decreed that it should be kept optional. Johnson was dissatisfied with this decision, and stopped attending conference. In 1859 he was censored for this action, and in 1861 he was expelled. Most of the Skippack congregation supported Johnson and seceded from the conference with him. They retained the Skippack Mennonite meetinghouse and became known as Johnson Mennonites.[60]

Johnson was not preserving tradition, as has sometimes been suggested, but he, too, was adopting patterns from surrounding evangelical groups. Foot washing was not practiced by Mennonites in the Franconia area in the eighteenth and early nineteenth centuries. It was observed by the German Revival groups: the Evangelical Association, the River Brethren, and some United Brethren in Christ.

---

[57] From the first church discipline of the Evangelical Mennonite Society, quoted in J. A. Huffman, *History of the Mennonite Brethren in Christ Church* (New Carlisle, Ohio, 1920), p. 66.

[58] "Doctrine of Faith and Church Discipline of the Evangelical Mennonite Society of East Pennsylvania, 1867," p. 3. Quoted in Huffman, p. 66.

[59] See "Letter of Jacob B. and Mary Mensch to John S. Kurtz, February 15, 1887," "Mensch-Oberholtzer Papers, XII," fn. 122, p. 380.

[60] Ibid., pp. 375-383, and John C. Wenger, "Johnson Mennonites," *ME*, s.v.

Upper Skippack meetinghouse, built by traditional group in 1848.

✕ Schism and Americanization

In the division of 1847 and the subsequent divisions in the Oberholtzer group, major Second Awakening concerns and trends are quite evident. Oberholtzer was interested in church programs, publications, and church organizations. Abraham Hunsicker and his followers emphasized education and progress. William Gehman wanted more evangelical revivalist emphases, and Henry Johnson wanted to practice foot washing. Those most influenced by cultural contact (approval of secret societies, open communion, etc.) were found to be too liberal to be contained by the new Mennonite group; those most influenced by revivalism were also rejected by the group.

The Oberholtzer division has been specifically related to influences in the American religious environment by Samuel F. Pannabecker and Robert Friedmann. Leland Harder acknowledges such influence, but has argued that the formation of the new Mennonite Church was a "Reformation," motivated by a desire to follow more closely basic Anabaptist principles.[61] Harder particularly wished to counter the position taken by Friedmann that the Oberholtzer division was a step in the direction of secularization for the New Mennonites.[62] Part of the disagreement between Friedmann and Harder rested on their differing interpretations of secularization. For Friedmann secularization was the acceptance by the Mennonites of American Protestant norms. For Harder the acceptance of such norms did not constitute secularization. Harder says that Oberholtzer had three overriding, positive concerns. The first was the unity of the church, the second the constitutive basis of the church, and the third the organization of the church.

This summarizes Oberholtzer's concerns well. In conclusion we will point out how we see these three emphases conflicting with the charter of the traditional group.

Concerning Oberholtzer's position on the unity of the church Harder says, "Much of his writing and activity was prompted by an impelling motive to do something about the provincial conventicle-type Christianity which negated the essential unity of the church."[63] To Oberholtzer the unity of the church meant giving and receiving fellowship with the broader Christian church, and subsequently open communion, intermarriage, and so forth. For the traditional community the unity of the church meant "peace" within the fellowship, with no member holding an offense against another member. Both emphases have validity in the history of the Christian church, but they stand in tension.[64] The tension here is not new, nor is it isolated to this time and setting. Troeltsch pointed out that the brotherhood emphasis of the sect is at the expense of the wider unity of the church. Furthermore, separation results in exclusiveness.

Harder says that Oberholtzer's second concern was the constitutive basis of the church. Oberholtzer argued that prospective members were not receiving adequate instruction before being admitted to baptism. In 1847 he organized catechetical instruction on Sunday afternoons for the young people of his congregation. He describes these sessions, and the materials used, in his letter to unknown friends in Germany.[65] There can be no argument that the Anabaptist position called for a personal confession of belief in Christ and for a mature, voluntary act of the individual in becoming a member of the church. The issue becomes clouded, however, when the initial affirmation of Christian belief and community are equated. Belief was the first step, but the Anabaptist-Mennonite charter called for commitment to the group in the daily living out of life in the community, not simply in a confession of faith.[66]

Oberholtzer's third concern was the organization of the church. The im-

---

[61] Leland Harder, "The Oberholtzer Division: 'Reformation' or 'Secularization'?" *MQR* 37 (October 1963):310-331.

[62] See Friedmann, *Mennonite Piety*, pp. 248-257; Harder, "Oberholtzer Division," p. 313.

[63] Harder, "Oberholtzer Division," p. 322.

[64] Ernst Troeltsch, *The Social Teaching of the Christian Churches* (Harper & Row: New York, 1960), vol. 1, pp. 337-343.

[65] "Letter of John H. Oberholtzer . . ." p. 403.

[66] This issue seems to have been a point of continuing disagreement between the two groups. In reviewing C. Henry Smith's *The Story of the Mennonites* (Berne, Ind.: Mennonite Book Concern, 1941) Harold S. Bender and Ernst Correll challenged Smith's interpretation on this point: "The reviewers feel that the major emphasis in Anabaptist thinking was on the commitment of the individual to the new and holy life of the brotherhood, not on the right for each to choose individualistically his own thought and pattern of living," *MQR* 15-16 (October 1942):273. See also Cornelius J. Dyck, "The Life of the Spirit in Anabaptism," *MQR* 47 (October 1973):309-326.

mediate purpose of the Constitution of the Mennonite Brotherhood, which was adopted by the new Mennonites in 1847, was the establishment of organized structures to direct and govern activities and behavior. It was designed to remedy what Oberholtzer felt were structural and functional weaknesses in the Mennonite Church. Two years after the division in 1849, he wrote:

> We have now properly organized by adopting a fixed written rule and constitution to govern our brotherhood. The Mennonites in this country have never had a written rule to manage the congregation. Now everything that is decided by the council or the conference of ministers is put down in writing.[67]

Organization represented order for Oberholtzer and laid the foundation for further development. He saw the outcome of his efforts as a Reformation, and uses that term in his letter to unknown friends in Germany. Yet his own group contained an uncontrollable number of divergent elements in the early years, and his charisma was not sufficient to unite the disparate fractions. The realities of disunity, including the insubordination of a number of leaders ordained for the group in the first dozen years, was a great disappointment to him.

In 1860 Oberholtzer met with representatives of scattered Mennonite congregations in Iowa in the interest of forming a general conference. The initiative for this meeting had come from two small Iowa congregations composed of recent immigrants from Germany. The churches represented at the meeting formed a working union, *The General Conference of the Mennonite Church of North America*. The following year eight congregations participated in a similar conference at Wadsworth, Ohio. The new association quickly expressed interest in combining efforts to make possible a seminary and missionary endeavors—initially the publication of tracts. These new areas of concern spawned change in other areas, particularly those affecting separation and withdrawal.[68] Some of these developments will be noted in the following chapters. The conference was greatly expanded after 1870 by the addition of new churches formed by Mennonites immigrating from Russia. During the first number of years Oberholtzer and his followers held a prominent role in leadership. As the number of Mennonite immigrants from Russian increased the western conferences became increasingly active.

Historian Samuel F. Pannabecker sees an underlying cause of the Oberholtzer division to have been the lack of a creative spirit in the traditional group, and the lack of sense of authority "to pass judgment on the many new questions that were being forced on the church by changes in the

American environment.... Critics of the time," he notes, "accused the [traditional] churches of deadness. This can hardly be substantiated on any general scale for there is much evidence of sincerity of purpose and of understanding of the Christian fundamentals—regeneration, faith in Christ, and a life of obedience." Then he adds, "The ability to recognize the moral and religious values in new situations, however, was not present."[69] Pannabecker recognizes that the adjustments made by New Mennonites to the American environment quickly resulted in a weakening of the sense of separation from society and a loss of traditional church discipline and pervasive nonresistance. Separation from society, nonresistance, and discipline were all charter values that the traditional conference was trying preeminently to preserve. This suggests that the ability of the traditional group to recognize moral and religious values in new situations may have been quite perceptive, even if not well articulated.

[67] "Letter of John Oberholtzer," pp. 402-403.
[68] Harder examines this development in detail in "Quest for Equilibrium."
[69] Pannabecker, "The Development of the General Conference," p. 110.

4
The Encounter with Revivalism

Central to the experience of Protestantism in America, and dominant in the historical interpretation of religion in America, are three Great Awakenings. The Awakenings were religious revivals that were accompanied by widespread religious reorientation including noteworthy changes in institutional structures and the adaptation of theology and practice to the cultural millieu.[1] In this chapter our primary concern will be with the manner in which Mennonite communities, and especially Franconia Conference, related to the revivalism of the Second and Third Great Awakenings.

Near the close of the Second Great Awakening, in 1844, Robert Baird wrote what became a religious classic: *Religion in America, An Account of the Origin, Progress, Relation to the State, and Present Condition of the Evangelical Churches in the United States, with Notices of the Unevangelical Denominations*. The intent of the book was to explain American religion to Europeans. Topics considered included voluntary support, relation of church and state, revivalism, missions, social influence, and types and effects of preaching. Baird listed the Mennonites as one of the unevangelical denominations, for they did not support revivalism or participate in other Second Awakening activities. From 1800-1840 many young people from Mennonite homes on the frontier, such as in the Ohio settlements, joined the River Brethren, the United Brethren in Christ, and the Dunkers, all of whom had favorable attitudes toward revivalism.[2]

Why did Mennonites not participate in the Awakening? Were they ignorant and petrified, as some claimed, or did they have positive grounds for their nonparticipation? To examine whether and in what ways the revivalism of the Awakening went counter to charter values, it will be necessary to examine variant manifestations of the Awakening. Both the evidence and the conflict in values tend to be implicit, yet with careful examination of the materials available a reasonably clear picture emerges.

The Second Great Awakening

The Second Great Awakening was a complex phenomenon with many facets. One of the early events in the Awakening, late in the eighteenth century, was a revival at Yale under the leadership of its president, Timothy Dwight. The Yale revival was furthered by Nathaniel Taylor who became an outstanding leader in reshaping Congregational theology, adapting it and making it more supportive of revivalism. His teaching, known as Taylorism, or the New Haven theology, was effectively promoted by the administrative and organizational skills of Lyman Beecher, who worked closely with him.

Charles Grandison Finney (1792-1875) became the central focus and most important force in spreading revivalism.[3] Finney, a converted lawyer, held that right means would result in right ends. Both Taylor and Beecher were initially uneasy with the preaching and tactics of Finney. In the end they found it necessary to cooperate with him. Finney developed specific techniques to induce conversion experiences. One of the most notorious was the "anxious bench," located near the front of the assembly, where persons could be seated while they were struggling with "conviction." Protracted meetings—meetings held night after night in an extended series—were another technique. Finney's revivals swept through upstate New York in the 1820s. In 1827-28 he introduced this phase of revivalism into Pennsylvania through his extended meetings in Philadelphia, most of which were held at the Race Street German Reformed Church.[4]

Revivalism was closely related to Pietism. Pietism stressed the experiential element in the Christian life. Revivalism, too, made the immediate, personal, subjective religious experience central. Conversion, usually a crisis experience, came to be considered the fundamental beginning and central focus of the Christian life. As one scholar noted, revivalism "gradually disengaged conversion from the classic Protestant doctrine of justification by faith and raised it to a position in which all other doctrines and all religious forms became subservient to it."[5] Mennonites considered the new birth essential, but repentance and the will were considered more important than experience or feeling. In the charter it was repentance and commitment, the willingness to follow Christ in obedience to his commandments, that was crucial in becoming a Christian.

Revivalism focuses on the individual. The redemption of the individual

---

[1] For a development of this thesis see William G. McLoughlin, Jr., *Modern Revivalism* (New York: The Ronald Press Company, 1959), especially p. 79f. In chapter 5 we will focus on institutional structures.

[2] See John Umble, "The Fairfield County, Ohio, Background of the Allen County, Ohio, Mennonite Settlement, 1799-1860," *MQR* 6 (January 1932):5-29; and "The Allen County, Ohio, Mennonite Settlement," *MQR* 6 (April 1932):81-109.

[3] See his *Revivals of Religion* (Chicago: Moody Press, 1962). Original published in 1868.

[4] See McLoughlin, *Modern Revivalism*, pp. 42-48, and John B. Frantz, "Revivalism and the German Reformed Church in the United States to 1850, with Emphasis on the Eastern Synod" (Ph.D. dissertation, University of Pennsylvania, 1961), p. 88f.

[5] Sem C. Sutter, "Mennonites and the Pennsylvania German Revival," *MQR* 50 (January 1976):37.

became the primary task of the church and the pastor. Theology and the individual's relation to the church were secondary. Sin itself came to be individualized, with the emphasis falling on sinful acts and sensuousness, not selfishness. The Mennonite charter, too, recognized the individual's response to Christ as primary. However, in the charter when regeneration was sealed by baptism, the recipient of the rite also became a member of a local fellowship with commitment to that group. Certain Second Awakening taboos, on the other hand, particularly the use of alcoholic beverages and tobacco, failed to permeate many Mennonite congregations in the nineteenth century. Some meetinghouses had spitoons on the rostrum, and members continued to make their own wine. These practices contributed to the judgment against Mennonites by Second Awakening enthusiasts.

Camp Meetings

A distinct aspect of the Awakening, the camp meeting, was a phenomenon primarily of frontier areas. It began as students converted at Yale, fired with enthusiasm for the revival, fanned out to remote areas carrying their zeal with them. Camp meetings grew spontaneously out of their attempts to preach to large crowds in frontier areas. After several phenomenal revivals had occurred in camp meeting settings, the camp meeting became a consciously planned technique for revival preaching.[6]

By 1810 camp meetings were being employed by the new churches growing out of the German Revival. The first meetings in Pennsylvania, sponsored by the Methodists in 1803 or 1804, were union meetings with many denominations participating, and were bilingual. The first German language camp meeting was sponsored by the Evangelical Association near New Berlin, Union County, Pennsylvania, in 1810. The German Revival churches prospered mainly on the fringes of the settlements, and among the poorer settlers. The camp meetings sponsored by the Methodists and the Evangelical Association in the new settlements in Ohio caused much religious unrest among the Mennonite settlers.[7]

Since their first appearance camp meetings have been elaborately praised and blamed. Contemporary accounts of camp meetings are numerous, and consistently describe an intense, exuberant experience, frequently accompanied by violent physical manifestations on the part of those seeking peace. The journal of the Evangelical bishop, Johannes Seybert, assumes both that emotional manifestations will occur, and that they are desirable.

> There is constant reference, year in and year out, to emotionalism in connection with Seybert's meetings. There is shouting, hand-clap-

ping, groaning, sighing, leaping, jumping, reeling with spiritual drunkenness, falling, even the "holy laugh." Weeping and emotional breakdowns in the meetings were frequent. Seybert had a word for it all. If these "exercises" were present, there was "life" in the meetings, or they were "lively."[8]

Leaders in the evangelistic churches repeatedly charged that the established churches—Lutheran, Reformed, Mennonite—were "dead" or formalistic. Understanding what the evangelistic groups considered to be a meeting with life, or a "lively" service, helps to bring the charge into perspective.

The emotional atmosphere of the camp meeting is legendary. The crowds, the continuous services, the type of preaching, the "rousing," military, marching songs," created an atmosphere in which paranormal phenomena became the norm.[9] The preaching placed great emphasis on the devil, both on his personal presence and his immediate participation in the struggle for possession of the individual's soul. The tension and anxiety which this conflict aroused often became unbearable and required physical expression.

> There were 5 or 6 under conviction, as they term it, laying on the floor, screaming, kicking, and some groaning; numbers of the congregation were singing over them.[10]

Two of the revivalistic emphases that made Mennonites uncomfortable were the prominence given to the confrontation of the individual with the devil, and the wrath of God. Mennonites believed that Christ had conquered Satan so that the believer in his own strength need not face confrontation with the powers of evil,[11] and that God's love, not his wrath, shaped his relationship with mankind.[12]

---

[6] Charles A. Johnson, *The Frontier Camp Meeting* (Dallas: Southern Methodist University Press, 1955).

[7] Don Yoder, in *Pennsylvania Spirituals* (Lancaster, Pa.: Pennsylvania Folklife Society, 1961), gives a colorful and scholarly account of the bush meetings, with special emphasis on their music. See also Umble, "Fairfield County," p. 10.

[8] Ibid., p. 56.

[9] Ibid., p. 10, pp. 41-94.

[10] *Extracts from the Journal of Eliabeth Drinker, from 1759 to 1807 A.D.*, edited by Henry D. Biddle (Philadelphia, 1889), p. 397, quoted in Yoder, *Pennsylvania Spirituals*, p. 26.

[11] See J. C. Clemens, "The Reign of Christ," *Christian Doctrine, Quarterly Supplement to the Gospel Herald* (July 19, 1934):346-348.

[12] Abraham Godshalk, *A Description of the New Creature* (Doylestown: Large, 1838), pp. 33-34, passim.

Perfectionism and Holiness

The doctrine of perfectionism as a second distinctive experience, attainable instantaneously, became widespread in the 1830s and 40s. Wesley had taught a moderate perfectionism—being perfect in love—but not sinlessness. The teaching was revived by Finney among the Congregationalists, and by Phoebe Palmer among the Methodists. The perfectionism of Finney and Palmer differed from that of Wesley in that they considered it an instantaneous occurrence and that it was necessary to give public testimony to the experience. It was variously known as "sanctification," "second work of grace," and "holiness," especially as the movement gained new impetus a third time, late in the nineteenth and early in the twentieth centuries.[13]

In the charter the Christian life is understood as a process of growth, and believers are to admonish and counsel one another. Both the will to do that which is right and obedience to Christ's commands are vital, but perffection is not achieved in this earthly life. The treatise by Godshalk, which we will examine below, has as a central concern the combatting of perfectionist teaching.

Finney's doctrine of perfectionism held, among other things, that if a person were completely consecrated it was possible for him to be restored to the condition of Adam before the fall. This idea was taken up by others, and applied in a manner that must have been a surprise to Finney. The most notable example is undoubtedly John Humphrey Noyes and his Oneida community.

Less well known, but of far more immediate concern to the Mennonites, was a small group led by Theophilus R. Gates, better known as Theophilus the Battle Axe.[14] Gates, after a considerable career in independent religious publishing, in 1837 established a small group of followers in Free Love Valley, several miles southwest of Pottstown, Pennsylvania. Gates anticipated the imminent establishment of the kingdom of God. He had personal contact with John Humphrey Noyes and was the first to publish Noyes' letter on free love, much to the latter's consternation.[15]

Following Noyes' lead, Gates began to teach that it was possible to attain perfection, and that those who achieved perfection were free from all behavioral restrictions, whether of biblical or human origin. Nudity was considered proper, since no clothes had been required in the Garden of Eden. Free love was the most notorious expression of this new freedom. Gates presented his views in a newssheet that was limited to three editions, entitled "Battle-Axe and Weapons of War."[16] From the news sheet Gates received his famous nickname, Theophilus the Battle-Axe.

The sect remained small, but its contact with Mennonites was more than academic. An ancestral couple of at least one respected contemporary

Mennonite family became involved with the group. Occasionally the Battle-Axes flouted their freedom.

> Once, howling and jubilant, they marched through the aisles of Shenkel Church, the scandalized brethren glowering at them from one side, the outraged sisters, gasping on the other, the pastor in a fury in the pulpit.[17]

The Mennonites experienced immediate confrontation with Awakening influences. Extreme perfectionism planted itself right on their doorstep. The new German Revival denominations were close at hand. Camp meetings (or bush meetings) were held along the fringes of the settlements, and Finney revivalism came early to Philadephia and the surrounding area. At the Franconia Conference held on October 5, 1893, members were discouraged from attending camp meetings. One item reads, "And about camp meetings, members are advised it is better not to go to them."[18] That the matter was discussed at all suggests that some members were in fact attending camp meetings at this time.

"Holiness" became a widespread Awakening emphasis in the second half of the nineteenth century. Closely related to perfectionism, it found expression in a number of denominations and became particularly pronounced in Methodism. Segments of that church withdrew to form holiness groups, beginning with the Wesleyan Methodists in 1843 and continuing through the turn of the century with the formation of various Pentecostal groups.[19]

A Methodist holiness revival in Kansas attracted the recently arrived Mennonite and Amish settlers from Pennsylvania in the 1890s, deeply influencing some of them. They embraced holiness teaching including divine healing, perfectionism, and the second work of grace. These doctrines were not acceptable to others in the congregation they had mutually formed, and schisms resulted in both 1903 and 1912-13, with those most deeply in-

---

[13] For a detailed treatment of perfectionism see John L. Peters, *Christian Perfection and American Methodism* (Nashville, Tenn.: Abingdon Press, 1956), and Timothy L. Smith, *Revivalism and Social Reform* (New York: Harper Torchbooks, 1959).

[14] For a description of the man and the movement, see Charles Coleman Sellers, *Theophilus the Battle Axe* (Philadelphia, 1930); see also Whitney R. Cross, *The Burned-Over District* (New York: Harper Torchbooks, 1965).

[15] Sellers, *Theophilus*, pp. 23-25.

[16] Vol. 1, no. 1, appeared in June, 1837. Subsequent issues were published in July and December. The title was taken from a quotation in Jeremiah.

[17] Sellers, *Theophilus*, p. 49.

[18] *Memorandum Book of Reverend Jacob B. Mensch*, tr. by Raymond E. Hollenbach (unpublished, 1972), EPMHL.

[19] Smith, "Revivalism."

A DESCRIPTION

OF THE

NEW CREATURE.

—:0:0:—

FROM ITS BIRTH UNTIL GROWN UP "UNTO A PERFECT MAN; UNTO THE MEASURE OF THE STATURE OF THE FULLNESS OF CHRIST."

WITH ITS NECESSITY, ORIGIN, GROWTH, AND FINAL GLORIOUS AND HAPPY STATE, THROUGH JESUS CHRIST.

"Prove all things; hold fast that which is good," 1 Thessalonians, 5 and 21.

BY ABRAHAM GODSHALK.

BOYLESTOWN, PA.
William M. Large, Printer.
1838.

A Mennonite response to Second Awakening emphases.

fluenced by holiness withdrawing from the congregation. The Kansas-Nebraska Mennonite Conference also passed a resolution rejecting these teachings.[20]

Brethren in Christ churches in Kansas were also influenced by the holiness movement and, contrary to Mennonites, accepted holiness teachings. Modified endorsement was given by their General Conference in 1910, and by 1937 the Brethren in Christ denomination officially and fully endorsed holiness and the doctrine of complete sanctification or second work of grace. Camp meetings became prominent among the Brethren in Christ after 1930. One of their camps, Roxbury, was within easy access of the Mennonites and eastern Pennsylvania. These camp meetings were specifically employed as a means of spreading the holiness emphasis. The promotion of this teaching by the Brethren in Christ was a particular threat to neighboring Mennonites, for their religious practices in many ways paralleled those of the Mennonites.[21]

Mennonites and Revivalism

The earliest substantial documentary evidence we have concerning the differing religious understandings of Mennonites and Second Awakening revivalism is a small book, *A Description of the New Creature*, written by Abraham Godshalk. Godshalk wrote the book in both German and English, and published both editions in 1838.[22] In intent Godshalk's book is not unlike John W. Nevin's *Anxious Bench*, which was a plea for the German Lutheran and German Reformed churches to stand by the traditional doctrine espoused by the Heidelberg and Augsburg confessions, and Horace Bushnell's *Christian Nurture*.[23] Godshalk's book appeared earlier than either of these two classics. Jacob Krehbiel, in his letter to Germany describing the American Mennonites, highly recommended the work.[24] Godshalk died the

---

[20] See Joseph S. Miller, "The Pennsylvania Mennonite Church near Zimmerdale, Kansas," *Pennsylvania Mennonite Heritage*, vol. 5, no. 3 (July 1982), pp. 14-19; and "The Kansas Movement: Paul Erb's Viewpoint," *Pennsylvania Mennonite Heritage*, vol. 5, no. 3 (July 1982), pp. 20-22; Interview with Joseph S. Miller.

[21] See Carlton O. Wittlinger, "The Impact of Wesleyan Holiness on the Brethren in Christ to 1910," *MQR* 49 (October 1975):259-283; and "The Advance in Wesleyan Holiness Among the Brethren in Christ since 1910," *MQR* 50 (January 1976):21-36. Wittlinger shows that this teaching conflicted with the historic theological position of the Brethren in Christ Church.

[22] Doylestown, Pa.: William M. Large. The subtitle reads "From its birth until grown up 'unto a perfect man; unto the measure of the stature of the fullness of Christ.' With its necessity, origin, growth, and final glorious happy state, through Jesus Christ." The German edition is Abraham Gottschall, *Eine Beschreibung der Neuen Creatur*.

[23] Chambersburg, Pa., 1843; Edinburgh: Straham, 1861. Bushnell held that the family is the ideal setting for the Christian nurture of the child, and that a child so nurtured can grow gradually into the acceptance of grace.

[24] "A Few Words About the Mennonites in America," tr. and ed. by Harold S. Bender, *MQR* 6 (April 1932):115.

same year that his book was published, at the age of 47 years.

Unlike Nevin or Bushnell, Godshalk did not directly discuss revivalism or the techniques of revivalism: "I did not undertake to write in order to judge more than what is indispensable with every writer and speaker; but to bring the truth to light with the least possible offence."[25] From the contents of the book it is nonetheless clear that Godshalk's understandings of regeneration, Christian conduct, and Christian growth stand in opposition to the revivalist emphasis on conversion and perfectionism.

The teaching of perfectionism seems to have been an immediate provocation for the book. The reader is reminded that by 1838 Finney's *Revivals of Religion* had already been written, and Theophilus the Battle Axe had moved his perfectionist group to Free Love Valley near Pottstown, Pennsylvania, at the edge of both the Lancaster and the Franconia conferences. In the preface Godshalk says,

> I had a desire to be profitable to my fellow creatures . . . believing that many of my fellow mortals have not yet a correct knowledge of regeneration, particularly the young, and that many preach a kind of regeneration in our day that is not well founded in scripture, namely, that the change is at once so perfect that no growth is necessary, or that the regenerated man is at once free from sin.[26]

Godshalk organizes the text around four points: (1) why a person must be born again; (2) the means by which regeneration is brought about; (3) what being born again, or regeneration is in itself; (4) what manner of being one is who is born again, or born of God.

Godshalk begins his discussion by quoting a passage from the Gospels, rather than from the Pauline Epistles:

> Jesus answered and said unto him, Verily, verily, I say unto thee, Except a man be born again he cannot see the kingdom of God.
> Nicodemus saith unto him, How can a man be born when he is old? can he enter a second time into his mother's womb, and be born?
> Jesus answered, Verily, verily, I say unto thee, Except a man be born of water, and of the spirit, he cannot enter into the kingdom of God.[27]

Godshalk speaks about being "born again" and about "regeneration." He does not speak of "conversion" or being "converted." Throughout the treatise he uses "being born again," "regeneration," and "entering the kingdom of God," as synonyms. Godshalk says, concerning being born again and thus being made a new creature, "This change is in itself the entrance into the Kingdom of God."[28] Here, almost immediately, we are introduced to one of the crucial differences between the view taken by Mennonites and the theology of the Second Awakening revivalists. Awakening revivalists thought of the kingdom of God as a thousand-year reign of peace and plenty. Already in the First Great Awakening Jonathan Edwards saw the thousand-year reign in this light, and as probably to begin in America, which he like many later revivalists saw as a chosen nation.[29] Charles Grandison Finney declared in 1835 that if the church would do her duty the millennium might come in this country in three years. The revivalists anticipated that the kingdom of God would be brought in as society was perfected through the conversion of individuals and their benevolent and reform activities.

For Mennonites the kingdom of God was the "rule of Christ" in the heart of the believers and found its expression in the church. Christ had already established the kingdom. The task of the believer was not to bring it in, but to become a member of it. "Why must man be born again before he can see or enter the kingdom of God?" Godshalk asks. Then he answers that it is because he did "not remain that which God originally made him, namely, an holy, guiltless and happy being." He continues:

> Herewith I will not assert that Adam, the first parent of us all, by this one transgression of the law of God, did so far fall from God, that there was no more any faith, any virtue, or any desire to worship God in him. The opposite doth much more shine forth from his own deeds and words, and those of his wife and children.[30]

Citing the statement of Eve after the birth of Cain, "I have begotten a man of the Lord," and the fact that Abel and Cain and Noah and Adam built altars to the Lord, he says, "I therefore conclude that something like an inclination to worship a superior being remained in Adam after the fall."[31]

Mennonites endorsed neither total depravity nor perfectionism, both common revivalist teachings. John M. Brenneman (1816-1895) from Ohio, who has been called "one of the finest and most insightful shepherds in the Mennonite church," a half century after Godshalk wrote in a similar vein. He

---

[25] Godshalk, *A New Creature*, p. 41.
[26] Ibid., p. 1.
[27] Ibid. The passage quoted is John 3:3-5.
[28] Godshalk, *A New Creature*, p. 74.
[29] Edwards stood at the head of the American postmillennial tradition with his *History of the Work of Redemption*, according to Martin Marty, *The Righteous Empire* (New York: Dial Press, 1970), p. 265.
[30] Godshalk, *A New Creature*, p. 2.
[31] Ibid.

published three essays which presented Mennonite understandings of obedience and commitment in opposition to revivalist teachings concerning perfectionism and the second work of grace. The essays were published in a pamphlet entitled *Hope, Sanctification, and a Noble Determination*.[32]

Godshalk's second point concerns the means God uses in regeneration. Conspicuously absent from the list is any reference to revival meetings, camp meetings, or prayer meetings, all proper means for proper ends, according to Second Awakening revivalists. Like the early Anabaptists, who spoke of *Bussfertigkeit* (repentance evidenced by fruits),[33] Godshalk places little emphasis on the emotional aspects of repentance. The test of regeneration is not the conversion experience, but the life that is lived following repentance. Christ, he says, is the great medium of regeneration from which all others flow. He existed before the foundation of the world and was a means for the patriarchs and prophets as well as those who lived after his life on earth.

The law, when truly observed, was a means of regeneration, but many failed in this. Jesus transformed the law into the nonresistant gospel. Permission to hate enemies was transformed into instruction to love enemies, "to bless them that curse us.... Moreover he cleansed the law of its permission to swear an oath." Simply to hate one's brother is to be a murderer. The pervasive nonresistance of the charter permeates the entire pamphlet, and is especially prominent in the discussion of Christian conduct:[34]

> Yea, Jesus Christ came to cleanse the church of its dead works; to do the will of God, both in word and deed; to be obedient unto the shameful death of the cross; and this is the new and living way, wherein we should follow him, whereby we would be so nearly allied to him as to have the privilege to be called his brother, sister or mother, Math. 12 and 50.[35]

All who are born again, Godshalk says, are a kind of secondary means of regeneration for those with whom they have intercourse, "for their wholesome words which are always mild and seasoned with salt, and their good walk in Christ are sometimes effectual to the seeding of others with the same spirit wherewith they are pregnant." He cites Peter's admonition to wives who have unconverted husbands—that without a spoken word such husbands might be won by the behavior of their wives. Parents, too, may be means of regeneration for their children by bringing them up in the nurture and admonition of the Lord. All institutions which are truly founded on the Word of God may be considered instruments of regeneration, including the assembling of believers. Sickness in ourselves and neighbors, or the death of friends or neighbors, may be the occasion for recalling Scripture or of awakening fears which cause the individual to seek God. Judgments from the Lord may likewise be a means, "as it is written, 'When thy judgments are abroad in the land, the inhabitants thereof learn righteousness.' "[36] Though all of these means may have a part in bringing about regeneration, none of them (excepting Christ) are sufficient means—not even "the whole sacred volume." Regeneration is a gift from God.

Later in the treatise Godshalk says "It would be hard to tell where regeneration begins in everyone (otherwise than that it comes from God)." He quotes Jesus' words to Nicodemus: "The wind bloweth where it listeth, and thou hearest the sound thereof, but canst not tell whence it cometh, or whither it goeth: So is everyone that is born of the spirit."

> Here we see that even he who receives the birth out of the spirit doth not exactly know whence this came upon him; it is like unto the wind which men can hear and feel, but cannot exactly tell from whence it cometh or whither it goeth. So it is with him that receives the birth, or is born out of the spirit of God. He feels the power, but doth not directly know from whence this comes unto him, or what is its end.[37]

This would seem to imply that regeneration can be a subtle, gradual change that comes over a person, contrasting sharply with the Second Awakening emphasis on a crisis conversion experience.

When Godshalk comes to the third consideration, what regeneration in itself is, he begins by saying what it is not. If it rests on a crying of peace when there is no peace it is not regeneration. It is not fanaticism, but a sober and rational thing which will show itself in conduct. It is a change of such a nature as not to be produced by humans alone, but by the cooperation of God with man:

> Regeneration is putting on Christ, by faith.... To put on Christ, is not merely to believe that he is, but to receive him in all, as he is, namely, in doctrine, in example, and in merits, as Paul says, "As ye have learned him, so walk in him."[38]

---

[32] Elkhart, Ind.: Mennonite Publishing Co., 1893. See Joseph C. Liechty, "Humility: The Foundation of the Mennonite Religious Outlook in the 1860's," *MQR* 54 (January 1980): 11, 29-30.

[33] See Harold S. Bender, "The Anabaptist Vision," *The Recovery of the Anabaptist Vision*, ed. by Guy F. Hershberger (Scottdale, Pa.: Herald Press, 1957), p. 39.

[34] Godshalk, *A New Creature*, p. 51f.

[35] Ibid., pp. 20-21.

[36] Ibid., p. 28.

[37] Ibid., p. 37.

[38] Ibid., p. 32.

The outgrowth of regeneration, and the test of its presence, is *love:*

> Now he that has truly put on Christ, cannot otherwise than love God, and his brother; for this Christ repeatedly taught, namely, "A new commandment I give unto you, that ye love one another." Again, "Thereby shall all men know that ye are my disciples, if ye love one another." And herewith St. John agrees, saying: "Beloved, let us love one another; for love is of God; and every one that loveth is born of God, and knoweth God . . . ." And when man has once such a love of God, by virtue of which he keeps his commandments, then he is indeed a NEW CREATURE.[39]

Half of Godshalk's entire work is devoted to the fourth question, namely, What manner of being he is who is born again, or born of God? Godshalk here is responding directly to the challenge of perfectionism. He speaks of stages of growth: the newborn babe in Christ is one who has experienced the first step in regeneration. By an act of the will he has received Christ, but the flesh still wars against the spirit. Though the will (which has been regenerated) desires to do that which is good, it is incapable of performing it. " 'For the good that I would I do not (mark he would do the good), but the evil which I would not, that I do.' " Godshalk fears that it is customary to remain at this stage of the Christian life.

> How many thousands there are who think themselves orthodox in faith, and were therefore children of God, and have not so much as the will to do that which is truly good. They may indeed be faithful in their attendance on religious meetings to hear preaching, and anxious to pray in order to be heard and seen of men, . . . [but] many are not yet willing to deal according to justice with their fellow men, to say nothing about love and mercy.[40]

The second stage in Christian growth is that of the young man in Christ. This is the stage Paul is writing about in Romans 8, and Godshalk says that the great advance from Romans 7, which Paul described the babe in Christ, "hardly happened in the few moments that were necessary to write the few intervening verses." There is perhaps a touch of sarcasm here, aimed against the prevalent teaching of instant perfection. In the second stage the deed is added to the will. The growth involves increase in faith, and charity grows with faith. Both show themselves in fruits and in the practice of Christian virtue.

The child of God does not willfully sin, according to Godshalk, not even as a babe in Christ. But if one argues that those who are born of God cannot sin, then their godly walk would be compulsion. Second, it would make all warnings against falling superfluous; and third, it would require disbelief in the biblical account of those falls of believers that have been recorded in Scripture. Here he is arguing against the teaching of sinless perfection.

Godshalk says there are sins both of commission and of omission. To avoid sins of omission the commandments must be kept. The first commandment is belief, and the second is repentance. Then one must learn meekness and lowliness of heart, and to love his neighbor as himself. Godshalk quotes numerous Scriptures relating to Christian conduct, climaxing them with the claim that he who abideth in Christ "ought himself to walk, even as he walked, 1 John 2 and 6. Now how did Christ walk touching these things? Answer—when he was reviled, he reviled not again, when he suffered, he threatened not; but committed himself to him that judgeth righteously, 1 Peter 2 & 23."[41] For nine pages Godshalk quotes Scripture after Scripture in support of the nonresistant gospel. Then he says,

> Here I presume, many will say, thou hast already described a state of perfection not attainable by any man, why wilt thou say yet more? To which I say, that we should make such a state our constant aim; and be running toward it continually, with full purpose of heart, whereby we should certainly get ahead much further, than by standing still, discouraged; for the whole matter has its origin in God, who can work in us both to will and to do of his good pleasure: for nothing is impossible with him.[42]

The ultimate state of perfection, according to Godshalk, involves not only the most difficult of all commandments—love of one's enemies, and the will to do what one knows he should do, but also perfect knowledge. While the first two are attainable in the present life, the third is not. In two respects the apostle Paul had achieved perfection: in faithfulness and complete self-denial. But perfection in knowledge belongs to another time. Not until persons have received their spiritual bodies, says Godshalk, will they finally achieve perfection: and here, finally, they are perfect humans.[43] He recognizes that many may think he has outlined a difficult course. But he softens it, saying,

---

[39] Ibid., p. 33.
[40] Ibid., p. 39.
[41] Ibid., p. 51.
[42] Ibid., pp. 59-60.
[43] Ibid., p. 63.

In conclusion, I would only say, that the work is principally a work of God, and I am so fully convinced of his perfect righteousness and love to man, that I can go to bed and sleep easy on this account—If I have only done as well as he has given me power to do.[44]

This little book from the pen of Abraham Godshalk is a positive statement concerning the Mennonite understanding of the Christian life. In it he affirms a number of charter values, placing special emphasis on nonresistance and walking as Christ walked. The contents of the manuscript stand in opposition to Pietism, individualism, reductionism, perfectionism, and Second Awakening millennialism.

Revivalism and the New Mennonites

Revivalism was divisive for the New Mennonites in eastern Pennsylvania, and an examination of their experience is instructive for understanding both resistance and accommodation to revivalism by Mennonites. Revivalism does not seem to have been an immediate issue in the Oberholtzer division of 1847. Godshalk had published his treatise almost a decade before the division; Oberholtzer and his followers who remained loyal seem not to have favored the emphases and techniques of revivalism. However, by 1853 a small group of New Mennonites under the leadership of William Gehman began holding prayer meetings, a common revivalist activity. By 1858 the new conference felt it could not tolerate the type of prayer meetings being held, and when Gehman and his followers refused to submit to the wishes of conference, they were excommunicated.[45]

Several groups stemming from the New Mennonites became involved in revivalism soon after 1860. An early record of "protracted meetings" comes from the *Minute Book of the Church Council of the Christian Society at Freeland*.[46] This church was founded by Abraham Hunsicker and his associates after they were excommunicated from Oberholtzer's group.[47] On June 1, 1863, it was reported at the church council meeting that 29 meetings had been conducted at the Christian Society at Freeland. At the same meeting it was thought necessary to discipline the deacon, Abram Tyson, for on December 12, 1862, at the Methodist meetinghouse in Schwenksville he had publicly expressed his wish to become a member of the evangelical Methodist denomination.

Protracted meetings were again held at Freeland from November 1, 1863, to December 6, 1863. Subsequent to these meetings 35 individuals were added to the membership of the Christian Society at Freeland: 26 by baptism, six by confirmation, and three by confession of faith. The names of these persons were recorded,[48] and it is interesting to note that the majority of persons who joined the group as a result of these meetings have traditional Mennonite surnames. The information is insufficient to enable one to draw any firm conclusions, but the names suggest that these meetings were affecting the Mennonite community even though the Christian Society at Freeland had not identified itself as Mennonite for some years.

Another fragment of the Oberholtzer schism was also considerably involved in revivalism, according to a letter written by Jacob B. and Mary Mensch in 1887. They reported that Joel Rosenberger, who was ordained to the ministry in 1864 by the Johnson Mennonites was "greatly taken up with a Methodist spirit,"[49] and as a consequence soon joined the Evangelical Mennonites.

In 1873 Johnson ordained another minister, Amos Bean. Bean, too, was interested in revivalism. The Mensches report: "Bean attends night (revival) meetings and prayer meetings a great deal, and at times he associates with the Evangelical Mennonites; . . . they often conduct night meetings every night for a whole week in order to convert people and draw others to themselves, by telling them they have never experienced conversion."[50] The letter implies that the other ministers in the Johnson group did not want their children to attend these night meetings but they tolerated Bean's participation. The Evangelical Mennonites, who were attracting Rosenberger and Bean, had formed their church in 1858 when William Gehman and a group of followers were expelled from the Oberholtzer group for holding prayer meetings.

Revivalism also influenced the New Mennonites through the Union Sunday School Movement, a direct outgrowth of the Second Great Awakening. The Sunday school movement during this era was aimed, not at providing Christian nurture, but at preparing the children for a conversion experience. The *Annual Report* of the Sunday School Union in 1857 reads: "Sunday school instruction must be regarded as only a means to an end *and that end is the conversion of the soul*...."[51] By 1876 the New Mennonites were holding annual Sunday School Conventions, and the minutes indicate

---

[44] Ibid., p. 74.
[45] Concerns similar to those of the Gehman group were finding expression in Canada. See Frank H. Epp, *Mennonites in Canada* (Toronto: Macmillan of Canada, 1974), Chapter 6. "Mid-Century Renewal Movements," especially pp. 141-154.
[46] Microfilm, EPMHL.
[47] Supra, pp. 140-143.
[48] See "Record of Joseph Hendricks, Pastor of Trinity Christian Church, Collegeville, Pa., 1864-1904," Microfilm, EPMHL.
[49] "Fragment of a Letter from Jacob B. and Mary Mensch to John S. Kurtz, 1880's" *MQR* 46 (October 1972):381.
[50] Ibid.
[51] See McLoughlin, *Modern Revivalism*, p. 157.

Revival preacher Daniel Brenneman was censured.

that they had adopted this viewpoint. At the Eastern District Sunday School Convention in 1885 a speaker said that children should be brought to Christ early. Another speaker said: "Never tell children that they must be good children, read the Bible, come to Sunday School and when they die they will go to heaven; this is false teaching as nothing but an interest in the saving blood of Christ will suffice."[52] In 1892 this same theme was repeated: "The immediate aim of the Sunday School is to lead the children to the truth as it is in Christ Jesus, to a knowledge of sin, to repentance, to faith in Christ and to love him and to swell the church membership; the ultimate aim is to number the children with the saints."[53]

Numbering the children with the saints was not new, but converting them before one could do so was a departure from the traditional Anabaptist-Mennonite position. The charter called for a believers' church which was built upon adult commitment and believer's baptism. Child evangelism was a threat to the foundational charter concepts of adult baptism and a responsible believers church.[54]

Mennonites and the Third Great Awakening

In 1872 John F. Funk and Daniel Brenneman, two Elkhart county, Indiana, ministers, held the first series of protracted meetings in the Mennonite Church at Masontown in western Pennsylvania. One of the reasons for the development of revivalism in America was the need to bring members into the churches in the new voluntary church environment. When Mennonites began to accept revivalism in the last quarter of the nineteenth century, this was also a primary concern for them. Many of their young people, normally not baptized until in their twenties, were attending revival meetings held by other denominations and subsequently joining those churches.

Revivalism proved to be divisive for the old Mennonites, just as it had been for the New Mennonites several decades earlier. Following the series of meetings at Masontown, Brenneman was eager to push forward with revivalism. Funk held back, both because he thought the Mennonite Church was not yet ready to accept revivalism, and because he had misgivings about the manner in which revival meetings and their accompanying prayer meetings were being conducted. That Funk had ample reason for concern is demonstrated by events in Elkhart County in the next several years.

---

[52] A. B. Grubb, "The Task of the Sunday School Superintendent," *Minutes, Twelfth Eastern District Sunday School Convention*, August 11, 12, 1885. Microfilm, EPMHL.

[53] William M. Gehman, "The Need and Opportunities of the Sunday School Today," *Minutes, Nineteenth Eastern District Sunday School Convention*, August 30, 31, 1892. Microfilm, *EPMHL*.

[54] See Harold S. Bender, "Evangelism," *ME*, s.v.

John F. Funk (1835-1930) was born and reared in Franconia Conference. As a young man he went to Chicago to assist in his brother-in-law's lumber business. He was converted during a period of revival in Chicago but elected to return to Franconia for baptism into the Mennonite Church. He went to preacher John Geil for his pre-baptismal instruction.[55] Back in Chicago he was very active in Sunday school work, and in 1864, on his own initiative, he began a churchwide periodical. In 1867 he moved his printing and publishing enterprise to Elkhart, Indiana, and quickly became very influential in the Mennonite Church.

Following the protracted meetings in Masontown, in 1873, Daniel Brenneman visited a revivalist group in Canada led by Solomon Eby, and soon began holding meetings in Elkhart County similar to those he observed in Canada. Funk describes these meetings in his diary:

> The meetings held were such prayer meetings in which much ado was made, loud crying and weeping—howling that could be heard a long distance—half a mile. Sitting or lying on the floor and making a great confusion, S. Sherk said, there comes the Lord! Catch Him quick—folly, when the Lord comes he will come in judgment.[56]

The type of meeting conducted by Brenneman was unacceptable to the Mennonite Church of Elkhart County, and when no reconciliation was possible Brenneman and his followers were excommunicated in 1874. In time they joined with Solomon Eby's group, which had been excommunicated from the Mennonite Church in Canada. In 1883, following a series of mergers which included the Evangelical Mennonites of the Franconia area, these groups united with an Ohio district of the Brethren in Christ. The combined groups called themselves the Mennonite Brethren in Christ Church and adopted a methodistic type of piety, activity, and church government.

Two letters written by Funk to a Franconia Conference bishop in 1876 indirectly suggest the attitude of the conference toward revivalism. Bishop Josiah Clemmer of the Franconia district appears to have written a letter of concern to John F. Funk. It was Clemmer's predecessor, Jacob Kulp, who had baptized Funk. No copy of the letter which Clemmer wrote to Funk has been located, nonetheless from the responses which Funk wrote we can learn something of the concerns of the Mennonites in the East. Clemmer apparently asked about prayer meetings, evening meetings, lights in the meetinghouses, and the Wisler schism.

We have two replies which Funk wrote to Clemmer, one written the day he received Clemmer's letter (February 21, 1878) but not completed or sent and the other written on March 12, 1878.[57] The first response of Funk, written but not sent, gives expression to Funk's frustration at continually being confronted by rumors: "Now comes the clamor. Funk holds protracted meetings, prayer meetings, and the like and that they have ornamental lamps in their meetinghouses. Now to resist all this and to undo it and tell people the truth, one must write many letters...."[58]

In his second letter Funk emphatically states that they do not hold prayer meetings:

> It must indeed have been a hostile man who reported such things, for there is not one word of truth in it that prayer meetings were held among us—*not one word*. Prayer meetings are not permitted among us at all. With the aged and infirm, the sick, widows, etc., there will be singing and admonishing and praying when we visit them just as among you, but nothing further. But of prayer periods and prayer meetings, we practice nothing.[59]

This objection to prayer meetings is often confusing to those who know only the sedate prayer meetings of a later time. Finney and his followers advocated prevailing prayer. Prevailing prayer was effectual, persevering prayer that sought a definite object and was intended to *move* God:

> Now, do not deceive yourselves with thinking that you offer effectual prayer, unless you have this intense desire for the blessing.... Prayer is not effectual unless it is offered up with agony of desire. The apostle Paul speaks of it as a travail of the soul. Jesus Christ, when he was praying in the garden, was in such an agony, that he sweat as it were great drops of blood falling down to the ground. I have never known a person to sweat blood; but I have known a person to pray until the blood started from the nose. And I have known persons to pray until they were all wet with perspiration, in the coldest weather in winter. I have known many persons to pray for hours, till their strength was all exhausted from the agony of their minds. Such prayers prevail with God.[60]

---

[55] For vignettes of John Funk and his relationship to John Geil and Franconia Conference, see John L. Ruth, *Maintaining the Right Fellowship*, passim.

[56] Diary, March 15, 1874. Quoted in Dean, "John F. Funk," p. 259.

[57] Copies of the letters are in the Mennonite Historical Archives, Goshen College, Goshen, Ind. The March 12, 1878, letter, "On the Wisler Schism: A John F. Funk Letter," was translated and printed in *MHB* (January 1971):7-8. The February 21 letter, "Another John F. Funk Letter: On the Wisler Schism," was translated and printed in *MHB* (January 1972):4-6.

[58] "Another John F. Funk Letter," ibid., p. 4.

[59] "On the Wisler Schism," p. 7.

[60] Charles G. Finney, *Revivals of Religion*, 55-56.

John S. Coffman made evangelistic meetings acceptable in the 1880s.

When intensity of this nature was experienced in a group, emotional phenomena were frequently expressed in ways that were unacceptable to Mennonites and many other Christians as well.

It was not prayer that was objected to, nor was it public prayer. Godshalk, in speaking of prayer, says of the young man in Christ:

> And when he prayeth, he is not like the hypocrites are, for they love to be seen standing in the synagogues, and at the corners of the streets, that they may be seen of men; but enters into his closet, and shuts the door, and prayeth to his Father which is in secret. Not that the child of God may not at all pray in public; but when he doeth it, it is in sincerity, to the glory of God and the salvation of man, and not to be heard or seen of men: And therefore, in his worship, with much propriety, calls God his Father.[61]

The final sentence should be noted in particular: in prayer, and in worship, the believer *with much propriety* calls God his Father. A loving Father can be trusted to supply the needs of his children without agonizing, prevailing prayer.

In response to the charge that they hold evening meetings, Funk says that occasionally in the country churches a meeting is held in the evening if they have a visiting minister. Evening meetings are allowed by conference in Indiana but protracted meetings (revival meetings) are not held. He says it is true that some churches are equipped with lights, but rather than being ornate they are the simplest type that is available. The concern over lights did not relate so much to modernity as to opposition to evening meetings and the overarching threat of protracted meetings.

Not long after Funk wrote this letter to Clemmer, revival meetings became a fact in the Mennonite Church west of the Alleghenies and in Canada. It was John S. Coffman, one of Funk's staff, who began to make revivalism acceptable in the Mennonite Church in the 1880s. Beginning in 1881, just three years after Clemmer's letter, Coffman began holding protracted meetings. His patience, personality, and the type of meetings conducted, together with effective Bible teaching, resulted in evangelistic meetings being widely accepted in the Mennonite Church by 1900.

Coffman preached at Doylestown, Deep Run, Blooming Glen, and Lexington, all of Franconia Conference, in 1896. He did not hold protracted meetings. He preached at these churches on consecutive days, in the daytime. Coffman's preaching was evangelistic but not revivalistic in the sense common at the time. His effort was constantly directed toward building

---

[61] Godshalk, *A New Creature*, pp. 52-53.

Hannah Rittenhouse Clemens and J. C. Clemens, c. 1940.

up the church, teaching the Word, and explaining the doctrines of the church. His efforts were effective. On January 31, 1897, forty young people were baptized at the Blooming Glen Church. It was the custom for young people to be married before they were baptized, but only eight of this group were married.[62]

Similar meetings were introduced into the Lancaster Conference by A. D. Wenger. Wenger was born in Virginia, attended Moody Bible Institute the summer of 1894, and was ordained at Versailles, Missouri, the following

November. In 1896 he returned east to Lancaster County, where he perceived the Mennonites to be greatly in need of evangelistic preaching. Protracted meetings were gradually accepted by the conference and Wenger led 10 series of revival meetings between 1905 and 1908. Shortly thereafter he moved back to Virginia.[63] Both Wenger and Coffman as young men had moved from Virginia to the Midwest. They began holding series of meetings in the Midwest, then brought revivalism back to the East.

In 1914 Franconia Conference granted, for the first time, permission to hold "continued" meetings. Although they were officially permitted following this time they were not generally accepted. J. C. Clemens, in his "Autobiographical Notes," complains of continuing objections to such meetings in the conference in spite of the fact that they had been officially approved.[64] This attitude persisted into the 1930s. This is not to say that no such meetings were held. One Franconia member recalls that in 1915, at a revival meeting at Providence, "the Evangelist cornered me and with all his effort tried to coerce me into 'standing up' in the meeting. But I resisted, and wished I didn't need to accompany my parents to other Revivals—but I must needs go with them,—and they went quite regularly. . . ."[65] Series of evangelistic meetings were held in churches on the edges of the conference soon after they were permitted. Doylestown early had evangelistic meetings. Clemens held a series of seven meetings at Providence in 1914. George R. Brunk held meetings at Coventry the same year. J. C. Wenger lists seven of the evangelists that were among those that held revivals at Vincent.

J. C. Clemens was widely used in the Mennonite Church as an evangelist between 1914 and 1941, but he held only a few series of meetings within Franconia Conference. It is evident from his record of sermons preached and his detailed sermon outlines that Clemens' sermons were biblical in orientation, emphasized key Anabaptist-Mennonite values, and were designed to teach the hearer. Yet considerable disjunction must have remained between the milieu of revivalism and the ethos of the Mennonite Church. It is touching to read the letters written to Clemens several months after a series of meetings was held. Repeatedly their content indicates that persons who had professed conversions during the meetings were not comfortable in joining the Mennonite Church. The following excerpt is typical of many:

---

[62] John C. Wenger, *History of the Mennonites of the Franconia Conference* (Telford, Pa.: Franconia Mennonite Historical Society, 1937), p. 183.

[63] Mark R. Wenger, "Ripe Harvest: A. D. Wenger and the Birth of the Revival Movement in the Lancaster Conference," *Pennsylvania Mennonite Heritage*, vol. 4, no. 2 (April 1981), pp. 2-14.

[64] "Autobiographical Notes," c. 1954, p. 4. Clemens Papers, EPMHL.

[65] Personal memorandum from Mary Mensch Lederach.

Enos and Rudy went to visit all the people that confessed. None came in but Frank Lilly. Mr. Rohrbaugh wanted to but he was not willing to give up his Russelism. They moved close to Harry's last fall and he comes quite regularly so we still have hopes for him. Mrs. Shaffer wanted to go to the Four square church. She did not want to give up her hat and he thought he should go with her.

Mrs. Winkler said she was saved every day and did not want to go any further. The Walter brothers were out to church once and we had prayer meeting there once. We expect to go back. They made arrangements to take that old sick man Brenneman in one Sun. But he got so bad that his mind failed him, but he had expressed his desire to be taken in and we were glad for that. He died since. Millers could not make a decision. They seem so ignorant of the way of salvation. We scarcely know what to do for them. She seems to enjoy the Prayer meetings but can never get the family to come in. Deitricks are not doing anything. She wants him to come to her church. He was along to one of our prayer meetings and gave a good testimony.

The Italian family seem very warm towards us but have not come as yet. We got into two new homes recently. One is a woman that has T.B. The other is a family in Wooster that lost a little child. Their little girl started to come to S.S. and church. We had a Prayer Meeting there two weeks ago, and are hoping to get them out tonight....[66]

Evangelistic meetings were not well established in Franconia Conference until after 1933, nearly 20 years after they had been formally allowed.[67] It is of special interest to note that revivalism, often regarded as the epitome of religious zeal, was considered by many Franconia Mennonites to be inappropriate to a people who believed in separation from the world:

> Not only were evangelistic meetings shunned as emotional phenomenon unworthy of those who believed in a life of separation from the world and of commitment to Christ, but also the giving of personal "testimonies" to the assurance of salvation and of God's dealings with the individual. Testifying was regarded as evidence of spiritual pride: it seldom if ever occurred in the church life of the Franconia Mennonites for the first two and a half centuries of their life in America.[68]

Franconians were not alone in their discomfort with revivalism. John M. Brenneman resisted revivalism his entire life.[69] Nor were Mennonites alone in their reluctance to adopt this mode. John Williamson Nevin (1803-1883), according to one authority, led an inspired movement to "repair the havoc which revivalism was working on Reformed church life in America."[70] For Mennonites, adaptations in theological understandings came with the acceptance of revivalism, just as they did for other denominations. Revivalism was a movement, a process of Americanization of the churches. The closely parallel developments of evangelical revivalism and the American democratic faith have been noted by a number of scholars in recent years.[71] This trend was evident to Alexis de Tocqueville already in 1835.

By the time the practice of holding evangelistic meetings was accepted in Franconia, the Third Awakening was in its final phases. Its ideological impact had differed from that of the Second Awakening, particularly its form of millennialism. The optimistic postmillennialism of the Second Awakening had become the focus of the social gospel movement. Much of conservative Protestantism embraced a new millennial interpretation, premillennialism, which we shall discuss in chapter 6. Franconia resisted premillennialism, but the Mennonite Church as a whole was greatly influenced by it.

As Mennonites accepted revivalism, a younger and younger age for baptism threatened the charter concept of adult baptism. Conversions that did not climax in church membership were another problem. Theological reductionism, making conversion the central feature of theology and of Christian experience, challenged the charter emphasis on obedience to the commandments of Christ and submission to the fellowship of believers. Hymnody changed, often to include rhythmic songs extolling the blood of Christ and less frequently the more sober songs calling for the believer to follow Christ and in obedience take up his cross. From its beginning phases in the First Great Awakening, revivalism caused divisions in the Mennonite Church, drawing off its most enthusiastic supporters into new denominations. Modernization and a growing acceptance of institutionalization in the Mennonite Church have also been associated with revivalism.[72]

---

[66] Letter from Rudy and Sylvia Stauffer, March 22, 1933. Clemens Papers. EPMHL.

[67] Wenger, *History of the Mennonites*, p. 329.

[68] John C. Wenger, "Franconia Mennonite Conference," *ME*, s.v.

[69] Liechty, "Humility," p. 29.

[70] Sydney E. Ahlstrom, "Theology in America," *The Shaping of Religion in America*, ed. James Ward Smith and E. Leland Jamison (Princeton, New Jersey: Princeton University Press, 1961) p. 267.

[71] See, for example, Stow Persons, *American Minds* (New York: Holt, Rinehart and Winston, 1958) chapter 9; Robert T. Handy, *A Christian America* (New York: Oxford University Press, 1971); and Martin Marty, *Righteous Empire* (New York: Dial Press, 1970).

[72] Theron Schlabach, "Mennonites, Revivalism, Modernity 1683-1950," *CH* 48 (December 1979):398-415.

5
The Encounter with Institutionalization

The period following the formation of the new republic was one of great optimism. Confidence in the ability of free persons in a free society to create a perfect life was augmented following the turn of the century by widespread religious revival. The spirit of the Enlightenment, religious revival, and a new nationalism fused to form a unique American outlook and a powerful impetus to activity. The outgrowth was a proliferation of educational, benevolent, and reform societies designed to perfect mankind in the American environment. The writings of a former minister of Franconia Conference echo this mood.

> I ... was willing to let each and every society organized for any purpose, stand or fall—as it inevitably would, by its own merits or demerits, in a community like this, where the scrutinizing vigilance of the public eye, the freedom of the press, together with the many means in our own power, individually, for information of every kind ... could easily arrest any evil tendency of associations; especially in a land like this, where no despotic monarch, with iron will, intercepts the light of learning and religion, from shedding their benign and holy influences upon the mind, but where the tide and current of improvement are mightily flowing onward, and upward, until knowledge shall assimilate man with his Maker, and enable him to realize the truth, "that man is created in the image of God."[1]

The creation of organizational structures in the American churches was an expression growing out of new modes of thought *and* a practical adaptation to the American environment: to voluntarism in the churches, to the westward movement of population, and to industrial and political centralization. It paralleled a similar proliferation of organizational development in the secular culture. Following 1820, church organization in America developed rapidly on three levels: voluntary societies that crossed denominational lines, programmed activities in the local church, and organized superstructures for the various denominations. We will use the term "institutionalization" to describe this general phenomenon.

Franconia Conference stood apart from many (but not all) of these trends toward institutionalization. Critics have attributed her stance to backwardness or indifference. In this chapter we will look both at the organizational structures operating in Franconia Conference, and at her resistance to institutionalization. Our basic question is whether the resistance by Franconia Conference to institutionalization was related to charter values.

In contrast to the traditional group, the New Mennonites of eastern Pennsylvania rapidly and intentionally organized structures to govern activities and behavior in an attempt to adapt the Mennonite way of life to the American environment.[2] That part of the Mennonite Church which had its center of activity at Elkhart, Indiana, during this period also made adaptations to institutionalization, yet segments of the group resisted this trend to the point of schism. We will briefly note these developments, and changes that concurrently took place in the value orientation of the Mennonite Church and the New Mennonites.

Institutionalization in the American Churches

One of the fundamental religious facts of the new republic was that the churches soon became voluntary associations, responsible for their own financial support and their own church government.[3] It also meant that the churches had to gain their own members by recruitment. Many of the church programs which developed out of the Second Great Awakening were designed to implement this recruitment and to nurture new members.

Among the first societies formed by the churches were those designed to establish home missions, primarily on the frontier settlements, but later also in the cities. Home mission societies were organized as early as 1798, and in 1826 a number of these endeavors combined to form the American Home Missionary Society. For two generations its missionaries significantly influenced the educational, cultural, and religious development of the West.[4] Closely associated with the home mission movements were the tract and Bible societies. Various Bible societies combined to form the nationwide New

---

[1] Abraham Hunsicker is here commenting on his position with reference to secret societies. Hunsicker was a member of Franconia Conference prior to the division in 1847 and had been ordained as a minister in the traditional conference. *A Statement of Facts* (Philadelphia: S. G. Harris, Printer, 1851), p. 5.

[2] For the development of this thesis see Samuel F. Pannabecker, "The Development of the General Conference of the Mennonite Church of North America in the American Environment" (Ph.D. dissertation, Yale, 1944).

[3] The last states to disestablish their churches were Connecticut, 1818; New Hampshire, 1819; Maine, 1820; and Massachusetts, 1833.

[4] William Warren Sweet, *Religion in the Development of American Culture, 1764-1840* (New York: Charles Scribner's Sons, 1952).

York Bible Society, 1809 (now the International Bible Society), the American Bible Society in 1816, and the American Tract Society in 1825. The American Tract Society became not only an agent of mission work in the cities, but through its subsidiaries was also responsible for extensive welfare and educational programs. Between 1820 and 1840 there was a gradual shift in the emphasis of benevolent societies in the cities from primarily evangelistic activity to the alleviation of social and moral problems. Within the same span of time, appointed professional workers began replacing volunteer staffs.

Education, too, was given a great forward thrust by the awakened churches. In Europe the relationship between church and state meant that it was the responsibility of the state to train ministers. In America, with the separation of church and state, this became the responsibility of the churches and it was subsequently necessary for them to found schools and colleges to provide for this need. The Presbyterian and Congregational churches, particularly, were greatly concerned that their ministers should be adequately trained, and to meet this need numerous colleges and seminaries were founded. An especially large number were established in the decade from 1820-1830. Nearly all of the 516 colleges and universities founded before the Civil War had a religious affiliation. Many of them are currently among the outstanding private colleges in America.

The American Sunday school movement, which was formally organized in 1824 as the American Sunday School Union, went hand in hand with both home mission and educational concerns. The first Sunday schools were taught by paid teachers and were primarily in urban areas. They were designed to give children otherwise deprived of a school experience the fundamentals of an elementary education. Children of families too poor to afford even the most elementary education, and children employed all week in factories, were on Sundays given basic instruction in reading, writing, and ciphering. Only gradually did Sunday schools become avenues for religious education and even later did they provide this function in connection with established churches.

Movements to reform society also touched the general population. The Temperance Crusade, the Peace Movement, and the Anti-slavery Crusade were all in this category. Most of the organizations for benevolent, educational and reform activity had their beginnings on the local level, but many became nationwide and subsequently required national organizations. These organizations tended to have overlapping boards of directors on the national level, and the resulting complex was sometimes referred to as the "benevolent empire." These societies required considerable amounts of money for their operation, and their total receipts in 1834 were in excess of nine million dollars.[5]

The trend toward institutionalization in American evangelical Protestantism was closely tied in with the concept of manifest destiny for America as a Christian nation with a mission to the entire world. The inevitability of progress was the undercurrent upon which the entire structure was built. "Men in all walks of life believed that the sovereign Holy Spirit was endowing the nation with resources sufficient to convert and civilize the globe, to purge human society of all its evils, and to usher in Christ's kingdom on earth."[6] In 1885 Josiah Strong, a Congregationalist minister serving in Ohio, wrote a stirring book entitled *Our Country*. Published by the American Home Missionary Society, it became a best seller. Anglo Americanism was in full flower. It seemed to Strong only a matter of time until manifest destiny would reach its zenith as American Christianity spread around the globe:

> Then this race of unequaled energy, with all the majesty of numbers and the might of wealth behind it—the representative, let us hope, of the largest liberty, the purest Christianity, the highest civilization—having developed particularly aggressive traits calculated to impress its institutions upon mankind, will spread itself over the earth. If I read not amiss, this powerful race will move down upon Mexico, down upon Central and South America, out upon the islands of the sea, over and upon Africa, and beyond.[7]

In stark contrast to this vision and mode was the pattern of life and understanding of Christianity found in the traditional Mennonite settlements of eastern Pennsylvania. Living in rural communities, they rejected higher education, contemporary modes of evangelism, and the institutional structures designed to foster these concerns. In resisting institutionalization they spoke of pride and worldliness, of becoming "high" and "mighty." The progressive ex-Mennonite minister, Abraham Hunsicker, comments on what he sees as the incongruity of the position taken by the traditionalists in the midst of a time filled with hope and expectation.

> It is evident to a common observer, that the Arts and Sciences, as well as the social, moral and political conditions of man, instead of

---

[5] For a treatment of these humanitarian crusades see Alice Felt Tyler, *Freedom's Ferment* (New York: Harper and Row, 1962). For treatments which relate reform activity to the churches see Timothy L. Smith, *Revivalism and Social Reform* (New York: Harper Torchbooks, 1957); Charles C. Cole, *The Social Ideas of the Northern Evangelists, 1826-1960* (New York: Columbia, 1954); and Donald W. Dayton, *Discovering an Evangelical Heritage* (New York: Harper and Row, 1976); Winthrop S. Hudson, *Religion in America* (New York: Charles Scribner's Sons, 1965), p. 154.

[6] Smith, *Revivalism*, p. 7.

[7] (New York, 1885), p. 175.

remaining where they were in the days of the Reformation, have been greatly and wonderfully changed and improved. There were not then, hundreds of literary and benevolent institutions throughout the land, all having for their object the cultivation and expansion of the human mind, and the amelioration of the condition of mankind generally; on the contrary, selfishness and bigotry, hatred, and religious intolerance, and a host of other passions—the invariable concomitants of ignorance—filled the place . . . and the faculty of thought—the privilege of reason—that great prerogative of the soul, lay dormant, and unconscious as to a true knowledge of its native birthright, its purposes, and its ultimate destiny. Who then could wish back that gloomy period, with all its disadvantages for improvement and happiness, even in a temporal respect? Yet . . . there are still to be found among us, those who cling tenaciously to the "good old times"—to their ancient discipline. . . .[8]

Like many others, Hunsicker could not understand why Franconia Mennonites would choose to hold Reformation-period values and customs in an age of enlightenment and progress.

The New Mennonites and Institutionalization

In contrast to the traditional group, John Oberholtzer and his followers consciously chose to adapt their church program to changes that were taking place in the American environment. The desire for more adequate formal structures was one of the main reasons for the Oberholtzer division. Before the division of 1847 Oberholtzer had pressed for the recording of minutes and for a constitution for the conference. These incidents and the circumstances surrounding them have already been discussed.[9] In 1847 Oberholtzer organized catechetical instruction on Sunday afternoons for the young people of his congregation. He describes these sessions, and the materials used, in his letter to unknown friends in Germany.[10] The first official Sunday school among the New Mennonites was begun at Flatland in 1853. At about the same time the Swamp congregation began using an organ in its worship services. In 1852 Oberholtzer began the publication of a church paper, *Der Religiöser Botschafter*.[11] The paper indicates that support was given to at least one of the contemporary voluntary societies. It repeatedly carried a notice encouraging readers to contribute to the American Tract Society: "We introduce ourselves as voluntary agents to receive gifts for the American Tract Society which we will then deliver every month."[12]

In 1860 Oberholtzer met with representatives of scattered Mennonite congregations in Iowa in the interest of forming a general conference. At least three ventures were discussed at this meeting: combining efforts on evangelism, on publication, and on founding a seminary. The few churches represented at the meeting formed a working union, *The General Conference of the Mennonite Church of North America*.[13] The following year the conference met at Wadsworth, Ohio, and eight congregations were represented. One of the first joint enterprises of the conference was a seminary, opened at Wadsworth, Ohio, in 1868.[14] Carl Justus van der Smissen, a north German Mennonite minister and scholar, whose 1838 letter had deeply moved Oberholtzer, was brought to America with his family to teach theology at the seminary.

By 1876 the Eastern District was holding annual Sunday school conventions, for which detailed minutes are extant.[15] The minutes of the first convention indicate that in 1876 West Swamp had an enrollment of 200 scholars, East Swamp had 100; the Zion Union Sunday School, 100 scholars; Springfield, 60; Deep Run, 40-45; Gottschall's, 1400; Upper Milford, 70; First Mennonite, Philadelphia, 289; Second Mennonite, Philadelphia, 240 scholars.

The minutes for the 1896 convention give a vote of thanks for the "well-rendered anthem by the choir," and "a vote of thanks was extended for all who made the convention a success, not forgetting the organist who acted her part so faithfully at every service."

Detailed records were kept of the talks given, and their content is of considerable interest. At the meeting held August 26 and 27, 1890, N. B. Grubb is reported to have said he "blesses God that he is living in the age of

---

[8] Hunsicker, *A Statement of Facts*, p. 5.

[9] See chapter 3.

[10] "A Letter of John H. Oberholtzer to Unnamed Friends in Germany, 1849," tr. by Elizabeth Bender, *MQR* 46 (October 1972):398-405.

[11] The enterprise was undertaken almost singlehandedly, and Oberholtzer found it necessary to give it up after three years. The articles tended to be interdenominational in character, and Oberholtzer himself made a rather curious statement about the content of the paper in the final issues: "For long we have understood that a Christian church, if it wants to hold together, ought to have a good paper founded on its basic principles. Yet, if a church has not accepted anything concrete and definite concerning the articles of faith *(nichts bestimmtes Festes)* then it is hard to edit a paper satisfying everybody, since too many opinions are present in such a body." Statement quoted in Robert Friedmann, *Mennonite Piety Through the Centuries* (Goshen, Ind.: The Mennonite Historical Society, 1949), p. 254.

[12] *Religiöser Botschafter*.

[13] For a brief discussion of the formation and purposes of the General Conference of the Mennonite Church of North America, see C. Henry Smith, *The Story of the Mennonites* (Newton, Kans.: Mennonite Publication Office, 1950), pp. 670-690.

[14] For a detailed history of the vicissitudes of the school, see H. P. Krehbiel, *The History of the General Conference of the Mennonite Church of North America* (published by the author, 1898).

[15] Minutes, Eastern District Mennonite Conference Sunday School Conventions, 1876-1900, Microfilm, EPMHL.

the Inter [national] les [son] system; when we are building up not a particular church or sect, but when we are learning to be more godly. It is the system." In 1892, by contrast, he says that "another need is the abolition of the International Lesson series, since the Sunday schools have outgrown them." He recommends instead the "C.E. [Christian Endeavor] Societies."[16] In 1894 it was reported that D. C. Cook's quarterlies were mostly used.

In 1891, "Are Young People's Christian Organizations Beneficial to the Sunday School and Church?" was debated affirmatively and negatively. It was partly an exercise, for after the debate the individual taking the negative side made a strong affirmative statement about young people's organizations.

In 1892 the Christian Endeavor Societies were enthusiastically promoted:

> The Christian Endeavor organizations can help.... The societies can be very helpful.... They bring new life and happiness into the churches, relieve the pastor of a part of his burden, overcome the hesitancy of the backward members, and greatly increase church activity. They also furnish the church with new members as reports of the United States prove; they aid in mission work by arousing greater interest in missions, and by contributing large amounts to the cause; they cultivate the reading and study of God's word among the church members; and spiritually edify all. They also promote the unity and cooperation of the different congregations and denominations.[17]

English secretarial notations were made on the speech of W. S. Gottschall, which was given in German. The English summary reads as follows:

> Inspiration is one of the chief achievements of the Christian Endeavor Society. The New York convention demonstrated this.... He referred to the fact that the C.E. Society was one of the indispensable things of today, and urged the Mennonite Church should not hesitate, but be abreast of sister denominations in this matter. *The churches that do not foster C.E. Societies are of necessity behind the times.*[18]

In 1897 at the Schwenksville Mennonite Church the secretary reports that they "found they were going to be entertained differently." The basement had been altered into a dining room and "sumptuous" meals were served. Several concerns about developments in the culture were expressed at this meeting. In protesting the desecration of the Sabbath, N. B. Grubb said that "one of the greatest evils is the bicycle," and Gehman added that the Sunday paper was the next evil to the bicycle.

At the Twenty-Fifth Annual Eastern District Sunday School Convention, Joseph B. Bechtel, who had the first topic, spoke on "An Up-to-Date Sunday School." He said, "Anything is up to date that brings about the best results in the shortest time, and this holds true in the spiritual world as well as the material...."

The New Mennonites were adapting to the spirit of the times. Oberholtzer felt keenly the need to adjust the Mennonite way of life to the North American environment. In this his vision was similar to that of many Mennonite immigrants from North Germany and Russia. Yet the adaptations made by the New Mennonites in Eastern Pennsylvania were recognized by one of their historians to have weakened both their sense of separation from society and nonresistance.[19] These were two of the charter values that the traditional conference was trying preeminently to preserve.

The Structure of Franconia Conference

John H. Oberholtzer was one of the earliest critics of Franconia Conference for her resistance to institutionalization. As early as the 1840s Oberholtzer was impatient with the failure of Franconia Conference to adopt contemporary organizational trends.[20] In his letter to unnamed friends in Germany, written in 1849, Oberholtzer deplores the backwardness of American Mennonites. He surmises that the first settlers were unable to organize as well as they would have liked because of the vicissitudes of their environment, particularly the hostility of the Indians. Later, he says, their descendants probably wished simply to follow the ways of their forebears. In addition, "under the circumstances their learning had naturally fallen to a considerable extent, for at that time and in such conditions it was impossible to set up schools and institutions of learning because of the poverty."[21]

Oberholtzer's understanding of the historical situation is debatable. In-

---

[16] The Christian Endeavor Society was founded in Maine in 1881 by Dr. Francis E. Clark. Within a decade it had become a highly successful and inspiring organization with more than a half million members. It crossed denominational lines and exerted a strong ecumenical influence.

[17] Seward M. Rosenberger, "Minutes, Eastern Mennonite Conference Sunday School Conventions, 1876-1900." The convention was held at Deep Run, August 30 and 31, 1892.

[18] Ibid.

[19] Pannabecker, "Development of the General Conference," *Digest*. Already in the Civil War, participation in military service was made optional for the New Mennonites of the Eastern District Conference. In 1942, 89.9 percent of the young men in the Eastern District accepted military service; 10.1 percent went into alternative service. See Leland Harder, "The Quest for Equilibrium in an Established Sect, A Study of Social Change in the General Conference Mennonite Church" (Ph.D. dissertation, Northwestern University, 1962), p. 324.

[20] "Letter of John H. Oberholtzer."

[21] Ibid., p. 401.

dications are that the settlers got along quite peaceably with the Indians the first half century. Even during the French and Indian War the main settlements were only minimally affected. The Mennonites early established schools, and James Pyle Wickersham, ex-superintendent of Public Instruction in Pennsylvania, in 1886 speaks highly of their efforts to educate their children from colonial times.[22] The Mennonites did not follow the vogue of the 1820s and 1830s to establish church colleges and seminaries, and Oberholtzer's frustration and judgment concerning education is probably related to this fact.

That Franconia's organized *program of activities* was extremely simple can be readily documented. The usual routine consisted of regular church services every two, or sometimes every four weeks. Special meetings were held on Good Friday, Ascension Day, for a Harvest Home Service, and on First and Second Christmas. Ordinations for the office of minister, bishop, or deacon, when required, took place at a special midweek service. Funerals were frequently held on Sundays, and were widely attended. Church weddings were uncommon before 1910. As late as 1940 it was still customary to hold church services only every second Sunday. That this infrequent meeting was a voluntary matter and not an arbitrary regulation of conference is suggested by the fact that the practice was not uniform: Deep Run held services every Sunday, and several congregations held evening services at Christmas.

Alternate Sundays were spent in quiet relaxation, Bible reading, and visiting friends and relatives. Visiting patterns were informal and were not dependent on an invitation. Hannah Rittenhouse Clemens says that sometimes numerous buggies would already be in the yard when still another family arrived in time for dinner. Documents from the period indicate that this visiting pattern was pervasive. No direct religious rationalization for the practice has been found in Franconia documents, but a very interesting verbalized argument can be documented from a sister group in the mid-nineteenth century. The Amish Mennonites traditionally held their church services on alternate Sundays in members' homes and barns. Whether or not meetinghouses should be built caused a division:

> The Old Order Amish objected that the building of a meetinghouse failed to provide for carrying out one Biblical aspect of congregational life, "fellowship of the saints," which they observed by eating a meal together in the home following the close of the morning service.... The "meetinghouse Amish" provided "fellowship of the saints" by holding church services only every other week and spending the intervening Sunday visiting at the home of some relative or friend.[23]

The practice of hospitality, visiting (especially the sick), and sharing in the work and ceremony of funerals were all considered the fulfillment of biblical injunctions and were a part of the believer's walk of life.

The budget of one congregation underscores the simplicity of the structured program of the conference. Until around the turn of the century the only money collected by the Plains congregation (except during a building project) was for the poor fund, which was in charge of the deacon. In 1905 the total amount collected was $33.00. In 1906 the amount increased to $52.75.[24] No offerings were lifted. Collection boxes were located on the walls near the doors, and contributions could be placed in these boxes as persons left the meeting.

If failure to adapt to changes in the surrounding culture makes a group "backward," Franconia *ipso facto* merits the charge. This is *not* to say that Franconia Conference lacked organizational structures. These two quite different matters have frequently been confused. Careful examination of the sources indicates that from an early date Franconia Conference had a simple but well-delineated structure to direct and govern activities and behavior. From a very early date assemblies were held for ministers and deacons in the conference. The first such meeting of which we have record in America was held in 1725. It appears that ordained officials met semiannually for discussion and counsel from at least 1806 and perhaps from 1750. These meetings were strictly for mutual counsel. No sermon was preached and no Scripture was read. No official minutes were kept until after 1909.[25]

The congregations in the conference were grouped into districts. Several congregations made up one district, and one bishop had oversight of each district. Other than this bishop oversight, church government was largely congregational.

Each congregation selected and ordained ministers from among its own membership, and their terms of service were for life unless for some gross offense it was necessary that they be removed from office. Usually several ministers and one or two deacons served each congregation. Sometimes the

---

[22] *A History of Education in Pennsylvania* (Lancaster, Pa.: Inquirer Publishing Company, 1886), pp. 164-167.

[23] John S. Umble, "From Meetinghouse to Church," *Gospel Herald* 48 (August 30, 1955), pp. 817-818, 837. Holding services every second Sunday made it possible to attend the services of neighboring congregations on alternate Sundays in the Franconia area. It also served the practical purpose of providing opportunities for contact between the young people of the various congregations, thus lessening the problem of intermarriage with relatives. Personal interview, John E. and Edith Lapp, September 20, 1975.

[24] "Autobiographical Notes," Jacob Cassel Clemens, c. 1954. Clemens Papers, EPMHL. The budget for the same congregation for 1954 was $15,000; for 1975, $100,693.

[25] John C. Wenger, *A History of the Mennonites of Franconia Conference* (Telford, Pa.: Franconia Mennonite Historical Society, 1937), p. 52.

Methacton Meetinghouse, built in 1773, still in use.

ministers served all of the churches in a single district on a circuit basis. In this way a group of ministers was responsible for all of the churches in one district, and they took turns preaching in the different congregations. Each deacon, however, was responsible for his own congregation only.

The structure of authority within the congregation was divided among four groups.[26] The first was "The Bench" which consisted of ministers, bishops, and deacons. The second group was the trustees. The trustees were responsible for the property and business aspects of the congregation. They also had the power to determine what the meetinghouse could or could not be used for. Trustees are listed for the first Franconia area church at Skippack in 1725. Trustee records are extant for the Salford congregation beginning in 1830.[27] Trustees were selected by several methods. In some congregations they were elected at a business meeting which was attended primarily by older men. In most congregations an elderly trustee appointed his replacement before he died. If he died before making an appointment, The Bench would make the appointment. Third, there were the song leaders. Song leaders remained seated to lead the singing. Usually older song leaders chose younger men as future song leaders and trained them in an apprentice-type manner. Sometimes these younger men were their sons.

The fourth group, Sunday school superintendents, began functioning only after about 1875, when Sunday schools became common in the conference. Sunday school superintendents were elected at an annual Sunday school meeting.

When a given congregation felt the need for an additional minister, this need was presented at the next meeting of Conference. If Conference agreed to the need, and the congregation voted in favor of an ordination, the next step was to give the members of the congregation an opportunity to vote for nominees for the office. Someone, usually a deacon, was designated to receive the votes. Each vote was presented to him in person by the individual giving the vote. All persons thus nominated were eligible to be placed in the lot, and a day was designated for the ordination. On the day appointed, usually a Tuesday, a large crowd would assemble at the meetinghouse. The nominees would sit on the front bench on one side, their wives on the front bench on the other side. As many identical hymnbooks were placed on the pulpit as there were nominees. In one book was placed a slip of paper containing Proverbs 16:33: "The lot is cast into the lap; but the whole disposing thereof is of the Lord." (In Franconia blank slips were placed in the other books.) Following prayer by the congregation each candidate chose a book. The person who selected the book containing the slip on which Proverbs 16:33 had been written was considered chosen by God and was ordained by the laying on of hands at the same service. No formal training was given to the candidate either before or after the ordination. J. C. Clemens describes his ordination in 1906:

> On the eleventh day of November, 1906, there was an announcement made in the church that there were five brethren nominated for the ministry.... Isaiah Lapp, father of John Lapp, 39 years of age; Abram C. Rittenhouse, 38 years; David Allebach, 34 years; J. C. Clemens, 32 years, Enos Godschall, 28 years. Bro. Lapp died in 1913 and Enos Godschall in 1945. These names, as stated, were announced on the eleventh, on a Sunday, and the statement was made that the following Wednesday morning there would be a special service for the ordination. I can't tell you how we felt through those few days. That time I was working in the bank in Lansdale and was living on Richardson Avenue. I was not seeking the office. My trends were in another direction. They should not have been. I did not have training, systematic Bible teaching, that our young people have today. I was a student, and had books; but my library was not Biblical. When Wednesday came there were three bishops here. There was Jonas Mininger, Samuel Detweiler from Rockhill, and Henry Rosenberger from Blooming Glen. Bro. Rosenberger preached the sermon. After the sermon was preached, they took five books, a German song book, and put them on the pulpit in a row. Isaiah Lapp took the first book, David Allebach took

---

[26] This structure was described by John E. Lapp, *Gemeinschaft II*, Salford Mennonite Church, June 15, 1974.

[27] Trustee Records, Salford Mennonite Congregation, 1830-1898. Microfilm. EPMHL.

John F. Funk founded and edited the Herald of Truth.

the second book, Abram Rittenhouse took the third, I took the fourth and Enos Godschall took the fifth. Enos Godschall was asked to bring his book back. They opened it and they told him he was free. I was then asked to hand mine back, and the Bishop read, "The lot is cast into the lap but the whole disposing thereof is of the Lord." It seemed to me like a mountain.... There was never a doubt in my mind but that it was of the Lord; I never doubted that the call came from God.[28]

Authority in the conference became more centralized following 1909, but the offices, and the methods of selecting candidates for office, remained the same. The conference did not adopt a constitution until 1947, one hundred years after the Oberholtzer division. In the meantime many changes occurred in the organizational structures of the Mennonite Church.

Resistance and Fragmentation

Following 1870 the Mennonite Church, too, began responding more directly to influences in the American environment. Mennonite historians have commonly termed this phenomenon the "Great Awakening" in the Mennonite Church. This Awakening in the Mennonite Church, which initially centered in the area surrounding Elkhart, Indiana, was brought about largely through the influence of contemporary religious forces.[29] By the latter third of the nineteenth century change was probably inevitable, particularly in frontier areas of the Mennonite Church. To assume that the Mennonite Church was "petrified," or ignorant, prior to this change, however, as has frequently been done, is to disregard the data. Change brought with it stress and dissension, but a certain vitality appears to have preceded both.

In 1862, while still resident in Chicago, the young John F. Funk visited the Mennonite community in Elkhart County, Indiana, and was moved and impressed by the vitality which he found in the church at that place.[30] It was Funk's intention to attend the Mennonite conference being held at Yellow Creek, but it was held on Friday and he arrived too late. He did attend a baptismal service at the Yellow Creek church (apparently on Saturday) at which 48 young people were baptized. He participated in his first communion service on the following day. Funk estimated that 600 persons participated in the service, and considered it most impressive. Five years later, when Funk was about to move to Elkhart, there was considerable dissension among Mennonites in this area. The difficulties were compounded (if not caused) by new migrations into the district that sometimes included ordained ministers whose ideas were at variance with the established practice of leaders already in the community. The acceptance or rejection of numerous innovations seems to have been a central issue.

Before Funk left Chicago for Elkhart he received a letter from Bishop John M. Brenneman of Ohio, who had ordained Funk and who encouraged him to begin a church paper. Brenneman counseled Funk to be a peacemaker upon his arrival in Elkhart. Speaking of Jacob Wisler, who was the presiding bishop at the time of Funk's visit to Yellow Creek in 1862, Brenneman says:

> Try to gain his favor and esteem, so that he can have confidence in you. And then I think you can get along with him. It is true, Wisler is opposed to the *Herald*, but for this I cannot blame him so very much, as Brother Rohrer is his counselor. He [Rohrer] has prophesied that we would all be Methodists before we were aware.[31]

---

[28] "Autobiographical Notes," Clemens, EPMHL.

[29] William Ward Dean has developed this thesis in "John F. Funk and the Mennonite Awakening" (Ph.D. dissertation, State University of Iowa, 1965). See also Theron F. Schlabach, *Gospel Versus Gospel* (Scottdale, Pa.: Herald Press, 1980). William G. McLoughlin considers "grave theological reorientation" to have been a fundamental aspect of each Awakening, which was "inevitably connected with a general reorientation in American society at large." See *Modern Revivalism* (New York: The Roland Press Co., 1959), p. 7.

[30] "An Address by John F. Funk," *MHB* 17 (July 1956):5.

[31] Letter of John M. Brenneman to John F. Funk, March 18, 1867, reprinted in John C. Wenger, "Jacob Wisler and the Old Order Mennonite Schism of 1872 in Elkhart County, Indiana," *MQR* 33 (April 1959):115.

Yellow Creek Mennonite Church, site of Wisler schism.

Critics of changes occurring in the Mennonite Church feared not only Funk's new religious periodical, the *Herald of Truth*, but the advancing inroads of the Sunday school movement into the Mennonite Church. One concerned observer succinctly expressed these concerns in a letter to Jacob Mensch of Franconia:

> Bro. Funk is inclined to follow the fast element favoring Sunday schools and other things inclined to bring our church into closer friendship with the high and most popular and warlike Christian denominations of the present time. In places where our membership is small no other than mixed Sunday schools or union Sunday schools could be had and I think there is no quicker way under heaven to exterminate a nonresistant church than by its going into a union Sunday school with the high and dressy fashionable warlike denominations of the present day by making them our equals in the eyes of our children.[32]

This letter expressed a pervasive concern: that through interdenominational cooperation the charter values of separation from the world and nonresistance would be lost. That such a concern was not without foundation has been acknowledged by strong supporters of the Sunday school movement:

> That there was some ground for opposition to Sunday schools as they were conducted by other denominations, or by the missionaries of the American Sunday School Union, cannot be denied, for these Sunday Schools often propagated a type of piety that was foreign to the Mennonite Church, a Methodistic sort of emotional religion which our people were instinctively unwilling to accept, and which they, with good reason, feared.... These Sunday schools were seldom in sympathy with the Mennonite principles of nonresistance, simplicity, and nonconformity to the world.[33]

The groups that separated from the traditional conference in Pennsylvania in 1847, making adaptations to American Protestantism, did indeed quickly modify their stands both on nonresistance and separation from the world. Military service was made optional for the New Mennonites already in the Civil War. The Hunsicker group seems to have participated fully in the military program.[34]

Most of the objections to union Sunday schools did not apply with equal force to Sunday schools administered by the local congregation. Between 1865 and 1875 Sunday schools were started in every state where there were Amish or Mennonite congregations, and all Mennonite conferences took action approving Sunday schools.[35]

Funk, unfortunately, did not prove to be a peacemaker in Elkhart County, and after years of alternate dissension and peacemaking, in 1872 Wisler and his followers permanently separated from the Mennonite Church. This story has been told in detail elsewhere, and we will not further elaborate its details here.[36] The restlessness in Elkhart County was not an isolated phenomenon. It was reflected in widespread areas of the church. Wisler and his supporters rejected numerous innovations, particularly the increasing use of the English language instead of the German in church services, and Sunday schools. Parallel schisms reached into Ohio (1872), Ontario (1889), Lancaster, Pennsylvania (1893), and Rockingham County, Virginia (1901). Jacob Mensch of the Franconia area opposed both Sunday schools and the

---

[32] Letter from Abraham Blosser to Jacob B. Mensch, May 16, 1885. Printed in *MHB* 31 (July 1970):6.

[33] Harold S. Bender, "New Life Through the Sunday School," chapter 7 in J. C. Wenger, *The Mennonite Church in America* (Scottdale, Pa.: Herald Press, 1966), p. 159.

[34] See Susan J. Schnabel, "Freeland Seminary," *Bulletin of the Historical Society of Montgomery Co., Penna.*, vol. 14, no. 2 (Spring 1964):81-103.

[35] Bender, "New Life," p. 154.

[36] Wenger, "Jacob Wisler."

192 *The Encounter with Institutionalization*

The Martindale meetinghouse, built in 1886, was shared by Old Order and Lancaster Mennonites.

use of the English language, and is reported to have told the leader of the schism in the Lancaster area that he would "feel much more comfortable to go along with his side of the division, but if he would, he would be the only one of his church [conference] to do so."[37] In the East, Mennonites who sided with Wisler became known as Old Order Mennonites. Additional fragmentation occurred within the Old Order Mennonites in the first years, reminiscent of the repeated splintering in the initial response to Pietism, and within the New Mennonites as they responded to Americanization. But over a period of time the larger group of Old Order Mennonites has demonstrated stability and prospered.[38]

Wisler was a native of Franconia Conference, and one historian says of the schism: "Looking back over the history of the Wisler schism one's heart must bleed for a man expelled from his church for trying to maintain the doctrine and practice which he had known from his boyhood."[39] There seems to have been some empathy in Franconia Conference for Wisler's position in the first years of the schism. Funk's letter to Josiah Clemmer[40] in 1878 indicates that Funk was offended by the inference in Clemmer's letter that Funk had broken off from Wisler.

In the end, Franconia stood aloof from the controversy. Mensch's memorandum for the conference held May 2, 1901, reports:

7th—Regarding the business affairs at Elkhart where they are much dissatisfied in the west and are split in Lancaster and Virginia our meeting discussed the matter and decided that the Western ministers and Canada who have come to the point of grips with Elkhart had better mind their business at home, and that our conference would take no part on either side, and if ministers on either side come to us to keep our doors shut against them and not to announce a meeting for either side, at least until after the fall meeting.

The report for the conference held on October 3, 1901, reads:

3rd—Regarding Elkhart, matters still stand as they stood in the spring.

By May 1, 1902, the situation had eased somewhat:

2nd—The matter of the western congregations and our dispute with Elkhart was brought up again. Our conference permits western preachers to have meetings among us, if they stick to the old rules and beliefs, but our conference forbids announcements for any strange [non-local] preachers.

Institutionalization in the Mennonite Church

The development of institutional activities in the Mennonite Church paralleled those of evangelical Protestantism, although admittedly somewhat belatedly. Basic reformulations resulted from the encounter:

> Mennonites awoke to a new concept of Christianity, a new vision of the Gospel, a fresh understanding of the church, and of the Christian life, and a new self understanding as Christians. Christianity was transformed for them into an active force for the evangelization of the world and the building of the kingdom of God, instead of being merely a quiescent, passive, conserving system that it seemed to be. The Christian life began to mean more than merely "keeping the command-

---

[37] Amos B. Hoover, *The Jonas Martin Era, 1875-1925* (Denver, Pa.: The Author, 1982), p. 392.

[38] For a contemporary treatment of the Old Order Mennonites see J. Winfield Fretz, "The Old Order Mennonites in Ontario," *Pennsylvania Mennonite Heritage*, vol. 3, no. 1 (January 1980), pp. 2-10.

[39] Wenger, "Jacob Wisler," p. 240.

[40] Supra, pp. 168-169.

ments," and obeying the church.... It was a new spiritual and intellectual atmosphere in which men's labors for Christ took on new colors and brought new joy, and in which young Christians grew up with a different outlook on life and religion.[41]

Finally, in 1898 one Mennonite editor complained that Christianity was now "all work—one continued earnest, active, hurrying, rushing, hustling, pushing whirl of active work."[42]

Within the scope of this chapter it is not possible to more than itemize some of the institutional adaptations that were made in the Mennonite Church between 1870 and 1898. Elkhart, Indiana, became the geographic center of this activity. Elkhart was central primarily because of one man, John F. Funk, and the gifted men which he gathered around him, including John S. Coffman, John Horsch, A. B. Kolb, George Bender, and H. A. Mumaw.[43]

Funk, on his own initiative, began a church paper in Chicago in 1864. It was published in both English and German editions, the *Herald of Truth*, and *Herold der Wahrheit*. In 1867 he moved his printing and publication enterprise to Elkhart, Indiana, and in 1875 organized it as the Mennonite Publishing Company. Funk organized a Mennonite congregation at Elkhart, Indiana, in 1871, and encouraged the building of a meetinghouse in the town.

In 1872, conjointly with Daniel Brenneman, he conducted at Masontown, Pennsylvania, the first series of protracted meetings to be held in the Mennonite Church. In the pages of the *Herald of Truth* he encouraged and promoted the establishment of Sunday schools. In the 1870s he played a very active role in organizing assistance for thousands of Mennonite immigrants from Russia. Franconia Mennonites supported the *Herald of Truth* and actively participated in giving aid for the immigration of large numbers of Mennonites from Russia and for their resettlement on the western plains of Canada and the United States.

In 1882 Funk organized a mutual fire and storm association, the Mutual Aid Plan.[44] In announcing the aid plan in the *Herald of Truth*, Funk had recognized the traditional, informal way of meeting this need, but said that sometimes it no longer functioned adequately. Mutual aid in case of fire was practiced informally in Franconia Conference, and they firmly resisted formalizing such aid. At the May 3, 1883, conference in Franconia, "thanks were received for the contributions collected for the loss suffered by Henry Clemmer of the Swamp congregation, when his barn burned."[45]

From the records of the October conference, 1883, we have the following statement:

> 4th—Concerning loss by fire, congregations are to make collections and when the first collections are insufficient another collection is to be made, etc., until sufficient money is raised.

The matter was dealt with again on October 1, 1885.

> 2nd—A request for permission to form a fire insurance organization was not allowed. The brothers out of love should take care of this between themselves.[46]

In October of 1930 the matter was again referred to, but it was not until May-2, 1935, that official action was taken reversing the former decision.[47]

In 1882 Funk and others organized the Evangelizing Fund, which later developed into the Mennonite Board of Missions and Charities. The Mennonite Home Mission opened in Chicago in 1893, and Funk presided at the ordinations of the first foreign missionaries in the Mennonite Church in 1898.

In 1894 a group of laymen and ministers sponsored the opening of a Mennonite secondary school at Elkhart, Indiana. The school, known as Elkhart Institute, operated independently for one year, then became incorporated. John S. Coffman gave the dedicatory address in 1896. The keynote of his speech was "progress."[48] He spoke of progress in the Garden of Eden and progress as an integral part of each successive development in the history of Christianity. In his speech Coffman attempted to combine contemporary thinking (i.e., progress) with traditional Anabaptist-Mennonite values such as humility and nonresistance.

The institute was moved to Goshen, Indiana, in 1903, where it became known as Goshen College. In 1906 it was turned over to a newly organized church agency, the Mennonite Board of Education.

In 1898 the Mennonite General Conference was formed, an advisory

---

[41] Bender, "New Life," p. 181.

[42] A. B. Kolb, "Sunday School and Church Workers," *The Herald of Truth* (March 1898):65.

[43] For a brief discussion of the life and contribution of Funk, see A. C. Kolb, "John F. Funk, An Appreciation," *MQR* 6 (July 1921):144-156 and (October 1932):250-263. For a popular biography see Helen Kolb Gates, et al., *Bless the Lord, O My Soul* (Scottdale, Pa.: Herald Press, 1964).

[44] Harold S. Bender, "Mennonite Mutual Aid Plan," *ME*, s.v.

[45] *Memorandum Book of Reverend Jacob B. Mensch and Proceedings of the Franconia Conference*, tr. by Raymond E. Hollenbach, 1972. Unpublished, EPMHL.

[46] Ibid.

[47] Minutes of Franconia Conference 1907-49. Recorded by Jacob C. Clemens, Secretary. Unpublished. EPMHL.

[48] For the full text of Coffman's speech see M. S. Steiner, *John S. Coffman, Mennonite Evangelist* (Spring Grove, Pa.: Mennonite Book and Tract Society, 1903), pp. 112-130.

body with representation from all but four of the oldest conferences in the Mennonite Church (Lancaster, Franconia, Washington-Franklin, and Ontario Amish Mennonite). When the matter came up for discussion in Franconia Conference in 1894 the vote against joining General Conference was unanimous except for one vote.[49]

Centralization of church government in a denominational organization threatened certain charter values. The concept of church government, and of what the essence of the church consists, differs fundamentally in the charter from Catholic or Protestant concepts. In the Schleitheim Articles the congregation *(Gemeinde)* is the church. Church order and hierarchy are repudiated. Church government is centered in the local congregation with the rule of Christ as expressed in Matthew 18 and obedient faith as the foundations of church organization. The emphasis on the congregation was tempered by assemblies designed to further unity and understanding through mutual discussion and sharing.[50]

Church government according to Matthew 18 necessitates face-to-face relationships, and that each situation be decided on its own merits. The crucial importance of flexibility in applying the rule of Christ has been well stated by a contemporary scholar: "The community's hermeneutic authority is binding, for that time and place; at the same time it remains permanently open to review if the same process of admonition again be initiated when another brother claims a new light or reports a new offense."[51]

Mutual counsel according to Matthew 18 was the first of the articles of the Brotherly Union to fall into disuse. Institutional structures mitigated its workability. Perhaps even more important, those leading in the direction of rational thought were adhering to the Dordrecht Confession, the official creedal statement of the American Mennonite Church. Dordrecht, unlike the Brotherly Union, makes no mention of Matthew 18 as a model for discipline. Franconia continued to refer to Matthew 18 as a guide for discipline, but once the carrying out of discipline was formally assigned to the deacon, Matthew 18 was greatly weakened.

The early leaders in institutionalization. John F. Funk. Menno S. Steiner (1866-1911), and John S. Coffman (1848-1899), were forward-looking men. By the turn of the century Funk was becoming aged, and both Steiner and Coffman died in mid-career. The next generation of leaders, among whom Daniel Kauffman (1865-1944) and George R. Brunk I (1871-1938) were particularly prominent, were conservative innovators. Kauffman spoke of "aggressive conservatism." Under his leadership various church agencies were consolidated to form a board of education, a board of publication, and a board of missions. Franconia did not become a member conference of these agencies.[52]

Gradually, organized activities in Franconia Conference increased. By 1878 Sunday schools were common. Following the turn of the century there was an increase in the activities sponsored by the local congregation. A few congregations organized young people's meetings. The first sewing circle was organized in the Doylestown congregation in 1908. Bible instruction meetings were allowed after 1912. After 1920 occasional Bible study classes were held.

The Franconia Mission Board was organized in 1917 and subsequently sponsored numerous local mission stations. A committee was appointed at the October 11, 1914, session of the conference to look into the construction of an old people's home, which began operation at Souderton in 1917. Plans for the development of the home encountered substantial opposition. Many felt it was wrong to put elderly people in a home, arguing that they should be cared for within the family.

There was no formal participation by Franconia Conference in benevolent or reform societies. Benevolent *acts* were performed, no doubt with considerable frequency and consistency. We will cite three examples of ways in which this concern went out to people surrounding the brotherhood community. The first is an account of preacher Jacob Mensch's response to a need:

> Known as the "friend of the tramp" because he has fed and sheltered them for years—as many as 300 of them in twelve months—Rev. Jacob B. Mensch, a plain Mennonite preacher-farmer has won for himself a warm place in the hearts and affections of the friendless and homeless wanderers who came his way.
>
> Down in Skippack Township, Montgomery County, Rev. Mensch has lived for over 40 years, and in all that time he has dispensed hospitality in his own quiet and original way. It is original because he fitted up a tenement directly opposite of his own large farm-house, into which he put beds for the tramps. After giving them suppers he would shelter

---

[49] Mensch records: "The matter was also brought up about having a general conference and on a rising vote every one stood up against this except [Deacon] Joseph Allebach of Rockhill." *Memorandum Book*, EPMHL.

[50] See Paul Peachey, "Anabaptism and Church Organization," *MQR* 30 (July 1956):213-228. See also Franklin Littell, *The Origins of Sectarian Protestantism* (New York: Macmillan, 1964).

[51] John H. Yoder, "The Hermeneutics of the Anabaptists," *MQR* 41 (October 1967):305.

[52] For a treatment of this era see Theron F. Schlabach, *Gospel Versus Gospel* (Scottdale, Pa.: Herald Press, 1980), especially chapter 3, "The Urge to Make Institutions," pp. 83-108. See also his article, "The Humble Become 'Aggressive Workers': Mennonites Organize for Mission, 1880-1910," *MQR* (April 1978):113-126; and Robert S. Kreider, "Discerning the Times," in *Kingdom, Cross, and Community*, ed. by John Richard Burkholder and Calvin Redekop (Scottdale, Pa.: Herald Press, 1976).

them and then give them their breakfasts; but in no instance would accept their labor for his hospitality.

But one night several of the ungrateful hoboes stole the beds and departed with them, and then Rev. Mr. Mensch hit on the plan of putting iron bars at the windows and locking the door securely so that his guests could not skiddoo at night, even if they had a mind to.[53]

Another illustration comes to us from the "Autobiographical Notes" of Jacob C. Clemens. Clemens records the incident as an example of the exigencies caused by the flu, but it also speaks to our point.

> At one time our neighbors had one son, Carl. He got influenza. At midnight the father came to our place to call for a doctor. Every doctor was out except old Dr. Moyer. He would come in the morning. All the others were out on account of this epidemic. But Carl died. They were Catholic people and the day before the burial the grave was not dug. They could not be dug fast enough. The father took the shovel and walked down to the cemetery to dig the grave. The neighbors told him not to do that and dug the grave for him. When the funeral was that day the priest would not come out. They were poor people, and asked me to come to the house and pray for Carl.[54]

Franconia Conference cemeteries frequently include the graves of persons who were not members of Mennonite churches. These are said to be graves of poor who could not afford a lot in any cemetery, and whom the Mennonites were willing to bury.

John E. Lapp tells of another kind of aid:

> There was always a concern for the poor members or neighbors who were not Mennonite. I will long remember the two occasions when the late bishop Jonas Mininger baptized persons who lived in Lansdale. One elderly couple were baptized in their home and Mininger reported this to the congregation on the next Sunday morning. He also informed the congregation that they would become responsible to keep these two persons who wanted to move into the Eastern Mennonite Home in Souderton. The congregation payed for the keep of these two as long as they lived. On another occasion bishop Mininger baptized a Mother and a daughter who were also needy people. These two also moved to Eastern Mennonite home and the congregation supported them as well. For the daughter it continued for many years, but the congregation cheerfully did this.[55]

Franconia Conference was curiously selective in its acceptance and rejection of institutional innovations. Sunday schools were accepted, and the Mennonite immigration from Russia was given strong financial assistance. Franconia accepted the *Herald of Truth* and gave encouragement to its publication. Abraham Blosser's letter reports that he was told that it was this Eastern conference that had in fact authorized the publication of the *Herald of Truth* as the official church paper. We do not have Mensch's reply, and know of no documentary evidence to support this rumor, but it does suggest that Franconia's support of the paper was well known. In contrast, Franconia rejected all organizations which appeared to take responsibility from the local congregation and the local conference. They were perhaps in part simply resisting changes in the familiar and customary structures, but this resistance was also related to key values as expressed in the charter. "The problem with institutional structures," one scholar has noted, "is that they tend to channel, limit, hinder, truncate, harden, and routinize human relationships in many ways contrary to the intent of the gospel."[56]

Institutionalization and individualism were two dangers threatening the full development of fellowship and brotherhood at mid-century.[57] Institutionalization, far more than accommodation to Pietism or Revivalism, directed Mennonitism toward mainstream American Christianity. Perhaps that is why those same leaders who furthered institutionalization in the early decades of the twentieth century also promoted the codifying of behavioral patterns. Daniel Kauffman, in his booklet entitled *The Mennonite Church and Current Issues*, outlined measures for maintaining the purity and standards of the Mennonite Church: first, there needed to be a definition of Mennonite standards, then proper organization to maintain them. This included pastoral oversight, home training, proper discipline, and proper indoctrination. Aggressive evangelism, freedom from entangling alliances, a spirit of loyalty, and progress were also concomitants. Kauffman found it reassuring that during the preceding century there had been "remarkable growth in effective organization and aggressive Christian work."[58]

The organization of boards and committees to carry on the work of the church continued to expand in the twenties, thirties, and forties. Each committee and organization tended to be formed to make possible cooperative ef-

---

[53] *The Pennsylvania-German*, vol. 10 (April 1909), p. 176.

[54] Sermon preached by Jacob C. Clemens on the fortieth anniversary of his ordination. Clemens Papers, EPMHL.

[55] John E. Lapp, "The Plains Mennonite Church," manuscript, to be published in the *History of Hatfield Township*.

[56] Calvin Redekop, "Institutions, Power, and the Gospel," in Burkholder, *Kingdom, Cross, and Community*, p. 142.

[57] Harold S. Bender, *These Are My People* (Scottdale, Pa.: Herald Press, 1962), p. 52.

[58] Scottdale, Pa.: Mennonite Publishing House, 1923, p. 81.

fort in meeting a specific need. The result was sometimes competition in fund raising and confusion in programming. Edward Yoder saw these developments as

> a rapid rush toward complete centralization and standardization. Machinery, consisting of committees and boards, has multiplied like a plague in Egypt, until one cannot make a slightest move without bumping into a committee. The ideal behind all this vast system of organization is control, complete and detailed control of every phase of church life and activity.[59]

The "rearrangement of the structures of General Conference"[60] was called for in 1946, and discussed more fully at a special meeting at Goshen, Indiana, February 17 and 18, 1948. Problems in the existing organization included lack of provision for inter-board or inter-committee planning, and lack of coordination in fund raising. The program planning of boards and committees was seen as too removed from the congregations. As a result of the meeting, the General Council of Mennonite General Conference was formed, a more broadly representative group bringing in representation from the Lancaster, Franconia, and Washington-Maryland conferences, as well as representatives from each of the standing boards and committees. This group met regularly to discuss and coordinate the planning of the various church programs until 1971, when an entirely new structure of organization was adopted after an extended study process.

---

[59] Edward Yoder, *Edward, Pilgrimage of a Mind*, ed. by Ida Yoder (Ohio and Pennsylvania: Ida Yoder and Virgil E. Yoder, 1985), p. 73.

[60] "Report of the General Conference Reorganization Study Committee," *Mennonite General Conference Report*, 1949, pp. 25-36. Quote from p. 25.

6
The Encounter with Fundamentalism

In the latter third of the nineteenth century an ominous gulf developed between scientific theories on the one hand and religion on the other. Most alarming to religious persons were those assumptions of evolution and biblical criticism which challenged the supernatural origin and accuracy of the Bible. Religious leaders who favored the adaptation of religious beliefs to modern thought became known as liberals or modernists. Shailer Matthews, one of their number, said that modernism was not a theory or a philosophy, but a method, "the use of scientific, historical, and social method in understanding and applying evangelical Christianity to the needs of a living people."[1] Conservatives opposed accommodation to modern thought, the most rigorous among them insisting on specific, readily identifiable creedal statements as safeguards. In time the most adamant of the conservatives became the Fundamentalists.

Development of Fundamentalism

As the debate mounted, four themes of dissension emerged: (1) the conclusions of biblical criticism in opposition to the claim of biblical inerrancy, (2) the theory of evolution over against the biblical account of creation, (3) whether Christ's millennial kingdom would unfold naturally or spiritually, and (4) patterns of leadership in relation to denominational structures. The issues had been fermenting for nearly half a century when the World's Christian Fundamentals Association was formed in 1919 making Fundamentalism a formally organized movement.

The initial formulation of the issues indicated to many Mennonites that they were Fundamentalists and by 1920 they were deeply involved in the controversy. Mennonite writer and historian John Horsch (1867-1941) authored *The Fundamental Truth Series,* published at the Fundamental Truth Depot, Scottdale, Pennsylvania. Titles in the series included "A Religious

---

[1] Shailer Matthews, *The Faith of Modernism* (New York: Macmillan, 1924), p. 24. Quoted in Willard B. Gatewood, *Controversy in the Twenties: Fundamentalism, Modernism, and Evolution* (Nashville, Tenn.: Vanderbilt University Press, 1969), p. 16.

Mennonite historian
and writer
John Horsch (1867-1941).

Revolution and Its Consequences," "The Inspiration of the Holy Scriptures," "The Social Gospel," "The Modernist View of Missions," and "What Ails Our Colleges and Seminaries?" The following year the pamphlets were combined into a book entitled *Modern Religious Liberalism*.[2] Mennonite General Conference, meeting in August of 1921, adopted a statement entitled "Christian Fundamentals."[3] The statement was initially prepared by a "Committee on the Investigation of Liberalism in the Mennonite Church," appointed by the Virginia Conference in 1918.[4] Articles concerning the controversy appeared in the denominational weekly, the *Gospel Herald*. Editor Daniel Kauffman authored "Liberalism vs. Fundamentalism." in two columns he outlined "What Fundamentalists Teach" and "What Higher Critics Teach."[5]

A major stronghold of American religious conservatism was located at the Presbyterian seminary in Princeton, New Jersey. From the time of its founding in 1812 the leaders of the seminary had based their theology and methodology firmly on an eighteenth-century conception of the use and power of reason. This "Princeton Theology" ignored both the influences of romanticism on theology, and the emotional piety of American Revivalism. "A startling confidence in the competence of human reasoning powers," one scholar has stated, "was a chief characteristic of the Princeton Theology."[6] The absolute inerrancy of the original biblical manuscripts was a foundation stone of this theology, which was supported by "proofs." The authenticity of the various biblical books was anchored to their authorship and to the historical claim of Christ's endorsement. The authority of the Church Fathers, the witness of the Spirit, and internal evidence—valued by other systems of theology—were deemphasized.[7] The structure of the Princeton Theology made it particularly vulnerable to biblical criticism, which included historical inquiry concerning texts and authorship and the cultural setting of biblical materials. Professor Charles Hodge's three-volume *Systematic Theology*, published from 1872 to 1875, was the classic formulation of the Princeton Theology. Several thousand ministerial students were directly influenced by Hodge's teaching, and many more by his writings.[8]

Not all Reformed theologians endorsed the Princeton Theology. By 1881 the issues raised by biblical criticism were being openly debated. The *Presbyterian Review* carried a symposium designed to present both liberal and conservative views. The first article, entitled "Inspiration," written by A. A. Hodge (1823-86) and Benjamin B. Warfield (1851-1921), was "one of the clearest and most balanced statements of the inerrancy of the Bible that the biblical controversy in America produced."[9] The series increased tensions between liberals and conservatives in the Presbyterian Church and in the next two decades three prominent seminary professors were subjected to heresy charges: Charles A. Briggs of Union Theological Seminary, 1891-93; Henry Preserved Smith of Lane Seminary, 1892-94; and Arthur Cushman McGiffert of Lane and Union, 1898-1900.[10]

Another group of conservative Christians began holding Bible conferences in the 1870s and some of the participants were soon sponsoring independent prophecy conferences. Prominent concerns included biblical inerrancy, evangelism, and a strong emphasis on premillennial prophecy. Focusing their attention on a literal interpretation of apocalyptic passages in the seventh chapter of the biblical book of Daniel and the twentieth chapter of

---

[2] Scottdale, Pa.: Fundamental Truth Depot, 1921. See Harold S. Bender, *Two Centuries of American Mennonite Literature* (Goshen, Ind.: Mennonite Historical Society, 1929), p. 80.

[3] L. J. Heatwole, *Mennonite Handbook of Information* (Scottdale, Pa.: Mennonite Publishing House, 1925), pp. 36-41.

[4] C. Norman Kraus, "American Mennonites and the Bible," *MQR* 41 (October 1967):318.

[5] (December 7, 1922), pp. 690-691; (January 4, 1923) pp. 770-771.

[6] Lefferts A. Loetscher, *The Broadening Church* (Philadelphia: University of Pennsylvania Press, 1954), p. 21.

[7] Ibid., p. 23.

[8] (New York, 1872-75. Reissued, Grand Rapids, Mich.: Eerdmans, 1929, 1952.) For bibliographical references to Hodge, see Nelson R. Burr, *A Critical Bibliography of Religion in America* (Princeton, N.J.: Princeton University Press, 1969), vol. 4, pp. 1001-1002.

[9] H. Shelton Smith, Robert T. Handy, and Lefferts A. Loetscher, *American Christianity*, vol. 2, 1820-1960 (New York: Charles Scribner's Sons, 1963), p. 324. For the text of the statement see pp. 325-332.

[10] Loetscher, *Broadening Church*, pp. 94, 48-74.

Revelation, they anticipated the imminent return of Christ to earth to establish a reign of peace and plenty that would last for one thousand years. This premillennial or millenarian view of the kingdom of God had ancient origins but was newly revived and reinterpreted by the Prophecy Conference Movement.[11]

Leaders of the Prophecy Conference Movement established a number of schools designed to train lay workers. Moody Bible Institute of Chicago, the first of these schools, was attended by a number of young Mennonite men near the turn of the century. These included A. D. Wenger (1867-1935), S. F. Coffman (1872-1954), Aaron Loucks (1864-1945), E. J. Berkey (1874-1945), and A. I. Yoder (1866-1932). These men were among the first members of the Old Mennonite Church in North America to receive any type of advanced, formal biblical training, and all of them became prominent leaders in the Mennonite Church.[12]

Dwight L. Moody, who was at the forefront of the Bible Conference Movement and the establishment of Bible Institutes, was also the preeminent evangelist of the Third Great Awakening. Moody's evangelistic meetings, held mostly in the cities, touched large numbers of persons. Some recent scholars, most notably George M. Marsden, have argued for a close tie between this evangelical awakening and the development of Fundamentalism.[13] Moody's theology was markedly reductionist, and may well have psychologically prepared the way for wide acceptance of five points as essential to the Christian faith.[14] The Mennonite Church, particularly in the Midwest, responded to this revival so extensively that it has been called the Great Awakening in the Mennonite Church.[15]

Three broad streams of conservative thought—the Princeton Theology, the Bible or Prophecy Conference Movement, and the Third Great Awakening—converged in the development of Fundamentalism. Mennonites who were beginning to reach out for new forms of education and expression had interacted with all three channels. Fundamentalism was initially a defense against modernism, but the codifying of beliefs to make them safe from the onslaughts of modernization resulted in a new actuality. Several events mark the development of Fundamentalism as a specific, identifiable entity.

In 1910 the General Assembly of the Presbyterian Church, in reaction to the modernist threat, adopted a doctrinal statement identifying five "essentials" of the Christian faith: "(1) the Holy Spirit so inspired the writers of Scripture 'as to keep them from error'; (2) 'our Lord Jesus Christ was born of the Virgin Mary'; (3) Christ offered up himself as 'a sacrifice to satisfy divine justice'; (4) 'he arose from the dead, with the same body in which he suffered'; and (5) Christ 'showed his power and love by working mighty miracles.'"[16] Reducing the essentials of Christianity to five points was distressing to many Presbyterian leaders, but the action passed, over strong dissent.

Mennonites were also concerned with this reduction of beliefs, not so much because of the content of the five points as because of their exclusiveness: not enough of the spirit and content of the Christian faith as Mennonites understood it was included. In an article on "Fundamentals and Fundamentalists," J. L. Stauffer defines Fundamentalism, prints the confession of faith of the World's Christian Fundamentals Association, then concludes by saying: "There are many commandments and teachings of the Word of God that need emphasis besides the nine that are included in the confession of faith in the World's Christian Fundamentals Association."[17] J. C. Clemens went further, asserting, "There are no non-essentials in religion."[18]

Another milepost in the development of Fundamentalism was passed when a series of books called *The Fundamentals* was released between 1910 and 1915. The project was sponsored by two brothers who were wealthy California oilmen, Lyman and Milton Stewart. The pamphlets contained 64 articles designed to treat the "essentials" of the faith in such a way as to provide a defense against modernism. Authors included representatives of both the Princeton Theology and the Bible Conference Movement. Three million copies of the books were mailed to Protestant leaders in America free of charge. The production and dissemination of these volumes is considered the beginning of the Fundamentalism Movement in America by Stewart G. Cole, early historian of Fundamentalism.[19]

In 1919, at what was initially billed as a prophecy conference, the World's Christian Fundamentals Association was organized. In the fall of 1918, after the close of World War I, prophecy conferences were held in both Philadelphia and New York. Another conference was planned for Philadelphia the following year. Before the second conference convened William Bell Riley and R. A. Torrey met with several other leaders and shifted the emphasis of the upcoming conference to the fundamentals of the faith. It was at this conference, held in Philadelphia from May 25 to June 1, 1919, that the

---

[11] For an account of the Bible or Prophecy Conference Movement in relation to the development of Fundmentalism, see Ernest R. Sandeen, *The Roots of Fundamentalism* (Chicago: The University of Chicago Press), 1970.

[12] J. C. Wenger, "Chiliasm," *ME*, s.v.

[13] *Fundamentalism and American Culture* (New York: Oxford University Press, 1980).

[14] For a discussion of Moody's revival theology see William G. McLoughlin, Jr., *Modern Revivalism* (New York: The Roland Press Company, 1959), p. 246f.

[15] J. C. Wenger, *The Mennonite Church in North America* (Scottdale, Pa.: Herald Press, 1966), especially pp. 144-208.

[16] Loetscher, *Broadening Church*, p. 98.

[17] "Fundamentals and Fundamentalists," *Sword and Trumpet* (April 1933):17.

[18] "Obedience," *Christian Doctrine* (January 15, 1931), p. 903.

[19] The History of Fundamentalism (Connecticut: Greenwood Press, 1971; original edition, 1931).

World's Christian Fundamentals Association was organized. With the formation of this association Fundamentalism became a formally structured movement crossing denominational boundaries.[20]

As a reaction to modernism, Fundamentalism became both a defensive and a combative movement. A struggle for control between liberals and conservatives created severe stresses in a number of denominations between 1920 and 1930. By 1924 the disputes were making national headlines. Adamant conservatives were resorting to rallies and circular letters to promote their cause. The five-point statement was widely heralded in 1924, "in religious weeklies, pamphlets, sermons, and addresses at conferences and public meetings."[21]

Alarm among the masses mounted as public schools began to teach evolution in their science curriculums. The conflict over this teaching climaxed in the Scopes trial at Dayton, Tennessee, in July 1925. There, a young science teacher, John Scopes, deliberately disregarded a law proscribing the teaching of evolution in high school classrooms. His case was argued by Clarence Darrow, a New York lawyer. William Jennings Bryan (1860-1925), prominent politician and Presbyterian churchman, served as chief witness for the prosecution. The highly publicized trial was ultimately rejected by the Tennessee Supreme Court on the basis of a technicality,[22] but it deepened the chasm between those who believed in a literal biblicism and the adherents of modern thought.

Although Charles Darwin was an Englishman, Darwinism and biblical criticism were both identified as German heresies by Fundamentalists following World War I, and the issues of the controversy became linked to patriotism. Communism, too, with its beginning triumphs in Russia, was associated with modernism. Karl Marx's *Communist Manifesto* had called for the dissolution of both religion and the family, and Christians were understandably concerned. Even John Horsch's *Modern Religious Liberalism* included a chapter on communism.

Fundamentalists believed that only they spoke for genuine Protestant faith, and called for a new reorganization of Protestantism.[23] They sought to ferret out liberals from church colleges, mission fields, institutions and pulpits. Fundamentalists saw themselves as the rightful proponents of Christianity, and modernists as errant deviants whose religion was not Christianity. This attitude found expression in the Mennonite Church as well, sometimes with a forcefulness that was shocking. In a 1922 article in the *Gospel Herald* John H. Mosemann responded to Harry Emerson Fosdick's pamphlet, "A New Knowledge of the Christian Faith." Mosemann, entitling his article "Shall the Liberals Be Driven Out of the Evangelical Churches?" asserted:

The Christian Church today should be as "intolerant" to these false friends as Elijah was to the false prophets of Baal when he slew them and exterminated them among the children of Israel.[24]

Pressures from sections of the Mennonite constituency, under strong conservative leadership, resulted in charges of liberalism against students and faculty at Goshen College and caused it to be closed for the 1923-24 school year. Daniel Kauffman's *Mennonite Church and Current Issues* includes an apology for the temporary closing of the college.[25] Kauffman says he had been opposed to the closing of the college, and that the board was unanimous in its desire to continue the college without interruption. In the meantime two additional Mennonite colleges had been established by persons with strong Fundamentalist leanings: Hesston College and Bible School in Kansas in 1909, and Eastern Mennonite College in Virginia in 1917. The Mennonite Board of Missions and Charities, too, was harassed by Fundamentalist critics attempting to gain support at the conference level.[26]

In 1925 the Mennonite Publishing House issued the *Mennonite Handbook of Information* written by L. J. Heatwole. Chapter five was entitled "How Mennonites Are Confronting the Menace of Modernism." Heatwole claimed that for 20 or more years it was evident that certain educational leaders in the Mennonite Church "had imbibed the idea that our doctrinal creed and methods of government were obsolete and out of date."[27] Professors at Goshen College in particular were suspected of teaching modernism, and the college was closed for one year. "Meanwhile," Heatwole continues,

> the fundamentals of the Christian faith and the dangers from modern liberalism were ably discussed in our church papers, in bible conferences, from the pulpit, and in a number of books written on these

---

[20] Sandeen, *Roots*, pp. 243-47.

[21] Robert Hastings Nichols, "Fundamentalism in the Presbyterian Church," *Journal of Religion*, vol. 5, no. 1 (January 1925), p. 28.

[22] Sydney E. Ahlstrom, *A Religious History of the American People* (New Haven: Yale University Press, 1972), p. 909.

[23] Robert T. Handy, "Fundamentalism and Modernism in Perspective," *Religion in Life* 24 (Summer 1955):381-394.

[24] (September 7, 1922), p. 435.

[25] (Scottdale, Pa.: Mennonite Publishing House, 1923). A 1931 *Sword and Trumpet* editorial by George R. Brunk entitled "Virginia Conference Vigilance" claims "the front of the fight against the covert disloyalty which sank the old Goshen was carried on from the Virginia district in connection with others." vol. 3, no. 4 (October 1931): 5.

[26] See Theron F. Schlabach, *Gospel Versus Gospel* (Scottdale, Pa.: Herald Press, 1980), pp. 127-147. See also a letter from John H. Mosemann to J. C. Clemens, January 18, 1929. Clemens papers, EPMHL.

[27] *Mennonite Handbook*, p. 35.

subjects. Among these publications may be named such books as "Fallacies of Evolution," by J. D. Charles; "The Conservative Viewpoint" and "The Mennonite Church and Modernism" by John Horsch. These books were put in circulation throughout the Church.[28]

The furor in the Mennonite Church may have been greater than the danger, for in responding to a critique of his book, *The Mennonite Church and Modernism*, Horsch wrote:

> The Modernists among us are a very small minority. The serious question confronting us is, shall a few men be permitted to slowly but surely revolutionize the doctrinal position of the Mennonites of North America?[29]

A crucial turn of events in the development of Fundamentalism occurred as distance developed between moderate conservatives and extreme Fundamentalists in two major denominations. The election of Charles Eerdman as moderator of the General Assembly of the Presbyterian Church in 1925 marked a defeat for the extreme conservatives, for although he termed himself a Fundamentalist he said he also stood for "Christian spirit and constitutional procedure."[30] In terms of the situation, this meant that he placed the voice and structure of the denomination above personal views. Similar struggles were occurring in a number of other denominations. The congregationalism of the Baptist Church prevented the controversy in that denomination from taking the doctrinal and institutional forms which it took in the Presbyterian Church. A number of strong, independent Fundamentalist leaders cooperated briefly in the formation of the Baptist Bible Union, initially a structure within the denomination. Differing from each other as well as from the church at large, their period of cooperation was short-lived, as was the Union.

The breach between moderate conservatives and adamant Fundamentalists was of major significance in the Presbyterian Church. In 1925 Dr. J. Ross Stevenson, president of Princeton Seminary, requested the assistance of the General Assembly in resolving tensions at the school. When the Assembly report and recommendations were accepted in 1929, four of the most conservative faculty members withdrew from the seminary. Led by J. Gresham Machen and Robert Dick Wilson, they immediately founded Westminster Seminary in nearby Philadelphia. Even more problematic for the denomination than the new seminary was the independent mission board which the same group promptly organized. Dissension ensued, climaxing in 1935 when Machen and the majority of his faculty "threatened to resign unless the trustees would formally endorse the aggressive type of ecclesiastical policy exemplified by the Independent Board.[31] One faculty member and 13 board members resigned rather than comply with the demand. When Machen and his followers were subsequently censored at the next General Assembly held in 1936, they organized an independent body called the Presbyterian Church of America. The following year a division occurred in the newly organized group, resulting in the formation of yet another denomination, the Bible Presbyterian Synod.

When their effort to gain control of denominational structures failed on a national scale, many Fundamentalists withdrew from their communions to form Independent Bible Churches. The Bible Institutes, which were a direct outgrowth of the Prophecy Conference Movement and millenarianism, served as a keystone in the development of Fundamentalism by giving it an institutional base that was not dependent upon denominational structures. The Bible Institutes frequently published a periodical, sponsored a radio station, and kept in close touch with alumni and their families. In so doing they provided a religious community for leadership, alumni, and supporters that was not dependent upon denominational affiliation.

Fundamentalism became a religious stance that both crossed and existed independently of denominational boundaries, based on the doctrine of biblical inerrancy and strict adherence to "essential" beliefs, combined with a spirit of attacking verbally one and all opponents. It was fostered by Bible Institutes, printed media, and radio and television programs. But not all Fundamentalists endorsed the same set of essentials. The nine points adopted by the World's Christian Fundamentals Association included a pronouncement on the premillennial return of Christ, a position not included in the 1910 five-point statement of the Presbyterian General Assembly.[32] Aggressive and independent leadership, that considered doctrinal positions more important than denominational loyalties, characterized Fundamentalism.[33] Militarism, and a strong, exclusive nationalism were also frequent concomitants.

In time many Mennonites recognized that they were not comfortable with Fundamentalism, even though adaptations of emphases had been made in that direction. The possibility of a third way, a biblical understanding that was neither Fundamentalist nor modernist, had earlier not seemed a viable

---

[28] Ibid., pp. 35-36.

[29] *Is the Mennonite Church Free from Modernism?* (Scottdale, Pa.: N.P., 1926), p. 27.

[30] Loetscher, *Broadening Church*, p. 154.

[31] Ibid., pp. 135, 136. Machen joined the Philadelphia Fundamentalist Association, but was expelled for not being a premillennialist.

[32] Sandeen, *Roots*, p. 243.

[33] C. Allyn Russel, *Voices of American Fundamentalism* (Philadelphia: The Westminster Press, 1976).

option to the most active leaders of the Mennonite Church. In 1924 Daniel Kauffman strongly rejected such an alternative, but by 1937 he hedged, writing: "The Mennonite Church is firmly committed to the Fundamentalist faith; including some unpopular tenets of faith which many so-called Fundamentalists reject." John L. Stauffer, in a perceptive article for the conservative *Sword and Trumpet*, outlined points of agreement and disagreement between Mennonites and Fundamentalists. In 1955 Harold S. Bender, dean at Mennonite Biblical Seminary, wrote: "Fundamentalism is currently the greatest danger confronting the Mennonite Church."[34]

A few Mennonite leaders quickly perceived that the theologies of both liberalism and Fundamentalism were foreign to their understandings. J. C. Clemens of the Franconia Conference was one such leader. According to a contemporary bishop, Clemens "preached against both liberalism and Fundamentalism, against both Harry Emerson Fosdick and Donald Grey Barnhouse."[35] The two most obvious differences between Mennonites and Fundamentalists concerned readily identifiable charter values: separation from the world, and the sword. Virtually all Mennonite leaders recognized that nonresistance stood juxtaposed to the militarism of the Fundamentalists. Mennonite nonparticipation in government did not mesh with a strong nationalism. Other differences also became apparent: the eastern Pennsylvania churches were still eschewing aggressive leadership styles, emphasizing rather a humble, servant model. The millenarian views of the Bible Conference Movement were adopted by many Mennonites, but Franconia Conference stood firm in officially resisting all premillennialism.

By the mid-thirties Mennonites began to realize that they understood the Bible differently than did Fundamentalists. The initial discussion concerning the Bible needed to be rephrased: the problem was not simply biblical criticism versus inerrancy; it concerned biblical interpretation as well.

Concerning Biblical Interpretation

Fundamentalists assert that they are the faithful bearers of historic Protestantism, basing their beliefs directly on the Bible, which is the Word of God. Mennonites, too, base their beliefs on the Bible, as did the Anabaptists. Yet on a number of issues, the most obvious of which is nonresistance, Mennonites understand the Bible quite differently from Fundamentalists. The divergences go all the way back to the Reformation. They continue through the development of scholastic theology and the endorsement of a rigid scholasticism by Fundamentalists, climaxing in the fundamentally variant interpretations of dispensational-premillennialism and the Scofield Reference Bible. It is one of the ironies of history that several core Anabaptist-Mennonite hermeneutical understandings were rather closely echoed in modernism: a historical approach to the Bible, appropriating the example of Jesus' life as well as his death, and an understanding of the kingdom of God as existing within the believing community.

American Mennonite leaders began discussing biblical inspiration and interpretation when scholarly study of the Bible engulfed many churches in controversy early in the twentieth century. Editor Daniel Kauffman formulated a series of questions for the *Gospel Herald* in 1919: "What have you to say to the statement: 'The Bible *contains* the Word of God, but the language is the language of men?'" "Does it affect our salvation not to believe in the entire Bible as being inspired and infallible?"[36] These two lead questions indicate that issues being discussed in American Protestant churches were also considered pertinent for Mennonites. Articles on biblical interpretation appeared frequently in the *Gospel Herald*. Two articles entitled "Methods in Bible Study" by I. R. Detweiler were published in December 1920.[37]

By 1922 roughly half of the articles on biblical topics appearing in the *Herald* were from non-Mennonite sources. American Mennonites had not yet systematically examined their own biblical hermeneutics, and Anabaptist research was in its initial stages. Those Mennonites who had received some biblical training, with several exceptions, had attended either Bible Institutes or Princeton Seminary, both strongholds of developing Fundamentalism. The defense against modernism subsequently tended to follow two alignments in the Mennonite Church: Bible school premillennialism, or the conservative orthodoxy of Princeton, and later Westminster seminaries.[38]

A number of attempts to state a Mennonite doctrine of Scripture were made following 1908. These efforts climaxed in a statement on *Christian Fundamentals* adopted by General Conference on August 25, 1921. The first article, "Of the Word of God," closely echoes Fundamentalist terminology (with the exception of the last phrase, which represents more traditional Mennonite understandings):

---

[34] Stauffer, "Modernism vs Fundamentalism," *Gospel Herald* (May 7, 1924); Kauffman, *Mennonite Cyclopedic Dictionary* (Scottdale, Pa.: Mennonite Publishing House, 1937), p. 116; "Fundamentals," pp. 16-20; and Bender, "Outsider Influences on Mennonite Thought," *Mennonite Life* 10 (January 1955):48. Kauffman and Stauffer sometimes distinguished a fundamentalist faith from a Fundamentalist one.

[35] John E. Lapp, Memorial Sermon, Jacob Cassel Clemens, May 18, 1965. Clemens Papers.

[36] Clemens Papers, 1919.

[37] (December 9, 1920), pp. 739, 740; (December 16, 1920), pp. 754, 755.

[38] For leaders who attended Moody Bible Institute, see above, p. 204. Harold S. Bender, dean of Goshen College, and Chester K. Lehman, dean of Eastern Mennonite College, attended Princeton Seminary. Exceptions were J. E. Hartzler, P. E. Whitmer, and N. E. Byers, who attneded either Chicago or Union. I. R. Detweiler received a B.D. from Garrett Biblical Institute and attended the University of Chicago a number of summers.

We believe in the plenary and verbal inspiration of the Bible as the Word of God; that it is authentic in its matter, authoritative in its counsels, inerrant in the original writings, and the only infallible rule of faith and practice.[39]

C. Norman Kraus has proposed that this statement represented a departure from Mennonite understandings of Scripture as expressed in earlier confessions.[40] The statement, first adopted by the Virginia Conference in 1919, was written by J. B. Smith, assisted by George R. Brunk, Sr., and A. D. Wenger.

The Mennonites of eastern Pennsylvania were somewhat insulated from the early accommodation to Fundamentalism. Conference leaders had attended neither seminaries nor Bible schools and they did not participate in Mennonite General Conference. John E. Lapp (1905-), ordained as minister in the Plains congregation in 1933 and bishop in 1937, outlined the characteristics of Franconia Conference biblical understandings before 1940 to a small gathering in 1974. He said that the church believed in the authority of the Bible, citing the reference in 2 Timothy 3:16. They knew how to read the Bible, he said, coming to the Word to hear God speak and reveal himself, and with a heart willing to obey the truth they heard. They came for personal searching. They knew the New Testament was the final authority. They read the Gospels and epistles for literal application to their daily lives (John 20:31). They believed the apocalypse was written in language that is highly symbolic, and looked to the Gospels and epistles for an understanding of the apocalypse. Lapp said that the increasing use of the radio, which had been discouraged in the thirties by Franconia Conference leadership, brought new questions to the people. From these concerns he named eternal security, the millennial myth (his phrase), and questions concerning loyalty to state and government.[41]

Significant research into the hermeneutics of the Anabaptists has been done in recent years, and the General Assembly of the Mennonite Church adopted a statement on biblical interpretation in 1977. This makes it now possible to delineate key ways in which the biblical interpretation of Mennonites differs from the biblicism of Fundamentalists. Four contrasts will be demonstrated in the following pages: (1) Scripture as the account of God's interaction with his people rather than Scripture as the basis for dogma, (2) an emphasis on obedience rather than inerrancy, (3) the precedence of the New Testament over the Old, and (4) literal interpretation of New Testament ethical directives and symbolic reading of apocalyptic passages. Changes in biblical hermeneutics as Mennonites interacted with Fundamentalism will also be noted.

History versus Dogma

Anabaptists and Mennonites read the Bible as the account of God's interaction with his people. "The Anabaptists seem to have been the only Protestants in the sixteenth century," one scholar observes, "who took a historical view of the Bible." They perceived the drama of God's redemption as a process, initiated by God in particular with Abraham, and moving forward to a climax in Jesus Christ. Jesus Christ was considered the most complete and final revelation of God to man: all else was measured against this standard.[42]

This theme was commonly reiterated in the sermons of American Mennonites. A written example has been preserved from 1782.[43] It begins with an account of God's interaction with mankind in creation, the temptation of Adam and Eve, and the breaking of God's commandment. It relates how God confronted man with his disobedience, the man's defense, and both the punishment and the promise given to Adam and Eve. The rivalry of Cain and Abel, the fiasco of the tower of Babel, and the destruction of Sodom and Gomorrah are all recounted as showing how God deals with man. The sermon goes on to the story of Joseph and the children of Israel, to the Exodus, and to the development of the kingdom under David and Solomon. The writer notes the unfaithfulness of the children of Israel, then draws his contemporary parallel:

> Likewise, I believe that the present back-slidden Christians are to be likened to those back-slidden children of God.... Because most people adhere to the New Testament and are baptized upon it, namely, upon the name of Jesus Christ, accepting the seal of obedience and of following Jesus, and confess themselves to be under his cross and suffering to build up a church for him, yet still live heathen lives, I call them back-slidden Christians or antichrists.[44]

The author then describes the true Christian:

> True Christians seek to walk in the path and bear the easy yoke of their Jesus, which is love, joy, peace, patience, chastity, gentleness, goodness, faith, meekness, being compassionate, patient in tribulation,

---

[39] Heatwole, *Mennonite Handbook,* pp. 36-37.
[40] Kraus, "American Mennonites and the Bible."
[41] *Gemeinschaft II,* Salford Mennonite Church, June 15, 1974.
[42] Walter Klaassen, "The Berne Debate of 1538: Christ the Center of Scripture," *MQR* 40 (April 1966):152-153.
[43] "A Mennonite Sermon of 1782," *MHB* 37 (July 1976):3-4.
[44] Ibid., p. 4.

not vengeful, not proud, but lowly, meek, not seeking wealth and honor or high office, but committing themselves to their Creator and putting themselves under the banner of their Jesus.[45]

Mennonites in the nineteenth century continued to take a historical view of the Bible. Abraham Godshalk, minister in the Doylestown Church, wrote concerning the issue in 1838.[46] He, too, begins by recounting God's dealings with man in the Old Testament and leading up to the New. Godshalk takes a historic view, not only of the content of Scripture, but of the processes by which it was recorded. Godshalk says God chose the agency of man to enlighten man. He is aware that this may not be received too well, adding, "Someone will perhaps say, I thank God we have something more permanent to depend on than man, or the agency of man. We have the written word of God, and therefore need not depend on man." Godshalk acknowledges that the Word is a precious treasure and a great source of light, "the foundation of all our spiritual light, and of all our hopes of a blessed immortality." This, however, does not undermine his deeper point:

> But how were the holy scriptures given? Most certainly not without the agency of man. The law was first given unto Moses and then through him to the children of Israel. The prophets of the Lord [were] inspired with what they should prophecy [sic], and thus they spoke as they were moved by the Holy Ghost. Jesus Christ preached in the presence of his disciples, but wrote no book. His disciples afterwards wrote down the most important part of what was said and done. Luke put on record the most important part of the apostle's doings, including some of their preaching. The apostles wrote epistles to the churches, and unto individuals. John the apostle, had a revelation in the island of Patmus [sic], and put it on record by the divine command. Here thou seest that the Holy Scriptures were given by the instrumentality of man; but thou wilt perhaps say they were very pious and godly men, who had the glory of God and the salvation of man at heart. So I believe, too, but had we lived in their days, that would we have thought of them?[47]

The story of God's interaction with his people was seen as instructive by Mennonites, showing them God's patience and love and man's repeated waywardness. Only by God's sending Jesus Christ into the world could man be redeemed and receive the power to live a new life.

Faith had been identified by Luther as the central aspect of man's salvation. Lutheran scholastic theology already in the sixteenth century saw the Bible as the basis for dogma, for the systematic and rational clarification of faith. Faith tended to become a matter of affirming certain correct beliefs. When faith became assent to correct doctrine it became more important than ever to have an infallible source of dogma, or doctrine. The infallibility of the Scriptures, and a trained theological expert to interpret them, very early became important in both the Reformed and the Lutheran theological traditions. In the early twentieth century, when scholarly historical study of the Bible threatened to undermine both the infallibility of the Bible and the certainty of doctrine, Fundamentalists, basing their position on scholastic Protestantism, countered by defining truth as dogma, insisting that certain doctrines were basic to Christianity.[48]

An emphasis on correct or "sound" doctrine developed in the American Mennonite Church following the turn of the century, paralleling increased Mennonite interaction with Fundamentalism. This developing stress on doctrine appears to have been both a response to Fundamentalist influences and a defense against some of the content of Fundamentalism. Prior to the appearance of *A Manual of Bible Doctrines*, written by Daniel Kauffman and published in 1898 at the Mennonite Publishing Company, the word "doctrine" does not appear in the title of any Mennonite publication. *A Manual of Bible Doctrines* was followed in 1908 with *Bible Doctrines Briefly Stated*, again by Kauffman, and *One Thousand Questions and Answers on Points of Christian Doctrine*. In 1914 he edited *Bible Doctrine*, a 701-page book compiled by a committee appointed by Mennonite General Conference. In 1923 J. R. Shank edited *Twenty-Six Studies in Christian Doctrine*, sponsored "by a committee appointed by the Eastern Amish Mennonite Conference, in co-operation with the General Sunday School Committee of the Mennonite Church." Daniel Kauffman, "assisted by a committee of twenty-one brethren," edited a new book on Bible doctrine published in 1928 and entitled *Doctrines of the Bible*. A 16-page *Christian Doctrine Supplement* was added to the *Gospel Herald* from 1925-1947. First it appeared quarterly, then bimonthly. The supplement was edited by Daniel Kauffman until 1943, then by Paul Erb, the new editor of the *Herald*, for the remaining four years that it was published.[49]

Bible conferences, popular in both the Second Great Awakening and in Fundamentalism, began to be widely held in the Mennonite Church following 1890. Bible conferences promoted doctrinal emphases. The topical method of Bible study, commonly used in these conferences, augmented the

---

[45] Ibid., p. 4.
[46] *A Description of the New Creature* (Doylestown, Pa.: William M. Large, Printed, 1838).
[47] Ibid., pp. 24-25.
[48] Kraus, "Mennonites and the Bible," pp. 310-311; John H. Yoder, "The Hermeneutics of the Anabaptists," *MQR* 41 (October 1967):291-308; Nichols, "Fundamentalism," pp. 14-36.
[49] See Bender, *Two Centuries*, pp. 59, 69, 73, 84, 89.

change in biblical hermeneutics that was occurring in the Mennonite Church. A *Herald* article noted that the topical approach to Bible study was the easiest and most popular method but also pointed out its weaknesses: a teacher may emphasize only those things which appeal to him and make it seem as though the subject is "about the whole of the Bible." The method should be used carefully, the article continues, for it is

> sometimes a misleading rather than a safe way to study the Bible. The reason why it is not always safe to use the topical method is because passages are taken out of their context and can easily be made to say something which the Bible does not teach.
>
> In order to understand the particular verses in their context it is also necessary that we give some consideration to the historical environment out of which the message has come.[50]

The author of the article, I. R. Detweiler, was born in Souderton, Pennsylvania, in the heart of Franconia Conference. A graduate of Goshen College, he later served as dean of the Bible school and was acting president of the college at the time the articles were written. The articles reflect long-standing Anabaptist-Mennonite understandings of biblical interpretation.

The eastern Pennsylvania churches were wary of Bible conferences. In spite of official objections, the first Bible conference was held at Doylestown in 1909. Although reservations continued, other conferences followed. The speakers were primarily from small, marginal settlements and were intent on preserving what they understood to be Mennonite distinctives. In the process, fundamental changes were occurring. Presentations had a rational base, following the Fundamentalist hermeneutic, rather than the relational thrust of Anabaptist tradition. These conferences subsequently became an avenue for compartmentalizing both faith and obedience and codifying them in practice, as we shall note in the next chapter.

Obedience and Inerrancy

> No one may truly know Christ, except
> one follow him in life.[51]

This motto of Hans Denk points to the centrality of obedience for the Anabaptists. Menno Simons, too, "stressed the obedient acceptance of the Bible, particularly the New Testament, as the basis of the Christian's faith, emphasizing the simple command of Christ."[52] The attitude toward obedience to New Testament commandments became a crucial difference between the

Anabaptists and the Reformers. When the Reformers compromised on the visible church and obedience to the Word, it was necessary for them to shift the locus of authority to the exact words of Scripture.

The infallibility of the inspired text was a keystone in the development of Protestant scholasticism and was assumed by much of American Protestantism until challenged by modern developments, including biblical criticism. The debate of emerging issues carried in the *Presbyterian Review* in 1881 included a classic statement of the Fundamentalist position. Because Mennonites highly valued the authority of the Bible they tended to identify with this position. Yet as it developed within Fundamentalism, it was at variance with Mennonite understandings.[53]

The Anabaptist concern was primarily for obedience rather than a preoccupation with literal words.[54] For Menno Simons

> the prerequisites of understanding are seen to lie in the attitude of the one who comes to the scriptures. Very briefly this attitude must be marked by obedience (willingness to submit to the cross), a willingness to be instructed both by the Spirit and by the brethren and a personal application in seeing the truths as they apply in everyday life.[55]

In a similar vein Hans Denk spoke of "Inner Word" and "Outer Word." He held the Bible to be "a true statement in the context of interpretation and 'reception' in which varying texts are related to one another and all are understood within a larger framework." To reinforce his point he drew up a series of scriptural statements that, read in isolation, appear contradictory, for example, "I am with you always," and "me ye have not always." His point was that to be adequately understood, Scripture required both testing within a wider context and personal appropriation.[56] This theme is echoed in American Mennonite sources. I. R. Detweiler pointed out in 1920 that in Bible study, "The first and most important element is the spirit of the student. Only as we give due recognition to God's spirit as the interpreter of his own word can we understand the meaning."[57] Although Detweiler was soon to be censored by Fundamentamentalist Mennonites in the struggle over the temporary closing of Goshen College, his words were very

---

[50] Detweiler, "Bible Study," pp. 739-740.
[51] W. F. Neff, "Hans Denk," *ME*, s.v.
[52] N. van der Zijpp, "The Early Dutch Anabaptists," *Recovery of the Anabaptist Vision*, ed. by Guy F. Hershberger (Scottdale, Pa.: Herald Press, 1957), p. 79.
[53] Kraus, "Mennonites and the Bible," especially pp. 310-312.
[54] Klaassen, "The Bern Debate," p. 153.
[55] Henry Poettcker, "Menno's Encounter with the Bible," *MQR* 40 (April 1966):115.
[56] Yoder, "Hermeneutics," pp. 298-299; Matthew 28:20; Matthew 26:11.
[57] Detweiler, "Bible Study," p. 739.

J. C. Wenger as a young scholar began speaking on biblical interpretation in the 1930s.

close in meaning to those of Hans Denk and Menno Simons, who, although they differed widely, agreed on this issue.

The gathered congregation formed a key locus for the discernment process as Anabaptists sought to understand the meaning of Scripture. Basing the practice on 1 Corinthians 14:29, they felt that the Spirit worked primarily in the midst of the believing community in helping them to understand the meaning of a given passage for their lives. The practice largely disappeared from the worship services of American Mennonites. A vestige perhaps remained in the custom of giving *Zeugnis* or testimony to the sermon. In the mid-nineteenth century, as Jacob Krehbiel noted, any member of the congregation was "given liberty" to share. By the first half of the twentieth century it was primarily the ordained brethren who were expected to respond briefly to the sermon. The hermeneutic community was de facto revived in the setting of adult Sunday school classes, and may be one reason for the exhilaration which Sunday schools initially brought to the Mennonite Church. In the 1920s and 40s, when church services in the Franconia area continued to be held only every second Sunday, informal biblical discussions were frequently the focus of Sunday afternoon visiting.[58]

We have noted that Bishop John E. Lapp said of Franconia Mennonites, c. 1940, that they "knew how to read the Bible, coming to the Word to hear God speak and reveal himself, and with a heart willing to obey the truth they heard." A number of Clemens' sermon outlines have obedience as their theme, either from a topical or historical perspective. Clemens' outlines include more than a dozen sermons on the Bible. He speaks of inspiration, preservation, translation, and the Bible as a guide for life. He speaks of the accuracy of the Bible *in the original autographs,* but does not use the term inerrancy—although he comes very close to doing so when he comments that the authors who wrote the books of the Bible were fallible as persons but their writings are infallible. A ninth-grade course for weekday Bible school in the conference outlines 30 lessons on the Bible in some detail. The outlines never mention inerrancy or infallibility, although they include reference to "other" sacred writings and to science.[59]

By the mid-thirties some of the language of inerrancy was appearing in conference publications. A brief article by J. C. Wenger entitled "What Does Your Church Stand for" appeared in the new conference mission magazine in 1937. Wenger was highly respected in the conference and his opinions were influential. He wrote:

> The Bible was written by men who were so guided by the Holy Spirit so that although the style of different authors is quite apparent, yet what they wrote is altogether free from error and is not merely the word of men; it is the very word of God and is to be received as the only infallible rule of faith and practice. All men are answerable to its demands and subject to its teaching.[60]

A few months later a series of articles by Wenger appeared in *Gospel Herald.* In them he notes Calvin's strict view of the inspiration of the Bible, and Luther's contempt for the book of James. He notes that Old Testament quotations which appear in the New are usually not verbatim. "In itself," he writes, "higher criticism was simply a branch of Biblical study, and dealt with date and authorship of the several books."[61] The views of higher critics became destructive, Wenger says, and he continues the article with a strong criticism of liberalism, then cites J. Gresham Machen and John Horsch as contenders of the faith. In a second article Wenger asks, "What of the common statement that faith is an attitude of trust toward a person and not belief in a list of concepts?" He answers: "As a matter of emphasis, the answer is 'Yes.' If it is meant absolutely the answer is, 'No.' " The New Testament faith is primarily a commitment to Christ in trust. It also includes obedience. But,

---

[58] Yoder, "Hermeneutics," pp. 300-302; "A Few Words About the Mennonites in America in 1841; A Contemporary Document by Jacob Krehbiel," tr. and ed. by Harold S. Bender, *MQR* 6 (April 1932):111; and John E. Lapp personal interview.

[59] Lapp, *Gemeinschaft II;* "Suggested High School Course for Use in Week Day Bible School. Ninth Grade Course" (no date; no author). Papers of Menno B. Souder. EPMHL. "Other" sacred writings are not specified.

[60] *Mission News,* vol. 1, no. 3 (July 1937), p. 1.

[61] *Gospel Herald* (August 5, 1937), pp. 402-403.

adds Wenger, faith also includes belief in certain propositions.[62] Persons like J. C. Wenger and J. C. Clemens tried valiantly to maintain Anabaptist-Mennonite emphases while sometimes employing terminology commonly used by Fundamentalists. It was an admixture that held some confusion for laypersons who were increasingly listening to radio preachers who spoke the same language about the Bible but in many ways preached a different gospel.

The Mennonite emphasis on obedience stood diametrically opposed to eternal security, a doctrine which came to be stressed by many Fundamentalists. In one of his sermon outlines, "Christian Assurance (not unconditionally)," Clemens quotes the prominent Fundamentalist preacher Donald Grey Barnhouse on eternal security:

> If a man is born again he is saved and safe forever. When a man is born he cannot be unborn, it is possible for such a man to commit terrible sin, but God definitely says that even in such a case he is saved, saved as by fire. Peter was saved even in the moment when he was denying Christ with oaths and cursings, had he died in that minute, he would have gone directly to heaven.[63]

Clemens carefully counters this position with three main points: (1) outstanding promises, (2) conditioned on faithfulness and watchfulness, and (3) saved people may drift and be lost. Franconia Conference twice formally stated its opposition to the teaching of eternal security.[64] Mennonites emphasized the covenantal aspect of salvation, considering willing obedience to the commandments of Christ as a necessary response to salvation. As a member of Christ's kingdom the believer is under the rule of Christ. This is a central theme in the "Brotherly Union" of 1527 and in the ceremonial practice of the Mennonites.

The Mennonite position on obedience was open to charges both of exclusiveness and legalism and such accusations were frequently made. This is the classic dilemma of groups that emphasize the Sermon on the Mount and New Testament ethical commandments.

Precedence of the New Testament

The most explicit contrast between Mennonite and Fundamentalist biblical hermeneutics concerns the relative authority given to the Old and New Testaments. Like other hermeneutical differences, this one, too, goes all the way back to the Reformation. One of the stipulations of the state clergy in the negotiations preceding a sixteenth-century debate between church authorities and Anabaptists was that the Old and New Testaments be given equal authority in the discussion.[65] The Reformers' conception of the church, its relationship to society, and the practice of infant baptism were all based on Old Testament passages. The Anabaptists accepted both Testaments; however, they held that:

> The earlier stands under the judgment of the later; the first word, the Old Testament, under the judgment of the last word, the New Testament. They agreed ... that the Old Testament was also the Word of God, but with one qualification; it is valid where Christ has not suspended it.... Any specific word in the Bible stands or falls depending upon whether it agrees with Jesus Christ or not.[66]

Menno Simons, too, stressed the obedient acceptance of the Bible, and particularly the New Testament, as the basis of the Christian's faith, emphasizing ... the simple command of Christ."[67] This granting of final authority to the New Testament was the basis for nonresistance:

> Menno was fully aware of the ethical issues which stemmed from his theological concerns. His statements about warfare and the use of the sword grew out of his position of seeing the difference between the Old and the New Testaments. Any vindictive approach to a person is ruled out because the New Testament forbids revenge, and the law of love must motivate the believer.[68]

This focus on the New Testament, and particularly the Gospels, is repeatedly demonstrated by the content of the "Brotherly Union." Article VI, which treats the Christian's participation in the magistracy and the use of the sword, is based directly on New Testament passages taken from the Gospels. "Many," they say, "who do not understand Christ's will for us will ask

> whether a Christian may or should use the sword against the wicked for the protection and defense of the good or for the sake of love.

---

[62] (August 12, 1937), p. 435. For a more recent view of Scripture by Wenger, see his book, *God's Word Written* (Scottdale, Pa.: Herald Press, 1966).

[63] Barnhouse, *Revelation* (February 1932):58. See also C. K. Lehman, "Eternal Security," *ME*, s.v.

[64] Minutes, May 5, 1932; October 5, 1939.

[65] Klaassen, "Bern Debate," pp. 148-156; see also Yoder, "Hermeneutics," and Willem Balke, *Calvin and the Anabaptist Radicals*, tr. by Wilem J. Heynen (Grand Rapids, Mich.: Ferdmans, 1981), pp. 309-327.

[66] "Bern Debate," p. 153.

[67] Zijpp, "The Early Dutch Anabaptists," p. 79.

[68] Poettcker, "Menno Simons' Encounter," pp. 120-121.

> The answer is unanimously revealed: Christ teaches and commands us to learn from Him for He is meek and lowly of heart and thus we shall find rest for our souls.[69]

Christ, they point out, models humility, not the use of physical force; and they assume that this modeling is an example for Christian conduct. The article continues:

> Second, is asked concerning the sword: whether a Christian shall pass sentence in disputes and strife about worldly matters, such as unbelievers have with one another. The answer: Christ did not wish to decide to pass judgment between brother and brother concerning inheritance, but refused to do so. So should we also do.[70]

The third question which they pose concerns whether a Christian should be a magistrate. Here they point out that Christ refused to be made a king. Followers of Christ, they say, should follow his example.

> "Whoever would come after me, let him deny himself and take up his cross and follow me." He himself forbids the violence of the sword when he says: "The Princes of this world lord it over them, etc., but among you it shall not be so."[71]

They believed that true Christians were to live together in peace, equality, commitment, and harmony. A modern scholar has argued that Mennonite nonresistance in the twentieth century lost its revolutionary character through interaction with Fundamentalist influences. These passages suggest that insofar as original Anabaptism was revolutionary it was not by intent, but because its understanding of New Testament passages contradicted dominant societal interpretations.[72] Anabaptists, like later American Mennonites, did not deny the necessity and legitimacy of government, but saw it as standing outside the perfection of Christ. In contrast, the Reformers took the Old Testament theocracy of Israel as their model and included all citizens in the church. Assuming the office of magistrate was seen by them as a high calling and the defense of one's country a moral obligation.

The continuing emphasis on the New Testament among Mennonites is indicated in early letters and sermons in America. The 1773 letter written by Pennsylvania Mennonites in response to inquiries from the Netherlands, says, "We recognize the Holy Scriptures, especially the Evangelists [Gospels], for our chief rule."[73] A Pennsylvania Mennonite sermon of 1782 again explicitly states this emphasis:

There would indeed be much more to mention from the Old Testament but because I want to make it short I will turn to the New; because the Redeemer, Jesus Christ has come, and he has brought us a New Testament—the other is now old.[74]

The 1820 edition of the Lancaster Mennonite hymnbook included an appendix which coordinates sermon texts and hymns. All of the references so cited are taken from the four Gospels, with the exception of one from Ephesians and three from the book of Acts.[75] Bishop Lapp said of his people, c. 1940, "They knew the New Testament was the final authority."

The two issues on which Mennonites generally differed from Fundamentalists, even when they otherwise identified with them, were nonresistance and separation from the world. Both are based on New Testament passages that for Mennonites took precedence over Old Testament patterns. "Will somebody please tell us," J. L. Stauffer wrote in 1933, "why these gifted Fundamentalist Bible-teachers cannot see the two most outstanding pillars of New Testament teaching, namely, nonconformity to the world and non-resistance?"[76] Nonconformity meant standing apart from the social order; nonresistance implied nonparticipation in all political and military activity.

Fundamentalists, like the Reformers, relied heavily on the Old Testament for their conceptions of nationalism and militarism. The Reformers, however, generally took a positive view of society and of the church in relation to society. Fundamentalists viewed society negatively, predicting that its evils were escalating to a catastrophic climax. Religious and social movements for the benefit of mankind were assessed with skepticism, or sometimes even hostility. These Fundamentalist views were closely associated with their understanding of end times, which were based on a literal interpretation of biblical prophecies.

Literal Interpretation

The claim that they interpret the Bible literally has been an important

---

[69] For the complete statement see "The Schleitheim Brotherly Union," *The Legacy of Michael Sattler*, tr. and ed. by John H. Yoder (Scottdale, Pa.: Herald Press, 1973), pp. 27-43.

[70] Ibid., pp. 39-40.

[71] Ibid., p. 40.

[72] Rodney Sawatsky, "The Influences of Fundamentalism on Mennonite Nonresistance 1908-1944" (M.A. thesis, University of Minnesota, 1973).

[73] "A Letter from Pennsylvania Mennonites to Mennonites in Holland," *MQR* (October 1929):230-231.

[74] "A Mennonite Sermon of 1782," *MHB* (July 1976):3-4.

[75] Martin E. Ressler, "*Ein Unpartheyisches Gesang-Buch*," *Pennsylvania Mennonite Heritage*, vol. 2, no. 4 (October 1979), pp. 13-19. See also Clarence Y. Fretz, "The Church Year?" *Gospel Herald* (December 29, 1981), pp. 960-962.

[76] Stauffer, "Fundamentals," p. 20.

emphasis of Fundamentalists. It was one of the great appeals of the movement to Mennonites. Yet careful investigation reveals that neither Fundamentalists nor Mennonites interpreted all of the Bible literally in relation to their own existential situations. Fundamentalists emphasized the Pauline Epistles and many of them insisted on a literal interpretation of all *prophetic* passages. Mennonites understood New Testament *ethical commandments* literally, paying particular attention to the Sermon on the Mount.

Mennonites were strongly influenced by the Fundamentalist emphasis on literal interpretation in two ways. First, they gave the New Testament epistles increasing emphasis. Then, unlike Fundamentalists, they applied a very literal interpretation to passages which related to ethical practice, such as those proscribing the wearing of gold for adornment and the injunction in 1 Corinthians 11 that women should have their heads veiled for worship. More will be said about this in the following chapter. Second, many Mennonites endorsed a literal interpretation of prophetic passages, which resulted in their acceptance of premillennialism.

The core idea of premillennialism is that Christ will physically return to earth and establish a political kingdom that will last for one thousand years. This kingdom will be established after the great battle of Armageddon, in which Christ and the saints will defeat the antichrist and his forces. The battle receives its name from its expected location: a valley in northern Palestine.[77] The teaching is based primarily on a literal reading of the seventh chapter of the book of Daniel and the twentieth chapter of the Revelation of John. The latter passage was early given a symbolic interpretation by Peter J. Twisk (1565-1636), elder in the Old Frisian Mennonite congregation at Hoorn, Holland. Twisk, in his booklet *The Peaceable Kingdom of Christ*,[78] understood the passage to be a spiritual description of the kingdom, which is already present in the heart of the believer, not as a prophecy to be literally fulfilled in history. Some Mennonites accommodated their views of prophecy to those of premillennialism, but others continued to hold that the Apocalypse was written in language that is highly symbolic, and looked to the Gospels and epistles for an understanding of the Apocalypse.[79]

Mennonites, from earliest times, measured all Scripture in relation to Jesus Christ.[80] In Fundamentalist hermeneutics the life and teachings of Jesus, particularly as they are expressed in the Sermon on the Mount, are generally thought to apply to a future fulfillment of the kingdom. In order to maintain both this emphasis and literal interpretation, dispensational premillennialists speak of "rightly dividing" the Word of truth. Biblical passages referring to the church, and those referring to Israel, are kept separate and distinct. The church is understood as a spiritual entity, and the appropriation of God's grace in Jesus Christ is the sufficient and necessary condition for salvation. In this system all kingdom passages refer to Israel. By this means kingdom passages can be understood literally, but do not apply to the believer in the present dispensation. The teachings of Jesus concerning the kingdom are set aside for a future Jewish political kingdom.[81] In essence, what is considered the core of biblical interpretation for Anabaptist-Mennonites is cut out and set aside.

These divergent interpretations of what is to be taken literally bode important consequences for evangelism and mission. In dispensational premillennialism Jesus Christ is significant for the church primarily as the means of grace. Grace is appropriated by assent to words of truth, or propositional truth. When grace has been received, it cannot become void or canceled. The appropriation of grace is the only, sufficient, and necessary condition for eternal salvation. In this system of thought only Jesus' birth and death have primary significance for Gentiles in the dispensation of grace. His commandments and teachings do not apply to Christians in the church. They are for the restored kingdom of Israel and the millennial reign of Christ. The missionary task of the church is to elicit conversions. This may be done through mass meetings, door-to-door evangelism, via radio and television, or by any means which makes possible the affirmation of truth. Confession of faith—more exactly, the assertion of belief—is the necessary response to Jesus Christ.

Those who understand the good news of Jesus Christ to be the gospel of the kingdom are often not comfortable with these modes of evangelism. They believe that to choose to enter the kingdom by repentance and faith in Jesus Christ, is to become a recipient of grace *and* a participant in the community of faith under the rule of Jesus Christ. "When anyone is united to Christ," the apostle Paul wrote, "there is a new world; the older order has gone, a new order has already begun."[82] Evangelization is not complete until the new believer has been drawn into the community of faith.

In modern Fundamentalism the Bible, as they understand it, is the final word. If an understanding arising from the chosen method of biblical interpretation and the message of Jesus Christ do not harmonize, the message

---

[77] See Timothy P. Weber, *Living in the Shadow of the Second Coming* (New York: Oxford University Press, 1979), pp. 13-42; and Clarence B. Bass, *Backgrounds to Dispensationalism* (Grand Rapids, Mich.: Baker Book House, 1960).

[78] Tr. from the German by John F. Funk (Elkhart, Ind.: Mennonite Publishing Company 1913).

[79] Lapp, supra.

[80] See William Klassen, "Anabaptist Hermeneutics: The Letter and the Spirit," *MQR* 40 (April 1966):83-94.

[81] Weber, *Living in the Shadow*, pp. 13-42; Bass, *Backgrounds*, pp. 37-38.

[82] 2 Corinthians 5:17, *New English Bible*.

of Jesus Christ is set aside. Walter Klaassen points to a similar Protestant pattern early in the Reformation, adding: "One is forced to the conclusion here that the clergy regarded the Bible as God's revelation rather than Christ, and all of their talk about Salvation through Christ alone was a hollow ring."[83] In contrast, Menno Simons wrote:

> All Scripture must be interpreted according to the spirit, teaching, walk, and example of Christ and the apostles.[84]

Mennonites and Millenarianism

The establishment of the kingdom of God was an active dream in America from earliest colonial times. Jonathan Edwards, the great New England theologian, anticipated a gradual unfolding and development toward perfection of society and the church until Christ himself would return to earth to claim his kingdom. In America this expectation, called *postmillennialism*, was tied in closely with belief in the manifest destiny of the nation. Second Awakening revivalists, liberals, and promoters of the social gospel generally held this view of end times. *Premillennialism*, expected social and political conditions to continuously worsen, climaxing in an apocalyptic end to the present age. Only then would Christ establish his kingdom, reigning in peace and prosperity for a thousand years. Both premillennialists and postmillennialists anticipated a material kingdom in time where the righteous would reign over others; both were strongly nationalistic.

A form of premillennialism was found in the early church. The more recent type was introduced into America about 1875. Its promoters gathered in prophecy and Bible conferences for study and discussion. Among the many conferences, the best known were the annual study and fellowship meetings held at Niagara-on-the-Lake and called the Niagara Bible Conferences.[85] The Bible Institutes, established by leaders of the movement, were highly influential in its development and perpetuation. The early Student Volunteer Movement was also to a considerable extent influenced by premillennialism. Excitement in the movement grew as adherents saw their political predictions seemingly being vindicated by the realignment of political boundaries following World War I.[86]

A phenomenal, popular resurgence of millenarianism occurred in the last third of the twentieth century. Hal Lindsey's book, *The Late Great Planet Earth*, published in 1969, by 1981 had gone into 31 foreign editions and sold 18 million copies. A significant segment of the electronic church heralded the imminent second coming of Christ and an accompanying economic and political crisis. Survivalist groups, perhaps the most extreme premillennialists, stockpiled freeze-dried foods, together with guns to protect their store from hungry neighbors when the end time arrives.[87]

Much of the Christian church has had a contrasting view of Christ's kingdom. Augustine said that the kingdom of Christ finds expression in the church. This view was subsequently held by the Catholic Church and by the major churches growing out of the Reformation. In the early Anabaptist-Mennonite view, the kingdom of Christ was understood to exist within the disciplined, gathered community, organized according to the rule of Christ and his law. The key values of a disciplined brotherhood community, separation from the world, and nonresistance to evil, which are expressed in the "Brotherly Union," all relate directly to this view of the kingdom. This amillennial or nonmillennial view holds that there will be no political territorial kingdom and that there will be no golden age spiritually before the second coming of Christ.

Each of these millennial positions encourages certain presumptions about power and its relation to the mission and message of Christ. Millenarians (a term used to denote those who expect the activation of a political, material kingdom of 1000 years' duration regardless of the specific details concerning its inauguration and form) see a material, political expression of power as the necessary fulfillment of the biblical promise that Christ will come in great glory and power. Catholicism, while it identified Christ's kingdom with the church, continued to see its expression as closely associated with material and political power. A third alternative is expressed by the phrase *Vicit Agnus Noster*, our Lamb has conquered. This position has been spelled out in detailed theological form in *Christ and the Powers* by Hendrik Berkhof[88] and by John Howard Yoder in *The Politics of Jesus*.[89] It sees the source and locus of power in Christ's kingdom as self-giving love, the power of the cross.

Dispensationalism, a distinctive form of premillennialism, has become widely accepted in America. The formulation of dispensationalism proposed by John Nelson Darby (1800-1882) was widely disseminated as he traveled throughout the United States and Canada, preaching and holding Bible study groups. The teaching was actively promoted in the British Isles before it became widespread in America. Although Darby did not wish to have his

---

[83] "Bern Debate," p. 152.

[84] *Complete Works* (Elkhart, 1871), vol. 1, p. 65. Quoted in John Horsch, *Mennonites in Europe* (Scottdale, Pa.: Mennonite Publishing House, 1950), p. 356.

[85] For a treatment of the Bible Conference Movement see Sandeen, *Roots*, especially chapter 6, and Weber, *Living in the Shadow*, especially chapter 5.

[86] Weber, *Living in the Shadow*, especially chapter 5.

[87] William Alnor, "Apocalypse Soon?" *Philadelphia Inquirer* (April 12, 1981), p. 16.

[88] John H. Yoder, trans. (Scottdale, Pa.: Herald Press, 1966, 1977).

[89] Grand Rapids, Mich.: William B. Eerdmans Publishing Company, 1972.

teaching follow denominational lines the (Plymouth) Brethren were the most active adherents of this teaching in Britain. The Brethren migrated to Canada and the United States in considerable numbers.

Dispensationalism was widely promoted by Darby but was further systematized by others.[90] The greatest impact for the spread of this teaching was made by Cyrus Ingerson Scofield (1843-1921) when he developed an annotated reference Bible supporting this system of thought. The Scofield Reference Bible, published in 1909 and revised in 1919 and 1966, was widely distributed and of immense importance in the dissemination of dispensationalist teaching. It contains extensive notations, together with cross references that explain the text according to the dispensationalist interpretation.

Dispensationalism carries to a logical conclusion ideas germane to premillennialism. A distinctive feature of dispensationalist teaching is the theory of the postponement of the kingdom. Dispensationalists hold that the sending out of the apostles by Jesus in Matthew 12 was a crucial watershed. Here the kingdom was offered to the Jews, and they rejected it. When this rejection was compounded by the crucifixion, the kingdom had to be postponed. The church and the dispensation of grace fill the subsequent period of time between Christ's ascension and his second coming. The kingdom is necessarily postponed until the future millennium, when Christ will reign over a physical Jewish kingdom on earth for a thousand years. In dispensationalism the church itself is a sort of parenthesis, and not a part of God's original plan. It is a purely spiritual entity, not necessarily related to denominational organizations and commitments. Dispensationalism specifically teaches that the blessings of the church are not conditioned on obedience. In contrast, the Mennonite charter insists that the church is a gathered group committed to mutual admonition and the encouragement of one another.

In the Mennonite Church persons who held the premillennial view often rejected dispensationalism as heresy.[91] The Scofield Bible was strongly censored in Franconia Conference, but there were members who owned and used copies. Two *Gospel Herald* articles outline in detail, and with care, ways in which the Scofield reference notes contradict Mennonite teaching.[92] Some Mennonite premillennialists stressed Mennonite emphases along with premillennialism and Fundamentalism. J. L. Stauffer's article "Fundamentalism and Fundamentalists" and his booklet *Premillennialism* are examples of this effort as is George R. Brunk's *Rightly Dividing the Scriptures*.[93]

Beginning contacts of Mennonites with millenarian teaching are identified by S. F. Coffman in a 1934 article. Coffman, a premillennialist, says he first heard of the idea of the millennial reign of Christ from an English minister who lectured at the Elkhart church in the 1880s. Additional exposure came through *Watchtower* magazine which was received as part of an exchange circulation for the *Herald of Truth*. Coffman writes:

> The idea of a "thousand-year reign of Christ" was the chief element in all these lectures and publications. It was a new thought to the ministers of the Mennonite Church at the time. But the idea of Christ, a King, and the Church as the Kingdom over which he now rules and over which He will reign eternally, was not new.[94]

Further exposure to the idea of the millennial reign came through the World Congress of Religions held in Chicago in 1893 at the time of the World's Fair. According to Coffman, the men in the Mennonite Church who heard millenarian teaching in Chicago did not immediately pick it up and include it in their preaching. The first persons to teach premillennialism in the Mennonite Church were A. D. Wenger and A. I. Yoder; both had attended Moody Bible Institute in Chicago. By the mid-1920s millenarianism had gained substantial support in the Mennonite Church. This view predominated among the faculty at Eastern Mennonite School in Harrisonburg, Virginia, and at Hesston College and Bible School in Hesston, Kansas. It was not supported at Goshen College in Indiana. The large Lancaster Conference was divided on the issue and the Franconia Conference strongly resisted the teaching.

Premillennialism and Fundamentalism were closely intertwined. They shared a rigid doctrine of inspiration and stressed the inerrancy of Scripture. But not all Fundamentalists were millenarians. Adherents of the Princeton theology in its pristine form were not millenarians. In the Mennonite Church, John Horsch, the well-known historian, identified with Fundamentalism but did not accept millenarianism. Daniel Kauffman, highly influential church leader and editor of the *Herald*, endorsed Fundamentalism but was not a millenarian. His reluctance to publish articles relating to millenarianism may have been a motivating factor in the inauguration in 1929 of a new Mennonite quarterly in Virginia, *The Sword and Trumpet*. Leaders in the Franconia Mennonite Conference perceived all millenarian teaching to

---

[90] For the history of dispensationalism see Bass, *Backgrounds*, and Kraus, *Dispensationalism in America*.

[91] J. A. Ressler and John H. Mosemann spoke out against it in the *Gospel Herald*. See *Christian Doctrine, A Quarterly Supplement to the Gospel Herald* (July 19, 1934), p. 52.

[92] Barney Ovensen, "Scofield's 'Helps'" (January 19, 1954), p. 53; and Aaron M. Shank, "What Is Wrong with the Scofield Bible?" (March 11, 1952), pp. 224-225.

[93] *Sword and Trumpet* (April 1933):16-20; (Harrisonburg, Va.: The Sword and Trumpet, Inc., 1952); and (Fentress, Va.: The Sword and Trumpet, 1935).

[94] S. F. Coffman, "The Kingdom of Our Lord Jesus Christ," *Christian Doctrine, A Quarterly Supplement of the Gospel Herald* (July 19, 1934), pp. 342-344.

be at variance with fundamental beliefs which they held.

In 1924, A. G. Clemmer, a bishop in the Franconia Conference, wrote a letter to J. C. Clemens, one of the leading ministers, expressing his concerns:

> For several years there has been something on my mind that is pressing me harder and harder as time goes on. Our church is being flooded with the doctrine of the Millennium or a literal reign of Christ that it seems to be a matter of only a few years till the teaching of our forefathers as well as most of our aged preachers of our days (who preach and teach the pure unadulterated Gospel of Jesus Christ) will be lost sight of and the coming generation will know little of a spiritual reign of Christ as taught by himself. And the church will thereby drift more and more into formality.
>
> Our quarterlies are so much filled with erroneous teachings that I feel it can hardly be tolerated longer....
>
> Some of the heads of our church schools are rank Millennialists. What shall we do? Shall we stand by and keep silent?[95]

Clemmer indicated that most of the ordained brethren in the conference opposed premillennialism but did not see how anything could be done to counteract the teaching.

Clemens had already been quite active in resisting the impact of premillennialism. A few days after the May conference in 1921, he had written a letter to Daniel Kauffman, chief editor at the Mennonite Publishing House. Reporting on the recent conference, he said:

> Our Bishops put up a solid front in condemning some of the teachings of the quarterly. Suggestions were freely made of dropping it altogether or sending a committee asking for fair play when it came to unfulfilled prophecy. We made a strong plea to keep the quarterly and finally it resolved itself into the fourth resolution which received a hearty vote.[96]

It seems that the Sunday school teachers were given specific help in following conference guidelines in at least some of the churches. Weekly meetings were held at which the Sunday school lesson was discussed before it was taught. There is some indication that one of the purposes of the meetings was to see that only approved teaching was presented.

On March 21, 1922, Clemens wrote a letter to the aged John F. Funk, expressing his concern regarding the propagation of millenarian teaching in the Mennonite Church. The supporters of millenarianism held it to be a teaching of the ancient church. Mennonites who endorsed this position also frequently held that they were supporting a traditional view. Clemens challenged this claim:

> A principal of one of our Bible schools made the statement at my home that Menno Simons and the other Reformers also believed in Literal Reign. So I got Menno Simons' complete works from my library and read to him extracts from the subject "*Spiritual Resurrection.*" He questioned your translation from the Dutch as being correct. So we visited the Library at Pennsburg, Pa. which contains S. W. Pennypacker's collection of Mennonite Books and compared the original, and then several of us Brethren asked this college Brother whether this was sufficient evidence that Menno did not believe in Literal Reign—He said "*It was.*"
>
> A Brother just placed in my hands a copy of the little booklet called the "Peaceable Kingdom of Christ," by Peter J. Twisk, and later translated by you in the English. I just read it this week and was moved to write to you for your encouragement.[97]
>
> Our Bishops came forward in a solid front against "Literal Reign," though every member of the conference has not the same view but a good majority.
>
> I also read Dietrich Philip on "Spiritual Restitution" and enjoyed it. I always had this view of the Kingdom and I am truly sorry that the "Faith of the Fathers," is not taught to our rising generation as it once was.
>
> Is it because their writings were not translated earlier or is it a departure from the *faith*?
>
> Are these essentials or non-essentials? I know we are almost afraid to talk about this matter at this time.[98]

In 1934 Daniel Kauffman, editor of the official church paper, the *Gospel Herald*, published a symposium on millennialism in the paper's quarterly

---

[95] Letter to J. C. Clemens dated January 1, 1924. Clemens Papers. "Quarterlies" were booklets issued four times a year to aid in the study of Sunday school lessons.

[96] Letter from J. C. Clemens to Daniel Kauffman, May 9, 1921. Original in the Mennonite archives, Goshen, Indiana. The resolution read: "*Fourth*—That this conference feels the necessity of urging the leaders of the churches to teach the new birth, separation from the world, nonresistance and other church essentials relative to the welfare of the church and not to speculate on unfulfilled prophecy as the doctrine of the Millennium." Minutes, Franconia Mennonite Conference.

[97] A complete, handwritten manuscript copy of *The Peaceable Kingdom of Christ* is among the papers of Clemens, suggesting the importance he attached to it when he first received it. Later he kept copies for sale to interested persons.

[98] Original in the Mennonite archives, Goshen College, Goshen, Indiana.

232   *The Encounter with Fundamentalism*

Molly and Daniel Kauffman.

doctrinal supplement. The articles were invited, and represented both sides of the issue.[99] Editor Kauffman, in his introduction to the symposium, says there had been numerous requests that he print articles relating to millennialism. He explains that considerable dissension had been aroused by the few articles that were printed previously, and he issues a plea for tolerance and patience on the part of both contributors and readers.

The articles demonstrate the complexity of the issues associated with millenarianism. The nature and locus of power, the significance of Jesus, the present power of Satan, and the importance given to the material are all closely associated with millennial views. Contrasting views concerning the locus of power and the significance of Jesus have already been noted. The articles also delineate contrasting views concerning Satan. Amillennialists believed Satan's power had been bound and limited by Jesus during his earthly ministry. Millenarians held that this would take place only after the second coming of Christ. The two contrasting views are spelled out in detail in the articles by J. C. Clemens and S. F. Coffman.

Millenarians saw real power as necessarily material and political. Amillennialists held it to be spiritual. "We are definitely taught, Clemens says, "that Christ's kingdom is a spiritual realm."[100] He applied this spiritual emphasis to the resurrection as well as to the kingdom:

> His [Christ's] varied appearances after His resurrection were physical only in so far as it was necessary to prove His identity, to prove that He is alive and of service. Wounded hands and flesh and bone were miraculous physical manifestations to assure His immediate disciples that he was living. We have no record that the world saw him at that time....
>
> The fact that resurrected glorified bodies are spiritual does not make them less real, but more so; for material things have no eternal existence....
>
> The Prophets speaking of this Kingdom say it is eternal; no end, so there is only one explanation; namely, it is spiritual. All material kingdoms have beginnings and ends.[101]

In his second point Clemens says that the rebuilding of the "Tabernacle of David," which premillennialists anticipated as the political restoration of the kingdom of Israel, took place when Gentiles, together with Jews from all of the tribes of Israel, were grafted into the church. The restoration of the throne of David, which premillennialists held was yet to be fulfilled, Clemens says, is now a reality and has been since Pentecost:

> When we think of a throne, it assures power. This thought filled and thrilled the disciples of the early Church. It was the keynote in the

---

[99] (July 19, 1934):338-352. The articles were: John Thut, "Is Christ's Coming Premillennial?" John H. Mosemann, "The Millennium, or Will There Be a Literal Reign of Christ on Earth 1000 Years?" S. F. Coffman, "The Kingdom of Our Lord Jesus Christ"; Oscar Burkholder, "The Premillennial View"; Jacob C. Clemens, "The Reign of Christ"; Elias Swartzendruber, "Is the Teaching of the Millennium a Bible Doctrine?" Ira D. Landis, "New Testament Eschatology"; and Harold S. Bender, "Christ's Spiritual Kingdom."

[100] Ibid., p. 346.

[101] Ibid.

J. C. and Hannah Rittenhouse Clemens relaxing.

Pentecostal sermon. The very thought that his Master was enthroned gave Peter dynamic power and brought marvelous results; for it emboldened him to lay hold on the Spirit of power. He uses the prophecy that "God would raise up Christ to sit on his throne." (Acts 2:30), in verse 33 he says it has taken place, and in verse 36 he makes further application and says He is, "both Lord and Christ" (King and Messiah).[102]

Harold S. Bender takes a similar position in his article, citing numerous New Testament passages which he says clearly indicate that Christ's kingdom has been established.[103] In this view Jesus' kingdom was inaugurated by his life and death. The teachings of the Sermon on the Mount are to guide the conduct of Jesus' followers in the present age. The beatitudes, found at the beginning of the sermon, are not arbitrary enactments but belong to the eternal nature of God.

Leadership Patterns

Traditional Mennonite leadership patterns stand in marked contrast to Fundamentalist leadership styles. Fundamentalist leaders saw their task primarily as that of preaching, for they placed paramount emphasis on sound doctrine. Their preaching styles tended to be highly dramatic, especially in their condemnations of modernists and modernism. Typically, only one minister presided over a congregation, frequently exercising almost exclusive authority. Relationships to colleagues, congregations, and denominations were considered incidental and sometimes deliberately rejected.[104] Among Mennonites, leaders were chosen from the congregation and usually served as part of a team ministry. Ordination was seen as a "high and holy calling,"[105] yet ordained leaders remained in close organic relation to congregations, fellow ministers, and conference. Key values of the group stressed the importance of mutual counsel and submission to the group, even in leadership selection.

By the 1930s, Fundamentalist Bible conference teachers were modifying Mennonite expectations for leadership. J. L. Stauffer, in his article on "Fundamentals and Fundamentalists," chided his readers, saying that they were making unfair comparisons and contrasts between ministers in their congregations and Fundamentalist preachers:

> It has often been noted that Mennonites who become frequenters of the Bible conferences and Union Bible Classes under the tutorship of Fundamentalist Bible-teachers, soon become very critical of the Mennonite Church and Mennonite preachers.[106]

Stauffer argued that the comparisons and contrasts were often unfair. The average Mennonite minister who needed to earn his own livelihood was often compared with a salaried Fundamentalist preacher who was a professional. "Compare the ablest Mennonite preachers or teachers with these Bible teachers, and the contrast will not be so noticeable, and it will be at least fair and consistent."[107] The Fundamentalist preacher may teach sublime truths, "but," Stauffer asks, "does he live them?" Mennonites strain at a gnat with reference to their own ministers, he continues, but sometimes discover they have swallowed a camel of inconsistency in relation to some Fundamentalist Bible teacher.

The charter refers to the leader as the shepherd of the flock. He is to be

---

[102] Ibid., p. 347.
[103] Ibid., p. 352.
[104] See Loetscher, *Broadening Church*; Russell, *Voices*; and Cole, *History of Fundamentalism*.
[105] "Bishop Ordained at Franconia," *Mission News* 1 (July 1937):2. Mennonite ministers continued to earn their own living, often by farming. J. C. Wenger points out that Menno Simons taught this vigorously. Personal note.
[106] Stauffer, "Fundamentals," p. 19.
[107] Ibid., p. 20.

one who is of good report both within and without the congregation. He is to preside in the congregation, "take care of the body of Christ," and to teach, warn, and admonish. He is not to "lord it over" others, but is to be the servant of all.[108] This ideal for leadership was carried well into the 1940s. "Ministers and Bishops are mentioned in the New Testament as having a place as Servants of the Church, never priests or popes or other names," Bishop Lapp wrote. In the fall conference sermon, 1950, he spoke on "The Purpose of Ordination." It was not, he said, "to elevate one above another. Every member fills a place. The ordained are a gift, servants, leaders in the congregation."[109]

Persons did not choose to become ministers, bishops, or deacons. They were *chosen*. They were selected by lot, but not at random. Those nominated had won the confidence of fellow members and had demonstrated ability in their chosen occupations. Rather frequently they had served as schoolteachers. Often they were relatively young at the time of their ordination. Bishop Jacob Godshall of Franconia, who died in 1845 at the age of 75 years, was ordained at age 34. He had taught school and was a song and hymn writer. He served as preacher for 41 years and as bishop for 32 years.[110] J. C. Clemens, ordained in 1906 in his early thirties, had been a schoolteacher and a banker. Menno B. Souder (1892-1969) was also a teacher. He had been valedictorian of his Souderton High School class of 1908, and had given an address entitled "Still Must I On."[111] He was ordained October 22, 1914, in his early twenties. These were gifted leaders, but none of them had had seminary training. This was not by default, but part of an approved pattern.

As early as 1892 questions were being raised concerning Mennonites receiving seminary training. John F. Funk, head of the Mennonite Publishing Company, located at Elkhart, Indiana, tried to explain to Abraham Leatherman of Franconia the attendance of one of his workers at a seminary:

> M. S. Steiner belongs to the old Mennonite Church and is a good solid member, and holds very closely to its doctrines. He is studying Bible studies, but not for the ministry unless God should some time call him to that work. You know in our church the ministers are chosen by lot so a man cannot study for the ministry but he can study to know the bible and when he knows the bible he will be able to preach if ever called to do so. Steiner has been working for me some as editor, and his education was not good enough, so he concluded to go to school another year and help himself out so as to be able to fill his place. He is in the theological department, but because he can go there cheaper than in any other. Oberlin is for classical scholars as well as for those who study theology.[112]

The descriptions of outstanding leaders by contemporaries are a commentary on the preferred style of leadership, indicating qualities and characteristics valued by the group. Bishop Andrew S. Mack (1836-1917), for many years moderator of the Franconia Conference, was seen as a gifted leader. "He took special pains," J. C. Clemens writes, "to find out the needs of the church and also the views of the different members of conference and then when conference convened he had things arranged to cope with the problems that came up." He continues:

> When he was an old man he took special care of the young members of conference and encouraged them in their work.
>
> He was blessed with a loving disposition and his messages from the pulpit appealed to young and old so that he faced receptive audiences. He used the German language mostly and had at his command a large vocabulary and with his ripe knowledge of the scriptures he would drive the message home. He preached the Gospel of Peace for more than fifty years not only to the various congregations in the Franconia district but visited the churches in the different conference districts of the Mennonite Church throughout the United States and Canada.[113]

The theme for his funeral service, chosen by the bishops, was "And they that be wise shall shine as the brightness of the firmament; and they that turn many to righteousness as the stars for ever and ever."[114]

Another outstanding leader, Abraham G. Clemmer (1867-1939), was ordained preacher for the large Franconia congregation on June 2, 1904, and as bishop on November 20, 1913. A local historian noted his self-denial and modest bearing, commenting that he cared more to please his Master than to achieve a finished style in order to gain the applause of men.[115] A second commentary is by Bishop Arthur D. Ruth, who as a young man was chosen to assist Clemmer. He saw Clemmer to be fair-minded, keen in his judgment, wise in his counsels, and richly endowed with the gift of what is known as foresight. In the deliberations on the various problems he freely expressed the possibility of being mistaken in his views and was considerate of the opinion of

---

[108] 1 Timothy 3:7. Qualification given in Article V of the "Brotherly Union," pp. 34-54.
[109] John E. Lapp to "Bro. Long," March 6, 1940. Lapp Letters, John E. Lapp Collection, EPMHL.
[110] John D. Souder. "Bishop Abraham G. Clemmer: Biographical Sketch," *Mission News* 3 (May 1939):1.
[111] Senior Class Program, Souderton High School, Menno B. Souder Papers, EPMHL.
[112] John F. Funk to Abm. Leatherman, February 18, 1892. EPMHL.
[113] J. C. Clemens Papers, 1929 Folder, EPMHL.
[114] Ibid.
[115] "Bishop Abraham G. Clemmer," p. 4.

others. He was a lover of sound literature and applied himself to reading until he was well informed on most any subject. When Bishop Clemmer died more than 1,360 persons attended the viewing which was held at his home.[116]

Phrases chosen to describe desirable leadership qualities include "to find out the needs of the church" and the "view of the different members of conference," "a loving disposition" "the Gospel of Peace," "they that be wise," "special care of the young members," "self-denial and modest bearing," "cared more to please his Master than to achieve a finished style," "fair-minded," "keen in his judgments," "wise in his counsels," "freely expressed the possibility of being mistaken," "considerate of the opinion of others."

Fundamentalist leaders, in accordance with the typical Protestant pattern, normally chose to attend a seminary or a Bible school, then became the pastor of a church. Their leadership was frequently described by phrases denoting decisive, independent thought, including "dogmatic," "adamant," and "aggressive." Fundamentalist leadership styles were epitomized by J. Frank Norris (1877-1952), simultaneously pastor of First Baptist Church of Fort Worth, Texas, and Temple Baptist Church of Detroit. Norris was among the most dramatic and controversial Fundamentalist leaders from the founding of the World Christian Fundamentals Association in 1919 to his death in 1952. His churches became increasingly independent of regional and denominational affiliations.[117]

Norris held that the one and only superintendent of the church is Christ through the Holy Spirit. In turn Christ works through the agency of the human pastor. "Repeatedly he emphasized," writes one biographer, "that there is no authority, ecclesiastical or otherwise, which has the right to interfere with any church or even advise a New Testament church how to order its affairs."[118]

The Independent Bible Churches were a flowering of this spirit. Fundamentalist leaders placed prime emphasis on dogma, and were subsequently unwilling to be subject to the authority of their own denominations when they believed sound doctrine was being threatened. The tactics employed by Fundamentalist leaders in this struggle were crucial to the rift that developed between conservatives and Fundamentalists in the major denominations, resulting in the withdrawal of the most adamant Fundamentalists to form independent churches.

In the larger Mennonite Church with activities centered at Elkhart, Indiana, and Scottdale, Pennsylvania, a new style of leadership was emerging, described approvingly with adjectives such as "active," "aggressive," and even "militant."[119] These leadership shifts were also in evidence in Virginia and to a lesser extent in the large Lancaster Conference. The resistance of Franconia to leadership with Fundamentalist sympathies was substantial in the years from 1910 to 1950. Inadvertently, the strictures contributed to strong Fundamentalist leadership in other areas of the Mennonite Church.

Franconia both resisted and was influenced by Fundamentalist leadership styles and the techniques being employed in other areas of the Mennonite Church. Evangelism, Fundamentalism, and a growing missions program aroused the zeal of numerous young people in the Franconia Conference in the early decades of the twentieth century. Traditional patterns of leadership selection made it difficult for them to promote their own placement in leadership positions. Strong sentiment supported the use of the lot, and leaders were to be chosen from and serve their own congregations. Aspiring to leadership was seen as inappropriate. Stresses developed, and a number of enthusiastic young persons were drawn from the conference to accept leadership in other areas of the church: Ohio, western Pennsylvania, Indiana, Kansas, Virginia, and Canada. These became noteworthy leaders, and their influence was far more widespread than their geographic locations. Most of them espoused a Mennonite Fundamentalism and endorsed premillennialism.

An open door to leadership was provided by the Altoona Mennonite Gospel Mission, Altoona, Pennsylvania, organized under the auspices of Southwestern Pennsylvania Mennonite Conference in 1910. John N. Durr (1853-1934), its vigorous bishop, actively solicited the assistance of gifted Franconia youths. As a young man Durr was converted at a Methodist revival meeting. The following year, on November 18, 1871, he was baptized and became a member of the Mennonite Church. In 1872, at the age of 19, he was ordained as a minister by John F. Funk and Daniel Brenneman while they were in Masontown holding the first series of meetings in the Mennonite Church. A year later, on November 26, 1873, Durr was ordained bishop. He was 20 years old.[120]

A call to serve at the Altoona Mission was given to the 23-year-old John L. Stauffer (1888-1959) of the Vincent congregation in Franconia Conference and he responded positively, going to Altoona in February, 1911. Stauffer joined the Southwestern Pennsylvania Mennonite Conference and was ordained as a minister the following June. In 1918 he responded favorably to another invitation, this time joining the faculty of Eastern Mennonite School in Harrisonburg, Virginia, where he was president from 1935 to 1950. Stauf-

---

[116] Arthur D. Ruth, "Bishop Abraham G. Clemmer: Service Together," *Mission News* 3 (May 1939):1.

[117] Russell, *Voices*, pp. 20-46.

[118] Ibid., p. 37.

[119] Schlabach, *Gospel*, makes this point repeatedly.

[120] Ellrose D. Zook, "John N. Durr," *ME*, s.v. Neither Brenneman nor Funk was a bishop. The custom of the period was that only bishops were authorized to ordain ministers, deacons, or other bishops.

240   *The Encounter with Fundamentalism*

Willis K. and Mary Mensch Lederach with son Paul, c. 1927.

fer was ordained as bishop in the Virginia Conference in 1934.

A dynamic and assertive young athlete of Souderton, Pennsylvania, joined the Mennonite Church in December 1911. Within two weeks of his decision to become a Christian, Clayton F. Derstine (1891-1967) was teaching Sunday school classes. The young Derstine was a printer by trade and soon caught the attention of Bishop Durr, who was publishing tracts and other items of literature that were being distributed door to door in Altoona. Derstine married his Methodist sweetheart, who became a Mennonite, and in 1912 at the age of 21 became assistant superintendent of the Altoona Mission. He transferred his church membership to the Southwestern Pennsylvania Mennonite Conference in 1913 and was ordained to the ministry the following year. He immediately began evangelistic work.[121]

The Philadelphia Mennonite Mission, under the auspices of the Mennonite Sunday School Mission, initially a laymen's organization, provided mission service opportunities for some youths. J. D. Mininger (1879-1941) and the young woman who was to become his wife, Hettie B. Kulp, both assisted in the program. In 1912 Mininger became superintendent of the Mennonite Gospel Mission in Kansas City, where he served until his death. Mininger was highly respected as leader in the Mennonite Church. He frequently taught Bible instruction meetings, served on numerous church boards, authored tracts and a book entitled *Exalting Christ in the City*.[122]

Some who desired to participate in mission programs found ready acceptance in the conference. A young couple volunteered to serve with the Mennonite Board of Missions and Charities in 1921. When the Elkhart board advised the Franconia Conference of their appointment to the 26th Street Mission in Chicago, conference approved the appointment, noting simply that if the question of ordination should arise they were to seek the advice of conference. When the Franconia Mission Board learned of their availability, they requested that the couple reconsider their place of service, inviting them to locate at the recently established Norristown Mission. They assented, and Willis K. and Mary Mensch Lederach lived and served at the mission from 1921 to 1928. When health reasons forced them to leave the mission residence, they continued to participate in the program, serving until 1945.[123]

Several other young men, both from the Blooming Glen congregation, were invited to city mission leadership positions by neighboring conferences. William G. Detweiler, about whom we shall have more to say later, was one of them. Clarence Y. Fretz, the other, attended Eastern Baptist Seminary. He was invited by the Lancaster Conference to serve at the Philadelphia Mission at Norris Square. When ordination was proposed he requested that it might be under the auspices of Franconia Conference and by his own bishop. This was not acceptable to the Lancaster Conference, but they did allow the participation of his bishop in the ordination service.[124]

Authoritarian control and the encroachments of Fundamentalism were frequently interrelated. The resistance of conference was formally encountered by one group that attempted to launch a local mission station. In 1921 several men proposed that a vacant church at Limerick would be an excellent place to begin a mission Sunday school. One of them, Solomon Good, was a charter member of the Franconia Mennonite Mission Board, organized in 1917. A second participant was an active layman, Abraham B. Mensch, who served for many years as superintendent of the Upper Skippack Mennonite Sunday school. Their proposal that the building be purchased was rejected, first by the mission board in May 1921, and then by conference in May 1922. Mensch decided to buy the building independently. His bishop, Warren Bean, responded to this news with an order stating that "no member be allowed to purchase a church alone." The restraint was circumvented by

---

[121] For a biography of Derstine see Urie A. Bender *Four Earthen Vessels* (Scottdale, Pa.: Herald Press, 1982).

[122] J. C. Wenger, *History of the Mennonites of Franconia Conference* (Telford, Pa.: Franconia Mennonite Historical Society), p. 176; Ruth M. Brackbill, "Jacob D. Mininger," *ME*, s.v.

[123] March Mensch Lederach, "*The Limerick Interlude*" (unpublished manuscript, 1978), pp. 9-10. EPMHL.

[124] Personal letter, June 18, 1982.

two additional persons contributing to the purchase price, monies which were later returned to the donors.[125]

Mensch and his supporters moved ahead unrelentingly, with the Sunday school scheduled to begin in April 1923, in the weeks between the agreement of sale and the deed of transfer of the property. Conference convened during this period, on May 3, 1923. The third action stated that members "taking steps in advance of Conference" would forfeit "their right to communion."[126] The action was ignored by the leaders of the Limerick project, and within a few months a conference announcement was circulated to all member churches:

> August 23 Announcement
>
> As the Brethren A. B. Mensch, Francis Bechtel Reuben Clymer and M. L. Plank were not subordinate to conference ruling, slip 2:8, namely, "That members are admonished against forwardness and be subject to those that have the rule over them according to Hebrews 13:17 and also slip 5:1, namely that the Sunday Schools are under the supervision of Conference," they therefore and others that have transgressed in like manner are not communicant members.
>
> This step has been taken after these Brethren [were] duly reminded of what they were doing by the Conference and by a committee appointed by the Bishops.
>
> Signed by the Bishops[127]

The brethren acknowledged their trespass and were reinstated at the October conference, 1924. They then promptly attempted to bypass conference restrictions by joining en masse a neighboring congregation belonging to another conference. It was only a temporary victory, for stresses soon developed between the two conferences and mediation was necessary.

The mediating group decided that sponsorship of the Sunday school should be given to the Franconia Conference, with workers being allowed to come from the Franconia, Lancaster, and Ohio and Eastern Amish Mennonite conferences. The Franconia Mission Board, in accordance with its policy, then conducted a survey of the town of Limerick. Their assessment was that nearly all of the residents attended churches already established in the town. Their policy was not to proselytize, so they determined that a Sunday school was not needed.

The founders of the Limerick Sunday school were clearly not in harmony with the charter principle of subordination to the group. Their actions did fit the Fundamentalist pattern of placing convictions above organizational relationships or structures. A sympathetic observer recognized the dichotomy when she reported that "some sincere seekers of opportunities not provided for them were labeled more in derision than admiration as having '*der Predig Geist*—the preaching spirit.' "[128]

Mensch, distressed with the conference decision to disband the Sunday school, once more independently went forward with the work. Soon preaching services were added. In 1929 B. B. King led a series of meetings and in 1930 another series was led by Maurice O'Connell. The final meeting of O'Connell's series, held on a Sunday afternoon, was advertised. His topic was to be "The second coming of the Lord." A sympathetic observer reported that Mensch and O'Connell were uncertain how well this meeting would be attended, but

> for years after this, O'Connell enjoyed to relate the particulars of a premillennial preacher's experience on this Sunday afternoon.
>
> When he and Mensch drove out onto Route 422 near the church, they were more than surprised to see the parking lot to the rear of the church filled with cars, and cars were parked on both sides of the highway. Already the church was filled, not even any more standing room, and groups were gathered outside the open windows to be within hearing of the message he would be bringing.[129]

This incident demonstrates that more was involved in the dissension than bypassing lines of authority. Mensch was a premillennialist and used a Scofield Bible. Teachers using the Scofield Bible were sometimes asked to no longer to use them or to quit teaching; at least one brother whose name had been proposed as a nominee had his name removed from the lot for minister because he used the Scofield Bible in his study. Both premillennialism and the Scofield Bible were widely endorsed in Fundamentalism. Fundamentalism, with its exclusivist emphasis, also did not hesitate to proselytize.

In June and September of 1932, the work of Limerick was again brought by Mensch to the mission board and the board took over and reorganized the program. In October 1936, the mission board voted to close the work because of lack of support in the immediate community. Mensch was no longer living, and in November, 1937, his widow sold the Limerick church building to a rapidly growing nonsectarian fellowship.

Ministers could be excluded from preaching in the conference, and institutional programs could be censored, but it was not possible to keep mem-

---

[125] Lederach, "Limerick Interlude," p. 8.
[126] "Minutes."
[127] Ibid.
[128] Lederach, "Limerick Interlude," p. 9.
[129] Ibid., p. 16.

bers from listening to radio preachers, and radio was a primary medium for the dissemination of Fundamentalism. The influence of radio multiplied when a former conference member began his own radio broadcast late in 1936.

William G. Detweiler (1903-1956), founder of the *Calvary Hour* religious radio broadcast, was from the Blooming Glen congregation in Franconia. At the May conference, 1928, he and his wife were appointed as workers for the Norristown mission. In 1931 they were called to the Mennonite mission in Canton, Ohio. Before this assignment there was an exchange of letters between J. C. Clemens and Bishop S. E. Allgyer, moderator of General Conference and fieldworker for the Mennonite Board of Missions and Charities. Among the questions asked by Allgyer was whether Detweiler was "completely settled in the Mennonite faith."[130] Clemens responded that he "seems to be more settled in the Mennonite faith. In fact his only trouble was a lack of patience. He is like a young horse ready to go."[131]

Detweiler and his wife went to Canton, where he was ordained on June 11, 1933. His ordination was recognized by Franconia Conference on May 7, 1936.[132] A few months later, on November 28, 1936, he began the *Calvary Hour* radio broadcast. The broadcast prospered, and Detweiler increasingly identified with national Fundamentalist leaders and programs. More will be said about his influence in the following chapter.

Congregational expectations of leadership often changed as members attended Fundamentalist Bible conferences and listened to radio preachers. These new expectations were frequently in conflict with traditional patterns, fostering a restlessness that sometimes erupted in schism. New mission programs, particularly in the cities, provided some opportunities for alternate modes of leadership style and selection.

Fundamentalism, like Pietism, revivalism, and institutionalization, made a significant impact on Mennonite religious forms. The interaction with Fundamentalism was not structured in the categories of the charter, although the belief orientation of the charter continued to be assumed.[133] The issues were framed in Protestant terminology, for the Mennonites had appropriated a Protestant debate. As contact with the surrounding culture increased, and Protestant influences pressed in upon the Mennonites, they developed defensive structures which were expressed in codification of practice.

---

[130] S. E. Allgyer to J. C. Clemens, April 6, 1931, Clemens Papers, EPMHL.
[131] Ibid. Response written by Clemens on back of letter.
[132] "Minutes."
[133] As late as 1955 to 1959, when *The Mennonite Encyclopedia* was published, each of the articles is spoken to as a fundamental belief.

7

Defensive Structuring and Codification of Practice

Events in the late nineteenth century created alarm among conservative Christians in America and resulted in several types of defensive response. These included an increased emphasis on the authority of the church, scholasticism, Pietism, and apocalypticism. Several of these defensive adaptations were brought into coalition and became the central focus of Fundamentalism.

While a number of Mennonite leaders formally endorsed Fundamentalism, they also recognized it as posing certain threats to specific beliefs and practices. They were particularly aware of its direct contradiction to the teaching of nonresistance and feared the threat which it posed to separation from the world (spoken of as nonconformity to the world by these leaders). Franconia, as we have noted, additionally opposed the premillennial position which often accompanied Fundamentalism.

The impact of ideological changes occurring in America between 1870 and 1920 was compounded by equal or greater changes in the economic and political structures of American society. These changes threatened the continuing existence of small, self-regulated communities which prior to 1870 had been a dominant feature in the structure of American society. Between 1870 and 1920 the structure of American society and its value system changed significantly. American cultural historian Robert H. Wiebe noted that by contrast to the personal, informal ways of the community, the new scheme was derived from the regulative, hierarchical needs of urban-directed life. Through rules with impersonal sanctions, it sought continuity and predictability in a world of endless change.[1]

By 1880, Mennonite leaders perceived the religious and cultural pressures encroaching upon them as a threat to key values. The new social, political, and economic developments particularly threatened the charter

---

[1] For a full development of this thesis see Robert H. Wiebe, *The Search for Order* (New York: Hill and Wang, 1967).

values of the disciplined brotherhood community, separation from the world, and nonresistance. These same key values were threatened by the encroachments of Fundamentalism. Problems concerning the disciplined community, separation from the world, and nonresistance received increasing attention from 1880 to 1920. By 1881 the large Lancaster Conference was codifying the authoritarian control exercised by its bishops.[2]

From the beginning of the American settlements, Mennonites continuously attempted to maintain a simple life and stressed separation from the world, but practice was not uniform. Ministers were admonished to warn, advise, or remind their members. Around the turn of the century structures changed significantly. Leadership became centralized, and practice was codified. Although we will document this process for one area, the Franconia Mennonite Conference, parallels were occurring throughout the Mennonite Church.[3]

Franconia Conference, located principally in Bucks and Montgomery counties, was relatively close to heavily populated urban areas and subject to the full impact of social and economic changes. First the train and then the automobile made urban areas much more accessible. Available diaries illustrate the frequent use made of the trolley and later of the automobile, and how both increased the mobility of members and ministers. Perhaps even more important, the economics of the area changed. Whereas agriculture had been dominant, increasing numbers of members now began working in factories.[4]

The defensive structuring which occurred in Franconia and other conferences was a response to both religious and secular encroachments upon key values. According to Bernard Siegel, defensive structuring as an adaptation, is a process whereby members of a group attempt to preserve a religious or cultural identity in the face of what they feel are pervasive and long-lasting threats to that identity.[5] The adaptive process selectively enforces beliefs already held in such a way that these beliefs can serve as a central focus for group-consciousness. Defensive structuring occurs with great regularity among groups that perceive themselves as exposed to environmental stress of long duration and with which they cannot cope directly or aggressively. Groups which resort to defensive structuring characteristically possess a highly integrated culture. Broad segments of the culture are related to a few key values which lend a sense of cultural identity to the group, and individuals are subordinate to the group. These characteristics aptly apply to the Franconia Conference.

Siegel proposed that the adaptive elements of defensive structuring include authoritarian control over members exercised by a small, specially knowledgeable elite; a high rate of endogamy; cultivation of cultural identity symbols; and early socialization of impulse control. Authoritarian control over members exercised by a small, specially knowledgeable elite can be readily documented for the conference, as can the cultivation of cultural identity symbols. A high rate of endogamy appears to have been a continuing norm for the conference. Early training for impulse control was almost certainly also present. However, no study of this phenomenon has been made, and data are not available. As codification of practice developed in Franconia Conference, it also attempted to protect other key values. Formal limitations on patterns of structural associations became increasingly dominant.[6] Rules were also passed concerning civil conduct and business affairs, particularly as they related to a broad interpretation of nonresistance.

Events in Franconia were not isolated from what was occurring in other areas of the Mennonite Church. On the contrary, explicit evidence suggests that defensive structuring as a means of coping with stress was introduced into Franconia Conference by leaders from other areas of the Mennonite Church. A primary avenue of influence was the Bible conference.

The Doylestown congregation sponsored such a meeting in 1909—the first to be held in the district—and news of the proposed conference apparently provoked a negative reaction. Conference minutes for October 7, 1909, noted that "the Doylestown congregation had worked ahead of conference in arranging for a Bible Instruction meeting. The brethren confessed and asked forgiveness. The congregation was then allowed to hold their proposed meeting for this one time." In 1910 the Vincent congregation was granted the privilege of holding a Bible instruction meeting. Blooming Glen held a similar meeting in 1911.

Apparently the speakers at these meetings strongly emphasized the importance of plain, distinctive attire. Concerning the first Bible conference at Doylestown, J. C. Clemens says, "Daniel Kauffman and S. G. Shetler were the instructors; this had a tendency to unify the church on Bible doctrine although some left the church on account of the teaching on nonconformity."[7] Vincent, following the 1910 Bible conference led by George R. Brunk I, was

---

[2] See Amos B. Hoover, *The Jonas Martin Era, 1875-1925* (Denver, Pa.: The Author, 1982), p. 686.

[3] See Sanford C. Yoder, *The Days of My Years* (Scottdale, Pa.: Herald Press, 1959).

[4] John L. Ruth, in *The History of the Indian Valley and Its Bank* (Souderton, Pa.: Union National Bank and Trust Company, 1976), has told the story of the economic development of the community.

[5] Bernard J. Siegel, "Defensive Structuring and Environmental Stress," *American Journal of Sociology* 76 (July 1970):11-32.

[6] The importance of structural associations in the maintenance of the ethnic community is a key focus in Milton Gordon, *Assimilation in American Life* (New York: Oxford University Press, 1964).

[7] Autobiographical Notes, unpublished manuscript, p. 6. EPMHL, Lansdale, Pa.

Preacher William S. Gross and family, c. 1902.

the first Franconia congregation to press for laymen to wear the "plain" coat.

Stringent dress restrictions adopted in 1911 appear to be directly related to Bible conferences that were being held in the area. The large Blooming Glen congregation held a Bible instruction meeting from August 27 to September 2, 1911, with Daniel Kauffman and Samuel G. Shetler from western Pennsylvania serving as speakers. Apparently support for the meeting was not unanimous. The sudden deaths of two of the meeting's sponsors (Abraham Hunsicker was killed in a train wreck and Sue Bishop was buried that week) "caused much comment." Supporters of the conference desired dress regulations. Topics included the "Devotional Covering," "Self Denial," "Idolatry of Today," and "Conformity to the World."[8]

The fall conference, held a few weeks later, enacted a stringent dress ruling. With this resolution Scripture references were used in relation to worldliness and dress for the first time in the official conference minutes. It was also the first explicit *regulation* on dress. The new stringency was not accepted passively. About a dozen families left the Blooming Glen church rather than comply with the regulation.[9]

Franconia both resisted and was influenced by the Fundamentalist practice of holding Bible conferences. Bible conferences, with their topical approach, tended to compartmentalize faith and obedience and codify them in practice by employing the categories of orthodox Protestantism (doctrine) to preserve a charter value (separation), which became codified as nonconformity. Evidence is quite explicit that defensive structuring as a means of coping with stress was introduced into Franconia conference by leaders from other areas of the Mennonite Church through the avenue of the Bible conference.

The tightening of controls across the Mennonite Church under authoritarian leaders after the turn of the century has sometimes been described as legalism. Labeling the phenomenon as legalism fails to provide an explanation for the content of the rules. Why *these* rules? Codification of practice in the Virginia Conference, in many ways similar to that which occurred in Franconia, has been discussed in terms of a revitalization movement.[10] The model has some merit for Virginia, where the conference had a strong charismatic leader in the person of George R. Brunk I, but does not apply equally well to other areas.

The pressures that resulted in defensive structuring were complex. We

---

[8] Printed conference program.

[9] For the text of the ruling see below, p. 257. See also J. C. Wenger, *History of the Mennonites of Franconia Conference* (Telford, Pa.: Franconia Mennonite Historical Society, 1937), p. 182.

[10] Robert S. Hardwick, "Change and Continuity in Two Mennonite Communities: The Effect of Urban and Rural Settings," Ph.D. dissertation, University of Virginia, 1974.

have noted social, economic, and religious forces that pressed into the community. Religious pressures were compounded by a modified endorsement of Fundamentalism, which contradicted certain key values. Furthermore, Fundamentalism emphasized sound doctrine. For the Mennonites sound doctrine included separation from the world, or nonconformity to the world, and the increased rigidity with which separation was promoted may have been partly an outgrowth of this influence. Mennonite practice was also influenced by holiness groups, particularly in the Midwest. Sanctions against neckties were adopted in the Midwest from the holiness movement, but were resisted in most of the Eastern conferences.[11] For instance, when the youthful minister A. D. Wenger (originally from Virginia) was on his way from Missouri to the Eastern communities, John F. Funk persuaded him to don a necktie. The *Herald of Truth* early contained a modest number of articles on dress, 13 appearing during the first 17 years of publication.

However, the emphasis being given to dress was itself an outside influence. Of the first 13 articles to be printed in the *Herald*, only one was written by a Mennonite, and it quoted freely from non-Mennonite periodicals.[12]

In the following pages we will document three adaptive elements of defensive structuring in Franconia Conference: (1) authoritarian control over members exercised by a small, specially knowledgeable elite, (2) cultivation of cultural identity symbols, and (3) formal limitations on patterns of structural association.

Authoritarian Control over Members

Bishops and ministers in Franconia Conference traditionally met semiannually for fellowship and counsel. Admonition was given and received, but there was no constitution and minutes were not recorded. "Conference," said one elderly bishop, "was conferring, then we went back [to our congregations] to discuss the issues."[13] In the second decade of the twentieth century the structure of leadership became centralized and codified. Beginning in 1909, minutes were officially recorded. The actions for the fall conference in 1912 structured leadership patterns. The resolutions served as guidelines for the next several decades. That this centralization of leadership was innovative, not simply a codification of existing practice has been affirmed by persons still living who were close to conference leadership during the period designated. The resolutions are so significant that we quote them in full:

October 3, 1912

First—That the bishops shall on each Wednesday afternoon

preceeding conference meet to consider the needs and desires of the several congregations, so that when difficulties arise they may have the opportunity to fully consider the questions and hold counsel before the regular sessions of conference.[14]

Second—That such as desire counsel shall present the same in a written and definite statement, or appear personally before the bishops.

Third—Questions may be asked while conference is in session, but if such questions are of great importance they will be held over until the next conference.

Fourth—Nothing shall enter into the church unless it be confirmed by two-thirds vote of conference.

Fifth—When discord arises in a bishoprick [sic], the Bishop, minister, or deacon of another district is not to take up the matter until called by the Bishop in whose district the matter arose.

Sixth—When the teachings of the Bishop are not gospel and not in accord with the nonresistance doctrine, so that the church is led astray, the members are privileged to inquire of the other Bishops in the conference.

Seventh—When the minister or deacon has any fault with the Bishop, he shall act according to Matt. 18. And the ministry in general shall seek the peace of one another in this spirit.[15]

Bishop John E. Lapp, when asked how he explained this centralization of power, responded: "I think the people wanted it.[16] In defensive structuring the legitimation of centralized authority stems from an urgent and apprehensive need for solutions to daily problems. When cultural survival is at stake, the matter of regulations cannot be left entirely to self-control. Instead, authority is vested in a few individuals whose qualifications include the ability to interpret the traditional and basic texts in such a way that they lend meaning to the culture.

The controls of leadership became ever more rigid in the next dozen years. At the October 2, 1913, conference an additional regulation was approved:

---

[11] Melvin Gingerich, *Mennonite Attire Through Four Centuries* (Breinigsville, Pa.: The Pennsylvania German Society, 1970), pp. 75-83; Joseph S. Miller, "The Pennsylvania Mennonite Church near Zimmerdale, Kans.," *PMH*, vol. 5, no. 3 (July 1982), pp. 14-19.

[12] Gingerich, *Mennonite Attire*, p. 145.

[13] Arthur D. Ruth in John L. Ruth, "Interview with Four Franconia Bishops," taped interview, January 6, 1981. EPMHL, Lansdale, Pa.

[14] The Lancaster Conference recorded a similar ruling in 1881. Hoover, *Jonas Martin*, p. 686.

[15] Minute Book, Franconia Mennonite Conference, EPMHL, Lansdale, Pa.

[16] *Gemeinschaft II*, Salford Mennonite Church, June 15, 1974.

> *First*—That when the Bishops agree upon a matter and bring it before conference, and the matter is not understood by any member of the conference, he is privileged to make inquiry, but not to gainsay the matter in question.

In May, 1915, Bishops were granted exclusive power to determine who should be permitted to preach within the conference:

> *Fourth*—That conference grant Bishops alone the privilege to decide which of the visiting Brethren, whose faith is in question, are safe to preach at regular or special services in their respective district. This is considered important because of the many new and strange doctrines afloat. Rom. 16:17.

At the same conference a regulation was passed stating that continued meetings, Bible instruction meetings, and Sunday school meetings were to be conducted by brethren from either the Franconia or the Lancaster Conference districts. The exclusion of other Eastern districts such as Virginia, Maryland, and Canada, is particularly interesting to note. The exclusion is also in distinct contrast to earlier practice. For example, the main sermon at the "Opening Service" of the new 1838 Rockhill meetinghouse was preached by a Sellersville Reformed Church minister. An 1887 conference notation by Jacob Mensch says that Quakers are granted the privilege of preaching in the conference, and John E. Lapp stated that Jacob C. Loux (1822-1895), who was ordained May 21, 1867, often preached or conducted services at St. John's Reformed Church in Lansdale.

The fourth resolution for the October conference in 1915 states that lay members of the church are not to make appointments for visiting ministers. Furthermore, a pointed resolution was passed at the fall conference, applying specifically to persons who had left the conference and been ordained elsewhere.[17] The new restriction limited the ministry of J. D. Mininger, J. L. Stauffer, and C. F. Derstine in the Franconia churches for the next 15 years. These well-known churchmen were originally from Franconia but were ordained by other conferences. In 1920 the leaders at Doylestown were required to make an acknowledgment for inviting J. D. Mininger of the Kansas City mission to preach, contrary to conference rules.

The *Rules and Discipline* published in 1921 further safeguarded authority in several areas. A bishop, minister, or deacon ordained in another conference was not to be accepted in Franconia unless specifically called by the conference, and unless he was also released by the conference of which he was formerly a member. Sunday schools were placed under the supervision of conference. Instruction in singing was to be encouraged, but bishops and ministers were to be consulted about appointees for leadership in this task.[18]

The *Rules and Discipline* of 1925 granted to bishops the right to reject "votes" from members for candidates for ordination if the bishop considered the nominee "not in harmony with Bible qualifications according to 1 Tim. 1:3-13; 1 Tim. 2:2; and Titus 1:6-9."

By 1929 stresses were becoming evident in the newly created authority structure. On October 3, 1929, "A plea for loyalty was made so that resolutions previously adopted could be carried out."

In 1930 Mininger and Stauffer were recognized "as ministers of the gospel in all churches of the Franconia district."[19] C. F. Derstine, who adopted a more demonstrative Fundamentalist style, was not included in the action. Two years later he was granted limited acceptance.[20] Derstine continued to await more inclusive acceptance by conference. "I am hoping," he wrote to Gerret Nice, member of the Franconia Mission Board, "the time will soon come in which I can come east for Bible conferences; some of the preachers have already discussed the same. This would allow me to come home a little oftener. For which I would be *very* glad."[21]

Loyalty is again called for May 3, 1934, and

> the members of Conference expressed by a rising vote a willingness to be faithful to the rulings of Conference and that any member who willingly and intentionally disobeyed Conference rulings, should fall under censure.

A response to complex forces, centralization of authority was a defensive response to pervasive, long-lasting threats beyond the control of the group. Fundamentalism was one of the forces influencing change, and strong, authoritarian leadership was characteristic of Fundamentalism. Yet even as authority became centralized in the conference it was the authority of a *group*. Typically, individualistic Fundamentalist-style leadership was little in evidence in the Franconia Conference.

---

[17] "October 7, 1915. *Second*—If any brother leave this conference district and be ordained different from our conference rules, his office is not recognized by this conference district, except by consent of conference." "Minute Book," EPMHL, Lansdale, Pa.

[18] *Rules and Discipline of the Franconia Conference of the Mennonite Church, November, 1921*. EPMHL, Lansdale, Pa.

[19] "Minute Book," EPMHL, Lansdale, Pa.

[20] Ibid. October 6, 1932.

[21] C. F. Derstine to Gerret Nice, July 22, 1935. Gerret Nice Ms., Folder 2. EPMHL, Lansdale, Pa.

Clayton F. Derstine and second wife, Mary E. Kolb, 1927.

Cultivation of Cultural Identity Symbols

✗ In defensive structuring a group typically selects and intensifies certain cultural items so that they become symbols of identity. Two prime examples of this among Mennonites were bonnets and the white caps worn by women members. These were not the only items of apparel that received increasing attention between 1882 and 1942. Dress in general was at issue. Jacob Krehbiel, writing in 1841, indicated that there was considerable emphasis on dress, but that practice was not uniform.[22] Plainness and simplicity of dress were everywhere accepted, but the amount of emphasis on dress varied. Mensch's memoranda indicate that from 1882 to 1907 repeated concern was expressed at conference about mustaches, ruffles, bustles, puffed sleeves, and ladies' hats.

> The matter was brought up that the older sisters complain about and regret that the younger sisters wear dresses with puffed up sleeves, and feel proud, and carry on in the fashions of the world. The conference voted that each minister should bring this to the attention of his congregation.[23]

The matter continued to be of concern in the ensuing years. The wearing of a uniform style of dress or suit was never made a conference regulation, although pressures to conform to a common standard were strong. An explicitly detailed leaflet was issued by conference, dated October 1, 1942, entitled "Position of the Franconia Mennonite Conference on Dress."[24]

This intensificaiton can be illustrated by the cases of bonnets and the white caps worn by women members. The wearing of a white cap by women was at one time a common custom in both Europe and America. In the eighteenth century in Pennsylvania it was worn by the Quakers, Moravians, Mennonites, and others. By the mid-nineteenth century American portraits show women wearing plain caps, fancy caps, and no caps.[25]

---

[22] "A Few Words About the Mennonites in America in 1841," tr. and ed. by Harold S. Bender, *MQR* 4 (April 1932):110-121.

[23] Jacob B. Mensch, *Memorandum Book of Reverend Jacob B. Mensch and Proceedings of the Franconia Mennonite Conference*, tr. and ed. by Raymond E. Hollenbach.

[24] The most complete study of dress in Franconia Conference is Mary Jane Hershey, "A Study of Dress of the Old Mennonites of Franconia Conference 1700-1953," *Pennsylvania Folklife*, vol. 9, no. 3 (Summer 1958): 24-45. See also Gingerich, *Mennonite Attire*.

[25] The magazine *Antiques* (August 1975) includes the following portraits: Watercolor portrait of a New England couple (dated as second quarter of the nineteenth century), p. 213. The woman is dressed simply, but wears no cap. Portrait of Elizabeth (nee Gibbs (1760-1843) and Jacob Peck (1756-1838), c. 1820, p. 273. Lady wears simple white cap with black ribbons. Mr. and Mrs. William Vaughan, c. 1845, p. 278. Sitters were residents of Aurora, Illinois. Lady wears a white cap, plain, except for a single ruffle. Portrait of Phoebe Welch from the Carr Collection, opposite p. 80. Lady wears white cap with ruffle, and a shawl over her shoulders.

The New Mennonites soon discontinued the practice of women wearing white caps. Conference minutes implied that the custom was also being disregarded by a significant number of Franconia Mennonite women prior to 1880. A note recorded by Jacob Mensch for the conference held on May 6, 1880, reads: "Earlier it had been voted that sisters wear caps to meeting, and this was again emphasized anew."[26] The custom must have been challenged by practice prior to this in order for the subject to have come up at conference. That the caps were left at the church house by many women, and worn by some only at communion time, is supported by a contemporary witness.[27]

Franconia women seem to have found a way of complying with the request that they wear caps to meeting. Apparently in the 1880s, if not before, they began leaving their white caps in boxes in the anteroom of the church from Sunday to Sunday. At least some of them, upon arriving at the meetinghouse, would put on their cap for the service. After the service the cap would be returned to the box and left there until the next Sunday. This practice is first mentioned in Mensch's minutes from 1892: "Sisters were again cautioned against bringing caps boxes to meetings." Perhaps the practice began when the custom of wearing a cap was being dropped in the surrounding culture, while the Mennonite ministers were continuing to urge women to wear caps to meeting.

There was considerable difficulty in getting sisters to comply with the request that they do not keep their caps in boxes at the meetinghouses, for the subject was again brought up on May 7, 1896; October 6, 1898; October 5, 1899; and May 3, 1900. On October 4, 1900, the matter of women leaving the meetinghouse wearing hats was mentioned.

References to cap boxes in minutes also frequently include mention of women wearing hats. In the nineteenth century both hats and bonnets were worn by women in the Franconia Conference. The bonnets that were worn were designed in an assortment of styles and types—often quite elaborate.[28]

Practice apparently varied among the different congregations. Women at the Salford and Franconia congregations are said to have worn mostly bonnets. Very few bonnets were born at Blooming Glen.[29] J. C. Wenger writes that

> A. D. Wenger preached at Blooming Glen in the general period 1895-1905, and stood—as he said—with a sea of coverings before him (the women occupied the huge center section between the two aisles, and the men the two "wall sections"). After the service A. D. was dumbfounded to see a vast number of women leaving the meetinghouse grounds with families in buggies, and *wearing hats*.[30]

John L. Stauffer, born in 1888, former president of Eastern Mennonite College, and earlier a member of the now extinct Coventry congregation in Chester County, wrote that when he was a child

> the great majority of the sisters were conformed to the world in wearing hats with ribbons and feathers. The covering was left at the church house by many and worn by some in times of worship and by others only at communion time. My own Mother and two of her sisters were received as members with their hats and without coverings.[31]

It is important to note that in all of the early references to hats and the cap in the conference minutes the matter is simply discussed. Ministers are urged to admonish their members, but there is no legislation. The manner in which the wearing of bonnets over caps was presented in 1896 is noteworthy:

> May 7, 1896—It was suggested that sisters might wear such bonnets or "strip bonnets" under which they can wear their caps and wear them at all times, as it is often pitiful to see what sisters have on their heads and sometimes nothing at times of prayer.[32]

Fifteen years later, in 1911, a resolution was passed requiring that all women members wear bonnets.

> *First*—That the Brethren and Sisters be required to submit themselves to the teachings of God's word according to 1 Tim. 2:8, 9 and 1 Peter 3:3, 4 and further that *none will be received into the church wearing fashionable clothing or gold for adornment or women wearing hats*. Sisters wearing hats are required to dispense with them before Spring communion and instead wear the plain protection covering, all complying with the foregoing resolution will be recognized as members of the church.[33]

As has been pointed out, this action resulted in a number of members withdrawing from the conference. The stance taken in this resolution held through 1940. Living members of the conference, with several exceptions,

---

[26] Mensch, *Memorandum*.
[27] See below, p. 257.
[28] Documented in detail by Hershey, "Dress of the Mennonites."
[29] Ibid.
[30] Personal letter, August 27, 1975.
[31] Hershey, "Dress of the Mennonites."
[32] Mensch, *Memorandum*.
[33] "Minute Book," EPMHL, Lansdale, Pa. Here the plain covering refers to the bonnet.

remember the conference as always having had very strict standards of dress, and bonnets and white caps or "coverings" as everywhere worn by women members.

The conference resolution is supported by appeal to passages of Scripture. The earliest references to the cap spoke of it as a custom. In the latter quarter of the nineteenth century the wearing of the cap was associated with 1 Corinthians 11:2-16 by leaders in the Mennonite Church.[34] After that time, biblical sanctions began to be invoked in support of the practice. There is no direct evidence that this was done in the Franconia Conference until late in the nineteenth century. By 1915 the "prayer veiling" was listed as one of the ordinances for the conference. The 1933 discipline of the conference reads: "Sisters shall not wear hats, fashionable clothing, or gold for adornment. They shall wear the plain devotional covering and use the strings for tying and not for ornament."[35]

Biblical sanctions used by the Mennonite Church in support of the cap related it both to prayer and to its significance as a symbol of submission. It was considered a symbol of the order of creation: God, Christ, man, woman, and as such signified the headship of man and the subordinate position of woman. This phenomenon corresponds with a characteristic of groups that develop defensive adaptation, namely, that the woman tends to be given a restricted and subordinate role.

Following the ruling in 1911 in Franconia Conference, bonnets became plainer and more standardized. From 1911 to 1940 bonnets and head coverings were emphasized in such a way that they served as a badge of membership widely recognized both within and beyond the Mennonite group.

Formal Limits on Structural Associations

Among the rules and regulations arising from 1909 to 1940 are many that limited where members may go and the organizations to which they might belong. The turn of the century was an era of associations, organizations, and societies. A new middle class was developing and seeking to establish its identity. A changing economy and changing society needed new forms of organization. These new structures were frequently intended to replace the more familiar patterns of the small community.[36] For this very reason they threatened the key values of a disciplined brotherhood community and separation from the world. The defensive response of the conference was to codify practice and thus protect key charter emphases.

The fundamental role played by structural associations in the maintenance of an ethnic group has been demonstrated by Milton Gordon in *Assimilation in American Life*. A network of structural associations makes possible the survival of the ethnic group in spite of acculturation. Contrariwise, structural associations beyond the ethnic group are a threat to group coherence and identity. Gordon does not specifically make this point, but Siegel notes of defensive groups that "their participation in the larger society is very selective—the greater the perceived stress, the greater the selectivity and severity of controls."[37]

The numerous regulations concerning social and business activities in Franconia Conference suggest that they were designed to limit the number and kinds of contacts which members had with nonmembers. Many of the regulations appear to have been designed specifically to limit the primary contacts and commitments of members to the in-group. Others were designed to protect charter values related to nonresistance and the use of the sword, particularly in everyday matters.

The leaflet entitled "Ordinances Passed by the Franconia Conference of the Mennonite Church, 1909-1912" contained no items that specifically limited business associations or events in which members were permitted to participate. In contrast, a leaflet bearing the same title—with the added the information "Revised 1918"—began with nine items, in three sections, that specified limitations to such activities. Business and social structures were changing rapidly, and the community responded with a rigid set of controls.

1

(a) Members shall not take advantage of the "Three hundred dollar law," unless the debts are all paid.
(b) Members shall not use the bankrupt law.
(c) Members shall not sell a mortgage except all parties interested agree.
(d) If a Brother makes an assignment and his debts can not all be paid, he is to seek the peace of the debtors, if possible, in the presence of another Brother before he can take steps to come back into the Church.
(e) If a Brother sues to recover a debt he is required to take another Brother with him and seek the peace of the debtor, if possible, before he can take steps to be reconciled to the Church.

2

(a) No Brother is allowed to hold a license to sell spiritous liquors except

---

[34] Clayton Vern Beyler, "Meaning and Relevance of the Devotional Covering," M.Th. thesis, Southern Baptist Theological Seminary, 1954. The covering was listed as an ordinance by Daniel Kauffman in his book, *Manual of Bible Doctrine* (1898).
[35] *Rules and Discipline of the Franconia Conference of the Mennonite Church*, Revised July, 1933.
[36] Wiebe, *The Search for Order*.
[37] Siegel, "Defensive Structuring," p. 26.

Workers at Eastern Mennonite Home, Souderton.

for medicine. Neither shall Brethren sign a petition for such a license. Neither shall any Brother become bondsman for license.
(b) Members that sign a temperance pledge and belong to a temperance union are not communicant members unless they withdraw from the union.

3

(a) Members are not allowed to belong to secret societies, life insurance, theft insurance, labor union, farmers' unions, attend fairs, excursions, picnics, surprise parties, moving picture shows, political meetings, parks, exhibitions, horse races, baby shows, and the like.
(b) The Brethren are not allowed to convey people to places of amusements where they themselves are forbidden to attend.

In the 1921 edition of the discipline several new items are added: members are not to accept any public office, and it was considered advisable to abstain from voting. They are also requested to refrain from uniting or working with breeders, poultry, milk, or similar associations.

As members increasingly began to work in factories the problem of joining labor unions threatened. The union option of force was in violation of the charter value of nonresistance. The issue came up repeatedly in conference minutes, always with negative sanctions against union membership.

Another category of restrictions does not seem to have been aimed at direct violation of charter values. Rather, these restrictions appear designed primarily to limit structural associations:

> *Third*—That we urge our members not to take part in home or state product shows, and the banquets are especially objectionable and to be avoided.[38]

They also helped to prevent attention from being focused on the individual rather than on the group:

> *Second*—That all organized quartet, chorus, solo, or duet singing in choruses or any other public gatherings shall no longer be continued or engaged in by our members. We encourage congregational singing and recommend that our faithful, talented members be encouraged to help.[39]

The tightening of restrictions on musical expression in the 1920s was resisted by a number of otherwise loyal members of the conference. One

---

[38] "Minute Book," May 1, 1930. EPMHL, Lansdale, Pa.
[39] Ibid., October 4, 1923.

Edith Nyce, 1921. Persons not yet baptized dressed like their non-Mennonite neighbors.

pious brother was banned from communion three times for singing in choral groups contrary to conference rules. Some persons withdrew their membership.

Defensive structuring and codification of practice constituted a distinctive phase in the life of Franconia Conference. While the content of defensive structuring seems for the most part to have been designed to preserve key values of the charter, the method used to implement the structuring, i.e., codification of practice and the centralization of power in authoritarian leadership, violated the principle of mutual counsel that is inherent in the charter. Until 1947, Matthew 18 continued to be cited in each conference discipline as a recommended procedure for dealing with differences. Yet the authoritarian structures, together with the fact that no one (not even a fellow minister) was allowed to gainsay the decision of the bishops, formalized the principle to a very serious degree.

Pressures to conform, similar to those emerging in the Franconia Conference, were appearing in most areas of the Mennonite Church during the second to fourth decades of the twentieth century. Hesston College teacher Edward Yoder in 1931 reflected on his pilgrimage with the plain coat, or garb, as he called it. Yoder had publicly volunteered to adopt the garb in a 1917 meeting at the Pennsylvania Church near Hesston, Kansas. For a time he was comfortable with his decision, giving it little thought. As Yoder's circumstances changed, however, and he found himself in graduate school, the plain coat cast him as a clergyman, and he found his natural shyness augmented by his peculiar appearance. Rather than enriching his witness, which was the acclaimed function of distinctive attire, it resulted in his withdrawing from social intercourse, a fact which he much regretted later.[40]

In 1939 at Mennonite General Conference some ministers asserted that in the previous 12 years there had been a continual struggle to maintain the rules against worldliness. A "Book of Standards," sponsored by the General Problems Committee of Mennonite General Conference, was circulated in the churches prior to the 1941 sessions of the conference, and three ministers were appointed to visit the various conferences in this regard.[41] The committee reported:

> In our fellowship with the various conference bodies, we note the vital issues are nonresistance and nonconformity to the world in all its various forms. Many are captivated by the spirit of worldliness, and the

---

[40] *Edward: Pilgrimage of a Mind*, ed. by Ida Yoder (Ohio and Pennsylvania: Ida Yoder and Virgil E. Yoder, 1986), pp. 8-11.

[41] The three men were Abner Yoder, Aaron Mast, and Jessie B. Martin. See "Minutes of the Twenty-second Mennonite General Conference Held at Wellman, Iowa, August 26-29, 1941," p. 28.

Gospel standards are endangered by the cares of this world, the deceitfulness of riches, and the lust of other things. Mk. 9:14.[42]

In spite of efforts during the previous biennium the General Problems Committee expressed continuing concerns in 1941, including church unity:

> The question of nonconformity in all its phases, life insurance, nonresistance, strifes and contentions, unionism, the diverse opinions on the second coming are ever before us. Because of a wide difference of opinion as to the interpretation of Scripture and application of principles, brethren are losing patience with one another and the fellowship is being marred and in some places broken.[43]

A 1943 study conference, called by the moderator of Mennonite General Conference and the Committee on Economic and Social Relations, concluded: (1) our century-long Mennonite ways of living are breaking up, and new patterns are being set; (2) the present war is hastening the process and adding new elements, through CPS [Civilian Public Service] and perhaps in other ways; and (3) in this changing situation the church means to go along with its members and to help them wherever in conscience they need to go and can go.[44] The formation of Mennonite Mutual Aid, about which we shall say more in the next chapter, followed this meeting.

Widespread tensions in the church concerning defensive structuring resulted in a special session of Mennonite General Conference which convened at Goshen College, Goshen, Indiana, from August 15-18, 1944. Forbearance among the differing factions was achieved at the conference, but the trends continued.

In June 1946, a special session of the Franconia Conference passed an extended resolution on Christian attire. Numerous biblical passages were cited supporting modesty, separation, and sex distinction in dress, and condemning immodesty and pride.

> The Bible teaching is clear on the manner of dress for Christians. Plain teaching is given in I Tim. 2:9 and I Peter 3:3 that modest apparel is to be worn. Isa. 3:16-24 and Jer. 4:30, 31 clearly condem [sic] immodest clothing and the use of make-up. Pride, which is often manifested in dress is condemned in Scriptures such as Prov. 16:18; James 4:6; Ezek. 16:49. Separation is definitely taught in Jn. 17:14-16; Rom. 12:12; II Cor. 6:14-18; James 1:27. Christians are taught not to love the world in James 4:4 and I Jno. 2:15-17. Deu. 22:5 teaches that sex distinction is necessary in dress.[45]

Many members internalized these Scriptures and the interpretation that was given to them. For them the prescriptions and proscriptions concerning attire that followed in the resolution were meaningful symbolic representations:

> For Brethren, the plain coat, without neck-tie, and the plain hat, and black shoes. All Brethren are encouraged to adopt this standard.
>
> For Sisters, long hair without any cutting and combed becomingly. A prayer veiling which covers according to I Cor. 11, should be worn at all times. The stiff bonnet, which is the only suitable protection covering to go with the prayer veiling, is the acceptable headgear. The capedress which is made modestly and long enough to go well below the knees is the standard, with black shoes and stockings. All Sisters are encouraged to adopt this standard.
>
> The following are prohibited for Brethren: Immodest clothing which does not cover the body, together with worldliness and jewelry of all kinds.
>
> The following are prohibited for Sisters: Cutting, waving and fashionable combing of the hair. Wearing of bandannas, soft-turban type head-gear, hats or other fashionable head-gear, except plain warm head-gear for extremely cold weather. Immodest dresses with low-cut necks, short sleeves and short skirts. Wearing of anklets, going without stockings, or wearing of shoes with openings at toes and heels. Wearing men's clothing of any type. Jewelry of all types including wedding rings. Make-up, lip-stick and nail polish.[46]

Some observers have positively associated the wearing of distinctive garb, including bonnets and head coverings, with the active mission outreach of the thirties and forties. Other persons active in mission work during this same period tell of the added stresses to mission endeavor resulting from codified forms of dress and limits on structural associations.[47]

Some chafed under the multiple rules and regulations. A former Mennonite expressed her response to defensive structuring when she wrote, "I never really left the Mennonite Church (which I joined in 1906) but the

---

[42] For reports concerning the work of the committee, see ibid., pp. 37-41.

[43] Ibid., p. 28.

[44] Guy F. Hershberger, "The Committee on Economic and Social Relations Is Important Too," *GH*, vol. 56, no. 18 (May 7, 1963):384.

[45] "Resolutions Adopted by the Franconia Mennonite Conference at a Special Session, June 11, 1946," Minutes, EPMHL, Lansdale, Pa.

[46] Ibid.

[47] See John L. Ruth, *Maintaining the Right Fellowship* (Herald Press, 1984); Mary Mensch Lederach, *The Limerick Interlude* (unpublished paper); interview with Elmer G. Kolb

church left me. Years ago at counsel meeting and communion the bishops used to say 'it is an expression of peace.' But the last few times (especially) I communed there it was said 'By this you show that you are agreed with conference rules.' "[48]

In 1947 a new *Doctrinal Statement, Constitution and Discipline of the Franconia Mennonite Conference, 1725-1947*, included the Dordrecht Confession of Faith for the first time, and a printed constitution. Between drafts of the publication and its printed form, reference to Matthew 18:15-17 was removed from the communion section and placed under nonconformity, where the passage was applied to the practice of gossip.[49] The revised discipline continued to protest the use of radio for either secular or religious programs, but it did allow special singing in many contexts.[50] Under "Doctrinal Teaching" only two items were included:

1. This conference feels the necessity of urging the leaders of the church to teach Christ and His Doctrine, the new birth, separation from the world, nonresistance and other essentials relative to the welfare of the church and not to speculate on unfulfilled prophecy or the doctrine of a Millennium.

2. We believe in the keeping power of God, offering Christian Assurance on condition of an enduring faith, but the doctrine of Eternal Security, that is once in grace always in grace, is unscriptural and dangerous in its effects, and is not to be taught.[51]

In the summer of 1948 President Paul Mininger of Goshen College addressed Mennonite World Conference concerning "The Limitations of Nonconformity." The ideal, he noted, though important to all Mennonites, had received particular emphasis among certain groups in America. While based on valid convictions and possessing value, nonconformity also had real limitations. It was negative in its meaning and lacking in power to motivate conduct. "It separates man from the world and its sins," Mininger noted, "but gives him no sense of responsibility for the separation of the world from its sin." Nonconformity tends to promote self-righteousness and clouds awareness "of the real conflict that exists between the church and the world." The Mennonite Church, he said, "must work more diligently at the task of properly relating the unchanging Christian message to culture and civilization of our time."[52]

A two-day conference on nonconformity in dress sponsored by Mennonite General Conference, was held in Chicago on October 19 and 20, 1948. Franconia asked its moderator and secretary to attend the meeting.[53] The topics presented at the conference were routine, except for Oscar Burkholder's address entitled "Adapting the Principles of Nonconformity to our Time."[54]

By 1950 the standard formulations of nonconformity were being openly discussed in areas of the church where they had earlier been vigorously supported, as exemplified by two contest orations delivered at Eastern Mennonite College in 1950 and published in the *Gospel Herald*. One, by Daniel Hertzler who in a few decades would himself become editor of the *Herald*, was entitled "What Basis Nonconformity?" The other, "What's Wrong with Nonconformity?" was presented by Richard Burkholder, later to become a professor in the department of religion at Goshen College.[55] In the next decade the formulations of defensive structuring would be increasingly challenged.

The growing stresses between the norms of members and the rules of conference in Franconia were brought to the fore in 1951 by a group in the large Blooming Glen congregation "that was being exposed to different interpretations by means of radio."[56] A core of persons had remained loyal to former member William Detweiler and his radio broadcast in spite of conference censure of radio programs. Many of these same persons also received Charles G. Trumbull's *Sunday School Times* as part of a subscription club sponsored by one of the members.[57] Acknowledged leadership problems existed in the congregation and several of the dissatisfied group wrote to the bishops, requesting new leadership and specifically recommending a young man who had recently received seminary training. Response to their request was delayed, and the tensions climaxed in a preparatory service for communion.

"Twice yearly," one of this group recounts, "we observed a Preparatory

---

[48] Letter from Mamie R. Freed, Dec. 21, 1949, in response to Mennonite Family Census Request. Elmer Kolb Papers, EPMHL, Lansdale, Pa.

[49] "VII. Nonconformity," 1. (1), Franconia, Pa.: Franconia Mennonite Conference, n.d.

[50] Ibid., "V. Meetings," 3. Special Singing," p. 49.

[51] Ibid., "VI. Doctrinal Teaching," p. 50.

[52] Paul Mininger, "The Limitations of Nonconformity," *MQR* 22 (April 1950): 163-169. Quotes from pp. 165, 168, 169.

[53] "Resolutions Adopted by the Franconia Mennonite Conference, October 7, 1948," EPMHL, Lansdale, Pa.

[54] *Mennonite General Conference Report, Eastern Mennonite College, August 23-26, 1949*, pp. 55-57.

[55] *GH*, vol. 43, no. 41 (October 10, 1950), pp. 996-997; *GH*, vol. 43, no. 36 (September 5, 1950), pp. 879-880.

[56] Alice Nase, "Calvary Church of Souderton" (unpublished private paper, March, 1982), p. 1.

[57] Clarence Y. Fretz, "The Influence of Fundamentalism on Franconia Conference Mennonites, 1900 to 1945" (unpublished paper).

268 *Defensive Structuring and Codification of Practice*

The 1882 Blooming Glen meetinghouse.

New building, 1939.

and Communion Service, over which the bishop himself presided. At these times the church book of rules and regulations was read from cover to cover, following which a strong admonition was given that we abide by these rules."[58] This practice must have been widespread in the Mennonite Church, for the 1955 article on "Counsel Meeting" in *The Mennonite Encyclopedia*

As remodeled, 1968.

notes that "after an appropriate sermon the bishop reads the entire conference discipline and current infractions."[59]

Any infraction of these rules, our informant continues,

> required a public confession before the congregation admitting to a transgression of the "law"—Biblical or otherwise.... One communion Sunday after the deacon had read the morning devotion, he announced to the congregation that he was requested to state that any church members who wore wedding bands, owned TV sets, had life insurance policies, sang in community or other church groups were being asked to refrain from taking communion. Some of these restrictions had been on paper but were never enforced in this way before.[60]

Some conference leaders were proceeding more tactfully. On March 20, 1950, John E. Lapp wrote to Joseph Gross: "We both feel that at this time when we read the Conference Discipline, that we should make a comment, that any member who has any conflict of any kind about the discipline should speak to us in private. I intend to do this in our Counsel Meeting at Plain on April 2. What do you think of this approach? It will certainly help to relieve some of the tension which exists at this immediate time."[61]

A number of men in the Blooming Glen congregation had taken out life

---
[58] Nase, "Calvary Church."
[59] *ME*, s.v.
[60] Nase, "Calvary Church."
[61] Lapp Letters, EPMHL, Lansdale, Pa.

insurance policies. "My husband was one of these men," our informant continues, "and so we were among the goodly number who were banned from communion table that morning. Now that we found ourselves excommunicated, and since there seemed no evidence of change in the forseeable future, we felt that the time had come to move out and begin a new fellowship."[62]

The initial group consisted of about 30 persons. William Anders, a minister who had been ordained at Towamencin, a sister congregation, became their first pastor. The new congregation, initially named the Calvary Mennonite Church, soon dropped the distinctive "Mennonite," becoming the Calvary Church of Souderton. In this series of events the outside influences were so strong that the original identity of the group was lost.

As the strong Fundamentalist direction of the new congregation became increasingly evident, a number of the initial members returned to the Blooming Glen congregation where Paul Lederach, the young man earlier requested by the group, was now serving as interim pastor. The leadership problem at Blooming Glen was resolved when one nominee withdrew his name from the lot, leaving only a single candidate, David F. Derstine, Jr., a Th.B. graduate of Goshen who had recently returned from a period of service under the Mennonite Central Committee in Europe. He was ordained without the use of the lot, and became the first minister in the conference to receive formal support.

When the Calvary group left the Blooming Glen congregation in 1950 to establish a congregation with a Fundamentalist emphasis, it signaled the necessity of adjustments in the conference. The proposed agenda for the fall conference, 1951, recommended that a sizable list of conference resolutions and practices be reconsidered:

(b) Does Conference approve study committees being appointed to restudy conditions that relate to the following resolutions?

May 6, 1920. That members are admonished to refrain from uniting and working with Breeders, Poultry, Milk and like associations.

October 7, 1937. "Our members are not to broadcast."

October 7, 1937. Television is prohibited from being brought into our homes, or business places of our members, either as an attachment for present radios, or new radios with these attachments. Members are not to distribute or take part in distributing the same.

(c) Is Conference willing to give the Executive Committee of Conference the privilege of using their discretion in employing the best Biblical methods, suited to the circumstances, in ordaining?

(d) Does Conference encourage weekly Sunday morning preaching services for each of the congregations?[63]

Opening up for discussion at conference the revision of these resolutions initiated the formal dissolution of defensive structuring.

For several more years conference attempted to specifically modify behavior. One bishop later assessed what had happened:

> For a certain period in our conference, there was an emphasis on the matter of pride and humility. This was seen as a life of faithfulness which was expressed in a certain form. So, consequently, our rule book continued to grow. The first conference rule book in my time was only several pages. Then when the 1940 discipline came out it was a little thicker. In 1947 another rule book came out and it was even thicker. By 1959 it was still larger and that is when we went over the cliff.[64]

In reflecting on the earlier era, the elderly bishop Amos Kolb pointed out that in the beginning days of his ministry, when nothing was written down, it was possible to work with issues and make changes without the kinds of struggles that were experienced when conference rules were written down. Leaders came together to confer, then went back and worked with their congregations in finalizing decisions. He cited the example of a bishop whose handling of administration and record keeping left something to be desired, but who was able to work with the conference when he was 30, and when he was 80. This bishop would say, "For the time being . . . this will be the policy of the conference."[65]

While codification of practice was a sincere effort to make possible the preservation of key values, the means employed in this process may well have reflected the spirit of the times. We are reminded again of Wiebe's statement, quoted at the beginning of this chapter. Like the society around them, the Mennonites were adopting regulative, hierarchical structures, and through rules with impersonal sanctions, were seeking continuity and predictability in a world of endless change. Edward Yoder sensed this already in 1931 when he wrote: "The naive faith many seem to have in the panacea of legislation and machinery is part of the spirit of the age no less than to follow its fashions in dress."[66]

---

[62] Nase, "Calvary Church." Members who experienced "being set back from communion" during this period commonly refer to it as excommunication.
[63] Elmer Kolb Papers. EPMHL, Lansdale, Pa.
[64] Ruth, "Interview with Four Franconia Bishops."
[65] Ibid.
[66] *Edward*, p. 9.

8
Change and the Nonresistant Faith

Mennonites in 1983 were surprisingly similar to those of 1683 and the decades following. As in the early 1700s, Mennonites were culturally little different from their religious neighbors and open to interaction. They identified themselves with their peace position as had the early immigrants who described themselves as "defenseless Christians."[1] Once again in the 1970s and 80s Mennonites found themselves surrounded by a plethora of new religious groups composed of people seeking a fervent, more expressive piety. Not a few of the seekers were from Mennonite background. There was again a search for meaning, with Mennonite members frequently being drawn off to more ardently expressive religious groups.

How did the Mennonite Church, and particularly the Franconia Conference, get from the withdrawal stance of c. 1920-1950 to the almost full cultural participation of the 1980s? Dramatic changes occurred in cultural interaction, religious forms, and structured programs. Virtually all of the well-known symbols of Pennsylvania Mennonites were abandoned in the span of a few decades. Yet the community remained relatively stable during this period. The change of cultural patterns from nonconformity to those of the surrounding society did not result in assimilation. How was it possible, within the span of one generation, to survive dramatic change in religious forms and patterns of life and yet remain a stable, integrated community?

In this chapter we will note some of the changes that were taking place in the Mennonite Church, and more particularly in the Franconia Conference, from 1950 to 1970. Events in the Franconia Conference in the fifties and sixties closely paralleled the concerns and actions of Mennonite General Conference. There was no formal affiliation between the two agencies at this time but some Franconia leaders were actively serving on General Conference committees. Glimpses into other conferences suggest patterns of change that were frequently very similar to those of the Franconia area. A significant exception is the Illinois Conference, where patterns of acculturation were considerably accelerated.

At midcentury, Mennonites continued to be influenced by American Protestant movements, particularly the mass revivals of the fifties and a beginning although belated response to institutionalization. Some leaders were active in the peace movement of the twenties and continued to relate closely to peace movements through the sixties. An examination of socioeconomic factors is beyond the scope of this study, but they no doubt also were a stimulus to change as Franconia and other areas metamorphosed from rural to semiurban.

In a previous chapter we noted the adaptations that segments of the Mennonite Church were making as they encountered Fundamentalism in the decades surrounding the turn of the century. These adaptations included a change in biblical interpretation toward doctrine/particularism, an emphasis on nonconformity to the world bounded by codification of practice, the centralization of authoritarian leadership, and a millenarian view of the kingdom. When doctrine/particularism was applied to separation from the world, it resulted either in specific prohibition, or in prescribed forms. Prohibitions included the wearing of gold or any form of jewelry, the cutting of their hair by women members, men joining business or agricultural associations, the owning of life insurance policies, and numerous other restrictions. Among the prescriptions was the wearing of bonnets for women members. Plain suits (coats without lapels) were recommended for men, particularly those in leadership roles. The charter values of separation from the world (renamed and codified as nonconformity) and nonresistance were now seen as "fruits" or "restrictions" rather than as an integral part of the gospel.

Defensive adaptations in the Franconia Conference from c. 1910 to 1940 included the centralization of authoritarian leadership, the cultivation of cultural identity symbols, and limitations on structural associations. Franconia Conference rejected millenarianism. It stressed the centrality of peace in the Mennonite understanding of the gospel, calling it a "root," not a "fruit." Most Franconia leaders strongly supported this view, as did the affirmation of faith which was expressed at the close of every conference session: "This conference is still willing to continue in the nonresistant and simple faith of Christ."[2]

Growing Peace Emphasis

As the Mennonite Church moved into midcentury, the strong pendulum swing toward Fundamentalism was increasingly challenged by a growing emphasis on peace and service. While the peace emphasis reached heightened articulation in the 1950s, it could be traced back through history to the "Brotherly Union" mandate to abandon all violence and to the early

---

[1] "The 1773 Letter to Holland Mennonites," *MQR* 3 (October 1929): 226.

[2] Following midcentury, the wording was altered several times but always included "continuing in the nonresistant and simple faith of Christ."

Clayton Kratz (front row, second from left), disappeared in 1920 while on a relief assignment in Russia.

settlers' declaration that "we have dedicated ourselves to serve all Men in every Thing that can be helpful to the Preservation of Men's Lives, but we find no Freedom in giving, or doing, or assisting in any Thing by which Men's Lives are destroyed or hurt."[3] The voice had been heard most clearly in times of war, or when brothers or sisters were in need. It came to the fore in the Civil War when John M. Brenneman wrote *Christianity and War* and John F. Funk stated his convictions in *Warfare: Its Evils, Our Duty.*[4] A few years later the needs of Mennonites in Russia called forth a response from American Mennonites, and at the turn of the century the famine in India evoked both material and spiritual response from American Mennonites.

In World War I neither Mennonite nor government leaders were prepared to handle a conscientious objector response to a military draft. Young Mennonites were frequently inducted into military camps, where they generally refused to wear military uniforms or participate in training. Many of them were in time furloughed to farm programs, but some felt an inner compunction to give themselves in service to needy war victims and, when released by the government, joined a relief unit in France under Quaker auspices. At least 60 young men from the Mennonite Church served in this program, including one Franconia participant who shared his experience in a letter to a conference leader.[5] In the summer of 1919 at a conference at Clermont-en-Argonne, France, these young men expressed their vision for the church. The dream included increased inter-Mennonite cooperation, a future Mennonite World Conference, greater missionary activity, and

> the development of a social conscience concerned with labor relations, prison reform, housing and urban problems; an aggressive peace program including a conference of peace churches, the production of literature, the development of peace curricula in the schools and colleges, and a program of witness to the state against military training and the imprisonment of conscientious objectors; serious inquiry into the causes of the world's spiritual and social ills, and the development of a relief and service organization ready to deal effectively with emergencies, such as wars and natural disasters.[6]

An American Mennonite Young People's Conference grew out of the Clermont meeting. The youthful Harold S. Bender was asked to become chairman of the group, although he had not been at Clermont. He consented, but with the stipulation that he would remain loyal to the church. Some Mennonite leaders were threatened both by the social programs envisioned at Clermont and the aggressive manner in which some of the young men proposed to carry them out, and the Young People's Conference was short-lived.[7] Yet a half century later all of the programs of which these young men dreamed were being carried forward in the Mennonite Church.

The Mennonite Church responded officially when fellow Mennonites were in need in Russia in 1920. A newly formed inter-Mennonite agency, the Mennonite Central Committee, sent several young men to investigate the situation, one of whom was Clayton Kratz from the Blooming Glen congregation in Franconia. Kratz disappeared early in the mission, never to be heard from again.[8] A second participant, Orie O. Miller, became the prime

---

[3] "The 1775 Declaration to the Colonial Assembly of Pennsylvania," John C. Wenger, *History of the Mennonites of the Franconia Conference* (Telford, Pa.: The Franconia Mennonite Historical Society, 1937), pp. 409-410.

[4] *Both* (Chicago: John F. Funk, 1863).

[5] Letter to J. C. Clemens, May 8, 1919, from Harvey G. Mack. Hist. Mss. 1-3, J. C. Clemens, Box 1, Correspondence 1920-25, Folder 25, Letters 1919, EPMHL, Lansdale, Pa. A second letter, dated September 17, 1919, concerned addresses of Franconia leaders to whom reports of the Clermont conference were to be sent.

[6] Guy F. Hershberger, "Historical Background of the Formation of the Mennonite Central Committee," *MQR* 44 (July 1970): 234.

[7] Guy F. Hershberger, "Harold S. Bender and His Time," *MQR* 38 (April 1964): 86-88. Orie O. Miller took a similarly cautious attitude toward the young people's conference. Concerning the 1923 meeting at Forks, Indiana, he wrote to Bender: "If I shall be at this meeting, and a spirit manifests itself like it did at Goshen last week either by one side or the other, I shall plan to immediately leave the meeting." Paul Erb, *Orie O. Miller, The Story of a Man and an Era* (Scottdale, Pa.: Herald Press, 1969), pp. 285-286.

[8] Hershberger, "Historical Background," pp. 241-243.

Orie O. and Elta Miller with daughter Lois.

moving force in the development of service programs in the Mennonite Church, embodying both creative vision and the executive leadership.[9]

Miller was sensitive to differing convictions yet aware of tensions between codification of practice and the service emphasis. In a 1921 letter to a co-worker in Near East Relief he explained that in the context of rural isolation certain customs had developed among Mennonites which amounted to "about as much as religion itself." In picking workers for relief, he said, he had tried to "keep in mind that only workers be sent who will as they get experience be able to distinguish between what is essential and what is not without letting it affect their spiritual lives."[10]

Following his participation in the emergency relief program in Russia, Miller tried to keep alive the peace and service program. In a 1927 *Gospel Herald* article concerning inter-Mennonite cooperation he noted:

> We have many differences, some deep-rooted and fundamental, others trivial and unessential.... We also have our common faith and characteristics. Mennonitism everywhere still includes a belief that the teachings of the New Testament were intended to be literally observed. This brings with a belief in the practice of the simple life, nonresistance, and brotherly love. This emphasis on simple living, this conviction that love shall be the Christian's only weapon in righting wrong and overcoming evil, this rallying to each other's aid whenever there is distress are the main points on which all Mennonites today have a common heritage.[11]

Miller both solicited support for the Mennonite peace and service program and kept in touch with the peace programs of other agencies. In response to criticism, however, he limited his participation in non-Mennonite agencies to that of an observer.[12]

The Peace Problems Committee of Mennonite General Conference, a standing committee initiated in 1919, was the official agency of the church for articulating peace concerns. Its responsibility included peace education, representation to government in matters affecting military service and conscientious objection, and a peace witness to other Christians. In the decades preceding World War II, the Mennonite Church issued 13 docu-

---

[9] For a discussion of the beginnings of the Mennonite Central Committee, see James Juhnke, "Mennonite Benevolence and Revitalization in the Wake of World War I," *MQR* 60 (January 1986): 15-30.

[10] Letter to James H. Nicol. See Erb, p. 286.

[11] Ibid., p. 86.

[12] See Paul Toews, "The Long Weekend or the Short Week: Mennonite Peace Theology, 1925-1940," *MQR* 60 (January 1986):38-57.

ments relating to peace and nonresistance, most of which were addressed to government officials.[13]

When the threat of World War II and conscription necessitated the planning of an alternative service program for conscientious objectors, the Mennonite Central Committee was the natural avenue for this cooperative effort. Segments of the church continued to vigorously question the resultant intergroup and interdenominational cooperation. A 1944 *Sword and Trumpet* article accused both the Mennonite Central Committee and the Peace Problems Committee of habitual association with "the *greatest of sinners*, the modernists." The same issue included four feature articles that rigorously promoted nonconformity in attire.[14]

Two highly significant statements concerning peace and Mennonite identity appeared in the beginning years of World War II. Guy F. Hershberger's *War, Peace, and Nonresistance*, published in 1944, articulated the Mennonite peace position more completely than had been done previously. The treatment included both Old and New Testament biblical exegesis, a history of pacifism in the Christian church with emphasis on the Anabaptist-Mennonite experience, and a discussion of the issues raised by the contemporary situation. It, too, received a sharply critical response from Fundamentalist-oriented Mennonites.[15] The second statement, Harold S. Bender's presidential address to the American Society of Church History in 1943, entitled "The Anabaptist Vision,"[16] set the tone for a new identity for Mennonites, although it would not be widely cited by them for another two decades.

Civilian Public Service, the finally agreed-upon alternative service program for conscientious objectors in World War II, broadened the vision of young men who participated, both in relation to fellow Christians of other denominations and opportunities for service. It was an intergroup program, administered by the Mennonite, Friends, and Brethren Service committees. The constituencies of these groups sponsored and financed the program. Eighty-seven additional religious denominations were represented by three or more participants in the program.[17] Many young men followed CPS with a term of foreign relief. Women voluntarily took part in both programs. Younger siblings often participated in the newly instituted voluntary service programs, in time greatly increasing the community's range of primary contacts. By 1950 many of these young people had returned to their home communities and were influential.

Both a widespread vision for peace and service programs and the organizational structures to implement them grew out of the CPS and relief programs during and following World War II. While the rejection of violence and weapons of war dated back to the beginning of the Anabaptist movement, it was the creative responses to military drafts—first in the French Reconstruction Unit and in Near East Relief following World War I, and then of Civilian Public Service in World War II—that opened both doors and the eyes of Mennonites to positive opportunities for service. The relief units of World War I touched only a few but did create leadership vision. The earlier belief that a peace position called for distinctive separation from the world was replaced in World War II by both the vision and the necessary structures for broadly supported peace programs which reached beyond Mennonite communities.

The CPS, relief, and voluntary service programs are seen by one Mennonite elder statesman and educator to have been the most influential inducement to change in the Mennonite Church.[18] As volunteers worked face-to-face with people with different ideas in communities and institutions, many of the assumptions behind defensive structuring were challenged. These Mennonites then took their new understandings back to their congregations. Doctrine/particularism and codified nonconformity, centralized authoritarian leadership and limitations on structural associations, appeared to be inadequate expressions of the gospel to these laypeople who were increasingly identifying being Mennonite with peace, service to humankind, and the priesthood of all believers.

New Wine in New Wineskins

The January 16, 1951, issue of the official Mennonite weekly magazine, *Gospel Herald*, carried two editorials, one entitled "New Wine in New Bottles" and the other "Prayer for Revival." In the first, editor Paul Erb noted that "new tasks and responsibilities require new means." The organizations

---

[13] Richard C. Detweiler, *Mennonite Statements on Peace, 1915 to 1966* (Scottdale, Pa.: Herald Press, 1968).

[14] Ernest G. Gehman, "Friends of the Enemies of God," *The Sword and the Trumpet*, vol. 12, no. 1 (March 1944), pp. 94-95. The articles on nonconformity were Clarence Fretz, "Nonconformity in Attire," pp. 96-104; John Horsch, "Worldly Conformity in Dress" (reprint), pp. 105-112; Mrs. A. D. Wenger, "Our Attire in Relation to Social Purity," pp. 112-119; and Bishop Geo. R. Brunk, "Dress" (reprint), pp. 120-122.

[15] For a further commentary see Theron F. Schlabach, "To Focus a Mennonite Vision, "*Kingdom, Cross, and Community*, ed. J. R. Burkholder and Calvin Redekop (Scottdale, Pa.: Herald Press, 1976), pp. 15-50, especially pp. 27-28. Two additional articles in the book focus specifically on the contribution of Hershberger: Leonard Gross, "History and Community in the Thought of Guy F. Hershberger," pp. 51-64; and Robert S. Kreider, "Discerning the Times," pp. 65-90.

[16] For the text of the address see *Church History* 13 (March 1944): 3-24; and *MQR* 18 (April 1944): 67-88.

[17] Melvin Gingerich, *Service for Peace* (Akron, Pa.: The Mennonite Central Committee, 1949), p. 452.

[18] Personal interview with Paul Mininger, June 1984. Others have strongly supported this view.

280   *Change and the Nonresistant Faith*

*Paul Erb,
editor of* Gospel Herald
from 1944 to 1962.

and methods of 1851 and 1901 are no longer adequate, he said, for the extensive programs and evangelism of 1951. "Our problem," he noted, "is to find an expression of true Biblical faith in ways that are consistent to that faith." The second editorial, entitled "Prayer for Revival," spoke of city-wide revivals all over the country that were drawing huge crowds and resulting in "thousands of professed conversions." A profound stirring of interest in things of the spirit was in evidence, Erb said, and the executive committee of Mennonite General Conference had called for January 21 as a day of prayer for revival throughout the Mennonite Church. The editorial listed how and what persons should pray for, urging that constitutents particularly pray "that we may know how to chart a course of non-resistant living amid the rising tides of fear and hate and war."[19]

The United States was involved in a limited war, was planning a permanent military draft system, and World War III was threatening. A new statement on nonresistance called "Peace and the Christian Witness" was adopted at Mennonite General Conference in August 1951. The conference noted that "a new statement of position is desirable, setting forth more completely the full meaning of our nonresistant faith, both for strengthening the faith and life of our membership and for a more adequate testimony to others."[20] The carefully prepared document continues to serve in the 1980s.

Mennonites were becoming highly trained and educated, full participants in business and the professions, as the moderator noted in his address to Mennonite General Conference in August 1951. Through the service and mission programs they were becoming world travelers. "We are becoming alarmingly dependent upon the efficiency of organization," he said, "and of necessity then, less dependent on the power of the Spirit."[21] These trends—professionalism, internationalism, and institutionalization—would become increasingly pronounced in the next decades.

Change was also affecting expressions of separation from the world. A book explicating the doctrine of nonconformity had been mandated at the special session of Mennonite General Conference concerning "world-ward drift" in 1944. Author J. C. Wenger shifted the vantage point, calling the book *Separated unto God*.[22] The move was significant. The proposed agenda for the 1951 fall conference in Franconia recommended that a sizable list of conference resolutions and practices be reconsidered, including membership in agricultural associations, radio broadcasting and television, methods of ordination, and the holding of weekly preaching services in the congregations.[23]

Erb's second editorial concern, "Prayer for Revival," presaged a course of events of unanticipated scope. The mass revivals sweeping through American Protestantism in the early fifties were soon to be echoed in the Mennonite Church. Two Virginia Mennonites, George R. Brunk II and his brother Lawrence, pooled their resources and purchased a large tent and other necessary equipment and began holding mass meetings in the summer of 1951.[24] A September article in the *Gospel Herald* tells of a revival campaign in Franconia extending from July 29 through September 3.[25] Twenty-five hundred persons were reported by writer Paul M. Lederach to have attended the meetings on weekday evenings, and from ten to twelve thousand on weekend and closing nights. The decorum of the meetings was above reproach, he said, and confessors were invited to testify each evening. "If you have no testimony you need a confession," became the slogan of the meetings. In the large Franconia congregation over 130 persons responded to a Sunday morning invitation for a confession of sin or renewed dedication. In the neighboring Blooming Glen congregation, on the morning of August 26, there were 85 confessions and testimonies and two conversions. Then in

---

[19] *GH*, vol. 44, no. 3 (January 16, 1951), pp. 51-52.

[20] *Peace and the Christian Witness* (Scottdale, Pa.: Mennonite Publishing House, n.d.).

[21] *Mennonite General Conference Proceedings*, pp. 18-19.

[22] (Scottdale, Pa.: Herald Press, 1951).

[23] Elmer Kolb Papers, EPMHL, Lansdale, Pa.

[24] The first series of meetings began on June 3, 1951, at East Chestnut Street in Lancaster, Pa., and continued for seven weeks. The second series was held at Souderton, Pa., beginning on July 29, 1951, and closing September 3. The third campaign was held in the late summer and fall at Orrville, Ohio, and the fourth at Manheim, Pa. For an in-group account see Katie Florence Shank, ed., *Revival Fires* (Broadway, Va.: published by the author, 1952).

[25] Paul M. Lederach, "Revival in Franconia," *GH*, vol. 44, no. 38 (September 18, 1951), pp. 902-903.

George R. Brunk II at podium during 1951 Souderton campaign.

response to a call for consecration, almost the entire audience stood. The "Franconia cowboys," a gang of rowdy Mennonite youths, became the Franconia Christian Workers. Even so, not all Mennonites supported the meetings. Some drove many miles to hear the messages, Lederach noted, while others closed their doors and windows so as not to hear. The fall conference in Franconia recorded "praise to God for the revival experienced among us," and added six points to guide ministers in shepherding their congregations.[26]

A Lancaster campaign, held from June 3 to July 22, had been given a laudatory report in the September *Gospel Herald*.[27] In November Mennonite Publishing House advertising manager Ford Berg reported on "A Week End at the Brunk Brothers' Revival in Ohio."[28] News releases of nationwide mass revival campaigns led by Billy Graham, John R. Rice, and others had been flooding his desk for months. Mennonites now were also experiencing the revival. Ford felt he was "standing on holy ground," yet he also recognized limitations to the method. In the same issue of the *Herald* a contributed article selected from the *Mennonite Weekly Review* sounded a dissonant note. "The large crowds of our time," it said, "give us a false sense of values. The man who can fill a big auditorium is by no means always the man with the most important message.... Every big crowd is pervaded by a strong emotional factor."[29] The mass tent revivals continued, augmented by a new unit in 1952 sponsored by Christian Laymen's Evangelism, Inc.[30]

At its April 9-10, 1953, meeting, the General Council of General Conference adopted a "Statement of Concerns on Revival and Evangelism." The statement, basically supportive, appeared in the *Herald* in June and was reprinted by popular demand in large type on the front page in August.[31] Between its two appearances, an Evangelism Study Conference was held at Goshen College Biblical Seminary. Three matters were considered of crucial importance by the conference: the primary-junior evangelism which had become so common; the phenomenon of mass evangelism both within and without the Mennonite Church; and evangelism for full discipleship as contrasted with an evangelism that aims only at crisis commitment to faith in Christ.[32] Two of these concerns related directly to the charter; all three had been concerns in the earlier waves of revivalism. This conference was a

---

[26] *Minutes*, fall conference, 1951.
[27] Maurice E. Lehman, "The Lancaster Revival," *GH*, vol. 44, no. 36 (September 4, 1951), pp. 852-853.
[28] *GH*, vol. 44, no. 46 (November 13, 1951), pp. 1093-1095.
[29] "The Auditorium Age," *GH*, vol. 44, no. 46 (November 13, 1951), p. 1092. From *Mennonite Weekly Review*. Selected by J. J. Hostetler.
[30] Nelson E. Kauffman, "Report of the First Annual Meeting of Christian Laymen's Evangelism, Inc.," *GH*, vol. 46, no. 5 (February 3, 1953), pp. 102-103.
[31] Vol. 42, no. 33 (August 18, 1953).
[32] Paul Erb, "The Evangelism Conference," *GH*, vol. 46, no. 19 (May 12, 1953), p. 435.

watershed concerning the acceptability of mass revivalism in the Mennonite Church.[33]

Paul Erb entitled his editorial a few weeks later "Evangelism for Full Discipleship":

> This honest search for truth may be something very different from a revivalistic intoxication that sends the addict reeling from one evangelistic meeting to another. It is sober business to search, and to see what things are so—a business entirely too prosaic for one who has only fallen under the spell of the flood-lights and the sawdust aisles and the bright singing and emotion-packed response to the invitation. If those things do not make the attendant a Biblical Christian their influence is shallow and in the long run harmful.... The Christian way is not a way of ease. It is not pleasant to bear a cross.[34]

As in earlier encounters with revivalism, both the emphasis and the methods caused discomfort to some. Pietistic and Fundamentalistic understandings of doctrine permeated the revival sermons of both Hammer and Brunk and are reflected in Erb's cautions. Brunk had a different approach than Franconia had ever had before, one leader noted, with some good and some questionable effects. Whereas the love of God had traditionally been the key emphasis, as explained in Abraham Godshalk's treatise on revivalism and the new creature in Christ Jesus, it was God's wrath that was brought to the fore in the tent meetings.[35] At the closing service of the Brunk revivals in September 1959 the moderator told the audience that if their preachers "would preach like Brother George has done, no doubt some would ... leave the church and say that they want to worship where preachers speak with authority but with a heart of love."[36] Many had been genuinely awakened spiritually. Not all would be comfortable with the theological presuppositions undergirding their experience.

Response to the meetings in local communities was mixed. For years, since nonconformity had been brought into the conference c. 1910 with the doctrine/particularism of the Bible conferences, consecration had been associated with plain clothes. The mass revivals reinforced this emphasis. Some persons became entranced with the evangelist, slighting local leaders. Others accepted the meetings with moderation, giving a generally positive evaluation of the experience. Testimony meetings followed the invitation each evening and must have had their own special appeal for a community with a propensity for gossip. A number of nervous breakdowns were attributed to the pressure to testify or confess. But the meetings were also, according to one informant, a very social experience. On Sunday evenings persons brought their suppers and all together had a fellowship meal.

Children responded to the invitations—sometimes lightheartedly, sometimes in fear. One informant said she was 13 at the time of the first Brunk campaign. Her family attended every night of the series, although they did not attend later series. She and her peers always sat on the front benches. Brunk was telling the audience how they could do better and she thought she could, too, so she went forward with her peers. "It was kind of fun," she said. But then the bishop came to see her and she didn't like that at all. It was a "heavy." A contemporary, attending the same meetings as a child, summarized his impressions as "hellfire and brimstone." He responded at age nine.

Mass revivals continued in the next decades, but their impact waned after the mid-fifties. Concern over child evangelism prompted an action at General Conference in 1955, lending support to a two-page prepared statement entitled "Position on the Nurture and Evangelism of Children."[37] Revivalism was resulting in the baptism of increasing numbers of children and threatening the charter principle of adult baptism. During 1956 only one article in Mennonite publications related to revivalism and evangelism and no article directly supported mass revivalism. Christian Laymen's Evangelism, Inc., dissolved in 1962, and local congregational revivals decreased markedly.

How can one understand the overwhelming response to the revivals, especially in light of their brief crescendo? Is William McLoughlin's thesis applicable?

> Great Awakenings (and the revivals that are a part of them) are the results, not of depressions, wars, or epidemics, but of critical disjunctions in our self-understandings. They are not brief outbursts of mass emotionalism by one group or another but profound cultural transformations affecting all Americans and extending over a generation or more.[38]

Were the mass tent meetings of the fifties part of a profound cultural transformation, a Great Awakening in the Mennonite Church? Mennonite

---

[33] Dale Franklin Dickey, "The Tent Evangelism Movement in the Mennonite Church: A Dramatic Analysis" (Ph.D. thesis, Bowling Green State University, 1980), p. 130.

[34] *GH*, vol. 46, no. 23 (June 9, 1953), pp. 539-540, 555.

[35] *A Description of the New Creature* (Doylestown: William M. Large, 1838).

[36] Elmer Kolb Papers, EPMHL, Lansdale, Pa. John E. Lapp was moderator. Repeatedly, Brunk had curtly reprimanded both ministers and church members from the pulpit.

[37] "Position on the Nurture and Evangelism of Children," *Mennonite General Conference Proceedings*, Hesston, Kansas, 1955, pp. 53-55.

[38] William G. McLoughlin, *Revivals, Awakenings, and Reforms* (Chicago: University of Chicago Press, 1978), p. 2.

communities were undoubtedly experiencing disjunction and the need for reorientation. One informant, who served as a counselor in the Brunk meetings in the Franconia Conference, called them "such an awakening, enlightening process. People thought of so many things they had not thought of before." The 1950s were undeniably the beginning of an Awakening in the Mennonite Church—if Awakening is understood in McLoughlin's terms, as an adjustment of religious understandings to the cultural milieu. The mass revivals of the fifties brought spiritual revival for many and made possible reorientation and the unleashing of energies to find expression in new programs. Mennonite communities in the next 30 years would also experience profound transformation in religious forms, structured programs, and cultural interaction. They would be searching for new means to implement new tasks and responsibilities.

The process of change in the Mennonite Church was probably forwarded by the appearance of the Revised Standard Version of the Bible in 1952. The new translation created a furor in conservative evangelical and Fundamentalist circles. Its publication was an affront to doctrine particularism, which ipso facto was challenged by multiple translations. While inerrancy was technically based on original manuscripts, lay people tended to understand the teaching as applying to the King James Version of the Bible. Variant wordings in the translation of passages that were considered of prime importance were unsettling at best.

The Mennonite Church quickly responded to the situation. A committee consisting of Chester K. Lehman, Th.D., from Eastern Mennonite College; Harold S. Bender, Th.D., of Goshen Biblical Seminary; and Millard C. Lind, B.D. (but soon also a Th.D.), from the Mennonite Publishing House, were chosen to evaluate the new translation. The committee published an extensive, thorough report in four issues of the *Gospel Herald* from January to May 1953. The report explicitly examined charges brought against the *RSV*, discussed the merits and weaknesses of the translation, and presented a general conclusion and evaluation. Among the merits were readability, an indication of poetry, accuracy of translation, a better understanding of biblical grammar than the King James Version, and a faithful translation of cardinal doctrinal passages. The study pointed out that "much of the progress of the *RSV* in accuracy of translation and the use of a better Greek text was already made in the American Standard Version of 1901."[39]

A few months later the "Virginia Conference Committee to Study the Revised Standard Version" published its conclusions. "While we do not endorse the hysteria and fanaticism which has been displayed against the Revised Standard Version," it reported, "we recognize there is ground for protest and disapproval."[40] The committee consisted of Menno J. Brunk, chairman, George R. Brunk II, and J. Otis Yoder.

While varying translations cast new light on some passages, they also fostered insecurity in the lay Bible reader. How could one know what the passage really meant if different translations seemed to be saying different things? Possible neglect of the Bible was one of the concerns expressed in the report submitted by General Council to General Conference in 1957. "We want to remain a Bible-reading, Bible-loving, Bible-obeying people," the statement asserted, but dangers threatened. Both modernism and Fundamentalism were to be eschewed, it noted, yet the greatest immediate danger seemed to be coming from "neo-orthodoxy with its low view of inspiration and its relativistic ethics and its inadequate doctrine of the church.... Unless we determine to keep true to our Anabaptist heritage of faith and life," the statement continued, "we can lose much of our distinctive doctrinal position in one generation."[41]

Separation and Structural Associations

Mennonite General Conference in August 1953 expressed concerns for unity, spiritual life, and the need for "separation to Christ and from the world system."[42] It was a time of both exhilaration and anxiety. Many found the new programs and freedoms invigorating. Others, those for whom codified expressions of nonconformity held deep meaning, felt profound concern. Churchwide, Mennonites were struggling with the issues. Following substantial groundwork by the Commission for Christian Education, an extensive "Declaration of Commitment in Respect to Christian Separation and Nonconformity to the World" was submitted by the General Council to General Conference at the 1955 meeting held in Hesston, Kansas. It was a broad, biblically based plea specifically touching many areas of life, but it did not call for codified forms.[43]

In the fall of 1955 simultaneous nonconformity conferences, conjointly

---

[39] Among Mennonites, listing degrees in this manner was most unusual. The reports were as follows: "Preliminary Report of the Special Committee on the Revised Standard Version," *GH*, vol. 46, no. 1 (January 6, 1953), pp. 1-2, 21; "The Revised Standard Version, An Examination and Evaluation," *GH*, vol. 46, no. 19 (May 12, 1953), pp. 433-434, 437; "The Revised Standard Version," *GH*, vol. 46, no. 20 (May 19, 1953), pp. 460-63; and "The Revised Standard Version," *GH*, vol. 46, no. 21 (May 26, 1953), pp. 484-491. Quote from vol. 46, no. 19 (May 12, 1953), p. 437.

[40] "Report of Virginia Conference Committee to Study the Revised Standard Version," *GH*, vol. 46, no. 30 (July 28, 1953), pp. 709-710.

[41] "General Problems Committee," *Reports Submitted to Mennonite General Conference at Harrisonburg, Virginia, August 26, 27, 1957*, p. 38.

[42] "Forward in 1953-1955," *GH*, vol. 46, no. 37 (September 15, 1953), p. 872.

[43] "Exhibit XVIII. Report of the General Problems Committee," *Mennonite General Conference Proceedings, Hesston, Kansas, 1955*, pp. 87-91.

MDS volunteer, Curt Nice, cleaning up after Wilkes-Barre flood.

planned by the Mennonite Commission for Christian Education and the General Problems Committee, were to be held in 44 locations across the Mennonite Church.[44] Anticipating the meetings, the Franconia spring conference declared: "All of our congregations are asked to work toward a better application of the principles of nonconformity as appearing in our discipline. . . . Special attention should be given to the matter of non-cutting of hair by sisters."[45] The conferences in the Franconia area were scheduled for September 17 and 18 at the Blooming Glen church where J. C. Wenger and Emanual Peachey were the speakers, and at Souderton, with Peter Wiebe and Sanford Shetler as leaders.

In the ensuing years in Franconia young women who were "Christian workers" or ministers' wives would especially feel the pressure to model cultural identity symbols, while lay members would increasingly ignore them. The minutes of the executive committee meetings of the conference during the 1950s repeatedly express concern over the disregard of conference rules relating to the cutting of hair by sisters, the wearing of jewelry, and similar items. The clandestine ownership of television sets was becoming an increasing embarrassment. In 1956 Franconia business men requested that the bishops meet with them to discuss the economic problems they were experiencing as a result of conference restrictions.[46]

By 1960 persons in leadership positions were sometimes bypassing dress codes. In the Franconia Conference the "plain coat" normally worn by ministers was being ignored in marginal geographic locations including Vermont, Philadelphia, Greystone Park, New Jersey, and later at Easton. By 1970 a number of ministers in the heartland of the conference had discontinued wearing it, and after considerable discussion the executive committee recommended, "In each situation work out the most satisfactory way with the person, congregation, and bishop involved."[47] In 1959 and 1960 faculty dress standards at Christopher Dock Mennonite High School received renewed attention. Repeated discussions by the board and the Religious Welfare Committee resulted in the issuing of a printed statement. It no longer specified the wearing of a plain coat by male teachers or the wearing of the cape dress by women faculty. It did appeal to loyalty and specified long hair and the devotional covering for women, while prohibiting short or tight skirts. Men were to eschew sport coats and crew cuts.[48]

While defensive structures were being defied, multiple congregational, conference, and churchwide activities were being organized, generally under the leadership of laypeople. The 1953 Mennonite General Conference Report included a "Report of the Lay Activities Committee" and a "Report of the Committee of Lay Worker Status."[49] Lay activity was not new. The Sunday school movement had largely been under the leadership of laypersons, as had the building of homes for the elderly and even the mission program in Franconia Conference. The multiplicity of activities was new. The trend continued, until in 1983 it took seven pages to list the 63 committees of one congregation, and an additional page to list the congregational members participating on conference and churchwide boards.[50]

This increase in structured activities for laypeople in local congregations may have been crucial for boundary maintenance as acculturation was breaking down defensive structures. In an extensive study on assimilation in American life, Milton Gordon concludes that, as ethnic or religious groups become acculturated, the creation of multiple structural associations through

---

[44] Hist. Mss. 1-278. H. S. Bender 81/15. Archives of the Mennonite Church, Goshen, Ind.

[45] Minutes, Franconia Mennonite Conference.

[46] Letter from John E. Lapp to Guy F. Hershberger, June 29, 1956. John E. Lapp Letters, EPMHL, Lansdale, Pa.

[47] "Executive Committee Minutes," January 7, April 28, and May 3, 1960; November 9, 1961; November 25, 1969; April 8, 1970; Elmer Kolb Papers, EPMHL, Lansdale, Pa.

[48] Ibid., February 12, 1959; February 29, 1960.

[49] Pp. 88-92.

[50] *Directory*, Blooming Glen Mennonite Church, 1983-84.

Harold Mininger consults with Wilkes-Barre resident.

which they experience their primary contacts enables them to retain their group identity.[51] During this period Mennonite parochial education also flowered, similarly providing a strong base for in-group identity. Donald B. Kraybill, a Mennonite sociologist, has noted that "the establishment of schools by an ethnic group for its members from elementary to college level can be understood as a defensive reaction by the group to a perceived threat in its external social environment."[52]

New peace and service structures increasingly reached beyond Mennonites and their community enclaves. From their experience serving in CPS units in mental hospitals in World War II, Mennonites had learned both of the chronic needs of the mentally ill and that they were gifted to meet that need. In the decades following the war they opened a number of mental hospitals and health centers designed to meet the needs of the larger community. One of these, the Penn Foundation, was located in the Franconia area and begun by one of its members, Dr. Norman Loux. The Mennonite Economic Development Associates (MEDA), an organization designed to aid in financing projects in economically underdeveloped areas, assisted with 422 projects in 25 countries from its beginning in 1953 to 1978. Mennonite Disaster Service, which dates from 1950, enabled people to come together, usually with their own tools and equipment, to clean up after floods and to rebuild after tornadoes, earthquakes, or fires. In the Franconia area the first major effort was in response to the Stroudsburg flood in 1955. Several local businessmen solicited interdenominational response among fellow entrepreneurs who had useful tools and equipment that could increase the effectiveness of the large number of lay volunteers. Following this incident the bishops wanted the Mennonite leaders to organize for future disasters. The businessmen said such an organization would need to be interdenominational because of the precedent, but they finally compromised by organizing it to include the peace churches of the area.[53]

The formalization of mutual aid received increasing attention in the fifties. Mutual aid societies, mostly on a conference level, had been functioning among Mennonites since the 1890s.[54] Franconia had resisted the formalization of aid until well into the thirties. As proposals for further development of mutual aid structures were under consideration by a committee of General Conference, John E. Lapp suggested Mennonite cooperatives, and then in a 1943 meeting supported a proposed investment-loan system.[55] But when Orie O. Miller inquired whether the proposed Mennonite Mutual Aid plan could be presented to the Franconia Conference in 1944, some leaders objected that such aid should be kept on a conference level, except for smaller conferences that could be united by the association.[56]

Mennonite Mutual Aid was formally organized under the sponsorship of General Conference in 1945 with Orie O. Miller as president. Providing loans to former CPS men to help them become reestablished was one of the initial functions. But change in employment, social, and cultural patterns was mandating other forms of organized insurance. A particularly difficult problem was posed by insurance for liability and property damage because litigation was likely. Litigation was, of course, prohibited by the charter.[57] Franconia Conference proposed a mutual plan for automobile aid to the state government in 1950.[58] General Conference in 1955 recommended that

> Mennonite Mutual Aid be requested to study with care the feasibility and advisability of . . . public liability and property damage . . . such a

---

[51] *Assimilation in American Life* (New York: Oxford University Press, 1964).

[52] "Religious and Ethnic Socialization in a Mennonite High School," *MQR* 51 (October 1977): 330.

[53] Elmer M. Ediger, "Influences on the Origin and Development of Mennonite Mental Health Centers," *MQR* 56 (January 1982): 32-46; J. Winfield Fretz, *The MEDA Experiment: Twenty-five Years of Economic Development* (Waterloo, Ont.: Conrad Press, 1978); and Interview with Harold and Myrtle Mininger, September 19, 1984.

[54] Lancaster organized in 1893 and Ohio in 1897. See "Mennonite Mutual," *ME*, s.v.

[55] Schlabach, "A Mennonite Vision," p. 35.

[56] Letters from John E. Lapp to Orie O. Miller, September 18 and September 28, 1944. Lapp Letters, EPMHL, Lansdale, Pa.

[57] Article VI.

[58] John E. Lapp to Mr. Keck, Department of Revenue, January 18, 1950; John E. Lapp to Mr. Randolf Rayder, Department of Justice, January 18, 1950; "Franconia Mennonite Association for Automobile Aid," Lapp Letters, EPMHL, Lansdale, Pa.

Neil Janzen, MCC India director, consults with Balumath villagers (India) concerning sandal-making.

company would have to accept litigation and would need to be set up to defend itself legally.... This it would seem, is a field which we are not set up to enter and which would involve our church in such a way as to be undesirable.[59]

Two years later General Conference postponed the issue of liability and automobile aid, recommending as a temporary solution that liability insurance be acquired through Goodville Mutual Casualty Company, Goodville, Pennsylvania.[60] In another four years the 1961 conference proceedings would report that Mennonite Automobile Aid was providing Collision-Comprehensive Coverage.[61]

Life insurance repeatedly came up for discussion after 1950. The "Report of the Life Insurance Study Committee" to General Conference in 1951 stated 16 conclusions but made no recommendations.[62] Two years later another report tacitly opened the way for life insurance, recommending that insurance needs be supplied by the brotherhood or MMA. But it added that "when 'circumstances mean other forms of insurance,' that this not prohibit persons from becoming members."[63] By 1961 a Survivors' Aid Plan would be functioning under the auspices of Mennonite Mutual Aid, Inc.[64]

One social historian has called the Mennonite community vision, of which Mennonite Mutual Aid was a part, "the most sharply focused alternative ever offered to the Mennonite Fundamentalist attempt to redefine Mennonitism through formulas of authority and orthodoxy."[65] MMA recognized changed social and economic circumstances. It took the basic principle of mutual aid and reshaped its practice in a way that made possible its continued functioning under new circumstances.

As codified forms of separation from the world were being dropped, new forms were being shaped that continued to express key values. Separation from the world was being expressed through peace and service programs rather than in prescribed nonconformity that emphasized distinctive appearance. Limitations on structural associations, a defensive adaptation designed to protect cohesiveness and separation, were being replaced by an in-group network of activities and organizations. Mennonite Mutual Aid was providing an organized avenue for aid to the brother. New associations such as MEDA and MDS provided expressive opportunities for service to the neighbor and effectively utilized practical Mennonite skills. Parochial education from elementary school through college, together with multiple church programs, gave positive reasons for primarily associating with other Mennonites. While de facto separation was continuing through these programs, so were those aspects of isolation which have a natural tendency to hinder mission.

Schism and the Sword

The changes in the church did not come without opposition. A distressing eruption in the Franconia Conference resulted from resistance to change on the part of the leadership of one congregation. The details of the incident are a commentary on change and therefore of wider significance than this one incident. Elwood Derstine, a minister in the large and always conservative Franconia congregation, defied both the counsel of fellow ministers in the congregation and leadership in the conference by the manner in which

---

[59] *Mennonite General Conference Proceedings, Hesston, Kansas, 1955.* "Exhibit XIV. Mennonite Mutual Aid," p. 73.

[60] *Mennonite General Conference Proceedings, Harrisonburg, Virginia, August 26, 27, 1957.* "Report, Mennonite Mutual Aid, Inc., 9. Liability Automobile Aid," p. 27. Goodville was a mutual insurance agency largely owned and operated by and for Mennonites.

[61] *Mennonite General Conference Proceedings, 1959*, p. 102.

[62] Pp. 67-75.

[63] *Mennonite General Conference Report, Aug. 26-30, 1953, Kitchener, Ontario.* "Report of the Insurance and Investment Study Committee," pp. 71-81.

[64] "Exhibit V. Mennonite Mutual Aid, Inc." *Mennonite General Conference Proceedings, August 22-25, 1961*, pp. 29-34.

[65] Schlabach, "A Mennonite Vision," p. 37.

he resisted modifications in the conference discipline. The resultant disruption of congregational life caused the executive committee of conference to assume direction of the congregation by an action taken on October 6, 1955. A further action was presented at conference a year later, calling for the silencing of Derstine and the suspension of his ministry. While these procedures were being enacted, the meeting was interrupted by two apologetic sheriffs serving a Bill of Equity on the three bishops of the Middle District of the conference, the three ordained brethren of the Franconia congregation, and its three trustees. The action was sponsored by three plaintiffs who were sympathetic to the suspended minister.[66]

The Bill of Equity listed numerous items which, the signatories charged, violated "long standing custom, usage, practice, and tradition" and therefore made void the deed that had been bequeathed to the Franconia congregation in 1834. Among the allegations were several relating to changes in the conference discipline as revised in 1947 and 1956. The 1947 discipline, the bill charged, had removed the right of congregations to resolve their own grievances. It noted that in 1951 prohibitions against joining breeders, poultry, milk, or like associations had been opened up for restudy, followed by the 1956 constitution that simply admonished members to refrain from accepting administrative duties in these organizations. The prohibition on union membership had been modified to read "non-union employment is to be preferred." The bill also noted that the 1956 discipline did not mention the exemption or bankruptcy law, which members for decades had been forbidden to invoke. The new discipline also failed to prohibit Sunday funerals and did not admonish members to clothe the dead in white. The Bill of Equity objected to the formalization of mutual aid, noting that the October 3, 1935, conference had favored an Aid Plan and urged the appointment of a committee to secure a state charter for such purpose, followed in 1946 by the call for a committee to study group, health and accident insurance.[67]

The authority structures in the conference were explicitly challenged by the Amended Bill in Equity which was submitted to the Court of Common Pleas in Montgomery County in September 1956. The 1956 Constitution and Discipline, it charged, "changed the function of the high office of the Bishops to one of rule and control . . . whereas custom, usage, practice and tradition of the Bishops since ancient times was to consult and advise and have general oversight of the church."[68] The conference response attributed far more historic authority to centralized structures than it would claim a decade later,[69] when it would identify the historic position as essentially that put forward by the plaintiffs.

The lawsuit finally came to the court in May 1958. J. C. Wenger, who served as expert witness for the defense, was also called on by the plaintiffs.

Their entire case was built on appeal to "custom, usage, practice and tradition." The Amended Bill listed 149 items which it claimed violated long-standing Mennonite forms. The argument contained a fatal flaw, however, for filing a petition for redress of a grievance in a court of law was itself a fundamental violation of tradition. The plaintiffs, confronted with this inconsistency, withdrew their case on June 17, 1958, admitting violation of "the letter of a historic Mennonite principle."[70] They also withdrew from the congregation and the conference, naming themselves the Franconia Conservative Mennonites. The group consisted of about 80 people. They constructed a small new church building for their use just a short distance from the large, old Franconia meetinghouse. A number of like-minded Lancaster ministers withdrew from their conference and affiliated with the Franconia group.[71]

Authoritarian Control Challenged

The nature and structure of authority was receiving widespread attention in the Mennonite Church in the second half of the fifties. Authoritarian leadership was characteristic of Fundamentalism and authoritarian control over members was one of the elements of defensive structuring. Like codified cultural identity symbols and limits on structural associations, centralized authority was being widely questioned. It was also becoming the object of formalized study.

The Ministerial Committee of Mennonite General Conference sponsored a study conference on church organization and administration in Chicago in March 1955.[72] Paul Mininger served as chairman of this and a number of subsequent committees on church organization. Four persons presented assigned topics relating to patterns of organization. New Testament patterns were not hierarchical, according to speaker Howard Charles, professor of New Testament at Goshen Biblical Seminary. They emphasized function rather than office, with the highest human authority residing in the congregation. Harold Bauman delineated characteristics of Episcopal, Con-

---

[66] John E. Lapp Papers, "Franconia Congregation Lawsuit, 1956." Hist. Mss. 1-1. Box 15. EPMHL, Lansdale, Pa. For more on the episode see Barbara Bowie Wiesel, "From Separation to Evangelicalism: A Case Study of Social and Cultural Change Among the Franconia Conference Mennonites, 1945-1970," Ph.D. dissertation, University of Pennsylvania, 1974.

[67] *Amended Bill in Equity* submitted to the Court of Common Pleas in Montg. C., Pa., September 1956, 8. A. (6) and 9.

[68] Ibid., 8. A. (5), p. 3.

[69] *Defendants' Answer to the Amended Bill in Equity*, September 1956, 2(b) 8. A. (1).

[70] "Statement of the Plaintiffs re Closure of the Case, June 17, 1958." See also "Field Note Sent to the *Gospel Herald*" by John E. Lapp, July 26, 1958. Hist. Mss. 1-1. Box 15.

[71] Executive Committee Minutes, Franconia Mennonite Conference, August, 11, 1960.

[72] A report of the conference was given to General Conference, August 11, 1960. *Proceedings*, "B. Church Organization and Administration," pp. 37-38.

John E. and Edith Nyce Lapp with their family in 1952. Counterclockwise: James (m. Nancy Swartzendruber), Mary (m. Willard Swartley), Sarah (m. Noah Kolb), Ruth (m.

Ron Guengerich), Joe (m. Hannah Mack), Dan (m. Shirley Yoder), John A. (m. Alice Weber). Behind ironing board: Rhoda (m. John Greenlee); behind sofa: Sam (m. Helen Longenacher).

Harold S. Bender, 1897-1962.

gregational, and Presbyterian forms of church government. Paul Peachey spoke on the history of Mennonite patterns of church organization. The early emphasis, he said, was not on organization. In the Schleitheim period the minister *(Diener* or servant) was preacher-teacher and the elder *(Alteste)* was responsible for pastoral ministry. When the bishop, minister, and deacon pattern developed, Peachey said, was not known. Only the office of shepherd is spoken of in the "Brotherly Union." John E. Lapp gave a "careful and well prepared" evaluation of the papers."[73]

John L. Horst reported on a study he had made of trends in the district conferences. He noted a widespread interest in representational, as opposed to hierarchical, authority. Three conferences reported a trend toward seminary training and three were licensing ministers. Trends included a one-man pastorate, setting a retirement age for ministers, giving more responsibility to the laity, organizing work by commissions, and a tendency to live below conference pronouncements. While the changing trends were significant, nevertheless in the mid-fifties most conferences were continuing to ordain ministers by lot and without seminary training.[74]

A report of the Chicago meeting was presented to the General Conference in August, together with a recommendation that each district arrange for a careful study of the true essence of the church, the offices of the church and their functions, New Testament and early church organization and administration, and conference trends in church organization and administration. The implications of the expression, "elevation to the office of deacon, minister, or bishop," also invited concerned discussion. The New Testament, the discussion noted, "knows of no such elevation." The Ministerial Committee study on "The Scriptural Basis for Ministerial Support" recommended financial remuneration for ministers at the same meeting.[75]

Changes relating to leadership patterns were prominent in the proposed revisions for the Franconia Conference Discipline dated August 2, 1956. They included the opening up of the "best Biblical method for ordaining suited to the circumstances," the option of issuing ministerial licenses, and the possibility of a bishop authorizing "the minister to perform duties usually performed by the bishop."[76]

The decades between 1910 and 1960 were an era of powerful leaders and at midcentury one of the foremost was Harold S. Bender. Bender became dean, first of the college and then of Goshen Biblical Seminary, founder of the Mennonite Historical Library and the *Mennonite Quarterly Review*, coeditor of *The Mennonite Encyclopedia*, chairman of the Peace Problems Committee, and secretary of the Mennonite Central Committee. He became president of the American Society of Church History and, in his presidential address, "The Anabaptist Vision," given in the midst of a war, gained respect for the Mennonite Church from his colleagues and challenged a generation of young scholars. Bender was respected by Mennonites of a Fundamentalist orientation and was recognized as a leader in peace programs. He supported authoritarian leadership and a federalist view of the church.[77]

Orie O. Miller, on the other hand, co-worker with Bender and leader in the peace and service area, voiced an alternative vision of leadership in the late fifties. "The Mennonite Church started out," Miller said, "as a lay movement with leaders chosen right out of the congregation."

> Around the turn of the century a tendency developed to put too much authority and responsibility into the hands of the ordained men.... The generation of J. S. Coffman, Daniel Kauffman, and D. D. Miller was the exception rather than the norm.

---

[73] Ibid.
[74] Ibid.
[75] "Recommendation B.," pp. 16-17; "Exhibit VII. Report of the Ministerial Committee," pp. 17-19, 58-60.
[76] "Proposed Revisions," *Rules and Discipline*, Elmer Kolb Papers, EPMHL, Lansdale, Pa.
[77] Mimeographed paper, "The History of the Conception of the Minister in the Anabaptist Mennonite Brotherhood," December 20, 1961.

Now the swing is back to the utilization of our lay resources. There is more of a conscious effort than a generation ago to use the total team. In this we are one of the leaders of Protestantism. The free use of lay talent and leadership gives our program a fluidity that others admire and envy.[78]

The pattern of leadership described by Miller would in the next dozen years increasingly become the norm in the Mennonite Church, and some would promote it as a return to Anabaptist practice. While the claim had a certain legitimacy, the extensive changes affecting all of American society were also profoundly influencing the church.[79] The 1967 report of the Ministerial Committee to General Conference recognized very rapid cultural and economic changes, then made the startling comment that these changes have "rendered the place and function of the church in the community uncertain. The image of the pastoral office is presently very fluid and this uncertainty is reflected among our own people."[80] Study documents concerning the role and task of the ordained minister and the meaning of ordination were included in the report. Commenting on the current study on ordination, executive secretary Paul M. Miller's report stated that "if, for the sake of the larger church unity, it seems wise to retain the word 'ordination,' ways will need to be found to shift its meaning to align with our beliefs."[81]

Ministers experienced considerable stress as authoritarian leadership gave way to a pattern in which pastor and congregation were together responsible for church government. In 1966 the executive secretary of Mennonite General Conference proposed a formal counseling resource for ministers, supported by funds from the Schowalter Foundation. He discerned four areas of concern: the confused role of the minister, the need for in-service training, the minister's need for a resource counselor, and the possible emergence of new forms of ministry.[82]

Another problem was recruitment. With a change in the pattern of ordination away from ordaining by lot out of the congregation, a dearth of candidates for ministry soon surfaced. Miller reported to General Conference that "every effort must be made to stimulate and offer suggestions to congregations until they begin to take seriously their duty to discern gifts and to call forward into service the gifted persons which God's Spirit has empowered in their midst."[83] In response to a letter from Elmer Kolb, secretary of the Franconia Conference, which sought help in finding ways to encourage persons to prepare for leadership positions, Edward Stoltzfus, coordinator of Church and Seminary Relations, shared a plan he had prepared. It was an eight-page design for discovering and encouraging potential church leaders that was intended for presentation to conference leaders in a seminar setting. The plan recognized the earlier pattern of calling leaders from the congregation and said the calling out continues to be the responsibility of the congregation.[84]

In May 1967 Moderator Lapp addressed the conference concerning "the State of the Church in the Franconia Mennonite Conference." Franconia, like many other district conferences, he said, found itself in a state of dilemma and uncertainty. The rapid urbanization of the area in the preceding decade had brought uncertainties, but potentially also held opportunities. Lapp told the conference, which had been unable to agree on a discipline, that differing opinions in the church enable one to see the whole of an issue. But he also had deep concerns.

Not all of the current discussions were fruitful, in Lapp's opinion, and he singled out opposing points of view on the matter of the Christian witness to the state. Some leaders were distributing literature that was militaristic in tone. "This violates the greatest principle taught by Christ," Lapp said, "the principle of love toward God and neighbors. What we ought to be doing is teaching nonresistance as an integral part of the Gospel of Jesus Christ."[85]

Lapp then turned his attention to the needs of ministers in the conference. "If we have been following certain ideas and have found that these do not work, are we ready," he asked, "to look at the situation with a willingness to face the needs of the hour as we ought to, and help toward a procedure which can work?"[86] Noting first some of the personal needs of ministers, he then turned to five important areas of concern to all ministers. The first centered on the person and work of Jesus Christ. "Sometimes," he said, "we tend to lose the meaning of the incarnation through our emphasis on the virgin birth of Christ. Surely we do believe that Jesus was born of a virgin, but our emphasis needs to be on the meaning of the incarnation."[87] The second great need he saw was for ministers to be instruments in God's

---

[78] Erb, *Orie O. Miller*, p. 26.

[79] See Sydney E. Ahlstrom, "The Radical Turn in Theology and Ethics. Why It Occurred in the 1960s," in *Religion in American History*, ed. by John F. Mulder and John F. Wilson (Prentice Hall: Englewood Cliffs, N.J., 1978), pp. 445-456.

[80] Linden M. Wenger, secretary. *Reports*, 1967, pp. 108-109.

[81] *Proceedings*, 1967, pp. 82-83.

[82] "Minutes, General Conference Executive Committee," Scottdale, Pa., November 2, 3, 1966. Hist. Mss. 1-1, John E. Lapp, Box 22, EPMHL, Lansdale, Pa. A. J. Metzler was executive secretary.

[83] *Proceedings*, 1967, p. 83.

[84] "Seminar on the Role of the Minister," Kolb Papers, EPMHL, Lansdale, Pa. Stoltzfus' letter was dated October 20, 1976.

[85] "Moderator's Message," May 4, 1967, p. 2. Lapp was chairman of the churchwide Committee on Peace and Social Concerns and experienced personally the tensions surrounding the Vietnam War as youth faced dilemmas and adults took variant positions at both the district and the national level.

[86] Ibid.

[87] Ibid., p. 3.

hands for the conversion of persons. The call, Lapp said, is to believe on Jesus Christ, but it also means taking up the cross and following him in a life of obedient discipleship. Conversion is never complete, Lapp added, until the individual has made a commitment to live in obedience and fellowship in the community of faith. His fourth and fifth points stated that the minister must be clear on the inspiration of the Scriptures, and must have the anointing of the Holy Spirit.

Ministers were doing too many things besides preaching the gospel, Lapp stated. "Are we willing," he asked, "to be freed from the demands for serving the tables of our own family, and to have the church to do this by way of regular support?"[88] He, together with the other bishops in the conference, had made a study of John 10:1-30 and he shared with his audience 12 things that the bishops had learned about shepherding from this passage.

The Ministerial Committee of the conference in 1967 had appointed Lapp to serve as "Adult Counsellor to Pastors and Church Councils." In this capacity he had interviewed the active pastors and many of the church councils. At the October 1967 conference he shared gleanings from these interviews: Some ministers who had served many years, but without formal training, had indicated feelings of inadequacy. A need for study seminars was commonly expressed. The role of the bishop frequently surfaced in the discussions. Many pastors wished for their bishop to be counselor to themselves, but questioned whether bishops needed to be administrative bishops. Some of the ministers felt that conference was not speaking to the great issues of the times. More ministers expressed weakness in the area of study than in any other area of activity. Conference in 1968 recommended that Lapp give further study to the "several offices of the ministry and the place of lay leadership and their function in the congregation."[89]

The Ministerial Committee of Mennonite General Conference sponsored a seminar on the role of the minister, August 27-28, 1968. The committee considered as urgent the relationship of the congregation to its leadership, both lay and ordained.[90] Those who participated in the seminar were expected to share its findings in local congregations. Paul M. Miller, who was designated to conduct similar seminars on a conference level, was invited to Franconia in March 1969 for a one-day seminar in each of four districts.[91]

A beginning in-service training program for ministers was initiated in Franconia in the fall of 1970. Meeting at the Plains meetinghouse for a period of eight weeks, two classes were offered. Ross Bender, on study leave from Goshen Biblical Seminary, led a class on family life education, and Richard C. Detweiler, one on current issues and concerns, including theological issues.[92]

Change Affirmed

The 1960s were a time of reinterpretation, characterized by leadership and organizational adjustments to a changed reality. A few more nonconformity conferences were held at the beginning of the decade. The Ohio and Eastern Conference called a special session concerned with "world ward drift" for January 14-16, 1960, at Smithville, Ohio. Stanley Beidler and Joseph Gross attended from Franconia. Beidler reported to the executive committee that "the entire field of nonconformity was covered."[93] The meeting, moderated by Harold Bauman, concluded by pointing out areas of agreement and disagreement. In March, Beidler reported that leaders of their local district had discussed nonconformity issues at their annual conference, but that they were hesitant to publish their position in local bulletins "unless it is definite that other districts take a similar rigid position."[94] In June, North Central Conference invited Franconia participants to share in a proposed conference relative to the "drift."[95]

Three articles on the charter values of discipline and separation from the world appeared in the *Gospel Herald* in the opening months of 1961. Author J. C. Wenger had just completed a term as moderator of General Conference and held the confidence of a broad segment of the church. The articles are highly significant because of their support of both traditional values and change.

The first article presented the importance of separation by contrasting "those who are in the kingdom of Christ and those who are in sin," but paid little attention to the Christian's relationship to the structures and values of the world.[96] The second article examined the "biblical application of abiding principles," which Wenger said meant applying these principles "to the issues of the day in an honest and fair manner."[97] Eleven long-standing foci of separation were listed in the article, including not taking a light attitude toward marriage and divorce. But Wenger noted that both the Dutch and the Swiss Mennonites had been willing to receive into membership divorced

---

[88] "Moderator's Message," October 5, 1967.

[89] "Actions," October 3, 1968.

[90] "Seminar on the Role of the Minister," Kolb Papers, EPMHL, Lansdale, Pa.

[91] March 10-13. "Ministerial Committee Minutes," January 30, 1969.

[92] "Minutes," Ministerial Committee, September 11, 1970.

[93] Executive Committee Minutes, January 7, 1960; January 28, 1960. Kolb Papers, EPMHL, Lansdale, Pa.

[94] Ibid., March 7, 1960. "Bro. Norman Yoder spoke on 'Cut Hair for Sisters' and Marvin Y. Benner on 'The Wedding Band.'"

[95] Ibid., June 9, 1960.

[96] "Abiding Principles of Separation," *GH*, vol. 56, no. 7 (February 14, 1961), pp. 137-138, 156-157.

[97] "Biblical Application of Abiding Principles," *GH*, vol. 56, no. 8 (February 21, 1961), p. 165.

and remarried persons who were converted. Avoiding immodest dress and outward adornment were long-standing expressions of separation, but this is "different from saying the church cannot tolerate change.... We not only can tolerate change, but we must.... In the final analysis," he wrote, "it is the church which must determine the application, not the leading thinkers, not even the ministry."[98] The third article in the series concerned church discipline. "By all means," he wrote, "we must enlist the congregation in the matter of church discipline."[99] The congregation, not the conference, had had the final word on discipline in Indiana until 1910. Before that time, following conference consultations, congregations would ratify or reject the recommendations that had been made. Wenger noted legitimate roles for conference, but firmly held that discipline properly rested with the congregation. He could have added, but did not, that both Matthew 18 and the Schleitheim "Brotherly Union" place discipline within the congregation.

In 1961 the General Problems Committee of General Conference became the Church Welfare Committee, and a change of orientation is seen in the description of its functions: whereas it had been concerned with unionism, nonconformity, divorce, and similar issues, it was now to consider problems affecting peace and unity and to give counsel on differences between a congregation and its conference or between conferences.[100]

A new confession of faith was presented to General Conference that same year. It had grown out of a 1957 action calling for the appointment of a committee to prepare a new doctrinal statement. In 1959, the committee recommended that instead of a doctrinal statement a new confession be written. "It is our plan," secretary J. C. Wenger reported, "to attempt to write a new statement of faith, thoroughly saturated with the convictions and insights of the Anabaptists...."[101] Other committee members were Harold E. Bauman, chairman, Clayton Beyler, John E. Lapp, and Chester K. Lehman. Paul Erb had been co-opted. Early drafts of the confession were presented to the General Council before its presentation to the General Conference in August 1961. Criticism of the draft introduced at General Conference was extensive and emotional. The confession was returned to the committee. Divisive issues included divine healing, divorce, and the prayer veiling.

The closing address of the 1961 conference was given by John R. Mumaw, long-term president of Eastern Mennonite College and moderator of the forthcoming 1963 General Conference. A few months later in a *Gospel Herald* article, Mumaw called for a "New Vitality." "Upon my return home," he wrote, "I turned to the Sermon on the Mount to see if a renewal of the application of its message might create such a vitality."[102] Mumaw enumerated changes among Mennonites in the preceding decade or two, counseling, "we should not dwell too long on our image of the past":[103]

It has become clear to most of us that the Mennonite Church is subject to the "winds of change"; in some areas it has taken the force of a hurricane. We are confronted with a complex array of causes and effects. Whether this is by process of revolution, or disintegration, of infiltration, of imaginative leadership, or of bold prophetic projection, new dimensions of church life are emerging in rapid succession. It becomes the responsibility of some agency to provide guidance in this process.[104]

The rewriting of the church's statement of faith was a part of this attempt to give guidance to inevitable change.

Responses to the proposed form and content of the new confession were numerous. Orie O. Miller considered the statement rather long and in parts too technical. The times, he felt, called for a confession that was not limited by time or culture, and one which could serve the younger churches.[105]

Change and the church-world issue was addressed by Paul Mininger in his annual report to the Mennonite Board of Education in 1962. He noted 14 areas of world change affecting the church and the college, including the expansion of technology, depersonalization and the breakdown of the community, secularization, and militarism. The recovery of the Anabaptist vision had inspired many students who were now serving throughout the world. The many contacts both at home and abroad made the always-present church-world issue critical. Goshen College, he wrote,

> acknowledges unashamedly its loyalty to the church of Christ and its commitment to its Anabaptist-Mennonite heritage.... We are committed to the strategy of Biblical faith which leads us to live our lives within two cultures, practicing the Christian life under the voluntary self-discipline of the Christian community and participating with discrimination in the cultural activities of the larger society, witnessing there to the Lordship of Jesus Christ.[106]

---

[98] Wenger, "Biblical Application," p. 163.

[99] John C. Wenger, "Methods of Discipline in congregation and Conference, *GH*, vol. 56, no. 15 (April 11, 1961), pp. 333, 349.

[100] John E. Lapp, Hist. Mss. 1-1. "Historical Development of the General Conference. II. Church Welfare Community," EPMHL, Lansdale, Pa.

[101] *Mennonite General Conference Proceedings, 1959,* "IX. Committee Statement of Doctrine," pp. 54-55. See also *Mennonite General Conference, Harrisonburg, Virginia. August 25-27, 1957,* "XXII. Plan for Preparing a Doctrinal Statement," pp. 79-80.

[102] John R. Mumaw, "A New Vitality," *GH*, vol. 55, no. 20 (May 15, 1962), pp. 441-442, 461.

[103] Ibid., p. 442.

[104] Ibid., p. 461.

[105] "Mennonite Confession of Faith" (1-4-35), Archives of the Mennonite Church, Goshen, Ind.

[106] Paul Mininger, "Our World, Our Church, and Our College," *MQR* 37 (October 1963): 279-309. Quote from pp. 303-304.

In the summer of 1962 the Seventh Mennonite World Conference was held at Kitchener, Ontario, with ten to twelve thousand persons in attendance. Another dream of the young men who gathered at Clermont en Argonne, France, in 1919 had been fulfilled beyond expectations. Harold S. Bender had been a prime mover in the development of Mennonite World Conference. His keynote address to this conference, "Who Is the Lord?" did not stress history, or the Anabaptist Vision, or the fulfillment of ecumenical dreams. From beginning to end it spoke of Jesus—as man, as the Christ, and as the risen Lord of history. The message was read in his absence because of his illness, but he did attend a part of the conference and led a closing inspirational prayer which has been preserved for us.[107] Bender passed away a few weeks later, September 21, 1962.

In the early months of 1963 the *Gospel Herald* carried numerous articles on the theme of change. David N. Thomas of Lancaster Conference listed five questions to consider in testing change, and 10 ways to strengthen the church in times of change.[108] Myron Augsburger proposed a "Neo-Conservatism," noting that "many leaders are struggling with what seem to them serious questions while young people of our churches, rightly or wrongly, have already answered these questions and are grappling with another set."[109] Dale Oldham, a frequent contributor, wrote, "The Church Must Change."[110]

Forthcoming moderator Mumaw wrote a series of articles entitled "Will the Spirit Speak Again.... At Mennonite General Conference," basing his comments on the messages to the churches in the Book of Revelation.[111] Anticipating the forthcoming sessions of Mennonite General Conference, the Confession of Faith Committee expressed the hope that "this Confession of Faith may serve to acquaint all men with the Biblical faith to which we witness, that it may also unify our brotherhood in its convictions, and deepen their consecration to the truth of God's Word."[112]

The conference met at Kalona, Iowa, August 1963. J. C. Wenger preached the conference sermon, entitled "Our Message in Today's World."[113] Paul Erb addressed the conference on "A Christian Philosophy of Change," and according to prearranged plan those in attendance broke into groups to discuss the address.[114] One newsman, later reporting on the conference, thought it was "obsessed with change."[115]

New issues before the conference included Peace Problems Committee statements on litigation and capital punishment (which were slated for action in 1965), a proposal for the reorganization of MMA, and a progress report from the committee preparing a new hymnal. Arnold Cressman reported that "come out from among them and be ye separate" and "go ye into all the world" had been held in realistic tension at the meeting, and new *Gospel*

Herald editor John M. Drescher noted a "strong sense of need to retrench ourselves in the faith. This was emphasized in particular . . . in the adoption of the Confession of Faith."[116] The delegates accepted the new confession by a unanimous vote, and the conference closed with an ascendant spirit of unity.

Change came as an avalanche. Many were exhilarated by new opportunities. A few were very vocal in their resistance to accommodation.

Accommodation and Dissension

Moderator Lapp's opening comments to the 1962 fall conference in Franconia reminded participants that the purpose of conference was to confer, to compare. "We come with our notions," he said, "but we need to discover the mind of God." This was to be found, not by "strong appeals, impassioned and influential persons, but by the Word of God, united prayer and hearing the still small voice and our brethren above our own preconceived ideas."[117] As it had done on numerous earlier occasions, conference recognized increasing "trends toward worldliness . . . in the wearing of the wedding ring, the sisters cutting their hair and omitting the wearing of the veiling."[118]

A lengthy resolution concerning trends toward worldliness was passed by the 1962 fall conference, but broader concerns were also included in the resolution such as a deepening of spiritual experience and a more helpful relationship between parents and youth. The resolution specified a program of teaching that included spiritual growth, family relationships, holiness of life, and the scriptural basis for approved nonconformity practices. It was accompanied by an explicit disciplinary mandate specifying that after appro-

---

[107] *Harold S. Bender Memorial Number*, *MQR* 38 (April 1964): 82-228, especially pp. 152-161, and 170-171.

[108] "Maintaining Biblical Principles in Times of Change," *GH*, vol. 46, no. 7 (February 19, 1963), p. 141.

[109] *GH*, vol. 54, no. 7 (February 19, 1963), pp. 142-143.

[110] *GH*, vol. 56, no. 24 (June 18, 1963), pp. 513, 516, 531.

[111] "As He Did to the Church in Ephesus," *GH*, vol. 56, no. 26 (July 2, 1963), p. 560; "As He Did to the Church in Smyrna," *GH*, vol. 56, no. 27 (July 9, 1963), p. 586; "To the Churches in Pergamos," *GH*, vol. 56, no. 28 (July 16, 1963), p. 608; "As He Did to the Church in Thyatira," *GH*, vol. 26, no. 29 (July 23, 1963), pp. 632, 643.

[112] "Mennonite confession" (1-4-35).

[113] *GH*, vol. 56, no. 43 (October 29, 1963), pp. 953, 956.

[114] *GH*, vol. 56, no. 46 (November 19, 1963), p. 1025.

[115] Quoted in Arnold Cressman, "General Conference Meets at Kalona," *GH*, vol. 56, no. 35 (September 3, 1963), pp. 769, 772.

[116] "Impressions at Kalona," *GH*, vol. 56, no. 35 (September 3, 1963), p. 771.

[117] "Minutes," October 4, 1962.

[118] Ibid.

priate teaching and pastoral counseling "communion privileges be withdrawn from those who do not comply with the above biblical teachings."[119]

Late in the summer of 1963 a questionnaire was sent to conference ministers to determine their experience in implementing the nonconformity resolution of the previous fall. Responses indicated that a substantial number of ministers had tried to follow the recommended program but, in response to a query concerning present conditions in the congregation, only nine reported improvement, 42 reported no change, and 19 said there had been more departure from accepted practices. Most important, 18 of the ministers who responded stated that they would be unwilling to deny communion to noncompliant members. Those willing to do so did not agree on the length of time that forbearance should be exercised before such action was taken.[120]

The executive committee examined the responses to the questionnaire at their September 23, 1963, meeting. Lack of agreement concerning the enforcement of the existing discipline in relation to communion indicated that the discipline was no longer viable. The possibility of rewriting the conference discipline precipitated extensive discussion. It was recognized that for several hundred years the conference had functioned with no written discipline. "A fresh approach seems the only satisfactory way to begin," the committee concluded, adding, "It is of highest importance that we keep the conference together."[121]

At the May 1964 conference, assistant moderator Richard C. Detweiler spoke on the meaning and significance of conference. It was, he said, an opportunity for inspiration and sharing of mutual faith, an opportunity for personal fellowship with Christ, and for bringing together information on the life and work of the church. It was conferring on the issues of the day and coming to responsible decisions.[122]

The theme of the 1964 fall conference was "The Holy Spirit in the Life of the Church." In the moderator's address, Lapp noted both renewed emphasis on finding the direction of the Spirit and current variations in expression. The Holy Spirit works in persons, Lapp said, and through them in congregations and conference. The limitations of human reasoning and convictions can be a strait jacket for the Holy Spirit. Sometimes it had appeared, Lapp said, as though the main purpose of conference was to take a "last-ditch stand" on preserving the problem resolutions of previous generations. Should not rather the work of conference be pioneering new territories of thought? The work of conference should be to rediscover the great and timeless principles of the Bible, to give more attention to the great doctrines of the Christian faith, and to discern the heart of problems. "Conference," he added, needed "to hear the voice of the Spirit of God; we can hear this voice through the voice of our brother."[123]

Authorization for the rewriting of the conference discipline was given at the conference. Anyone having suggestions was to submit them to the secretary before October 31. A special session of conference would be held in March 1965 to review the proposed discipline. In February 1965, a copy of the suggested discipline was mailed to conference members for their perusal. They were invited to share it with their congregations and to solicit responses in Sunday school classes, evening services, or special meetings. "These involvements will enable us all to be truly representative," wrote secretary Elmer G. Kolb, "as we seek to discover the consensus regarding the form of an acceptable discipline."[124] Kolb, secretary of the conference since 1950, had been the primary author of the new discipline.

A city mission worker since the 1930s, Kolb warmly welcomed the new discipline. Certain conference restrictions had been painful to implement in an urban mission setting. One breadwinner in his congregation, for example, had been excluded from membership for years because his job required that he be a union member. Union membership potentially involved the use of force and was therefore forbidden by conference regulations. Kolb knew the individual as a very nonmilitant person and was pained to see him censured. "In those years," Kolb said, referring to the period of defensive structuring, "it was the people who came into the church and who could adjust who were the 'big' people, and not the other way around."[125]

The special session of conference convened on March 11, 1965. Lapp gave a historical sketch of conference, and outlined procedures for the day, which included opportunity for detailed comment by conference participants on every section of the proposed discipline. The new discipline accommodated changed realities by not mentioning certain items such as women cutting their hair or wearing slacks, life insurance, or employment in union shops. In the course of the day, ballots were distributed and conference members were invited to "express themselves as to their agreement to proceed with further preparation for the discipline to be presented at the May 6, 1965, session of conference for possible adoption."[126] Seventy-three voted in favor of proceeding with the discipline, and 13 voted no.

At the May conference a few months later, assistant moderator Richard C. Detweiler called for unity in his opening remarks. "The mind of Christ is

---

[119] Ibid.
[120] Kolb Papers, EPMHL, Lansdale, Pa.
[121] "Minutes of an Executive Committee Meeting, Souderton Mennonite Church, Mon. Eve. Sept. 23, 1963."
[122] "Minutes."
[123] "The Call to Conference," October 1, 1964.
[124] Kolb Papers (no date).
[125] Personal interview.
[126] "Minutes," Special Conference, March 11, 1965.

most clearly revealed," he said, "where we recognize the Spirit's leading in the total conference brotherhood. J. C. Wenger had been invited to bring the conference sermon, and spoke on "The Role of Christian Love." Correction without love hardens, Wenger advised, and correct doctrines and good intentions apart from love are empty and ineffective. The closing meditation, led by John L. Ruth, endeavored to help conference members see ways to be truly the body of Christ in changing situations. "We need to have a balance in our emphasis, right attitudes and open dialogue," Ruth admonished, "otherwise we become afraid of ourselves and develop unfair judgments of others." No vote was taken at the conference on the new discipline.[127]

Mennonite General Conference was also focusing on new structures. Almost immediately following the acceptance of the 1963 Confession of Faith, attention churchwide had focused on reorganization. During the 1963 to 1965 biennium the Committee on Coordination of Church Program recommended to General Council that a study be made of the organization and functions of the various General Conference agencies. The issue became the biennium's most dominant focus and a report presenting the need "for a careful review of the existing organizational structure" was brought to the 1965 conference for consideration. It was the consensus of the recommending body that the proposed study should "include all levels of organization, but especially ... the structure of the local congregations, the district conferences, and General Conference."[128] Part A of the report recommended a comprehensive study with professional-sounding expectations: to clarify aims, state objectives, define mission, identify roles, define relationships, delineate functions, outline methods, assess facilities, and explore new areas of programming. The guidelines in Part B had a very different tone. They called for a structure that "follows a very simple pattern," "expresses our concept of the nature of the church," "allows initiative in developing new programs," "provides flexibility," and "provides services to the local congregations"[129] Some Franconia leaders were cooperating closely with the churchwide program.

David N. Thomas of Lancaster brought the conference sermon at the fall Franconia Conference, October 7, 1965. Entitled "Christ's Last Words to the Church," it was based on the first three chapters of Revelation. Moderator Lapp once again introduced the proposed discipline and said it was being brought for adoption. At this point a relatively new conference member, Dr. Fred S. Brenneman, asked for the privilege of reading a prepared paper. Although the request was highly unusual, it was granted. Brenneman, originally from Alberta, had served a term with the churchwide mission board in India, practiced medicine in Kansas, and more recently had served as a medical doctor with the Mennonite Central Committee. Only recently had he moved into the conference. Brenneman opposed the adjustments in discipline and had rallied the support of a group of conservatives. His paper raised several questions:

> Why rewrite the former discipline? Is the former discipline unscriptural? Have we ministers taught the scripture attached to the former discipline? Bro Brenneman then commented on a number of district practices, church-wide conditions, publication, institutional and historical items and raised the question whether we want this? He then made a motion that we reaffirm our position on the previous discipline and reminded us unless we adopt this motion, we do not see the danger, hope all will come out alright, or we don't care.[130]

The motion was seconded, and a long and emotional discussion followed. Finally a vote was taken to see whether the conference body would reaffirm the former discipline. The motion was defeated by a vote of 55 to 33. A subsequent vote to approve the new discipline was 55 in favor and 33 against. The vote lacked the necessary two-thirds majority required to pass the proposal. Lapp pointed out that this in effect left the conference without a discipline. Once again discussion was rigorous. Following a statement of supportive affirmation by David Derstine, Jr., the moderator broke down, and asked the assistant moderator Richard C. Detweiler to chair the remainder of the meeting. Action was taken that plans be made for the conference body to meet for a special session of prayer and fellowship and the meeting was soon brought to a close.

The special session of conference, in February 1966, provided opportunity for prayer and fellowship but not for specific discussion of the discipline.[131] At the May conference a proposal recommended that "while we are in the process of preparing an acceptable form of conference discipline, we recommend that our congregations use the Mennonite Confession of Faith as adopted by Mennonite General Conference in 1963 and the Franconia Mennonite Conference in 1964."[132] At the 1966 fall conference considerable discussion again centered on how to proceed concerning a discipline, but no consensus was reached.

By December the executive committee recognized that conference had reached a stalemate in its ability to provide an acceptable discipline. A

---

[127] "Minutes," May 6, 1965.
[128] *Mennonite General Conference Proceedings, Kidron, Ohio, August 24-27, 1965*, p. 17.
[129] Ibid., p. 18.
[130] "Minutes," October 7, 1965.
[131] Kolb Papers.
[132] "Minutes," May 5, 1966.

number of dissatisfied brethren were acting on their own, outside the framework of conference.[133] A Ministers' Prayer Fellowship was the base for this discord. In February 1967 the bishops received a letter of concern from a number of these brethren. The executive committee agreed to meet the signers of the letter at the Plains Church on March 27, 1967, at 7:00 p.m.[134] Concerns included women cutting their hair, participation in peace marches, loss of the veiling, the wearing of jewelry, the contents of Sunday school literature and the *Gospel Herald*, discipline and communion, Vietnam, and war-tax resistance. Secretary Kolb noted that some of the discussion revealed "the popular 'fundamentalist' patriotic emphasis."[135]

In the summer of 1967 General Conference was held at Lansdale, Pennsylvania. Paul Mininger, chairman of the Study Committee on Church Reorganization, addressed the conference. In the New Testament, he explained, organization in the church is simply the bringing together of persons for specific tasks. The nature of the church and the nature of the task should determine the structures. Many of his points echoed long-standing Mennonite concepts of the church: obedience to Jesus Christ, quality of relationships, counsel among members in decision-making, and mission. But to implement the aims of the restructuring, the study commission expressed an "urgent need to obtain the help of experts in the field of the professional management of large corporations."[136]

The Mennonite Board of Education, Goshen College, and Mennonite Mutual Aid had recently employed the management firm of Cresap, McCormick, and Pagent, and the study commission proposed also hiring this firm as soon as it could arrange the financing. Thus while the goals and purposes of the study commission appear to have been deeply rooted in Mennonite understandings of the gospel, it was a contemporary corporate agency that was called in for counsel in creating new structures to implement these goals. J. Howard Kauffman, sociology professor at Goshen College, was appointed to coordinate the studies being done on a conference level and by the churchwide agencies.

The churchwide plans for reorganization were presented in Franconia in the fall of 1967—first to the executive committee of conference, then to the conference body. Although the conference had participated in Mennonite General Conference for a score of years, it had not become a member agency. An action taken at the 1967 fall conference in Franconia authorized the formation of a committee to conduct a conference organization self-study in line with the General Conference plan.[137] The first meeting to discuss reorganization was held at the Christopher Dock Mennonite High School the evening of December 5, 1967. J. Howard Kauffman, General Conference representative, visited the conference in March, and the May conference approved the planning of a workshop to discuss reorganization.

As it became increasingly evident that change was neither temporary nor by default, conservatives throughout the Mennonite Church began to unite in their opposition to reorganization and to cultural accommodation. In July 1966, A. J. Metzler, executive secretary of Mennonite General Conference, wrote to officers of selected committees concerning the "current rash of divisive forces in our North American fellowship." He noted that it was a recurring problem, recalling that 30 years earlier when as a young minister he began to travel throughout the church, he "felt things were about ready to go to pieces." He had proposed to veteran leader Daniel Kauffman that much of the difficulty could be resolved if 30 or 40 leaders throughout the brotherhood could get together for a week or two of prayer, study, fellowship, and discussion. "I well recall," Metzler continued, "as I made this proposal, dear Bro. D. K. struck his desk and said, 'That's what I proposed 40 years ago.'" Now, Metzler wrote, Paul Peachey as executive secretary of the Peace and Social Concerns Committee, was making a similar request in response to parallel problems.[138] In November the General Council considered Peachey's proposal that a study conference be arranged, but their response was diffuse and cautious.[139]

In September 1968, three Franconia brethren speaking for the Ministers' Prayer Fellowship made an impassioned plea to the executive committee of conference. They recommended that several congregations be formally designated as churches where standards of the past would be preserved and that like-minded members from throughout the conference be publicly invited to join these congregations.[140] They saw the failure to enforce the 1962 conference action on nonconformity as a watershed. They accused

---

[133] "Executive Committee Minutes," December 7, 1966. Kolb Papers.

[134] Ibid., February 21, 1967.

[135] Ibid., April 14, 1967.

[136] *Reports, Mennonite General Conference, Lansdale, Pa., August 21-24, 1967*, pp. 138-142. Quote from p. 140.

[137] The entire process is recorded in detail in five reports: "District Conference Organization Self-Study Committee Meeting, Souderton Mennonite Church, Thursday, March 28, 1968, 3 P.M."; "Progress Report of the Study Committee on the Organization of the Franconia Conference, May 1, 1969"; "Report of Franconia Mennonite Conference to the Mennonite General Council, February 24, 1970"; "Progress Report of the Study Committee on the Organization of the Franconia Conference, February 1, 1970"; and "Minutes of a Special Session of the Franconia Mennonite Conference, Souderton, Pa., Saturday, December 11, 1971." Kolb Papers.

[138] Letter to John E. Lapp, Carl Kreider, Paul Peachey, Truman Brunk, Linden Wenger, Newton Gingerich, Harold Bauman, Howard Zehr, and John Rudy, July 27, 1966. Lapp Collection, Hist. Mss. 1-1, General Conference folder, EPMHL.

[139] "Minutes, General Conference Executive Committee," Scottdale, Pa., November 2-3, 1966. Lapp Collection, Hist. Mss. 1-1, Box 22, EPMHL.

[140] Minutes of an interview with the executive committee and Jacob Z. Rittenhouse, Jacob Kolb, Norman H. Bechtel, Franconia, Pa., September 12, 1968. Kolb Papers.

Richard C. Detweiler became moderator of Franconia Conference in 1971.

conference leaders of being more interested in organizational than spiritual unity.

Conference leaders firmly resisted the proposal that publicly designated congregations provide a haven for conservatives. The executive committee believed that such a plan would be divisive, pointing out that "congregations need the leavening effects of members who hold more strongly to certain principles.[141]

Lay delegates were among the conference representatives invited to attend the conference workshop on church organization held October 1 and 2, 1968. Topics included "The Nature of the Church," "The Function of the Church," and "Total Mobilization." Participants had been asked to read Richard C. Detweiler's presentation to the May conference on "A Theology of the Church." Paul G. Landis and Myron Augsburger were guest speakers. In late fall, 1968, Richard Detweiler represented Franconia at a churchwide meeting in Chicago. At the meeting the Study Commission presented its projected organizational plan to representatives from the various conferences, and they in turn shared plans that had been made for their respective conference organizations. At the spring conference in Franconia, April 30 and May 1, 1969, the Franconia plan was presented to the conference and approved. It was adopted October 1, 1970. Both the Lansdale and the Haycock congregations, together with their respective leaders, requested releases from conference, which were granted at the fall conference which was held on

September 30 and October 1, 1970. Parallel withdrawals were experienced in Virginia, Maryland, and Lancaster.[142]

The proposed model for the national organization was presented to the constituency in two articles in *Gospel Herald* in June and July, 1969, prior to its presentation to the General Conference meeting in Turner, Oregon, August 15-19.[143] The plan was formally approved at the Constitutional and General Assembly at Kitchener, Ontario, August 16-19, 1971.[144]

The new structures at first glance appear to embody major change in Franconia: lay delegates, administrative responsibility for conference administration lodged in a conference council, former committees and boards merged into five commissions, a formal shift from conference to congregational decision making, and major changes in the role of the bishop.[145] Perhaps even more, it was the adjustment of the formal structure to changes that had already occurred. In a presentation by the study committee to conference members, dated May 1, 1969, the committee reported:

> Our study takes into account developments in our Church-wide picture. Educational levels have advanced, activities in the congregation have multiplied, members have more nonchurch-related involvements, there is less group conformity, attitudes toward authority and methods of church discipline have changed, the role of lay persons in decision-making and leadership has come to the fore, church life has become more congregationally oriented rather than Conference-centered, changes in members' vocational, social, and economic life have come through urbanization, new methods of ministerial call have evolved, and new ways of viewing the church's mission have developed.[146]

Long-standing expressions of charter values were being challenged by the sweep of change. Some saw separation from the world dissolving in the

---

[141] John E. Lapp, "Answer to Proposal Made to the Bishops on September 12, 1968." Kolb Papers. The executive committee did later allow bishops to share with the ministers in their respective districts the possibility of membership transfers in the normal manner, and prepared a statement for the bishops to use in this process. "Copy of A Statement Authorized By the Executive Committee," February 6, 1969, and "A Proposed Statement from the Bishop to be Given Orally to the District Ministers, February 6, 1969.

[142] "Executive Committee Minutes, February 6, 1969," pp. 3-4. Kolb Papers. For a discussion of the parallel schism in Lancaster, see Robert B. Graber, "An Amiable Mennonite Schism: The Origin of the Eastern Pennsylvania Mennonite Church, *Pennsylvania Mennonite Heritage* 4 (October 1984): 2-10.

[143] Vol. 62, no. 24 (June 17, 1969), pp. 545-546; vol. 62 no. 26 (July 1, 1969), pp. 578-80.

[144] For the complete records see "I. Mennonite Church Study Committee on Church Organization," Official Files, Boxes 1-3, Mennonite Historical Archives, Goshen, Indiana.

[145] See Executive Committee Minutes, March 14, 1970. Kolb Papers.

[146] "Progress Report . . . May 1, 1969."

dissolution of defensive structuring. Changes in discipline (the ban) and how discipline related to communion were also undergoing fundamental change. Yet the demise of well-known forms did not necessarily mandate the loss of the underlying charter value. We have already noted that modes of separation from the world were changing, but that separation—with its negative as well as its positive implications—continued. Expressions of the ban and the breaking of bread were also being transformed.

Centuries-old Mennonite communion practices were significantly altered in the 1960s. "Close communion"—which meant that only members in good standing and who had expressed peace and unity within the congregation were allowed to participate, was defended as late as 1955 in a *Gospel Herald* article by Harold S. Bender.[147] A letter by Lapp that same year says close communion is practiced everywhere in Franconia as it had been throughout the history of the group.[148] Close communion implied a counsel meeting prior to communion, where differences could be aired and digressions confessed. Only those who expressed peace and unity with each other and the standards of the church were allowed to participate in communion. While the practice was intended to insure peace and unity in the breaking of the bread, the actual result was sometimes just the opposite. Uneven congregational support for formalized standards had for years resulted in counsel meetings and communion being surrounded by tension. Required confessions were sometimes simply acknowledgements that the individual had broken a conference ruling.

Almost two-thirds of the Franconia ministers personally interviewed by John E. Lapp in 1967 believed that discipline needed to be separated from the communion service.[149] A communion and foot-washing service held during Mennonite General Conference at Lansdale in Franconia Conference, August 21 to 24, 1967, heralded a shift away from communion being closely tied to a uniform expression of discipline. It was the first time a communion service was observed during General Conference sessions.[150] The following June, Bishop Joseph Gross informed the executive committee of Franconia Conference of "requests coming to him for a more 'open' type of communion service," and the committee agreed to consider the matter.[151] A major pressure for open communion was the regular presence in some congregations of spouses or other persons who were devout Christians, but not members. Soon after this request some Franconia congregations were welcoming to the communion table all who expressed faith in Christ and peace with others.

Had a key value, oneness and unity in the body of Christ in the breaking of bread, been lost? A marked change in practice had unquestionably occurred. Participants whose experience spans the two eras would be divided in their response, some affirming increased spiritual unity and oneness in the more open practice, others feeling a key value had been lost. The change undeniably marked the demise of the ban as it had been practiced for half a century. The only mode of discipline remaining was a return to Matthew 18:15-17, a personal encounter with the person who had caused offense. Congregations once again became the base for decision-making, with conference providing opportunity for fellowship and conferring. Inadvertently, practice had returned to that of an earlier era.

Witness and Peace

Rumors of a renewed draft for compulsory military service in 1950 prompted Mennonite leaders to design a new program for conscientious objectors. When a law requiring their induction was enacted the following year, Selective Service accepted the alternative program proposed by peace church leaders. Known as I-W Service, it included domestic assignments and certain types of foreign service called Pax.[152] The draft continued from 1952 to 1973, and the widespread service assignments of young Mennonites increasingly aroused awareness of the need for witness to government both concerning policies exacerbating the likelihood of war and the suffering of the disadvantaged.

Race relations were the focus of a substantial statement adopted by Mennonite General Conference in 1955. Prepared by the Committee on Economic and Social Relations (CESR), the statement closely associated reconciliation and redemption. Proclaiming that in Jesus Christ God has made persons of diverse races into a new people, it asserted that "he has called this new people to the ministry of reconciliation.... This is the essence of our missionary task, and only as we rise above the differences of race and class are we truly engaged in Christian witness."[153] By invitation Guy F. Hershberger, executive secretary of the CESR, attended some of Martin Luther King's Southern Christian Leadership conferences. Hershberger, like a number of other Mennonite peace leaders, was open to a wide range of contacts with other Christians when there was opportunity to discuss peace issues. In 1958

---

[147] "Communion, Open or Close," *GH*, vol. 48, no. 2 (January 11, 1955), pp. 25-26.
[148] Letter to E. Jane Nyce, April 26, 1955. Lapp Letters, EPMHL.
[149] "Report to Conference on the Interviews with the Ministers," October 5, 1967, p. 5. Kolb Papers.
[150] *Proceedings, Mennonite General Conference, Lansdale, Pa., August 21 to 24, 1967*, p. 106.
[151] "Executive Committee Minutes," June 25, 1968. Kolb Papers.
[152] For a discussion of the I-W program see Dirk W. Eitzen and Timothy R. Falb, "An Overview of the Mennonite I-W Program," *MQR* 56 (October 1982): 365-381.
[153] *Report*, pp. 25-26.

his new book, *The Way of the Cross in Human Relations*, developed the ethical framework for a Christian position of peace in personal as well as group relationships.[154]

Peace concerns came increasingly to the fore as the fifties progressed. In 1957 Mennonite General Conference adopted a resolution recognizing that the world is "torn with suspicions, military rivalries and threats" and that the United States "cultivates fear in people abroad as well as at home, exhaustive experimentation with terrifying weapons." Each generation of the church must speak out against evil. Commending President Dwight D. Eisenhower for his efforts toward peace, the resolution challenged him to "place spiritual defenses above material ones, and to use every power at his disposal to curtail further testing of nuclear weapons."[155]

At the 1958 conference in Franconia, a New York speaker "held the rapt attention of the conference body as he shared . . . the reason for much of the unrest in our country and over the world because of racism."[156] In response the conference reflected that Mennonites may know how to be peaceable but they are weak as peacemakers, for nonresistance is often thought of as noninvolvement.

In a 1959 letter, signed by moderator J. C. Wenger and secretary Paul Erb, General Conference again addressed President Eisenhower. The letter spoke of continuing distress concerning the further development and testing of nuclear weapons which potentially bring "mankind to the brink of immeasurable and heretofore undreamed of depths of horror and tragedy."[157] Mennonites had experienced both persecution and totalitarianism, the letter went on to say, yet

> should we be forced to the extreme choice . . . we would prefer facing the risk of possible totalitarian domination to assuming responsibility for a nuclear holocaust bringing certain annihilation of whole peoples, with its resultant disorder and chaos, whether this be called offense or defense.[158]

Obligation to witness to the state was formally acknowledged in the 1951 General Conference statement on peace, but a decade later its formulations seemed inadequate for the times. A supplementary statement, "The Christian Witness to the State," was submitted to and adopted by General Conference in Johnstown, Pennsylvania, in 1961.[159] The 1951 statement, which gave basic reasons for the nonresistant faith, was retained in full. The new statement sought additionally to provide a rationale for Christian witness to the state and to give guidance concerning the character of that witness.

In Franconia the next several conferences gave strong attention to peace concerns. Moderator John E. Lapp for several decades had been a member of the Peace Problems Committee, and after the death of Harold S. Bender in 1962 became its chairman. Four consecutive Franconia conferences passed major resolutions relating to peace. The first discouraged participation in Civil War anniversary celebrations with a militaristic emphasis and expressed appreciation for religious freedom.[160] The second recognized the sin of racism and urged members to welcome persons of all races into their homes and churches. Those able to provide employment opportunities were encouraged to do so on a nondiscriminatory basis.[161] Conference at its next session authorized that a "letter be sent to our Senator(s) expressing our position on race and civil rights, and encouraging them to early bring to reality a practical, workable Civil Rights Bill."[162] The fourth statement registered "convictions on the spirit of hate visible in many present day circles," and called on conference participants "to express the love of Christ to all men on all occasions." It admonished members to avoid both secular and religious associations that promote hate and encouraged them to lend support "to community efforts which promote fair treatment and help to alleviate unjust and unwholesome conditions." Ministers and churches were called upon "always to preach and practice not only salvation by grace through faith, but also the necessary expression, the love of Christ to all men."[163]

The Franconia actions echoed widespread concerns in the nation. According to historian Edwin S. Gaustad,

> the country and its churches were deeply divided over civil rights, over communist and anticommunist crusades, over moral obligations to the culturally and economically deprived, and over moral integrity—or the conspicuous absence thereof—in the nation's highest offices.[164]

In the Franconia area the visit of a delegation of Russian Baptists in the summer of 1964 created high drama. Fundamentalist preachers Carl McIntire and E. Robert Jordan for several days denounced the visit over the

---

[154] Scottdale, Pa.: Herald Press.
[155] *Mennonite General Conference Proceedings, 1957, Harrisonburg, Virginia,* "XVIII. Resolutions Adopted," p. 70.
[156] "Minutes," May 1-2, 1958.
[157] *Mennonite General Conference Proceedings,* 1959, p. 72.
[158] Ibid.
[159] "Part II. The Christian Witness to the State," *Peace and The Christian Witness.*
[160] "Minutes," May 2, 1963.
[161] "Minutes," October 31, 1963.
[162] "Minutes," May 7, 1964.
[163] "Minutes," October 4, 1964.
[164] *A Documentary History of Religion in America Since 1865* (Eerdmans: Grand Rapids, 1983), p. 431.

Carl McIntire (right) led the protest against meeting the Russian Baptists at Plains meetinghouse in 1972. Walt Hackman, MCC Peace Section (left), and William T. Snyder, MCC executive secretary (center).

airwaves as communist-inspired and promised to disrupt it. MCC and Franconia leaders moved ahead as planned, and on Sunday evening, June 7, 1964, the large Blooming Glen meetinghouse was packed for the service, while placard-carrying supporters of the radio evangelists marched in the church parking lot. The meeting was uninterrupted, even though McIntire had seated himself at the front of the auditorium on a chair he had himself carried in. Similar demonstrations protested the 1972 visit of Russian Baptist leaders at the Plains church.

By the mid-sixties it became apparent that some Mennonite leaders had not been fully aware of the implications of the 1961 statement on "The Christian Witness to the State," and that others disagreed with its import. In February 1964 the General Council of Mennonite General Conference requested that the PPC and the CESR accept joint responsibility "for a careful study of church-state relationships as they affect the Christian ethic of our time." The committees reported to General Conference in August that their study would be integrated with a larger one under MCC sponsorship. Twelve regional conferences in ten geographic areas were planned for June 15, 1965. Specific church and state issues to be examined included biblical, theological, and historical perspectives; the Christian witness to the state and

Christian political participation; national loyalties; the establishment of religion; public morality and the state; education, welfare, and other financial benefits derived from the state.[165]

Following the regional meetings a general study conference convened in Chicago on October 7 to 9, 1965, to examine the papers presented at the regional meetings and to discuss the findings. A major point of discussion growing out of the meetings concerned church cooperation with government programs designed to ameliorate suffering and hardship.[166] The findings left room for cautious cooperation with government programs, but encouraged the church repeatedly to penetrate new areas where government awareness of need had not yet reached. It also encouraged individual-government cooperation wherever possible rather than government-church cooperation.

By 1965 the escalating war in Vietnam was causing widespread consternation among Americans. Mennonite General Conference, assembled at Kidron, Ohio, in August sent President Lyndon B. Johnson a lengthy telegram. It praised his efforts to promote racial equality, but continued:

> At the same time, however, we are mindful of the mandate laid upon the church to witness concerning the righteousness which God requires of all men and nations, and therefore in the particular instance of Vietnam, we are impelled to register with you our deep concerns and misgivings regarding both the moral basis and the direction of American policy there.[167]

The same conference sent a letter to its constituent congregations concerning the war in Vietnam.[168] Both documents strongly challenged the escalating American military presence in Vietnam.

Peace-related activities intensified in the next biennium. The Committee on Peace and Social Concerns (CPSC),[169] the peace committee of the General Conference of the Mennonites of North America, and the MCC Peace Section prepared special issues of both the *Gospel Herald* and *The*

---

[165] *Report, Mennonite General Conference, Kidron,* p. 26.

[166] See "Findings of the MCC Peace Section Church-State Study Conference, Chicago, Illinois, October 7-9, 1965." Hist. Mss. 1-1, John E. Lapp. EPMHL, Lansdale, Pa. For an account of the MCC Peace Section see John A. Lapp, "The Peace Mission of the Mennonite Central Committee," *MQR* 44 (July 1970): 281-297. By the mid-sixties the MCC had developed an extensive international peace witness program.

[167] *Proceedings, Mennonite General Conference, Kidron, Ohio, August 24-27, 1965,* pp. 142-143.

[168] "A Message from Mennonite General Conference to the Constituent Congregations Concerning the War in Vietnam," ibid., pp. 113-115.

[169] The Committee on Economic and Social Relations and The Peace Problems Committee had been combined in 1965 to form the Committee on Peace and Social Concerns.

Mennonite in January 1966. The magazines were taken personally to the White House and discussed with a presidential aide. Following other peace witness efforts, MCC and the CPSC leaders recognized anxieties in many congregations over the "mild" protests which had been made. By September 1 the executive committee of the MCC Peace Section decided that before further protests were planned it was necessary for the agency and the constituency "to get up to date with each other."[170] Subsequently the MCC Peace Section held a consultation with constituency representatives in Minneapolis to discuss the relation of the Christian to the state and to society. At the meeting Orie Miller expressed the conviction that "Mennonites must find a way of engaging in social protest that will be acceptable to a peace-loving people." He reminded the conference that

> the Anabaptist movement from which the Mennonites came was born in a radical protest against evils that had come to be taken for granted. But, he said, "having forgotten how to protest through long disuse of that faculty, and now being aroused to the need for it, and finding some protesters using arrogant means to that end, Mennonites must find a Christian way of performing this ministry."[171]

The meeting ended with the consensus that the way had been cleared for renewed efforts to articulate a peace witness. Details concerning witness to government officials remained problematic. Increased conversation with other Christians on peace issues was strongly urged, and the CPSC, upon the endorsement of the General Council, prepared a letter to be sent by the moderator of General Conference to the Council of Methodist Bishops, who had called for consultations on peace among religious leaders.

While pacifism, especially pacifism based on religious conviction, had a long history in the nation, never before the war in Vietnam had it been so widespread. Many Protestants, Catholics, and Jews questioned the war. Some Mennonites sensed a unique opportunity to share their peace witness. Others were wary of the widespread resistance to the war. In February 1967, the General Council of Mennonite General Conference devoted two sessions to peace and social concerns. Richard C. Detweiler, assistant moderator of the Franconia Conference and student at Princeton Seminary, presented an analysis of Mennonite statements on peace from 1915 to 1966.[172] Detweiler held that actual practice had not changed as much as had the stated rationale giving support to witness to government, which since the mid-fifties had relied heavily on the work of the Swiss theologian Oscar Cullmann. Cullmann, on an American tour in 1955, had given a series of lectures later published as *The State in the New Testament* in 1956.[173]

Formal respondents to the paper were John Howard Yoder whose 1964 book entitled *The Christian Witness to the State* carefully delineated why nonresistant Christians should witness to the state,[174] and George R. Brunk II who represented persons considering the salvation of the individual as the primary concern of the Christian. Brunk said Detweiler's paper stressed the incarnation rather than redemption, with no emphasis placed on the substitutionary death of Christ. "How much have we borrowed from current theological thought," he asked. "Eschatology," he commented, "has an important place in our thinking on this issue." He also noted concerning Detweiler's paper that "a complete shift in the view of the world is noted."[175] Yoder pointed out that past emphasis had been on separation from the world without a sense of responsibility for the society in which we live. He also asked how we should relate to persons and groups who do not accept our position.

At the same meeting John E. Lapp, chairman of the CPSC, addressed the General Council. According to Lapp, radio preachers who preach salvation but encourage militarism were considerably influencing Mennonites. Many Mennonites were quite sympathetic to the National Association of Evangelicals. "Indeed," he continued, "there are a large number of people who listen to McIntire in his 'holy war against communism.' "[176] This meant that many Mennonites were even sympathetic to the extreme right, the American Council of Churches.

Protestant influences of both the right and the left were pressing in upon Mennonites. Lapp observed that some young Mennonite men were finding more in common with the National Council of Churches than with the evangelical and fundamentalist coalitions. "If we are silent on issues such as the war in Vietnam in our times," he continued, "this puts our stamp of approval on these war efforts. If we are silent on the sins of segregation and other social evils, this again adds our approval to the sins of society."[177] Lapp called for a "third way," one which would express the whole gospel, with concern for the economic and social well-being of the individual as well as his personal salvation.

---

[170] *Proceedings, Mennonite General Conference, August 21-24, 1967, Lansdale, Pa.*, p. 34.
[171] Erb, *Orie O. Miller,* p. 226.
[172] "An Examination of Mennonite Peace Witness Documents," Exhibit V. Minutes, General Council of General Conference, Chicago, February 24-25, 1967. Hist. Mss. 1-1, Box 22. John E. Lapp. EPMHL, Lansdale, Pa. Published as *Mennonite Statements on Peace, 1915-1966* (Scottdale, Pa.: Herald Press, 1968).
[173] New York: Charles Scribner's Sons, 1956.
[174] Institute of Mennonite Studies, series number 3 (Newton, Kans.: Faith and Life Press).
[175] "Minutes," p. 3.
[176] Exhibit V-A, General Council Meeting, February 25, 1967. Hist. Mss. 1-1. John E. Lapp. EPMHL, Lansdale, Pa.
[177] Ibid.

The growing sense of responsibility for policies spawning poverty and need was a spontaneous response arising from person-to-person contacts of Mennonites in service programs around the globe. As J. Richard Burkholder pointed out in yet another consultation on peace issues in 1985, it was the mission and service efforts that plunged Mennonites "into painful awareness of just how pervasive and determinative are the actions (or neglects) of government in affecting the lives of people we care about, next door or across town or around the world."[178] When returned mission or service personnel sought hearings with Congresspersons it was, for them, not a partisan political act, but a step of faithful obedience to the command to love one's neighbor as oneself.

In the spring of 1967 a draft bill was in process with no provision for conscientious objectors until they had been inducted into the armed forces. MCC Peace Section representatives together with Guy F. Hershberger and John E. Lapp, as well as representatives of other concerned groups, were instrumental in getting an amendment to the bill which resolved the problem.[179] Acknowledging with appreciation the results of their efforts, the CPSC proposed several resolutions to Mennonite General Conference meeting in Lansdale, Pennsylvania, in the summer of 1967. The first resolved "that we seek to be more faithful in witnessing as vigorously against the evils of war by our own and all governments as we are in witnessing concerning our own conscientious-objector interests." The second called for a new study of biblical teaching relating to war taxes. An extended resolution recognized problems and tensions causing urban riots and urged the constituency to both religious and appropriate economic responses.[180]

Continuing criticism of peace policies by some Mennonites instigated yet another consultation. In September 1967 the CPSC appointed a committee to study issues relating to the Christian witness to the state and to identify points of difference and commonality among those of opposing views. This committee met in a series of study conferences in the 1967 to 1969 biennium. It consisted of Edward B. Stoltzfus, chairman; George R. Brunk II, J. Richard Burkholder, Paul G. Landis, John A. Lapp, Sanford G. Shetler, John H. Yoder, and J. Otis Yoder. They met for a total of eight days, and through the CPSC submitted a report to General Conference in 1969.[181] The report listed 17 points which continued to confront them. A churchwide meeting to discuss the issues was held at Archbold, Ohio, in April 1970. Among their 17 points of agreement, the committee recognized the General Conference statements of Turner, Oregon, 1937; Goshen, Indiana, 1951; and Johnstown, Pennsylvania, 1961, as "authentic, adequate statements of the church's position although open to interpretation."[182] Thirteen continuing problems were listed, including biblical interpretation, the relation of the Old Testament to the New Testament, and the affinity between eschatological views and positions on state-church relations.

A number of questions emerging from the group process would be of continuing concern: What are the forms in which the individual Christian, and the church as a body, may witness to civil authorities? When? How often? About what? With whom do we and should we cooperate and to whom should we relate in peace witnessing? What about political involvement? What are the proper methods for dealing with social injustice? What are the theoretical and practical problems as well as moral issues?[183]

Those who resisted witness to the state by a nonresistant Christian supported their position as traditional. But it was an admixture of contemporary Protestant emphasis on separation of church and state with the nonparticipation in government office-holding expressed in Article VI of the "Brotherly Union." Article VI forbids the believer to function as a magistrate. This is a different issue from witnessing to the state concerning its policies.

At the May 6, 1970, Franconia Conference John E. Lapp's address was entitled "I Am Distressed." He was distressed by the president's speech giving reasons for the invasion of Cambodia. He was distressed because of what had already happened in Vietnam. He was distressed by the appearance of armed forces on university campuses, and that the lives of unarmed students had been snuffed out. He suffered still more, he added, when he sees Christians support the use of force. Some Mennonites, he added, accept the word of the president but reject the word of the Lord through their ministers. The same concerns were expressed in a guest editorial in *Gospel Herald* a few weeks later.[184] In October he spoke on "God's Reconciling Agents," calling reconciliation the task of every Christian in order to complete the work of Christ. But there was a sad note, for he recognized that Mennonites believe in nonresistance but have not caught the spirit of reconciliation.[185]

---

[178] "Continuity and Change: An Analysis of Mennonite Experience in the Political Order." Paper presented at Conversations II, Laurelville, Pa., March 7-9, 1985.

[179] *Reports, Mennonite General Conference*, Lansdale, Pa., August 21-24, 1967, p. 34.

[180] *Proceedings, Mennonite General Conference*, Lansdale, Pa., August 21-24, 1967, pp. 118-119.

[181] "Church-State Study," *Proceedings, Mennonite General Conference*, Turner, Oreg., August 15-19, 1969, pp. 41-42. Tensions peaked at this conference. A number of young Mennonite draft resisters challenged the acceptability of conscientious objectors registering for the military draft in a statement which they submitted to the conference. Although discussion was heated, conference officially voted to support those who opposed registration. *Proceedings*, pp. 119-121.

[182] Ibid., p. 42.

[183] Ibid.

[184] *GH*, vol. 45, no. 21 (May 26, 1970), p. 473. A virulent response by Samuel Wenger in "Readers Say" appeared a few weeks later, June 9, 1970, p. 554.

[185] Address given at Franconia Mennonite Conference, held September 30 and October 1, 1970. Kolb Papers.

Jim Longacre became youth peace and service representative for Franconia in 1966, conference moderator in 1975, and conference coordinator in 1981.

National and international conditions forced Mennonites, and all Americans, to focus on war and peace in the fifties and sixties. Some Mennonites were critical of the growing service and witness emphasis, but opportunity for service to the needy expanded so that virtually any member could participate. Mennonite Disaster Service provided a structure that enabled adults who could spare only a few days from their jobs to meet need meaningfully, as voluntary service and foreign relief did for those who could spare a year or more. The compulsory draft forced the choice for some; others volunteered to share the mandate to service. The service programs provided opportunity for a nonverbal expression of Christian faith for many who would have felt incapable of articulating their beliefs in a mission setting.

As Mennonites attempted to refocus identity in the fifties and sixties, major issues were laced through with charter values. An exception might be institutional structuring, which can be seen as an adaptation to American Protestant norms. Institutionalization itself was not new. Some have seen the era from 1920 to 1970 as a half century with major emphasis on organization. But the professionalization of the structures on a national level, and their proliferation on a local level, were new. Although a strong reaction to defensive structuring can be seen in these adjustments, institutionalization itself may be seen as a form of defensive structuring. We have argued that the creation of multiple structural associations effectively maintained isolation, with both its strengths and its drawbacks.

Major adjustments were being made on the role of the shepherd, which is embodied in Article V. Continuing questions were being raised concerning discipline, the subject of Article II; and inadvertently the confused status of discipline sometimes brought about a return to earlier ideals. A trend toward a younger and younger age for baptism was reexamined as congregational revivals were supplanted by large tent meetings. The result was a reemphasis on a sufficiently mature age of baptism to make possible responsible commitment, echoing Article I of the charter. The earlier interpretation of Article III, Concerning the Breaking of Bread, changed in the sixties when discipline was disassociated from communion and close communion was replaced by open communion. Only the oath, the subject of Article VII—which was not challenged by changing circumstances—did not appear as a subject of the discussions.

The influences of American Protestant movements continued to be felt in the fifties and sixties. The mass revivalism of the period was followed by a marked waning of all revivalism. Institutional and structural associations continued to bound the community, making mission endeavors difficult. Fundamentalism continued to create stresses within the group, especially through the power of radio and later television. The influences of Pietism were revived in the charismatic movement. Much of the religious expression of the main body was to be found in patterns of life. Pietistic expressions might be sung in church or hung on a wall, but they were rarely recorded in a diary or spoken in conversation. As the seventies dawned, the charismatic movement spreading across America began to infiltrate the laity, and sometimes the leadership, to a marked degree.

It appears that absorption into American Protestantism was most threatening in the mid-sixties. Steeples went up on some churches, symbolizing the vast changes in cultural forms. But the pendulum swung past the low point, and in 1970 Mennonites were in many ways similar to those of c. 1700. There was little outward difference in appearance from neighbors, and there was free interaction with other religious groups. They found their identity in the idea of peace as had the "defenseless Christians" of the early Pennsylvania settlement. Religious emphases continued to be primarily ethical, and the Mennonites continued to be criticized for their lack of expressive spirituality. It is a human story, and it is ongoing.

Despite unresolved dilemmas, the Mennonites demonstrated an alternate understanding of the gospel—one that was more lived than spoken, more relational than dogmatic, one seeking peace rather than conquest. Endeavoring to live within the kingdom was not a search for utopia, but an attempt to live in community under the rule of Christ.

This study refutes the widespread assumption that American Mennonites were spiritually dead prior to an awakening in the late nineteenth century. Mennonites to a considerable degree did stand apart from the dominant Protestant religious and secular culture, and this gave them the appearance of being both obstinate and backward. The roots of their differences with American Protestantism can in many instances be traced back to the Reformation in the early sixteenth century. Other differences stem from the initial Mennonite rejection of Protestant adjustments to conditions of the American environment. For instance, the Great Awakenings in America were adaptations of religious expression to the new cultural setting. Revivalism was a response to voluntarism in the churches and a means of bringing in new members. Institutionalization provided structures for benevolent societies and educational endeavors. In the midst of these changes the steadfast adherence of the Mennonites to the same forms over an extended period of time did make them an anachronism.

Stresses caused by beliefs that seemingly pulled in contradictory directions were accentuated as Mennonites had increasing contact with modernity. Separation from the world and evangelism frequently stood in tension, although throughout their history in America persons from non-Mennonite background had joined the Mennonite Church, primarily as a result of intermarriage. Voluntarism in church membership was preserved by a late age for baptism and is attested to by continuing large numbers of offspring that did not join the mother church. As Mennonites began home mission programs, particularly in the cities, codified practice as an expression of separation sometimes appeared to be an almost impossible barrier to winning converts. Even more important, the unspoken understandings of the indigenous Mennonites bewildered and baffled those trying to become part of a close-knit community.

Nowhere is antinomy—the opposition between one law, rule, or principle and another—more clearly illustrated in the Mennonite faith than in the matter of unity and schism. The Mennonite church in America consists of three major, and numerous smaller subgroupings. Some of these units have their basis in national origin or time of migration, just as almost every denomination has variant units resulting from these circumstances. But unity and schism among Mennonites has a more integral base. Unity may be overarching, as in the Catholic Church, or be seen as primarily within the gathered group, as it was among Mennonites. Lack of an overarching authority, and the need for complete unity in the gathered congregation before the breaking of bread could take place, has repeatedly resulted in schism. Unity in the congregation was necessary on a practical, relational level, not just confessional; and this unity was sometimes not realized. Fragmentation was the byproduct.

An emphasis on obedience, and the literal interpretation of ethical passages of the Bible sometimes left the conscientious with an unresolved burden of guilt. Persons of this genre in each generation were drawn to more pietistic expressions of the Christian faith.

In the quarter century following 1950, virtually all of the elements of defensive structuring disappeared from Mennonite practice. During the period of sloughing off of cultural identity symbols it appeared to some Mennonites that their only difference from Protestant neighbors was a certain inability to articulate beliefs concerning redemption, the teaching of nonresistance, and the practices that had been codified as symbols of identity. Others became increasingly aware that distinctives remained, distinctives which they often had difficulty identifying.

An inner consistency and integrity that was religious, not simply ethnic, provided the basis for continuity in the Franconia Mennonite Conference and other Mennonite communities. Mennonite religious forms were imbedded in patterns of life and for the lay person largely nonverbal. Relationships were more important than dogma; and religion was expressed in life, whole, entire, and undiminished. Key values, a charter centered in the "Brotherly Union," undergirded religious forms and shaped both resistance to American religious patterns and the adaptations that were made by the group.

Bibliography

I. Archival Collections

The excellent collections of Mennonite Historical Libraries and Archives were indispensable for this research. The Eastern Pennsylvania Mennonite Historical Library and Archives at Lansdale, Pa., was the most extensively used. Also important were the Mennonite Historical Library and Archives at Goshen College, Goshen, Ind.; the Lancaster Mennonite Historical Library and Archives, Lancaster, Pa.; and the Menno Simons Historical Library at Eastern Mennonite College in Harrisonburg, Va.

The papers of Jacob C. Clemens (1874-1965), a leading minister in the Franconia Conference from 1906-1954, were made available for this study, first by the family, then by EPMHL. The personal collections of John E. Lapp, Menno B. Souder, Jacob Gross, Gerret Nice, and Elmer G. Kolb, all located at EPMHL, Lansdale, Pa., were also significant. Taped interviews—most pertinent of which was John L. Ruth's "Interview with Four Franconia Bishops," January 6, 1981—were also helpful. Extensive perusal of conference and committee minutes, as well as back issues of *Gospel Herald, The Mennonite Quarterly Review, Pennsylvania Mennonite Heritage, Herald of Truth, Sword and Trumpet, Mission News*, and numerous other materials were made possible by the library collections.

II. Minutes, Diaries, and Record Books

Alms Records, Franconia Mennonite Congregation, 1765-1945. Microfilm. EPMHL. Lansdale, Pa.

Constitution and Charter of the Christian Society. Freeland, Pa., 1854. Microfilm. EPMHL. Lansdale, Pa.

Ehst, John M. *Diary of John M. Ehst*. Vol. I, 1873-1913; Vol. II, 1913-1923. (Twenty-six handwritten volumes.) Abstracted and typed by Raymond E. Hollenbach, Royersford, Pa., August 1970.

Gehman, John. *Diary of John Gehman, 1829-1882*. Translated and arranged from the original by Raymond E. Hollenbach, Royersford, Pa., 1965.

Krupp, Henry C. *Diary of Henry C. Krupp, 1888-1929*. Copied and arranged by Raymond E. Hollenbach.

Memorandum Book of Reverend Jacob B. Mensch and Proceedings of the Franconia Conference. Begins March 26, 1880; ends October, 1907. Translated by Raymond E. Hollenbach, Royersford, Pa., 1972.

Mensch, Jacob B. *Diary of Jacob B. Mensch, 1880-1911*. Copied and rearranged by Raymond E. Hollenbach, Royersford, Pa., April, 1966.

Minute Book of the Church Council, Christian Society, Freeland, Pa. Microfilm. EPMHL, Lansdale, Pa.

Minutes, Eastern District Mennonite Conference Sunday School Conventions, 1876-1900. Microfilm. EPMHL. Lansdale, Pa.
Minutes of Franconia Conference, 1907-1949. Recorded by Jacob C. Clemens, secretary. Microfilm. EPMHL. Lansdale, Pa.
Minutes of Franconia Conference, 1950-1970. Elmer G. Kolb, secretary. EPMHL. Lansdale, Pa.
Organization and Progress of the Freeland Sabbath School. Microfilm. EPMHL. Lansdale, Pa.
Record of Joseph Hendricks, Pastor of Trinity Christian Church. Collegeville, Pa., 1864-1904. Microfilm. EPMHL. Lansdale, Pa.
Skippack Alms Book, 1738-1954. Transcribed and translated by Raymond E. Hollenbach, 1968.
Trustee Records, Salford Mennonite Congregation, 1830-1898. German to 1889, English beginning August 1889. Microfilm. EPMHL. Lansdale, Pa.
Tyson, Isaac B. *Journal.* Covers material from 1820-1876. Original in Schwenkfelder Library, Pennsburg, Pa.
Verhandlungen des Hohen Rathes der Mennoniten Gemeinschaft (Abraham Hunsicker, *Vorsitzer,* Johannes H. Oberholtzer, *Schreiber). Gedruckt bey* Johann H. Oberholtzer. Broadside, 1848.
Worcester Mennonite Sunday School Record Book. Minutes and treasurer's reports, 1898-1919.

III. Formal Letters

"The 1773 Letter to the Holland Mennonites," March 1, 1773. Signed by Andreas Ziegler, Isaac Kolb, and Christian Funk. First published by Samuel W. Pennypacker, *Hendrick Pannebecker, Surveyor of Lands for the Penns, 1674-1754,* Philadelphia, 1894, pp. 46-63. Reprinted as "A Letter from Pennsylvania Mennonites to Mennonites in Holland," with editorial comments by Harold S. Bender, *MQR* 3 (1929):225-234. Included by J. C. Wenger in the *History of the Mennonites of Franconia Conference.*
Gross, Jacob. To Br. Peter Weber at Hardenberg. Historical Archives of the Mennonite Church, Historical Mss. 1-536, Box 1, Weber Collection.
Krehbiel, Jacob. "A Few Words About the Mennonites in America." Translated and edited by Harold S. Bender. *MQR* 5-6 (1932):43-57, 110-112.
Oberholtzer, John. "A Letter of John H. Oberholtzer to Unnamed Friends in Germany, 1849." Translated by Elizabeth Bender. *MQR* 46 (1972):398-406.
Geil, John. "Farewell Message of Preacher John Geil (1778-1886) to His Lexington Congregation." Reprinted in John C. Wenger, *History of the Mennonites of Franconia Conference.*
Funk, John F. "Another John F. Funk Letter of the Wisler Schism." *MHB* (1972):4-6. Letter written to Josiah Clemmer, February 21, 1878. Apparently not sent.
_____. "On the Wisler Schism: A John F. Funk Letter." *MHB* (1971):7-8. Letter written to Josiah Clemmer, March 12, 1878.

IV. Publications

Ahlstrom, Sydney E. "The Radical Turn in Theology and Ethics: Why It Occurred in the 1960's." In *Religion in American History*, edited by John F. Mulder and John F. Wilson. Englewood Cliffs, N.J.: Prentice Hall, 1978.

_____. *A Religious History of the American People*. New Haven: Yale University Press, 1972.

Albanese, Catherine L. "Research Needs in American Religious History." *Bulletin, The Council on the Study of Religion* 10 (1979):103-105.

Albright, Raymond W. *History of the Evangelical Church*. Harrisburg, Pa.: Evangelical Press, 1942.

Allen, G. W. "Boehme." *Encyclopedia of Religion and Ethics*. Edited by James A. Hastings. 2 (1951):778-784.

Augsburger, Myron. "Neo-Conservatism." *Gospel Herald* 54 (1963):142-143.

Ausbund, das ist: Etliche schone Christliche Lieder. Germantown: *Gedruckt bey Christoph Saur*, 1742.

Baird, Robert. *Religion in America*. New York: Harper & Bros., 1845.

Balke, Willem. *Calvin and the Anabaptist Radicals*. Translated from the Dutch by William J. Heynen. Grand Rapids, Mich.: Eerdmans, 1981.

Barr, James. *Fundamentalism*. Philadelphia: The Westminster Press, 1977, 1978.

Bass, Clarence B. *Backgrounds to Dispensationalism: Its Historical Genesis and Ecclesiastical Implications*. Grand Rapids, Mich.: Baker Book House, 1960, 1977.

Bauman, Harold Ernest. "The Believer's Church and the Church College." D. Ed. dissertation, Teacher's College, Columbia University, 1972.

Beachy, Alvin J. "The Theology and Practice of Anabaptist Worship." *MQR* 40 (1966):163-178.

Bender, Harold S. "The Anabaptist Vision." *Church History* 13 (1944):3-24; *MQR* 18 (1944):67-88.

_____. "Baptism." *ME* 1 (1955):224-228.

_____. "Church." *ME* 1 (1955):594-597.

_____. "Communion, Open or Close." *Gospel Herald* 48 (1955):25-26.

_____. "Effects of Revivalism on the Mennonites Since the Mid-Nineteenth Century." Manuscript, Goshen College, 1946. Archives of the Mennonite Church, Goshen, Ind.

_____. "Evangelism." *ME* 2 (1956):418-419.

_____. "The Founding of the Mennonite Church at Germantown, 1683-1708." *MQR* 7 (1933):227-250.

_____. "Hymnology of the American Mennonites." *ME* 2 (1956):879-886.

_____. "John Fretz Funk." *ME* 2 (1956):421-424.

_____. "The Mennonite Conception of the Church and Its Relation to Community Building." *MQR* 19 (1945):90-101.

_____, and Smith, C. Henry, eds. *The Mennonite Encyclopedia*. 4 vols. Scottdale, Pa.: Herald Press, 1955-1959.

_____. "The *Mennonite Encyclopedia*: Report of the Editor to the Publishing Committee." *MQR* 38 (1964):361-367.

_____. "The Office of Bishop in Anabaptist-Mennonite History." *MQR* 30 (1956):128-132.

———. "Outside Influences on Mennonite Thought." *Mennonite Life* 10 (1955):45-48.

———. "A Swiss Mennonite Document of 1754 Bearing on the Background of the Origin of the Brethren in Christ Church." *MQR* 34 (1960):308-309.

———. *These Are My People: The Nature of the Church and Its Discipleship According to the New Testament*. Scottdale, Pa.: Herald Press, 1962.

———. *Two Centuries of American Mennonite Literature*. Goshen, Ind.: The Mennonite Historical Society, 1929.

———. "Walking in the Resurrection." *MQR* 35 (1961):96-110.

Bender, Ross. *The People of God: A Mennonite Interpretation of the Free Church Tradition*. Scottdale, Pa.: Herald Press, 1971.

Bender, Urie A. *Four Earthern Vessels*. Scottdale, Pa.: Herald Press, 1982.

Berger, Peter. *The Sacred Canopy*. New York: Doubleday. Anchor Books, 1969.

Bestor, Arthur. *Backwoods Utopias*. Philadelphia: University of Pennsylvania Press, 1950, 1971.

Beyler, Clayton Vern. "The Meaning and Relevance of the Devotional Covering." M.Th. thesis, Southern Baptist Theological Seminary, 1954.

———. "The Values and Limits of Nonconformity." *Gospel Herald* 44 (1951):481-482.

Boorse, John C. "The Towamencin Mennonite Meetinghouse." In *Historical Sketches. A Collection of Papers Prepared for the Historical Society of Montgomery County, Penna.*, vol. 3. Norristown, Pa., 1905.

Bruce, Dickson D., Jr. *And They All Sang Hallelujah: Plain Folk Camp Meeting Religion, 1880-1845*. Knoxville: University of Tennessee Press, 1974.

Brunk, George R. *Ready Scriptural Reasons*. Scottdale, Pa.: Mennonite Publishing House, 1926.

———. *Rightly Dividing the Scriptures*. Fentress, Va.: The Sword and Trumpet, 1935.

Brunk, Harry Anthony. *History of Mennonites in Virginia, 1900-1960*. Vol. 2. Verona, Va.: McClure Printing Co., 1972.

Burkholder, J. Lawrence. "An Examination of the Mennonite Doctrine of Nonconformity to the World." Th.M. thesis, Princeton Theological Seminary, 1951.

Burkholder, John Richard, and Redekop, Calvin, eds., *Kingdom, Cross, and Community*. Scottdale, Pa.: Herald Press, 1976.

Burkholder, Richard. "What's Wrong with Nonconformity?" *GH* 43 (1950):879-880.

Burr, Nelson. *A Critical Bibliography of Religion in America*. Religion in American Life. Edited by James Ward Smith and A. Leland Jamison, vols. 3 & 4. Princeton, N.J.: Princeton University Press, 1961.

Bushnell, Horace. *Christian Nurture*. Edinburgh: Strahan, 1861.

Caplow, Theodore, et al. *All Faithful People: Change and Continuity in Middletown's Religion*. Minneapolis: University of Minnesota Press, 1983.

Cassel, Daniel K. *History of the Mennonites*. Philadelphia: Daniel K. Cassel, 1888.

Coalter, Milton J., Jr. "The Radical Pietism of County Nicholas Zinzendorf as a Conservative Influence on the Awakener, Gil Tennet." *Church History* 49 (1980):35-46.

Coffman, Barbara F. *His Name Was John*. Scottdale, Pa.: Herald Press, 1964.
Cole, Charles C., Jr. *The Social Ideas of the Northern Evangelists, 1826-1860*. New York: Columbia, 1954.
Cole, Stewart G. *The History of Fundamentalism*. Westport, Conn.: Greenwood Press, 1931, 1971.
Cronk, Sandra. "Gelassenheit: The Rites of the Redemptive Process in Old Order Amish and Old Order Mennonite Communities." Ph.D. dissertation, University of Chicago, 1977.
Cross, Barbara. *Horace Bushnell: Minister to a Changing America*. Chicago: The University of Chicago Press, 1959.
Cross, Whitney R. *The Burned-Over District*. New York: Harper Torchbooks, 1950, 1965.
Crous, Ernst. "Anabaptism, Pietism, Rationalism, and German Mennonites." In *The Recovery of the Anabaptist Vision*, edited by Guy F. Hershberger. Scottdale, Pa.: Herald Press, 1957.
Cullmann, Oscar. *The State in the New Testament*. New York: Charles Scribner's Sons, 1956.
Dayton, Donald W. *Discovering an Evangelical Heritage*. New York: Harper and Row, 1976.
Dean, William Ward. "John F. Funk and the Mennonite Awakening." Ph.D. dissertation, State University of Iowa, 1965.
Delp, Priscilla, and Hostetler, John A. "History Makes Bonnets." *Christian Living* 2 (1955):14-18.
Detweiler, I. R. "Methods in Bible Study." *Gospel Herald* 13 (1920):739-740, 754-755.
Dillenberger, John, and Welch, Claude. *Protestant Christianity*. New York: Charles Scribner's Sons, 1954.
Douglas, Mary, and Tipton, Steven, eds. *Religion in America: Spiritual Life in a Secular Age*. Boston: Beacon Press, 1982.
Drescher, John M. "The World Today, A Threat and a Challenge." *Gospel Herald* 56 (1963):1001, 1004, 1021.
Drury, C. A. W. *History of the Church of the United Brethren*. Dayton, Ohio, 1924.
Duerksen, Rosella Reimer. "Doctrinal Implications in Sixteenth Century Anabaptist Hymnody." *MQR* 35 (1961):38-49.
Durnbaugh, Donald F. *The Believer's Church*. New York: The Macmillan Co., 1968.
_____, ed. *The Brethren in Colonial America*. Elgin, Ill., Brethren Press, 1967.
_____, ed. *European Origins of the Church of the Brethren: A Source Book on the Beginnings of the Church of the Brethren in the Early Eighteenth Century*. Elgin, Ill.: Brethren Publishing House, 1958.
_____, ed. *Every Need Supplied: Mutual Aid and Christian Community in the Free Churches, 1525-1675*. Philadelphia: Temple, 1974.
_____. "John Adam Gruber," *The Pennsylvania Magazine of History and Biography* 83 (1959):387-408.
_____. *On Earth Peace: Discussions on War/Peace Issues Between Friends, Mennonites, Brethren and European Churches, 1935-1975*. Elgin, Ill.: The Brethren Press, 1978.

———— "Relationships of the Brethren with the Mennonites and Quakers, 1708-1865." *Church History* 35 (1966):35-39.

———— "Religion and Revolution: Options in 1776." *Pennsylvania Mennonite Heritage* 1 (1978):2-9.

———— "Work and Hope: The Spirituality of the Radical Pietist Communitarians." *Church History* 39 (1970):72-90.

Dyck, Cornelius J., ed. *An Introduction to Mennonite History*. Scottdale, Pa.: Herald Press, 1967, 1981.

———— "European Mennonite Motivation for Emigration." *Pennsylvania Mennonite Heritage* 6 (1983):2-9.

———— "The Place of Tradition in Dutch Anabaptism." *Church History* 43 (1974):34-49.

Dyck, Peter J. "A Theology of Service." *MQR* 44 (1970):262-280.

Eby, A. *Verhandlungen der Ost-Pennsylvanischen Conferenz der Mennoniten Gemeinschaft, 1847-1872*. No title page.

Eby, Benjamin. *Briefe an die Mennoniste Gemeine in Ober Canada*. Berlin, Canada: Gedruckt bey Heinrich Eby, 1840.

———— *Kurzgefasste Kirchen-geschichte und Glaubenslehre der Taufgesinnten-Christen oder Mennoniten*. Berlin, Canada: Gedruckt bey Heinrich Eby, 1841.

———— *Zweyter Brief aus Daenemark an die Mennonisten Gemeine in Canada*. Berlin, Canada: Gedruckt bey Heinrich Eby, 1841.

Edwards, Morgan. *Materials Towards a History of the Baptists in Pennsylvania*. Microfilmed. American Baptist Historical Society, 1970.

Ensign, Chauncy David. "Radical German Pietism, c. 1675-1760." Ph.D. dissertation, Boston University School of Theology, 1955.

Epp, Frank H. *Mennonite Peoplehood*. Waterloo, Ont.: Conrad Press, 1977.

———— *Mennonites in Canada*. Vols. 1 & 2. Toronto: Macmillan of Canada, 1974, 1982.

Erb, Paul. *The Alpha and the Omega: A Restatement of the Christian Hope in Christ's Coming*. Scottdale, Pa.: Herald Press, 1955.

———— *Orie O. Miller: The Story of a Man and an Era*. Scottdale, Pa.: Herald Press, 1969.

Erb, Peter C. "Dialogue Under Duress: Schwenkfelder-Mennonite Contact in the Eighteenth Century." *MQR* 50 (1976):181-199.

Finney, Charles G. *Revivals of Religion*. 1835. Reprint. Chicago: Moody Press, 1962.

Franklin, Benjamin. "William J. Campbell Collection of Benjamin Franklin Manuscripts." Philadelphia: Curtis Publishing Co., 1918.

Frantz, John B. "The Awakening of Religion Among the German Settlers in the Middle Colonies." *William and Mary Quarterly*, 3rd series, 33 (1976):266-288.

———— "Revivalism in the German Reformed Church in the United States to 1850, With Emphasis on the Eastern Synod." Ph.D. dissertation, University of Pennsylvania, 1961.

Fretz, Clarence Y. "The Church Year?" *Gospel Herald* 74 (1981):960-962.

Fretz, Herbert. "Germantown Anti-Slavery Protest." *Mennonite Life* 13 (1958):183-186.

Fretz, J. Winfield. "The Old Order Mennonites in Ontario." *Pennsylvania Mennonite Heritage* 3 (1980):2-10.

Friedmann, Robert. "Conception of the Anabaptists." *Church History* 9 (1940):341-365.

―――――― "The Encounter of Anabaptists and Mennonites with Anti-Trinitarianism," *MQR* 22 (1948):139-162.

―――――― "The Encounter of Anabaptists and Mennonites with Anti-Trinitarianism," *MQR* 22 (1948):139-162.

―――――― "On Mennonite Historiography and on Individualism and Brotherhood." *MQR* 18 (1944):121.

―――――― *Mennonite Piety Through the Centuries, Its Genius and Its Literature.* Goshen, Ind.: The Mennonite Historical Society, 1949.

―――――― "The Schleitheim Confession (1527) and Other Doctrinal Writings of the Swiss Brethren in a Hitherto Unknown Edition." *MQR* 16 (1942):82-99.

―――――― *The Theology of Anabaptism.* Scottdale, Pa.: Herald Press, 1973.

Funk, Henrich. *Eine Restitution.* Philadelphia: *Gedruckt bey* Anton Armbruester in Moravian Ally, 1763.

―――――― *Ein Spiegel der Tauffe mit Geist, mit Wasser, and mit Blut.* Germantown: *Gedruckt bey* Christoph Saur, 1744.

Funk, John R. *Biographical Sketch of Pre. John Geil.* Elkhart, Ind.: Mennonite Publishing Co., 1897.

―――――― *The Mennonite Church and Her Accusers.* Elkhart, Ind.: Mennonite Publishing Company, 1878.

Furniss, Norman H. *The Fundamentalist Controversy, 1918-1931.* Hamden, Conn.: Archon Books, 1954, 1963.

Gates, Helen Kolb; Kolb, John Funk; Kolb, J. Clemens; and Sykes, Constance Kolb. *Bless the Lord, O My Soul: A Biography of Bishop John Fretz Funk, 1835-1930.* Edited by J. C. Wenger. Scottdale, Pa.: Herald Press, 1964.

Gatewood, Willard B. *Controversy in the Twenties: Fundamentalism, Modernism, and Evolution.* Nashville, Tenn.: Vanderbilt University Press, 1969.

Gaustad, Edwin Scott. *A Documentary History of Religion in America.* Vols. 1 and 2. Grand Rapids, Mich.: Eerdmans, 1982, 1983.

Geon, C. C. "Jonathan Edwards: A New Departure in Eschatology." *Church History* 29 (1959):25-40.

Gingerich, Melvin. "Change and Uniformity in Mennonite Attire." *MQR* 40 (1966):243-259.

―――――― *Mennonite Attire Through Four Centuries.* Breinigsville, Pa.: The Pennsylvania German Society, 1970.

―――――― "Significant Dates in Germantown Mennonite History." *MHB* 33 (1972).

Glazer, Nathan. *American Judaism.* Chicago: The University of Chicago Press, 1957.

Godschalk, Abraham. *A Description of the New Creature.* Doylestown, Pa.: William M. Large, 1838.

Gordon, Milton M. *Assimilation in American Life.* New York: Oxford University Press, 1964.

Gottschall, Abraham. *Wahrer Gerechtigkeit.* Doylestaun: J. Jung U. Krapf, 1837.
Graber, Robert B. "An Amiable Mennonite Schism: The Origin of the Eastern Pennsylvania Mennonite Church." *Pennsylvania Mennonite Heritage* 4 (1984):2-10.
Grater, Abraham. *An Explanation of Incidents That took Place Among the So-called Mennonites.* Perkiomen, Pa.: J. M. Schueneman Co., Skippack, Pa.
Groh, John E. "Revivalism Among Lutherans in America in the 1840's." *Concordia Historical Institute Quarterly* 43 (1970):29-43.
Gross, Leonard. "History and Community in the Thought of Guy F. Hershberger." In *Kingdom, Cross, and Community,* edited by J. R. Burkholder and Calvin Redekop. Scottdale, Pa.: Herald Press, 1976.
———. "Paul Erb's Era." *Gospel Herald* 77 (1984):519.
Gross, Wesley. "Mahlon G. Gross: Life and Labors." *Pennsylvania Mennonite Heritage* 4 (1981):6-11.
Hall, Edward T. *Beyond Culture.* New York: Anchor Press/Doubleday, 1976.
Handy, Robert T. *A Christian America.* New York: Oxford University Press, 1971.
———. "Fundamentalism and Modernism in Perspective." *Religion in Life* 24 (1955):381-394.
———. *History of the Churches in the United States and Canada.* New York: Oxford University Press, 1976.
———. "The Protestant Quest for a Christian America, 1830-1930." *Church History* 22 (1953):8-20.
Harder, Leland C. "An Empirical Search for the Key Variable in Mennonite Reality." *MQR* 45 (1971):331-351.
———. "The Oberholtzer Division: 'Reformation' or 'Secularization'?" *MQR* 37 (1963):310-331.
Hardwick, Robert. "Change and Continuity in Two Mennonite Communities: The Effect of Rural and Urban Settings." Ph.D. dissertation, University of Virginia, 1974.
Hark, J. Max, trans. *Chronicon Ephratense: A History of the Seventh Day Baptists at Ephrata.* Lancaster County, Pa., 1889.
Hartzler, J. S., and Kauffman, Daniel. *Mennonite Church History.* Scottdale, Pa.: Mennonite Book and Tract Society, 1905.
Harvey, Van Austin. *The Historian and the Believer: The Morality of Historical Knowledge and Christian Belief.* New York: Macmillan, 1966.
———. "Resurrection of the Dead." *A Handbook of Theological Terms.* New York: The Macmillan Co., 1964.
Hatch, Nathan O., and Noll, Mark A., eds. *The Bible in America.* New York: Oxford, 1982.
Hayes, Samuel P. *The Response to Industrialism, 1885-1914.* Chicago: University of Chicago Press, 1957.
Heatwole, L. J. *Mennonite Handbook of Information.* Scottdale, Pa.: Mennonite Publishing House, 1925.
Heckler, James Y. *History of Lower Salford Township in Sketches Commencing with a Story of Harleysville.* Harleysville, Pa.: Weekly News Office, 1888.
Hershberger, Guy F. "Harold S. Bender and His Time." *MQR* 38 (1964):83-112.

_____, ed. "Harold S. Bender Memorial Number." *MQR* 38 (1964):83-228.

_____. "Historical Background to the Formation of the Mennonite Central Committee." *MQR* 44 (1970):213-244.

_____. "The Modern Social Gospel and the Way of the Cross." *MQR* 30 (1956):83-103.

_____. "The Pennsylvania Quaker Experience in Politics, 1682-1756." *MQR* 10 (1936):187-221.

_____, ed. *The Recovery of the Anabaptist Vision*. Scottdale, Pa.: Herald Press, 1957.

_____. "The Times of Sanford Calvin Yoder: The Mennonite Church and the First Fifty Years of Goshen College." *An Evening to Honor Sanford Calvin Yoder*. Goshen, Ind.: Goshen College, 1974.

_____. *War, Peace, and Nonresistance*. Scottdale, Pa.: Mennonite Publishing House, 1944.

_____. *The Way of the Cross in Human Relations*. Scottdale, Pa.: Herald Press, 1958.

Hershey, Mary Jane. "A Study of the Dress of the Old Mennonites of Franconia Conference, 1700-1953." *Pennsylvania Folklife* 9 (1958):24-27.

Hertzler, Daniel. "What Basis Nonconformity?" *Gospel Herald* 43 (1950):996, 997.

Hoover, Amos B., ed. *The Jonas Martin Era*. Muddy Creek, Pa.: The author, 1982.

Hopkins, Charles Howard. *The Rise of the Social Gospel in American Protestantism*. New Haven: Yale University Press, 1940.

Horsch, John. *The Failure of Modernism*. Chicago: The Bible Institute Colportage Association, 1926.

_____. *The Fundamental Truth Series*. Scottdale, Pa.: Fundamental Truth Depot, 1920.

_____. *Is the Mennonite Church of America Free from Modernism?* Scottdale, Pa.: n.p., 1926.

_____. *Modern Religious Liberalism*. Scottdale, Pa.: Fundamental Truth Depot, 1920.

Horst, Irvin B. "The Dordrecht Confession of Faith: 350 years." *Pennsylvania Mennonite Heritage* 5 (1982):2-8.

Horton, Robin. "African Traditional Thought and Western Science." In *Rationality*, edited by Brian Wilson. New York: Harper Torchbooks, 1970.

Hostetler, Beulah. "The Charter as a Basis for Resisting the Impact of American Protestant Movements." *MQR* 52 (1978):127-140.

_____. "Franconia Mennonite Conference and American Protestant Movements, 1840-1940." Ph.D. dissertation, University of Pennsylvania, 1977.

_____. "Leadership Patterns and Fundamentalism in Franconia Mennonite Conference, 1890-1950." *Pennsylvania Mennonite Heritage* 5 (1982):2-9.

_____. "An Old Order River Brethren Love Feast." *Pennsylvania Folklife* 24 (1974-1975):8-19.

Hostetler, John A. *Amish Society*. Baltimore: Johns Hopkins, 1968, 1980.

_____. "The Amish Use of Symbols and Their Function in Bounding the Community." *The Journal of the Royal Anthropological Institute* 94 (1963):11-22.

———. *God Uses Ink.* Scottdale, Pa.: Herald Press, 1958.
Hough, Samuel. *Christian Newcomer: His Life, Journal and Achievements.* Dayton, Ohio: United Brethren Publishing House, 1941.
Hudson, Winthrop S. *American Protestantism.* Chicago: University of Chicago Press, 1961.
———. *The Great Tradition of the American Churches.* New York: Harper and Bros., 1953.
———. *Religion in America.* New York: Charles Scribner's Sons, 1965.
Huffman, J. A. *History of the Mennonite Brethren in Christ Church.* New Carlisle, Ohio, 1920.
Hull, William I. *William Penn and the Dutch Quaker Migration to Pennsylvania.* Swarthmore, Pa., 1935.
Hunsburger, Willard. *The Franconia Mennonites and War.* Scottdale, Pa.: Peace and Industrial Relations Committee of Franconia Conference, 1951.
Hunsicker, Abraham. *A Statement of Facts: and Summary of Views on Morals and Religion, As Related with Suspension from the Mennonite Meeting, 1851.* Philadelphia: G. S. Harris, Printer, 1851.
Hunsicker, Henry A. "Church Division in 1847." *Mennonite Year Book and Almanac,* 1907.
———. *A Genealogical History of the Hunsicker Family.* Philadelphia: J. B. Lippincott Co., 1911.
Hunter, James Davidson. *American Evangelicalism.* New Brunswick, N.J.: Rutgers University Press, 1983.
Hutchinson, William R. *The Modernist Impulse in American Protestantism.* New York: Oxford University Press, 1982.
Jamison, A. Leland. "Religions on the American Perimeter." *The Shaping of American Religion.* Edited by A. Leland Jamison and James Ward Smith. Princeton, N.J.: Princeton University Press, 1961.
Jeschke, Marlin. *Discipling the Brother.* Scottdale, Pa.: Herald Press, 1972.
Johnson, Charles A. *The Frontier Camp Meeting.* Dallas: Southern Methodist University Press, 1955.
Jones, Rufus M. *Spiritual Reformers in the Sixteenth and Seventeenth Centuries.* Boston: The Beacon Press, 1914.
Juhnke, James C. *A People of Mission: A History of General Conference Mennonite Overseas Missions.* Newton, Kans.: Faith and Life Press, 1979.
———. *A People of Two Kingdoms.* North Newton, Kans.: Faith and Life Press, 1975.
Kauffman, Daniel. *The Mennonite Church and Current Issues.* Scottdale, Pa.: Mennonite Publishing House, 1923.
———. "The Two Standards." *Gospel Herald* 15 (1922):690-691.
Kauffman, J. Howard, and Harder, Leland. *Anabaptism Four Centuries Later.* Scottdale, Pa.: Herald Press, 1975.
Kauffman, J. Howard. "Boundary Maintenance and Cultural Assimilation of Contemporary Mennonites." *MQR* 51 (1977):227-240.
———. "Report on Mennonite Sociological Research." *MQR* 37 (1963):126-131.

———. "Toward a Sociology of Mennonites." *MQR* 30 (1956):163-212.
Keim, Albert N. "Service or Resistance? The Mennonite Response to Conscription in World War II." *MQR* 52 (1978):141-155.
Kenney, William Howland, III. "George Whitefield and Colonial Revivalism: the Social Sources of Charismatic Authority, 1737-1770." Ph.D. dissertation, University of Pennsylvania, 1966.
Klaassen, Walter, ed. *Anabaptism in Outline*. Scottdale, Pa.: Herald Press, 1981.
———. "The Bern Debate of 1538: Christ the Center of Scripture." *MQR* 40 (1966):148-156.
———. *Neither Catholic nor Protestant*. Waterloo, Ont.: Conrad Grebel Press, 1973.
———. "Speaking in Simplicity: Balthasar Hubmaier." *MQR* 40 (1966):139-147.
Klassen, William. "Anabaptist Hermeneutics: The Letter and the Spirit." *MQR* 40 (1966):83-96.
Kolb, A. C. "John F. Funk, 1835-1930, an Appreciation." *MQR* 6 (1932):144-156, 250-263.
Krahn, Cornelius. "Pietism." *ME* 4 (1959):176-179.
———. "Smissen, Carl Justus van der." *ME* 4 (1959):550.
Kraus, C. Norman. "American Mennonites and the Bible." *MQR* 41 (1967):309-329.
———. *Dispensationalism in America*. Richmond, Va.: John Knox Press, 1958.
———. "Reexamining Mennonite Reality: Shapes and Meanings of the Future." *MQR* 32 (1978):156-169.
Kraybill, Donald B. "A Content and Structural Analysis of Mennonite High School Songs." *MQR* 51 (1977):52-66.
———. "Religious and Ethnic Socialization in a Mennonite High School." *MQR* 51 (1977):329-351.
Krehbiel, H. P. *The History of the General Conference of the Mennonites of North America*. The author, 1898.
Kreider, Robert. "Discerning the Times." In *Kingdom, Cross, and Community*, edited by J. R. Burkholder and Calvin Redekop. Scottdale, Pa.: Herald Press, 1976.
———. "The Impact of MCC Service on American Mennonites." *MQR* 44 (1970):245-261.
Landis, Ira D. *The Faith of Our Fathers in Eschatology*. Lititz, Pa.: The author, 1946.
Lapp, John A. "Christopher Dock's Message for 20th Century Christians." *Mennonite Life* 24 (1971):149, 162-164.
———. "The Peace Mission of the Mennonite Central Committee." *MQR* 44 (1970):281-297.
Learned, Marion Dexter. *The Life of Francis Daniel Pastorius*. Philadelphia: William J. Campbell, 1908.
Lederach, Mary Mensch. "The Limerick Interlude." Unpublished manuscript, 1978. Lansdale, Pa.: EPMHL.
Lederach, Paul M. *A Third Way*. Scottdale, Pa.: Herald Press, 1980.
Lehman, James O. *Creative Congregationalism*. Smithville, Ohio: Oak Grove Mennonite Church, 1978.

Liechty, Joseph C. "Humility: The Foundation of the Mennonite Religious Outlook in the 1860's." *MQR* 56 (1980):5-31.

Littell, Franklin H. *The Origins of Sectarian Protestantism*. New York: Macmillan, 1952, 1964.

———. *Wild Tongues*. Collier-Macmillan Ltd. London: The Macmillan Company, 1969.

Lodge, Martin E. "The Crisis of the Church in the Middle Colonies, 1720-1750." *The Pennsylvania Magazine of History and Biography* 95 (1971):195-220.

Loetscher, Lefferts A. *The Broadening Church: A Study of Theological Issues in the Presbyterian Church Since 1869*. Philadelphia: University of Pennsylvania Press, 1954.

MacMaster, Richard K.; with Horst, Samuel L.; and Ulle, Robert F. *Conscience in Crisis: Mennonites and Other Peace Churches in America, 1739-1789*. Scottdale, Pa.: Herald Press, 1979.

———. *Land, Piety, and Peoplehood: The Establishment of Mennonite Communities in America, 1683-1790*. The Mennonite Experience in America. Vol. 1. Scottdale, Pa.: Herald Press, 1985.

Malinowski, Bronislaw. *A Scientific Theory of Culture*. North Carolina: University of North Carolina Press, 1944.

Marsden, George M., ed. *Evangelicalism and Modern America*. Grand Rapids, Mich.: Eerdmans, 1984.

———. "Everyone One's Own Interpreter? The Bible, Science, and Authority in Mid-Nineteenth Century America." In *The Bible in America*, edited by Nathan O. Hatch and Mark A. Knoll. New York: Oxford, 1982.

———. *Fundamentalism and American Culture: The Shaping of Twentieth-Century Evangelicalism: 1870-1925*. New York: Oxford University Press, 1980.

———. "Preachers of Paradox: The Religious New Right in Historical Perspective." In *Religion and America: Spirituality in a Secular Age*, edited by Mary Douglas and Steven Tipton. Boston: Beacon Press, 1982.

Marty, Martin. "Religion in America Since Mid-Century." In *Religion and America: Spiritual Life in a Secular Age*, edited by Mary Douglas and Steven Tipton. Boston: Beacon Press, 1982.

———. *Righteous Empire: The Protestant Experience in America*. New York: Dial Press, 1970.

———. "Sects and Cults." In *Religion in American Society*, edited by Richard D. Lambright. *The Annals of the American Academy of Political and Social Science* 332 (1960):125-134.

May, Henry Farnam. *The End of American Innocence: A Study of the First Years of Our Own Time, 1912-1917*. Chicago: Quadrangle Books, 1959.

———. *Protestant Churches in Industrial America*. New York: Harper & Bro., 1949.

McLoughlin, William G. *The Meaning of Henry Ward Beecher: An Essay on the Shifting Values of Mid-Victorian America, 1840-1870*. New York: Knopf, 1970.

———. *Modern Revivalism*. New York: The Ronald Press Company, 1959.

———. *Revivals, Awakenings, and Reform*. Chicago: University of Chicago Press, 1978.

McNeill, John T. *Modern Christian Movements*. Philadelphia: Westminster Press, 1954.

Mead, Sidney E. *The Lively Experiment: The Shaping of Christianity in America*. New York: Harper and Row, 1963.

———. *Nathaniel W. Taylor, 1786-1858: A Connecticut Liberal*. Chicago: University of Chicago Press, 1942.

———. "Professor Sweet's Religion and Culture in America." *Church History* 22 (1953):

Mennonite General Conference Proceedings, 1939-1969.

"A Mennonite Sermon of 1782." *Mennonite Historical Bulletin* 37 (1976):3-4.

Mennonite Yearbook. Scottdale, Pa.: Mennonite Publishing House.

Millennial Symposium printed in *Christian Doctrine*, A Quarterly Supplement to the *Gospel Herald* 27 (1934):338-352.

    Thut, John. "Is Christ's Coming Premillennial?"

    Mosemann, John H. "The Millennium, or Will There Be a Literal Reign of Christ on Earth 1000 Years?"

    Coffman, S. F. "The Kingdom of Our Lord Jesus Christ."

    Burkholder, Oscar. "The Premillennial View."

    Clemens, Jacob C. "The Reign of Christ."

    Swartzendruber, Elias. "Is the Teaching of the Millennium a Bible Doctrine?"

    Landis, Ira D. "New Testament Eschatology."

    Bender, Harold S. "Christ's Spiritual Kingdom."

Miller, Joseph S. "The Kansas Movement: Paul Erb's Viewpoint." *Pennsylvania Mennonite Heritage* 5 (1982):20-22.

———. "The Pennsylvania Mennonite Church Near Zimmerdale, Kansas." *Pennsylvania Mennonite Heritage* 5 (1982):14-19.

Mininger, Paul. "Limitations on Nonconformity." *MQR* 24 (1950):163-169.

———. "Our World, Our Church, and Our College." *MQR* 37 (1963):279-309.

Minnich, R. Herbert. "First Mennonite Charismatic Conference Attracts 2,500." *Gospel Herald* 67 (1974):504.

Mouw, Richard J. "The Bible in Twentieth-Century Protestantism: A Preliminary Taxonomy." In *The Bible in America*, edited by Nathan O. Hatch and Mark A. Noll. New York: Oxford, 1982.

Mowry, George E. *The Era of Theodore Roosevelt, 1900-1912*. New York: Harper Torchbooks, 1962.

Muller, Dorothea R. "The Social Philosophy of Josiah Strong: Social Christianity and American Progressivism." *Church History* 28 (1959):183-201.

Mumaw, John R. "A New Vitality." *Gospel Herald* 55 (1962):441-442, 461.

Musser, Daniel. *The Reformed Mennonite Church*. Lancaster, Pa.: Inquirer Printing and Publishing Co., 1878.

Neff, Christian. "Deknatel, Jerne." *ME* 3 (1956):28-29.

———. "Imbroich, Thomas von." *ME* 3 (1956):12-13.

———. "Peter Weber." *Christlicher Gemeinde-Kalander* (1930):61-102.

Neufield, Vernon. "The Mennonite Mental Health Story." *MQR* 56 (1982):18-31.

Newcomer, Christian. *The Life and Journal of the Rev'd Christian Newcomer*.

Transcribed, corrected, and translated by John Hildt. Hagerstown: Printed by F. G. W. Kapp, 1834.

Niebuhr, H. Richard. *Christ and Culture*. New York: Harper and Brothers, 1951.

———. "Fundamentalism." *Encyclopedia of the Social Sciences* 5 (1930):527.

———. *The Kingdom of God in America*. New York: Harper and Brothers, 1969.

———. *The Social Sources of Denominationalism*. New York: World, 1929.

Nieper, Friedrich. *Die Ersten deutschen Auswanderer von Krefeld nach Pennsylvanien*. Neukirchen (Moers): Buchhandlung des Erziehungsvereins, 1940.

Nichols, Robert Hastings. "Fundamentalism in the Presbyterian Church." *Journal of Religion* 5 (1925):14-36.

"Oberholtzer Division Issue." *MQR* 46 (1972).

Oberholtzer, John H. *Der Wahre Character von John H. Oberholtzer*. Milford Square, Pa.: Herausgageben vom Verfasser, 1860.

———. *Ordnung der Mennonitischen Gemeinschaft*. n.d., n.p. [1848].

Oldham, Dale. "The Church Must Change." *Gospel Herald* 56 (1963):513, 516, 531.

Ovensen, Barney. "Scofield's Helps." *Gospel Herald* 47 (1954):53.

Pannabecker, Samuel F. "The Development of the General Conference of the Mennonite Church of North America in the American Environment." Ph.D. dissertation, Yale, 1944.

———. *Open Doors: A History of the General Conference Mennonite Church*. Newton, Kans.: Faith and Life Press, 1975.

Pastorius, Franz Daniel. "The Beginnings of Germantown." *MHB* 33 (1972):2.

Peachey, Paul. "Anabaptism and Church Organization." *MQR* 30 (1956):213-228.

———. "Identity Crisis Among American Mennonites." *MQR* 42 (1968):243-259.

———. "The Meaning of the Life and Work of Harold S. Bender: A Symposium." *MQR* 38 (1964):200-202.

———. "The Modern Recovery of the Anabaptist Vision." *The Recovery of the Anbaptist Vision*. Edited by Guy F. Hershberger. Scottdale, Pa.: Herald Press, 1957.

Pennypacker, Samuel W. *Hendrick Pannabecker, Surveyor of Land for the Penns, 1674-1754*. Philadelphia: Privately printed, 1894.

Persons, Stow. *American Minds: A History of Ideas*. New York: Holt, Rinehart and Winston, 1958.

———. "Religion and Modernity, 1865-1914." In *The Shaping of Religion in America*, edited by James Ward Smith and A. Leland Jamison. Princeton University Press, 1961.

Peters, John L. *Christian Perfection and American Methodism*. Nashville, Tenn.: Abingdon Press, 1956.

Philip, Dietrich. *Enchiridion or Handbook of Christian Doctrine and Religion*. Elkhart, Ind.: Mennonite Publishing Company, 1910. German editions in 1811, 1851, 1872.

Poettcker, Henry. "Biblical Controversy on Several Points." *MQR* 40 (1966):127-138.

———. "Menno's Encounter with the Bible." *MQR* 40 (1966):112-126.

Ramseyer, Dr. Lloyd. "Christian Nonconformity in a Conformist Age." *MQR* 33 (1959):335-346.

Ramseyer, Robert L., ed. *Mission and the Peace Witness.* Scottdale, Pa.: Herald Press, 1979.

Rauschenbusch, Walter. *Christianity and the Social Crisis.* Edited by Robert Cross. New York: Harper Torchbook, 1964.

Reports Submitted to Mennonite General Conference, 1939-1969.

Ressler, Martin E. "Ein Unpartheyisches Gesang-Buch." *Pennsylvania Mennonite Heritage* 2 (1979):13-19.

Rosenberg, Carroll Smith. *Religion and the Rise of the American City.* Ithaca: Cornell University Press, 1971.

Rosenberg, Charles. "Science and Social Values in Nineteenth Century America: A Case Study of the Growth of Scientific Institutions." *Science and Values.* Edited by Arnold Thackery and Everett Mendelsohn. Atlantic Highlands, N.J.: Humanities Press, 1974.

Ross, George. *Semi-Centennial Sketch: Biography of Elder John Winebrenner.* Harrisburg, 1880.

Roth, Dwight E. "Reflections of Elderly Mennonites." Mimeographed. Lansdale, Pa.: EPMHL, 1982.

Russell, C. Allyn. *Voices of American Fundamentalism.* Philadelphia: The Westminster Press, 1976.

Ruth, Arthur D. "Bishop Abraham G. Clemmer: Service Together." *Mission News* 3 (1939):1.

Ruth, John L. *The History of the Indian Valley and Its Bank.* Souderton, Pa.: Union National Bank and Trust Company, 1976.

_____. *Maintaining a Right Fellowship: A Narrative Account of the Oldest Mennonite Community in North America.* Scottdale, Pa.: Herald Press, 1984.

_____. "The Story Behind Franconia Conference's Outreach." *The Franconia Conference News,* October 1976 to November, 1978.

_____. *'Twas Seeding Time.* Scottdale, Pa.: Herald Press, 1976.

Sachse, Julius Friedrich. *The German Sectarians of Pennsylvania, 1708-1742.* Philadelphia: The author, 1899.

_____. *The German Sectarians of Pennsylvania, 1742-1800.* Philadelphia: The author, 1900.

Sandeen, Ernest R. *The Roots of Fundamentalism: British and American Millenarianism, 1800-1930.* Chicago: The University of Chicago Press, 1970.

_____. "Towards an Historical Interpretation of the Origins of Fundamentalism." *Church History* 36 (1967):3-20.

Sanders, Thomas G. *Protestant Concepts of Church and State.* New York: Holt, Reinhart and Winston, 1964.

Sawatsky, Rodney James. "History and Ideology: American Mennonite Identity and Definition Through History." Ph.D. dissertation, Princeton University, 1977.

_____. "The Influence of Fundamentalism on Mennonite Nonresistance, 1908-1944." M.A. thesis, University of Minnesota, 1973.

Schaff, Philip. *America: A Sketch of Its Political, Social, and Religious Character, 1855.* Reprint. Edited by Perry Miller. Cambridge: Belknap Press of Harvard University, 1961.

Schlabach, Ervin A. "The Rule of Christ Among the Early Swiss Anabaptists." Ph.D. dissertation, Chicago Theological Seminary, 1977.

Schlabach, Theron F. *Gospel Versus Gospel*. Scottdale, Pa.: Herald Press, 1980.

———. "The Humble Become 'Aggressive Workers': Mennonites Organize for Mission, 1880-1910." *MQR* 52 (1978):113-126.

———. "Mennonites, Revivalism, Modernity, 1683-1850." *Church History* 48 (1979):398-415.

———. *A New Rhythm for Mennonites: The Mennonite Church and the Missionary Movement, 1860-1890*. Elkhart, Ind.: Mennonite Board of Missions, 1975.

———. "To Focus a Mennonite Vision." In *Kingdom, Cross, and Community*, edited by J. R. Burkholder and Calvin Redekop. Scottdale, Pa.: Herald Press, 1976.

Schnabel, Susan J. "Freeland Seminary." *Bulletin of the Historical Society of Montgomery County, Pennsylvania* 16 (1964):81-103.

Schrag, Martin Homer. "The Brethren in Christ Attitude Toward the World." Ph.D. dissertation, Temple University, 1967.

Schrock, Paul M. "The Mennonite Church in 1960." *Gospel Herald* 56 (1961):5.

Seguy, Jean. *Les Assemblees Anabaptistes-Mennonites de France*. Paris, The Hague: Moulton, 1977.

Sellers, Coleman. *Theophilus the Battle-Axe*. Philadelphia, 1930.

Sessler, Jacob John. *Communal Pietism Among Early American Moravians*. New York: Henry Holt and Company, 1933.

Shank, Aaron M. "What Is Wrong with the Scofield Bible?" *Gospel Herald* 45 (1952):224-225.

Siegel, Bernard J. "Defensive Structuring and Environmental Stress." *American Journal of Sociology* 76 (1970):11-32.

Simons, Menno. *The Complete Writings of Menno Simons*. Translated by Leonard Verduin. Edited by John C. Wenger. Scottdale, Pa.: Herald Press, 1956.

Smart, Ninian. *A Theory of Religious Change and Ideological Change: Illustrated from Modern South Asian and Other Religious Nationalisms*. The University Lecture in Religion. Tempe, Ariz.: Arizona State University, 1984.

Smith, C. Henry. *The Mennonite Immigration to Pennsylvania*. Norristown, Pa., 1929.

———. *The Mennonites of America*. Goshen, Ind.: The author, 1909.

———. *Story of the Mennonites*. Berne, Ind., 1941. 3rd rev. ed. Newton, Kans.: Mennonite Publication Office, 1950. 5th ed., rev. Cornelius Krahn. Newton, Kans.: Faith and Life Press, 1981.

Smith, H. Shelton; Handy, Robert T.; and Loetscher, Lefferts A. *American Christianity: An Historical Interpretation with Representative Documents*. Vol. 2, 1820-1860. New York: Charles Scribner's Sons, 1963.

Smith, James Ward, and Jamison, A. Leland, eds. *Religious Perspectives in American Culture*. Religion in American Life, vol. 2. Princeton: Princeton University Press, 1961.

———. *The Shaping of American Religion*. Religion in American Life, vol. 1. Princeton: Princeton University Press, 1961.

Smith, Tilman R. "The Legacy of Paul Erb." *Gospel Herald* 77 (1984):518.
Smith, Timothy L. *Revivalism and Social Reform.* New York: Harper Torchbooks, 1957.
Snyder, C. Arnold. "Revolution and the Swiss Brethren: The Case of Michael Sattler." *Church History* 50 (1981):276-287.
Souder, John D. "Bishop Abraham G. Clemmer: Biographical Sketch." *Mission News* 3 (1939):1.
_____. "The Life and Times of Dielman Kolb, 1691-1756." *MQR* 3 (1929):33-41.
Spangenberg, A. G. *Life of Nicholas Lewis, Count Zinzendorf.* Translated by Samuel Johnson, 1838.
Spener, Jacob Philip. *Pia Desideria.* Translated, edited, and with an introduction by Theodore G. Tappert. Philadelphia: Fortress Press, 1964.
Stauffer, Ethelbert. "The Anabaptist Theology of Martyrdom." *MQR* 19 (1945):179-214.
Stauffer, John L. "Fundamentalism and Fundamentalists." *Sword and Trumpet* 2 (1933):16-20.
Steiner, M. S. *John S. Coffman, Mennonite Evangelist.* Spring Grove, Pa.: Mennonite Book and Tract Society, 1903.
Stoeffler, F. Ernest. *Continental Pietism and Early American Christianity.* Grand Rapids, Mich.: Eerdmans, 1976.
_____. *German Pietism During the Eighteenth Century.* Leiden: E. J. Brill, 1973.
_____. *Mysticism in the German Devotional Literature of Colonial Pennsylvania.* Pennsylvania German Folklore Society, vol. 14. Allentown, Pa.: Schlechter, 1950.
_____. *The Rise of Evangelical Pietism.* Leiden: E. J. Brill, 1965.
Stoltzfus, Grant M. "A People Apart and a People Involved—the 'Old' Mennonites." *Christian Living* 17 (1970):20-26.
Stoudt, John Joseph. "Count Zinzendorf and the Pennsylvania Congregation of God in the Spirit." *Church History* 9 (1940):370-376.
_____. *Jacob Boehme: His Life and Thought.* New York: Seabury Press, 1968.
Strong, Josiah. *Our Country: Its Possible Future and Present Crisis.* New York, 1885.
Studer, Gerald C. *Christopher Dock: Colonial Schoolmaster.* Scottdale, Pa.: Herald Press, 1967.
_____. "The Dordrecht Confession of Faith, 1632-1982." *MQR* 58 (1984):503-519.
_____. "What Place Confessions?" *Pennsylvania Mennonite Heritage* 6 (1983):2-6.
Sutter, Sem C. "Mennonites and the Pennsylvania German Revival." *MQR* 50 (1976):37-57.
Sweet, William Warren. "The Churches as Moral Courts of the Frontier." *Church History* 2 (1933):3-21.
_____. *Religion in the Development of American Culture, 1765-1840.* New York: Charles Scribner's Sons, 1952.
_____. *Revivalism in America: Its Origin, Growth, and Decline.* Gloucester, Mass.: Peter Smith, 1965.

Thomas, David N. "Maintaining Biblical Principles in Times of Change." *Gospel Herald* 46 (1963):141.
Tinkcom, Harry M. and Margaret B.; and Simon, Grant Miles. *Historic Germantown*. Philadelphia: The American Philosophical Society, 1965.
Tocqueville, Alexis de. *Democracy in America*. 1835. Reprint. New York: Knopf, 1945.
Toller, Frederick B. *Meetinghouse and Counting House: The Quaker Merchants of Colonial Philadelphia, 1682-1763*. New York: W. W. Norton & Co., 1948.
Troeltsch, Ernst. *The Social Teaching of the Christian Churches*. Vols. 1 and 2. 1911. Reprint. New York: Harper and Row. Harper Torchbooks, 1960.
Turner, Victor W. *The Ritual Process*. Chicago: Aldine Publishing Company, 1969.
Tuveson, Ernest Lee. *Redeemer Nation: The Idea of America's Millennial Role*. Chicago: University of Chicago Press, 1968.
Twisk, Peter J. *The Peaceable Kingdom of Christ*. Translated by John F. Funk. Elkhart, Ind.: Mennonite Publishing Co., 1913.
Tyler, Alice Felt. *Freedom's Ferment: Phases of American Social History from the Colonial Period to the Outbreak of the Civil War*. New York: Harper and Row, 1944, 1962.
Ulle, Robert. "Materials on Mennonites in Colonial Germantown." *MQR* 57 (1983):354-387.
Umble, John S. "The Allen County, Ohio, Mennonite Settlement." *MQR* 6 (1932):81-109.
──────. "The Fairfield County, Ohio, Background of the Allen County, Ohio, Mennonite Settlement, 1799-1860." *MQR* 6 (1932):81-109.
──────. "From Meetinghouse to Church." *Gospel Herald* 48 (1955):817-818, 837.
Visser't Hooft, Willem A. *The Background of the Social Gospel in America*. 1928. Reprint. St. Louis, Mo., 1963.
Wacker, Grant. "The Demise of Biblical Civilization." In *The Bible in America*, edited by Nathan O. Hatch and Mark A. Noll. New York: Oxford, 1982.
Wallace, Philip B., and Dunn, William Allen. *Colonial Churches and Meetinghouses, Pennsylvania, New Jersey, Delaware*. New York, 1931.
Weber, Timothy P. *Living in the Shadow of the Second Coming: American Premillennialism, 1875-1925*. New York: Oxford University Press, 1979.
──────. "The Two Edged Sword: The Fundamentalist View of the Bible." In *The Bible in America*, edited by Nathan A. Hatch and Mark A. Noll. New York: Oxford, 1982.
Weinlick, John R. "Colonial Moravians: Their Status Among the Churches." *Pennsylvania History* 26 (1959).
──────. *Count Zinzendorf*. Nashville: Abingdon, 1956.
Wenger, John C. "Abiding Principles of Separation." *Gospel Herald* 56 (1961):137-138, 156-157.
──────. "The Alms Book of the Skippack Mennonite Church, 1783-1936." *MQR* 10 (1936):138-148.
──────. "Biblical Application of Abiding Principles." *Gospel Herald* 56 (1961):165, 180-181.

———. "The Biblicism of the Anabaptists." In *The Recovery of the Anabaptist Vision*, edited by Guy F. Hershberger. Scottdale, Pa.: Herald Press, 1957.

———. "Bruderlich Vereinigung." *ME* (1955):447-448.

———. "Chiliasm." *ME* 1 (1955):557-559.

———. *Even unto Death*. Richmond, Va.: John Knox Press, 1961.

———. *Faithfully, Geo. R*. Harrisonburg, Va.: *Sword and Trumpet*, 1978.

———. "Franconia Conference." *ME* 2 (1956):368-370.

———. "Franconia Mennonites and Military Service, 1683-1923." *MQR* 10 (1936):222-245.

———. *Glimpses of Mennonite History and Doctrine*. Scottdale, Pa.: Mennonite Publishing House, 1940.

———. *God's Word Written*. Scottdale, Pa.: Herald Press, 1966.

———. *History of the Mennonites of Franconia Conference*. Telford, Pa.: Franconia Mennonite Historical Society, 1937; Th.D. edition, 1938.

———. "Jacob Wisler and the Old Order Mennonite Schism of 1872 in Elkhart County, Indiana." *MQR* 33 (1959):108-132, 215-241.

———. *The Mennonite Church in America*. Scottdale, Pa.: Herald Press, 1966.

———. "Mennonites Establish Themselves in Pennsylvania." *Mennonite Life* 3 (1947):28.

———. "Methods of Discipline in Congregation and Conference." *Gospel Herald* 56 (1961):333, 349.

———. "The Schleitheim Confession of Faith." *MQR* 19 (1945):243-253.

———. *Separated unto God*. Scottdale, Pa.: Mennonite Publishing House, 1951.

———. "Some Observation on the Word of God and Present Thought." *Gospel Herald* 30 (1937):402-403, 434-435, 446.

———. "T. T. Van Sittert's Apology for the Anabaptist-Mennonite Tradition, 1664." *MQR* 49 (1975):5-21.

———. "What Does Your Church Stand For?" *Mission News* 1 (1937):1.

Wenger, Mark R. "Ripe Harvest: A. D. Wenger and the Birth of the Revival Movement in Lancaster Conference." *Pennsylvania Mennonite Heritage* 4 (1981):2-14.

Whitefield, George. *George Whitefield's Journals*. London: Banner of Truth Trust, 1960.

Wichersham, James Pyle. *A History of Education in Pennsylvania*. Lancaster, Pa.: Inquirer Publishing Company, 1886.

Wiebe, Robert H. *The Search for Order*. New York: Hill and Wang, 1967.

Wiesel, Barbara Bowie. "From Separation to Evangelicalism: A Case Study of Social and Cultural Change Among the Franconia Conference Mennonites, 1945-1970." Ph.D. dissertation, University of Pennsylvania, 1974.

Williams, George H. *The Radical Reformation*. Philadelphia: The Westminster Press, 1957.

Wilson, Bryan. *Religious Sects: A Sociological Study*. New York: McGraw-Hill, 1970.

Wittlinger, Carlton O. "The Advance of Wesleyan Holiness Among Brethren in Christ Since 1910." *MQR* 50 (1976):21-37.

———. "The Impact of Wesleyan Holiness on the Brethren in Christ to 1910." *MQR* 49 (1975):259-283.

———. "The Origin of the Brethren in Christ." *MQR* 48 (1974):55-73.
———. *Quest for Piety and Obedience*. Nappanee, Ind.: Evangel Press, 1978.
Yoder, Don, ed. *American Folklife*. Austin: University of Texas Press, 1976.
———. "The Bench Versus the Catechism: Revivalism in Pennsylvania's Lutheran and Reformed Churches." *Pennsylvania Folklife* 10 (1959):14-23.
———. "Folk Costume." In *Folklore and Folklife*, edited by Richard M. Dorson. Chicago: University of Chicago Press, 1972.
———, ed. "Mennonite Contacts Across the Atlantic: The van der Smissen Letter of 1838." *Pennsylvania Folklife* 19 (1969):46-48.
———. "Men's Costumes Among the Plain People." *The Pennsylvania Dutchman* 4 (1953):6-9.
———. *Pennsylvania Spirituals*. Lancaster, Pa.: Pennsylvania Folklife Society, 1961.
———. "Plain Dutch and Gay Dutch: Two Worlds in the Dutch Country." *The Pennsylvania Dutchman* 8 (1956):34-56.
———. "Research Needs in Pennsylvania Church History." *Pennsylvania Folklife* 9 (1958):48-52.
———. "Sectarian Costume Research in the United States." In *Forms upon the Frontier*, edited by Austin and Alta Fife and Henry H. Glassie. Logan, Utah: Utah State University Press, 1969.
Yoder, Edward. "The Mennonites of Westmoreland County, Pennsylvania." *MQR* 15 (1941):155-186, 219-242.
———. *Edward, Pilgrimage of a Mind*, ed. by Ida Yoder. Ohio and Pennsylvania: Ida Yoder and Virgil E. Yoder, 1985.
Yoder, John H. *The Christian Witness to the State*. Institute of Mennonite Studies, no. 3. Newton, Kans.: Faith and Life Press, 1964.
———. "The Hermeneutics of the Anabaptists." *MQR* 41 (1967):291-309.
———. *The Legacy of Michael Sattler*. Scottdale, Pa.: Herald Press, 1973.
———. "The Otherness of the Church." *MQR* 35 (1961):286-296.
———. *The Politics of Jesus*. Grand Rapids, Mich.: Eerdmans, 1972.
Yoder, Paul M.; Bender, Elizabeth; Graber, Harvey; and Springer, Nelson P. *Four Hundred Years with the Ausbund*. Scottdale, Pa.: Herald Press, 1964.
Yoder, Sanford C. *The Days of My Years*. Scottdale, Pa.: Herald Press, 1959.
Zijpp, N. van der. "The Conception of Our Fathers Regarding the Church." *MQR* 27 (1953):91-99.
———. "Socinianism." *ME* 4 (1959):565-569.
Zinzendorf, Nicholaus Ludwig. *Pennsylvanische Nachrichten von dem reiche Christi, Anno 1742*. Johann Christoph Stohr, 1742.

Index

A

"A Few Words About the Mennonites in America." *See* Krehbiel, Jacob
Albright, Jacob, 68-69
Alternative service, 278
Altoona Mennonite Mission, 239-240
American churches and organizational structures, 176-177
Americanization and schism, 146-149
American Protestantism and mass revivals, 281, 283
American society
   changing structures of, 245-246
   and charter values, 245-246
   and hierarchical structures, 245, 271
American Society of Church History, presidential address to, 278
Amillennialism defined, 227
Amish, immigration of, 31
Amman, Jacob, and half-Anabaptists, 33
Anabaptists' historical view of the Bible, 213
Anabaptist Vision, The, 278
Andenken Einiger Heiligen Martyrer, Das, 62
Anders, William, 270
Anfechtung, 61
Antes, Henry
   letter of invitation to the synods, 42-44
   mentioned, 54
   visited by Zinzendorf, 42
   and Whitefield's visit, 41
Anxious bench, 151
Arndt, Johann, 32
Ashmead, Mr., host of fourth synod, 47
Associated Brethren of the Skippack
   formed, 40
   hosted Whitefield, 40
   and Zinzendorf, 42
Associations, limits on, 258-261
Augsburger, Myron
   on confronting change, 306
   guest speaker, 314
Ausbund, 54-57
   and communion parable, 86
Authoritarian control, 246-247, 250-253
Authority
   centralized, 188
   structure of, 186
Awakening influences and Mennonites, 155

B

Baird, Robert, 150
Ban
   in "Brotherly Union," 82-84
   in America, 105-108
   in the twentieth century, 108
Baptism
   and the *Ausbund*, 58
   Mirror of, 59-60
   of suffering, 61
   and the "Brotherly Union," 81-82
   Henry Funk on, 98-99
   mode of, 99
   age of, 99, 175, 327
Baptism, Mirror of, 59-60, 98-100
Baptismal service, 101-105
Baptist Bible Union, 208
Baptist Church, congregationalism and Fundamentalism, 208
Barnhouse, Donald Grey
   mentioned, 210;
   on Eternal Security, 220
Bauman, Harold
   and nonconformity conference, 303
   speaker on church organization, 295, 298
Bean, Amos, and night meetings, 165
Bean, Warren, and Limerick mission, 241
Bebber, Isaac Jacob van, immigrant, 24-25
Bebber, Matthias van, purchased land tract, 29
Bechtel, John, 42
Bechtel, Joseph B., on the Sunday school, 183
Becker, Peter, and Conrad Beissel, 35-36
Beecher, Lyman, 151
Beidler, Israel, 143
Beidler, Stanley, and nonconformity conference, 303

Beissel, Conrad
  and the Ephrata community, 35-38;
  and Zinzendorf, 40
Beliefs, doctrinally essential, 77
Bench, the, 186
Bender, Elizabeth, and *Ausbund* hymns, 55
Bender, Harold S.
  and the Anabaptist Vision, 76, 278
  on the dangers of Fundamentalism, 210
  view of the kingdom, 234
  and peace education, 278
  committee on the Revised Standard Version, 286
  leadership of, 299
  and Mennonite World Conference, 306
  on close communion, 316
Bender, Ross, and training program, 302
Berkey, E. J., and Moody Bible Institute, 204
Berkhof, Hendrick, 227
Bethlehem, named by Zinzendorf, 42
Bible conferences
  and Fundamentalism, 203-204
  among Mennonites, 215-216, 247, 249
Bible doctrine, 215
Bible Doctrines Briefly Stated, 215
Bible Institutes
  activities of, 209
  and Fundamentalism, 209
  and prophecy conference movement, 209
Bible Societies, 177-178
Biblical criticism and Princeton Theology, 203
Bible Presbyterian Synod, 209
Biblical interpretation
  Anabaptist-Fundamentalist contrasts, 211-226
  and General Assembly statement, 212
  historical view of, 213-214
  and the hermeneutic community, 218
  inner word-outer word, 217
  and Jesus Christ, 213
  literal, 223-225
  and obedience, 217
  and missions and evangelism, 224-225
  relationships of Old and New Testaments, 220-223
  and Sermon on the Mount, 224-225
  topical approach to, 216
Bishops and power, 252-253
Bishop, Sue, 249
Blooming Glen
  and Bible conferences, 249
  and stresses, 267

Blosser, Abraham
  on *Herald of Truth*, 199
  on Sunday Schools, 190
Body of Christ, 86
Boehler, George, 40
Boehme, Jacob
  Protestant mystic, 34
  and Radical German Pietism, 98
Boehm, Martin
  and the German Revival, 65-67
  and the ideas of Jacob Boehme, 70-73
  and excommunication, 69-72
Bonnets, 255-258, 265
Boyertown Court Case, 134
Braght, Thielman J., 61
Breaking of bread
  and the ban, 83-84
  in the "Brotherly Union," 84-86
  in the nineteenth century, 108
  practice in Bucks and Montgomery distinctive, 109
  and Oberholtzer's constitution, 109
Brenneman, Fred S., opposed new discipline, 310-311
Brenneman, Daniel
  ordains Durr, 239
  and protracted meetings, 167-168
Brenneman, John M.
  advice to Funk, 189
  Christianity and War, 274
  and revivalism, 159-160, 174
Brethren in Christ and holiness, 157
Briggs, Charles A., 203
Brotherhood community and changing structures, 246
"Brotherly Union of a Number of Children of God Concerning Seven Articles"
  the initial charter, 77, 92; 77-92, *passim*
  the charter in America, 93-124, *passim*
Brunk, George R., I
  and Bible conferences 173, 247
  and Christian Fundamentals statement, 212
  conservative innovator, 196
  and revitalization movement, 249
Brunk, George R., II
  and RSV committee, 286-287
  respondent at peace conference, 323
  and tent revivals, 281-287, *passim*
Brunk, Lawrence, 281
Brunk, Menno J., 286-287
Burkholder, Richard
  article on nonconformity, 267
  on peace and service witness, 324

Index 353

Bushnell, Horace, and *Christian Nurture*, 157-158
Business associations, 259, 261
Bussfertigkeit, 160
Bryan, William Jennings, 206

C

Calvary Church, 267-270
Calvary Hour, origins of, 244
Calvin
  and the "Brotherly Union," 79
  on office holding, 89, 91
  and the oath, 92
  and the Lord's Supper, 85
Cambodia, 325
Camp meetings, 152-153, 157
Canton Mission and ordination of Detweiler, 244
Cap boxes, 256
Capital punishment, 306
Capito, Wolfgang, 92
Caps, prescriptions on, 255-258
Change and revivals, 285-286
Charismatic movement, 327
Charles, Howard, on church organization, 295
Charles, J. D., on evolution, 208
Charles II, debt of, 23
Charter, the
  and the Seven Articles, 92
  for midcentury Americans, 93-124
  and the Oberholtzer division, 149
  and religious forms, 76
  served widely, 123
Children
  "Position on Nurture and Evangelism of," 285
  and revivals, 285
Christ
  present in the community of believers, 84-85
  example of, 90-91
  followers to be separate, 87
  putting on of, 161-162
  and the Christian walk, 163
Christ and the Powers, 227
Christian witness to the state, 318, 320-21, 323
Christian Witness to the State, 323
Christian Doctrinal Supplement, 215
Christian Endeavor Societies, 182
Christian Fundamentals statement, 202, 211-212

Christianity and War, 274
Christian Laymen's Evangelism, Inc., 283, 285
Christian walk, 213-214
Christopher Dock dress standards, 289
Church
  activities developed, 176
  as a disciplined community, 87
  invisible, 85
Church government
  and charter values, 196
  vulnerable to schism, 126
Church membership and voluntary societies, 177
Church of God in the Spirit, 42-51
Church organization, conference on, 295-299, 310, 312-313, 314-315
Church service, mid-nineteenth century, 117-118
Church Welfare Committee, 304
Civilian Public Service 74
Christian Laymen's Evangelism, Inc., 283, 285
Christian walk, 213-214
Christopher Dock dress standards, 289
Church
  activities developed, 176
  as a disciplined community, 87
  invisible, 85
Church government
  and charter values, 196
  vulnerable to schism and Fundamentalism alien, 210
  calling and ordination, 236
  essentials in religion, 205
  on eternal security, 220
  on millennialism, 230-231, 233-234
  and ministerial support, 116
  ordination of, 187-188, 236
  quoted on Mack, 237
  and revival meetings, 173-174
Clemmer, A. G.
  leadership and service, 237-238
  on the reign of Christ, 230
Clermont-en-Argonne
  conference at, 274-275
  dream fulfilled, 306
Close communion, 316
Coercion, abandonment of, 88
Coffman, John S.
  dedicatory address, 195
  forward looking, 196
  and revival meetings, 170-173

Coffman, S. F.
  Mennonites and millenarianism, 228-229, 223
  and Moody Bible Institute, 204
Conference affirmation, 273
Conference discipline, rewriting of, 300
Confession of Faith
  accepted, 307
  new statement of, 304
Cole, Stewart G., beginnings of Fundamentalism, 205
Committee on Peace and Social Concerns, 319-322
Communion
  changes in, 316
  close, 110
  communion parable, 86
  and the Constitution, 140
  and discipline, 109-110, 267-270, 316-317
  and spiritual government, 110
Communism and Fundamentalist writings, 206
Community of True Inspiration, 39
Confessio Schlattensis, 85
Congregational order, 123
Conscientious objectors
  and the 1967 draft bill, 324
  Pax service, 317
  in World War I, 274
Constitutional and General Assembly, 315
Constitution of the Mennonite Brotherhood, 136-140
  and the American environment, 133-134
  conceived by Oberholtzer, 129
  and the division, 130, 137
  and organizational structures, 148
  printed, 129-130
  and self-defense, 134
Conversion
  and the charter, 151
  crisis experience, 151, 161
Counsel meeting, 106
Countess Agatha of Salm, 33
Coverings, 258, 265
Cover letter, 77-78
Cramer, Samuel, and the "Brotherly Union," 92
Cresap, McCormick, and Pagent, 312
Cronk, Sandra
  on the ban, 108
  and Mennonite values, 76
Cross of Christ, Anabaptist and Pietist conceptions of, 55-58
Cultural identity symbols
  cultivation of, 246-247
  women model, 288
Cultural survival and defensive structuring, 251

D

Darby, John Nelson, 227-228
Darrow, Clarence, 206
Darwin, Charles, 205
Deep Run and meetinghouse, 131-132
Defensive structuring adaptive elements of, 250, 246-271, *passim*
Deknatel, John, and Moravians, 40, 42
Denk, Hans, on obedience, 216-217
Derstine, Clayton F., leadership of, 240, 252, 253, 254
Derstine, David F.
  pastor at Blooming Glen, 270
  statement at conference, 311
Derstine, Elwood, charges brought by, 293-294
Description of the New Creature, A, 95, 157-164
Detweiler, I. R., on biblical interpretation, 211, 216-217
Detweiler, Richard C.
  addresses conference, 309-310
  assistant moderator, 311
  and ministerial education, 302
  on Mennonite peace statements, 322-323
  on significance of conference, 308
  on theology of the church, 314
Detweiler, William
  and Blooming Glen, 267
  and city mission leadership, 241
  and radio broadcast, 244
Devotional covering
  Bible conference topic, 249
  See also "cap."
Discipline
  and communion, 267-70
  and communion parable, 86
  demise of the ban, 317
  enforcement of, 308
  face-to-face, 136
  Gospel Herald article on, 303-304
  new statement of, 309

Dispensationalism
  beginnings of, 227-228
  and biblical interpretation, 224-225
  influence of, 228
  and Mennonite leaders, 228-229
Divorce among Swiss and Dutch, 303-304
Doctrinal emphasis among Mennonites, 215
Doctrine, 215, 250
Doctrines of the Bible, 215
Donatist controversy, 88
Dordrecht Confession
  and the charter, 93-94, 93 n63
  selected by Pennsylvania settlers, 38-39
  and shunning, 84
Doylestown, Bible conference at, 247
Drescher, John, *Gospel Herald* editor, 306
Dress codes
  adopted, 249
  articles on, 250
  and plain coat, 289
  and prohibitions, 273
  and restrictions, 255-58
  special session concerning, 264-266
  women's hair, 288
  Dunkers and baptism, 99
  origin and immigration 34-35
  and revivalism, 150
  and spiritual awakening, 34-35
Durr, John N., ordination and leadership, 239-240
Dwight, Timothy, 151

E

Eastern District Sunday School Convention, 167
Eastern Mennonite College, founding of, 207
Eby, Benjamin
  on baptism, 101-105
  on communion, 108
  and *Kurzgefasste Kirchen-geschichte*, 95
Eby, Solomon, 168
Economic and Social Relations, Committee on, 264
Eckerlin, Israel, and the Ephrata community, 37-38
Ecumenicism and the Hunsickers, 141-142
Education and the churches, 178
Edwards, Jonathan
  and postmillennialism, 226
  and the thousand-year reign, 159
Eerdman, Charles and constitutional procedure, 208

Ein Spiegel der Taufe, see Baptism, Mirror of
Ein Warhafftiger Bericht, 59
Eisenhower, Dwight D., letter to, 318
Elkhart and Mennonite Publishing Company, 194
Elkhart Institute, 195
Endogamy, high rate of, 246-247
Engle, Jacob, 65, 68
Ents, Theobald, hosted conference, 44
Ephrata community
  and *Martyrs Mirror* 62-63
  origin of, 35-38
Erb, Paul
  editorials and change, 279-281
  editor of *Gospel Herald*, 215
  "Evangelism . . ." 284
  letter to Eisenhower, 318
  on a philosophy of change, 306
Ernsthafte Christenpflicht, 63
Eternal security, opposition to, 220, 266
Evangelical Association
  beginning of, 65, 68-69
  and camp meetings, 152
  and foot washing, 145
Evangelical Mennonites, 165, 169
Evangelism
  and biblical interpretation, 225
  study conference, 283-284
Evangelistic meetings, in Franconia Conference, 173-175
Exalting Christ in the City, 241

F

Finney, Charles Grandison
  on the millennium, 159
  and perfectionism, 154
  on prevailing prayer, 169
  revivalist, 151
Foot washing
  and the Franconia Mennonites, 93-94
  and Johnson Mennonites, 145-146
Fosdick, Harry Emerson, and Fundamentalist Controversy, 206, 210
Fox sisters, 98
Fragmentation, causes of, 125-126, 328
Franconia Mennonite Conference
  and benevolent activities, 197-198
  and Dordrecht Confession, 93-94
  and foot washing, 93-94
  meetings of, 185
  and Matthew 18, 94

and reorganization, 312, 314-315
  resistance to institutionalization, 177, 179-180
  and shunning, 94
  special meetings of, 184
  1946 special session, 264-266
  1966 special session, 311
  and social change, 245-246
  structure of, 183-188, 197
  and the Wisler Schism, 191-192
Franconia cowboys, 283
Franconia Mission Board, organized, 197
Franconia Conservative Mennonites, origin of, 295
Freeland Seminary, 141-142
French Camisards, 98
French Reconstruction Union, 279
Fretz, Abraham, commissioner and county treasurer, 119, 120
Frey, Andrew, 50
Friedmann, Robert
  and "the Brotherly Union," 92
  on the Oberholtzer division, 127, 146
Fundamental Truth Series, 201-202
Fundamentalism
  and charter values, 210
  combative, 206
  definition of, 209
  differences from Anabaptism, 212
  influence of, 212
  Mennonite position and 209ff.
  militarism of, 209-210
  origins of, 201-206
  and premillennialism, 229
  and separation from the world, 115
  and sound doctrine, 250
  themes of dissension, 201
  threats to beliefs, 245, 250
Fundamentalist leadership
  and authority, 235
  descriptions of, 238
  and preaching, 235
  styles, 209
Fundamentalists
  called for reorganization of Protestantism, 206
  and political alarm, 206
Fundamentals, The, 205
Funk, Christian
  and the oath of allegiance, 121
  and shunning, 94
  and war tax, 125*n*
Funk, Henry
  on baptism, 59-60, 95
  and *Martyrs Mirror*, 62

Funk, John F.
  defends seminary attendance, 236
  and institutionalization, 194-196
  and necktie, 250
  ordains Durr, 239
  visits Yellow Creek, 189
  Warfare: Its Evils, Our Duty, 274
  and Wisler Schism, 189-93

G

Gates, Theophilus R., 154
Gavstad, Edwin S., 319
Gehman, William, 144, 146, 164
Geil, John
  capable, 143
  on congregation and minister, 116
  farewell address of, 95-98
  and John F. Funk, 168, 169
  on love, 107-108
  and external forms, 113
  and recording of minutes, 128-129
General Conference of the Mennonite Church of North America, 148, 181
German Baptist Brethren, *see* Dunkers
German Reformed, problems of organization, 30, 54
German Revival, the, 65-72
  and camp meetings, 152
Germantown
  church, 27-29
  established, 25
  early report concerning, 26
  government of borough, 118
  and Hunsickers, 143
  and Indians, 26
Godschalk, Abraham
  and *A Description of the New Creature*, 95, 157-164
  on baptism, 99
  combatting perfectionism, 154
  and God's love, 284
  historical view of the Bible, 214
  and the nonresistant gospel, 114
  on prayer, 171
  and external forms, 113
Godschalk, Jacob, 28, 116
Godshall, Jacob, 236
Golden Apples in Silver Bowls, 62-63
Gordon, Milton, on assimilation, 289
Gospel Herald
  articles on discipline and separation, 303-304
  report on RSV, 286-287, 287 *n* 39
  reports mass revivals, 281-282

Goshen College
  beginning of, 195
  closing of, 207
  commitment to world change, 305
Graham, Billy, 283
Gross, Joseph
  and communion, 269, 316
  attended nonconformity conference, 303
Gottschall, Moses, 144
Gottschall, W. S., on Christian Endeaver Societies, 182
Gotwals, John, 120
Government
  in Pennsylvania, 118
  attitudes toward, 119-120
Grater, Abraham, 143, 145
Great Awakening
  in the Mennonite Church, 204,
  Second, 150-157
Gross, Jacob, 68
Grubb, N. B., on Sunday schools, 181-182
Gruber, John Adam
  Inspirationist, 39
  and appeal for union, 40

H

Hamburg, Altona, letter from, 28
Harder, Leland, and Oberholtzer division, 146
Hats, 256-257
Haycock congregation, withdraws from conference, 314-315
Heatwole, L. J., and modernist controversy, 207
Hendricks, Garret, signs slavery protest, 26
Herald of Truth, 189-190, 194
  and articles on dress, 250
  supported by Franconia, 199
Hermeneutic, Anabaptist, 92
Herold der Wahrheit, 194
Hermits of the Wissahickon and Boehmist Theosophy, 34
Herr, Christian
  letter to, 107
  on the Constitution, 138
  and Hunsicker letter, 128
Hershberger, Guy F.
  and draft legislation peace concerns of, 317
  publication activity, 278
  and *War, Peace, and Nonresistance*, 278
Hertzler, Daniel, 267
Hesston College, founding of, 207
Hierarchical structures and discipline, 271

Hirten Lieder von Bethlehem, 54
Hodge, A. A., "Inspiration," 203
Hodge, Charles, and the Princeton Theology, 203
Holy Spirit
  in the life of the church, 308
  speaks again, 306
  born of, 99
Holiness
  and Amish and Mennonites, 155-156
  and Brethren in Christ, 157
  and neckties, 250
Home Mission Societies, 177, 179
Hoover, Amos, 80
Hope, Sanctification, and a Noble Determination, 160
Horsch, John
  conservative viewpoint, 208
  and Fundamentalism, 201-202
  and Modernism, 208
  and premillennialism, 229
Horst, John L., study of leadership trends, 298
Hostetler, John, and the charter, 76
Hubmaier, Balthasar, and discipline, 83
Hubner, George, hosted second synod, 47
Hunsberger, Henry, moderating conference, 129-130
Hunsicker, Abraham
  active politically, 119-120
  appeals to Lancaster 119
  and Christian Society at Freeland, 164,
  founds Freeland Seminary 141-142
  and dissension at Skippack, 106-107
  and division, 140-143
  education and progress, 146, 179-180
  letter to Christian Herr, 128-129, 137-138
  politically active, 141.
  See also Oberholtzer division
Hunsicker, Abraham, of Blooming Glen, 249
Hunsicker, Francis R., 143
Hunsicker, Henry, 141-143, 145
Hunsicker, John
  and Constitution, 129-130
  died, 141;
  and Oberholtzer Division, 127
  moderator, 141
Hymnody
  and Pietism, 54-58
  revivalism changed, 175

I

Imbroich, Thomas von, statement on baptism, 58
Immigration
  to Pennsylvania, 30
  Russian Mennonite, 194
I-W Service, 317
Independent Bible churches
  formation of, 209
  and leadership styles, 238
Indians
  baptized, 47
  friendly, 26
Individualism and revivalism, 151-152
Inerrancy and Princeton Theology, 202
Inter-Mennonite cooperation
  in alternative service, 278
  in MCC, 275-279, 289-291, 320-322
  in relief, 277
Inquiry meeting, 105-106
Isaac Long's barn, 65-66, 69
Inspirationists come to America, 39
Institutionalization
  Franconia, 199-200
  and values, 193-194
Insurance, problematic, 291

J

Jesus Christ
  in "Brotherly Union," 77, 123-124
  and biblical interpretation, 224-226
  complete and final revelation, 213
Johnson, Henry G., 145-146
Johnson Mennonites
  and division, 145
  and revivalism, 165
Johnson, Lyndon B., message to, 321
Jordan, Robert E., protests of, 319-320

K

Kauffman, Daniel
  and Bible conferences, 247, 249
  cited by Metzler, 313
  and closing of Goshen College, 207
  conservative innovator, 196
  doctrinal writings, 215
  and Fundamentalism, 202, 207, 210-211
  letter from Clemens, 230
  and Mennonite standards, 199
  and premillennialism, 229
  symposium on millennialism, 231-234

Kauffman, J. Howard, and reorganization study, 312
Kelpius, Johannes, 34-35
King, B. B., meetings at Limerick, 243
King, Martin Luther, contacts with, 317
Kingdom of God
  and rule of Christ, 159
  and regeneration, 159
Kingdoms, two, 87
Klaassen, Walter, and biblical interpretation, 226
Kleine Davidische Psalterspiele, Das, 54
Kolb, Amos, 271
Kolb, Dielman, 62
Kolb, Elmer
  and conference discipline, 309
  reports complaints, 312
  on training leaders, 300
Kratz, Clayton, 275
Kraus, C. Norman, and biblical interpretation, 212
Kraybill, Donald B., 289
Krefeld, emigrants from, 283-284
Krehbiel, Jacob
  on American Mennonites, 95-97
  and the hermeneutic community, 218
  on the oath, 121
  and plain dress, 255
  on selection of ministers, 117
  on separation, 111-112
  and shepherds of the flock, 115, 117
  on the sword, 118-119
Kulp, Hettie B., 240
Kurzgefasste-Kirchen-Geschichte
  See Benjamin Eby

L

Lancaster Conference
  and authoritarian control, 246
  and the Constitution, 137-138
Lancaster ministers
  support solicited, 127
  response to Nice, 138-140
Landes, Elias, 106
Landis, Eli, 120
Landis, Felix, persecution of, 58
Lapp, John A., on baptism, 105 n 84
Landis, Paul G., 314
Lansdale congregation withdraws from conference, 314-315
Lapp, John E.
  address of 1970, 325
  adult counselor to pastors, 302

aid to poor, 198-199
on biblical interpretation, 212, 218
and centralization of power, 251
chairman of Peace Problems Committee, 319
and discipline, 269
and draft registration, 324
evaluated study conference, 298
on the function of conference, 308
and guest preachers, 252
peace witness concerns, 323
the state of the church, 302-303
and witness to the state, 318-319
on worship and obedience, 218
Late Great Planet Earth, The, 226-227
Lawsuit: re Elwood Derstine, 294-295
Lay activity
and conference reports, 289
delegates, 314
encouragement of, 302
role of, 315
volunteer work, 290
Leadership
authoritarian pattern challenged, 295
and the charter, 235-238
centralization of, 250-258
changing trends, 238-239
concerns of ministers, 301-302
new patterns, 238-239
resistance to Fundamentalist styles of, 238
styles of, 235-238
trends at midcentury, 298-299
Lederach, Paul
report on revivals, 281
pastor at Blooming Glen, 270
Lederach, Willis K., and Mary Mensch, call to Norristown Mission, 241
Leatherman, Abraham, 236
Legalism, 249
Lehman, Chester K., and RSV Committee, 286
Lehman, Peter, and Snow Hill community, 38
Lensen, Jan
Mennonite immigrant, 24
and jury duty, 118
Letter to Holland, 73
Liechty, Joseph C., on humility, 76
Life insurance
prohibitions, 269-270
acceptance, 293
Limerick, work at, 241-243
Lind, Millard, committee work on RSV, 286
Lindsey, Hal, 226

Line Lexington, farewell address to
See Geil, John
Literal reign, bishops against, 231
Litigation
problems of, 292
and Goodville Company, 292
issue of concern, 306
Longacre, James C., 326
Lord's Supper
See Breaking of bread
Lot, the, 117, 138-139, 187-188
Loucks, Aaron, and Moody Bible Institute, 204
Loux, Norman, and Penn Foundation, 290
Love, test of regeneration, 162
Luther
and the ban, 84
and priestly office, 89
Lutherans and church organization, 30-31
Lutheran theology, scholasticism and dogma, 214-215

M

McGiffert, Arthur Cushman, 203
Machen, J. Gresham, 208-209
McIntire, Carl, 319-320
Mack, Alexander, 34
Mack, Andrew S., 237
McLoughlin, William, on Awakenings, 285-286
Magistracy, the, and the Christian, 90-91
Malinowski, Bronislaw, and the Charter, 76-77
Manifest Destiny and institutionalization, 179
Manual of Bible Doctrines, A, 215
Marsden, George M., on Fundamentalism, 204
Martyrs Mirror, 60-62
Matthew 18
and the ban, 83
and bishops, 251
and church government, 196
and communion, 317
and defensive structuring, 263
and discipline, 106-108
and gossip, 266
Matthews, Shailer, 201
Meetinghouses, claimed by Oberholtzer group, 131
Mennonite Board of Education, organized, 195, 312
Mennonite Board of Missions and Charities, organized, 195

Mennonite Brethren in Christ, 145, 169
Mennonite Central Committee
    formed, 275
    and alternative service, 276-277
    service of 275-279, 290, 293, 299, 317-326, *passim*
Mennonite Church
    Awakening in, 188-189
    and defensive structuring, 247, 249
Mennonite Church and Current Issues, 207
Mennonite Disaster Service, 290-291, 326
Mennonite General Conference
    formed, 195-196
    and Franconia Conference, 272
    and nonconformity, 281
    and nonconformity conference, 266-267
    prayer for revival 280
    reorganization of, 310
    statement of fundamentals, 211-212
    witness to government, 318
    and worldliness, 263-264
Mennonite Gospel Mission, 240
Mennonite Home Mission, 195
Mennonite Mental Hospitals, 290
Mennonite Mutual Aid, 291-293
Mennonite Publishing Company, 194
Mennonites
    and the American Revolution, 73-74
    and Awakening influences, 155
    charges of ignorance, 143
    colonial church organization, 54
    and colonial publications, 54-63
    and the Ephrata community, 36-37
    judgments against, 152
    key values and Pietism, 53-63
    and the Pennsylvania synods, 44, 45-47
    practice at midcentury, 94-124
    revivalism divisive for, 167
    and revivalistic emphases, 153
    rumors concerning, 45-47
    synod report, 49
    and Zinzendorf, 42
Mennonite Young People's Conference, 275
Mennonite World Conference, 275, 306
Mennonite Weekly Review, 306
Menno Simons
    on biblical interpretation, 226
    on literal reign, 231
    on obedience, 217, 221
    and precedence of the New Testament, 221
Mensch, Abraham B., and the Limerick Mission, 241-243
Mensch, Jacob
    letter to, 190
    opposed Sunday schools, 191-192
    and tramps, 197-198
    note on worldliness, 111
Mensch, Jacob, and Mary
    and the Oberholtzer division, 135
    on revivalism, 165
Mensch-Oberholtzer papers, 127 n 3
Methodist itinerants, 65
Metzler, A. J., executive secretary of Mennonite General Conference, 313
Midcentury changes, 272
Millenariansim
    and the charter, 227
    and conference regulation, 266
    and power, 227
    and prophecy conferences, 203-204
    rejected, 273
    and Satan's power, 233
Millennialism
    defined, 226-227
    and J. C. Clemens, 230-233
    symposium on, 231-234
    views of S. F. Coffman, 233
Miller, John Peter
    joins Ephrata community, 38
    and *Martyrs Mirror*, 62
Miller, Paul M.
    on ordination study, 300
    seminar on leadership, 302
Militarism
    and biblical interpretation, 233
    and Fundamentalism, 209
Mininger, J. D., 240-241; 252-253
Mininger, Jonas, 187, 198
Mininger, Paul
    on change, 305
    conference speaker, 312
    on nonconformity, 266
    and reorganization of General Conference, 312
    and service programs, 279
    on social and world changes, 305
Ministerial support, 116
Minister, seminar on role of, 302
Minister's Prayer Fellowship
    concerns of, 312-313
    opposes change, 312-314
Minute Book of the Church Council of the Christian Society at Freeland
    minutes, 164-165
    and the American environment, 133
    and the Oberholtzer division, 127-129, 133, 136
    objections to, 136
    recording of 127-128, 250

Mirror for All Mankind, 94
Mission and biblical interpretation, 225
Modernism
  a method, 201
  similarities with Anabaptism, 210-211
Modern religious liberalism, 202, 206
Miller, Orie O.
  on lay leadership, 299-300
  and Mennonite Mutual Aid, 291
  and policy on social protests, 322
  and peace activism, 322
  and relief program, 275-277
  and new Confession of Faith, 305
Moody Bible Institute and Mennonite leaders, 172, 204
Moody, Dwight L., 204
Moravians
  and hymnody, 54, 56, 57
  origins and immigration to Pennsylvania, 39-40
Mosemann, John H., and modernist controversy, 206-207
Moyer, Isaac, and Boyertown court case, 135-136
Muhlenberg, Henry Melchior, 33, 53
Muller, Joseph, 50-51, 61
Mumaw, John R.
  series of articles, 306
  on social changes, 304-305
Mutual Aid Plan, 194-195

N

Nägele, Rudolph, and the Ephrata community, 36
National Association of Evangelicals policy on militarism, 322
Nazareth visited by Zinzendorf, 42
Near East Relief, 277
Neues, Hans, chosen preacher, 28
Nevin, John William
  Anxious Bench, The, 157-158
  and revivalism, 174-175
New birth, 151
Newcomer, Christian, 66-68
New Mennonites
  and adaptations 140
  and organizational structures, 177, 180-183
  and revivalism, 164-167
New Republic and optimism, 176
"New Wine in New Bottles," 279-280
Niagara Bible conferences, 226
Nice, Henry, and Constitution, 137-138
Nonconformity
  and Bible conferences, 247, 249
  conferences on, 287-288, 303,
  emphasis in 1944, 281
  openly discussed, 267
Nonresistance
  and *A New Creature*, 160
  and biblical interpretation, 221-223
  to evil and Article IV, 113-114
  and Fundamentalism, 115, 210, 245
  modifications of, 191
  statement on, 280
  teaching of, 301
  and union Sunday schools, 190-191
Nonresistant gospel, 114, 163
Nonverbal expression
  of religious forms, 329
  in service opportunities, 326
Norris, J. Frank, as Fundamentalist leader, 238
Norristown mission, 241, 244
Noyes, John Humphrey, 154
Nuclear weapons protests, 318

O

Oath, the
  and American Revolution, 121
  and the "Brotherly Union," 91-92
  and persecution in America, 91
O'Connell, Maurice, meetings at Limerick, 243
Obedience
  and biblical interpretation, 217
  to Christ's commandments, 151
  and eternal security, 220
Oberholtzer division
  and the American environment, 132-134
  and American religious influences, 146-149
  issues challenged charter, 127, 134-140
  congregations involved, 131, 126-140, *passim*
Oberholtzer, John H.
  critical of Franconia Conference, 183-184
  and effective organization, 133-134
  and the lot, 117
  letter to Germany, 95-97
  no mention of dress restrictions for laypersons, 113
  and organizational structures, 180, 183
  and the plain coat, 132-135
  and preparation for baptism, 101
  and prayer meetings, 144, 126-140, *passim*
Old Order Mennonites, 123, 125n, 191-193
Old Order River Brethren hymnody, 57-58
One Thousand Questions and Answers on Points of Christian Doctrine, 215

Ordination of ministers, 186-188
Otterbein, Philip William, 65-66
Our Country, 179

P

Palatinate and Swiss immigrants, 29-30
Palatine Mennonites arrive in Germantown, 28
Palmer, Phoebe, and perfectionism, 154
Pannabecker, Samuel F., on the Oberholtzer division, 127, 146, 148-149
Pastorius, Daniel Francis
  immigration of, 24
  leader at Germantown, 25
  protest against slavery, 26
  visited Krefeld, 24
Pax service, 317
Peace activities in the twentieth century, 273
Peace and service
  concerns regarding, 312
  mental hospital work, 290
  resolutions, 317-319
  service opportunities, 326
"Peace and the Christian Witness," 280
Peace Declaration of 1775, 273-274
Peace Problems Committee
  origins, 277
  work of, 277
Peace Section, 320, 322
Peace statements, 277-278
Peace witness, policy on, 322
Peaceable Kingdom of Christ, The, 224, 231
Peachey, Emanuel, speaker on nonconformity, 288
Peachey, Paul
  on church organization, 298
  requests conference on unity, 313
Penn, William
  assisted Germantown settlers, 26
  his Holy Experiment, 23
  and land grant, 25
Penn's Sylvania, laws of, 23
Penn's Woods, taming of, 26
Pennsylvania synods, 42-52
Pequea, settlement at, 29
Perfectionism, 154-157, 160, 162-164
Philadelphia Mennonite Mission, 240
Phoenixville, 143
Pia Desideria, 32-33
Pietism
  beginning of, 32
  characteristics of, 33
Pietists
  fellowship with, 32

  religious values of, 53-63
Plain clothes and consecration, 284
Plain dress, Krehbiel on, 224
Plain coat
  and Oberholtzer division, 127, 129, 132, 135
  and Vincent, 249
  wearing of, 289
Plymouth Brethren and dispensationalism, 221
Polish Brethren
  See Socinians
Politics of Jesus, The, 227
Postmillennialism and Manifest Destiny, 226
Power and millennial views, 233-234
"Prayer for Revival," 279-281
Prayer meetings
  and the Gehman division, 144
  and revivalism, 169, 171
Premillennialism
  and biblical interpretation, 224-225
  development of, 226
  opposed by Franconia, 210
  relationship to Fundamentalism, 229
Presbyterian church: and the "Five Points," 204
Presbyterian Review, 203
Princeton Seminary
  and conservatism, 202
  and Fundamentalist controversy, 208-209
Princeton theology, 202-203
Prophecy conferences
  and Fundamentalism, 203-204
  and Bible institutes, 209
Protest against slavery, 24, 26
Protestant movements, influences of, 327
Protracted meetings, 151, 164-165, 167
Providence, 143

Q

Quaker
  missionaries, 23
  preaching, 252
  Quaker Relief Unit, 274
Questionnaire to ministers, 308

R

Race relations, 316-317, 319
Radical German Pietism and Jacob Boehme, 98
Radical Pietists
  and *Martyrs Mirror,* 63
  persecution and migration, 33

and suffering, 61
Radio and new questions, 212
Reductionism and revivalism, 175
Reform societies, 178
Regeneration, Godschalk on, 158, 160-162
Relationships and key values, 123-124
Reorganization study
  cited, 312
  opposition to, 313
  report cited, 315
Repentance
  before baptism, 99
  and the Charter, 151
Resurrection of Christ and baptism, 82, 105
Revised Standard Version, 286-287
Revivals
  campaigns, 281
  interest in, 280
  and the New Republic, 176
  responses to, 284
  statement of concerns, 283
Revivalism
  and camp meetings, 152-153
  and church membership, 167
  divisive for New Mennonites, 164
  focused on individual, 151-152
  and Mennonite values, 157-164
  and prayer meetings, 169-171
  and Pietism, 151
  and Protestant understandings, 284
Ribeaupierre, Eberhard, benefactor of Anabaptists, 33
Riley, William Bell, and fundamentals conference, 205
Rittenhouse, William, elected minister, 27-28
River Brethren
  and baptism, 99
  origins of, 65, 68, 70
  and foot washing, 145
  and revivalism, 150
Rosenberger, Henry, 187
Rosenberger, Joel, and revivalism, 165
Roxbury holiness camp, 157
Rule of Christ and the ban, 84
Rule of Paul and reputation of ministers, 88
Russia and Mennonite aid, 274-275
Russian Baptists, visit of, 319-320
Russian Mennonite immigration, 194
Ruth, Arthur D., 237
Ruth, John L.
  on changing situations, 310, 315
  and John Geil, 169 n 55
  Maintaining the Right Fellowship, 19
  and the Oberholtzer division, 127 n2

S

Sammelband, A., and the "Brotherly Union," 80
Satan and millenarianism, 233
Sattler, Michael
  author of the "Brotherly Union," 55
  on the ban, 84
  hymn of, 55-56
  and the Seven Articles, 92
Sauer, Christopher, 39, 54
Schisms
  and Americanization, 125, 127
  elements operative in, 125-126
  recurring phenomenon, 125-126
Schlabach, Theron F.
  Mennonites and modernization, 76
  on mutual aid, 292-293, 293, n 65
Schlatter, Michael, 33, 53
Schleitheim, town of, 77-78
Scholasticism and infallibility, 217
Schwenkfeld, Caspar, 31
Schwenkfelders, 31, 46
Schwenksville Mennonite Church, 182
Scofield, Cyrus Ingerson, 228
Scofield Reference Bible, censored 228, 243
Scopes trial, 206
Scripture
  authority of, 135-136
  and church regulations, 138
Second Great Awakening
  activities of, 97
  emphasis on external forms, 113
  and Mennonite values, 75
Second work of grace, 157, 160
Seguy, Jean, 92
Secret societies and the Hunsicker division, 142-143
Secularization and the Oberholtzer division, 146
Seminary training and Mennonite leadership, 236
Separation from the world
  articles in *Gospel Herald*, 303-304
  and American Mennonites, 110-115
  in the "Brotherly Union," 86-88
  and churchwide meetings, 288
  and doctrinal statement, 287-288
  and Fundamentalism, 115, 245-246, 250
  Krehbiel on, 111-112
Separation
  and Catholics, 88
  and Protestant Reformers, 88
Separated unto God, 281
Separatists in America, 39

Sermon on the Mount
  attempt to follow, 91
  guide to conduct, 234
  and the oath, 91
  and separation, 87
Sermon of 1782, 213-214
Seven Articles, the
  and American Mennonite religious forms, 98-124
  and the charter, 92, 94
  formulation and content, 77-78, 81-92
  and key values, 123-124
  relational in content, 123
Seventh-day Baptists
  See Ephrata community
Seybert, Johannes, 152-153
Shank, J. R., 215
Shepherds of the Flock
  and American Mennonites, 115-118
  in the "Brotherly Union," 88-89
  character or training, 115
Shetler, Samuel G., and Bible conferences, 247, 249
Shetler, Sanford, speaker on nonconformity, 288
Schowalter Foundation and leadership study, 300
Siegel, Bernard, and defensive structuring, 246-247
Simons, Menno, on shepherds, 89
Singing, restrictions concerning, 261
Smissen, Carl Justus van der, 97, 97 n 71, 181
Snow Hill community, 38
Skippack
  constitution meeting at, 129-130
  dissension at, 106-107
  and the Hunsickers, 141, 143
  and the Johnson division, 145
  powerful congregation, 127
  settlement began, 29
  Whitefield preached at, 40-41
  Zinzendorf invited to preach, 47
Slavery
  in Philadelphia, 26
  protest against, 26-27
Smith, C. Henry, 118, 127
Smith, Henry Preserved, 203
Smith, J. B. and Christian Fundamentals, 212
Smith, Joseph, 98
Socialization for impulse control, 247
Society of Friends
  See Quakers
Socinians, beliefs similar to Mennonites, 46
Song leaders, 186

Souder, Menno B., 236
Spangenberg, August Gottlieb, 39-40, 51
Spener, Philip Jacob, 32-33
Spiritualism and the Fox sisters, 98
Stauffer, John L.
  on Fundamentalism, 205
  on Fundamentalist Bible teachers, 223
  on Fundamentalist preachers, 235
  leadership of, 239-240, 252-253
  on Modernism vs. Fundamentalism, 210-211
Steiner, Menno S., 196, 236
Stevenson, J. Ross, and Princeton controversy, 208
Stewart, Lyman and Milton, sponsored *The Fundamentals*, 205
Strong, Josiah, 179
Stoltzfus, Edward, on training leaders, 300
Structural associations, limits on, 247
Student Volunteer Movement and premillennialism, 226
Submission and devotional covering, 258
Sunday school conventions and Eastern District, 181
Sunday schools
  organized, 191
  origins of, 178
  and superintendents, 186
Suffering
  baptism of, 59-60
  theology of, 61
Sunday School Times, 267
Suing at law, 119
Swamp congregation, Oberholtzer ordained, 127
Swearing an oath and the American Revolution, 74
Swiss persecution, Articles cited, 79
Sword, concerning the, 90-91, 118-121
Sword and Trumpet
  and accusations, 278
  and millenarianism, 229
  on peace and nonconformity, 278, 279 n 14
Systematic Theology, 203
Symbols abandoned, 272
Syndic, the, and Pennsylvania synods, 45-48

T

Taylor, Nathaniel, 151
Teaching of the Twelve Apostles, 86
Telner, Jacob
  and land purchase, 23
  immigrant, 23

Tennet, Gilbert, visited by Zinzendorf, 42
Theophilus the Battle Axe, 154
Third Great Awakening and development of Fundamentalism, 204
Thirty Years' War, 30
Thomas, David N.
  brought conference sermon, 310
  on social change, 306
Torry, R. A., 205
Trends
  revivalism, 327
  age of baptism, 327
Trustees, responsibilities of, 186
Türk, John de, hosted third synod, 47
Twenty-six Studies in Christian Doctrine, 215
Twisk, Peter J.
  on the apocalypse, 224
  Peaceable Kingdom of Christ, 231
Tyson, Abram, 164

U

Union Sunday School Movement and child evangelism, 165, 167
Union Sunday Schools, 190-191
Unitas Fratrum
  See Moravians
United Brethren in Christ
  origins, 65-66, 69
  and foot washing, 145
  and revivalism, 150
Upper Milford, 144
Urbanization, problems of, 301
Urban-directed life, hierarchical needs of, 245

V

Vicit Agnus Noster, 227
Vietnam War, concerns and protests, 321
Vincent, Bible conferences at, 247
Violence, weapons forbidden, 88
Virginia Conference
  and codification of practice, 249
  committee on liberalism, 202
  on Revised Standard Version, 286-287
  statement on Fundamentals, 212
Visiting and fellowship of the saints, 184-185
Visiting preachers, 252
Voluntary Service, 278
Voluntary societies, 176-177

W

Warfare: Its Evils, Our Duty, 274
Warfield, Benjamin B., on inspiration, 203
War, Peace, and Nonresistance, 278
War taxes, resolution on, 324
Watchtower magazine and literal reign, 229
Way of the Cross in Human Relations, The, 318
Weber, Peter, 68
Wenger, A. D.
  and *Christian Fundamentals*, 212
  and hats, 257
  attended Moody Bible Institute, 204
  and necktie, 250
  and premillennialism, 229
  and revival meetings, 172-173
Wenger, J. C.
  articles on nonconformity, 303
  on biblical interpretation, 219-220
  conference sermon, 306, 310, 340
  concerning hats, 257
  letter to Eisenhower, 318
  and new confession of faith, 304, 306
  nonconformity conference speaker, 288
  nonconformity publications, 288
  and Oberholtzer division, 131
  on recording of minutes, 136
  Separated unto God, 281
  on T. T. van Sittert, 114
  witness in court, 294-295
Wesley, John, on perfectionism, 154
Wesleyan Methodists, 155
Westminster Seminary, founding of, 208
White caps, 255-258
Whitefield, George
  and New Light preachers, 66
  visited Pennsylvania, 40-41
  and Zinzendorf, 49
Wiebe, Peter, speaker on nonconformity, 288
Wiebe, Robert H., 245, 271
Wiegner, Christopher
  and Spangenberg, 40
  visited by Zinzendorf, 42
Wilson, Robert D., and Westminster Seminary, 208
Wisler, Jacob, 189-193
Wisler Schism, 191-193
Witness to government, concerns expressed, 320-322
Witness to the state, committee on, 324-325

Wohlfahrt, Michael, and the Ephrata community, 36
World, the, separated from, 87
World Congress of Religions and millenarianism, 229
Worldliness, and conference discussions of, 307
World's Christian Fundamentals Association, 201, 205-206
World War I
  and conscientious objectors, 274-275
  and Franconia Mennonites, 14-115
  and political climate, 120
World War II and alternative service, 120-121

Y

Yellow Creek Mennonite Church, baptism at, 189
Yoder, A. I.
  and premillennialism, 229
  attended Moody Bible Institute, 204
Yoder, Edward
  on institutionalization, 200
  and plain coat, 263
Yoder, John H.
  Anabaptists and tradition, 133
  and the "Brotherly Union," 78-79
  on Christ and power, 227;
  respondent at peace conference, 323
Yoder, J. Otis, and RSV committee, 287

Z

Zinzendorf, Count
  visits Indians, 50
  and the Moravians, 40
  and the Pennsylvania synods, 32, 41-51
  reception in Pennsylvania, 49-51
  mentioned, 53-54
Zwingli, Ulrich,
  and baptism, 81
  and the ban, 84
  on the "Brotherly Union," 79
  and the Lord's Supper, 85

The Author

Beulah Stauffer Hostetler was born at Tofield, Alberta. Her pilgrimage took her to Hesston and Goshen colleges, the Mennonite Central Committee headquarters at Akron, Pennsylvania, and to Herald Press at Scottdale, Pennsylvania. After returning to Alberta for three years where her husband, John A. Hostetler, was teaching at the provincial university in Edmonton, the family—which now included three daughters, Ann, Mary, and Laura—returned to Pennsylvania and selected a home midway between Franconia Mennonite Conference and center city Philadelphia.

Beginning graduate school when her youngest child was in second grade, the author earned a Ph.D. in Religious Thought at the University of Pennsylvania in 1977. She has served on numerous Mennonite church committees and boards, including the Editorial Council of *The Mennonite Encyclopedia V*; the committee to write a new inter-Mennonite Confession of Faith; the Council on Faith, Life, and Strategy; the Leadership Commission of Franconia Conference; and on the boards of trustees of Christopher Dock Mennonite High School and Eastern Mennonite College.

In the summer of 1986 she was selected to participate in a National Endowment for the Humanities summer seminar at Harvard University on Religion and Cultural Change in American History. She is presently Associate Director of the Center for the Study of Anabaptist and Pietist Groups at Elizabethtown College, Elizabethtown, Pennsylvania, and assistant professor of sociology.

Beulah and her husband, John, are members of Blooming Glen Mennonite Church.

www.ingramcontent.com/pod-product-compliance
Lightning Source LLC
Chambersburg PA
CBHW030604230426
43661CB00053B/1836